Business studies
for AS

Business studies for AS

David Dyer, Ian Dorton,
David Grainger and
Peter Stimpson

CAMBRIDGE
UNIVERSITY PRESS

PUBLISHED BY THE PRESS SYNDICATE OF THE UNIVERSITY OF CAMBRIDGE
The Pitt Building, Trumpington Street, Cambridge, United Kingdom

CAMBRIDGE UNIVERSITY PRESS
The Edinburgh Building, Cambridge CB2 2RU, UK
40 West 20th Street, New York, NY 10011-4211, USA
10 Stamford Road, Oakleigh, VIC 3166, Australia
Ruiz de Alarcón 13, 28014 Madrid, Spain
Dock House, The Waterfront, Cape Town 8001, South Africa

http://www.cambridge.org

First published 2000
Reprinted 2000

Printed in the United Kingdom at the University Press, Cambridge

Typeface Minion   *System* Apple Macintosh Quark® 4.04

A catalogue record for this book is available from the British Library

ISBN 0 521 78606 1 paperback

Cover photo by courtesy of Telegraph Colour Library

Contents

v

Authors

David Dyer
Director of Cambridge Business Studies Trust

Ian Dorton
United World College, Singapore

Peter Stimpson
Hurtwood House, Surrey

David Grainger
Coleraine Boys' Secondary School, Northern Ireland

Preface

This book has been written specifically for the A level specifications in Business Studies developed by OCR and meets the requirements of the three AS components of the Business Studies course. It will meet the needs of those who will complete the AS qualification and provide a foundation for those who intend to go beyond AS and complete the A level course. It will also be useful to students on courses requiring a business background.

The book has been produced by four authors, all of whom have knowledge and experience of teaching the subject to Advanced level and were involved, at some stage, in the development of the new Business Studies specification.

The book contains features designed to support teachers and students in the successful completion of the AS course and prepare them effectively to continue into the A2 course.

- It is divided into two distinct parts. Part 1 (Sections 1–7) covers the course for Businesses: their objectives and environment and Part 2 (Sections 8–18) fulfills the requirements for Business decisions and Business behaviour, the two final teaching modules of the AS course.
- Each section begins with a clear statement of objectives and contains opportunities throughout, in the form of Case studies and Activities, to extend and enrich understanding of the subject. Some of these test understanding but most are concerned with bringing the business world and the way it operates into the learning process. It is essential to a good understanding of business studies that it is seen as a dynamic study of what actually happens in the world and is not confined to the classroom or textbook.
- The book is written on the assumption that students are observant and curious and will bring their perceptions of what is happening at a local and national level into their studies. There is also the expectation that students will update their knowledge through the continuous use of libraries, the media and the internet.

- An equally vital assumption is that students will learn from one another and turn each other's weaknesses into strengths. Most of the activities are best tackled in a group and much of the real learning will come from working together and through discussion.
- Each section highlights key issues and vital subject vocabulary. It is a feature of the new specifications that students are able to define, explain and exemplify concepts, ideas, theories and techniques which are central to the subject. To this end, there is a glossary at the end of the book. But good results will come not just from understanding the language of business studies but from the confident use of it in course work and in examination answers. This is as much a matter of good learning and practice as it is of memory.
- From a student point of view the existence of examinations is a challenge. Students need to both understand the process of examinations and know how to prepare for them. Section 19 provides this support. It should be read in preparation for every examination and not just at the end of the year. It suggests the most effective ways of preparing and helps students avoid the most common ways of losing marks. In particular it suggests ways in which the pre-issued case, which is a feature of the third assessment unit in AS, can best be used in the run up to the examination.

I would like to express my thanks to the following, who have made this book possible: my fellow authors for all their work; John Harris for his constructive review of the draft; my wife Margaret (Meg), who proofread the text; my long time friend Roger Blackmore who came to the rescue when two chapters needed his computing skills; Anne Rix for her support as we put the book together.

David H. Dyer
Director Cambridge Business Studies Project
Chief Examiner OCR Business Studies
April 2000

Part 1

Businesses: their objectives and environment

1 Introduction

About this book

The OCR A level in Business Studies is taken in two distinct stages. The first stage is **AS level** and this book is solely concerned with that stage. You may take AS on its own or continue the course through A2 to complete the full advanced level qualification.

In this book you will find:

◆ Part 1: Sections 1–7 designed to support your studies for teaching module 1 called Businesses: their objectives and environment.

◆ Part 2: Sections 8–18 designed to cover teaching module 2 which is assessed by two examination units. Each covers the whole of the specification for teaching module 2. The first is called Business decisions and the second Business behaviour.

These three examination units are all compulsory and make up the examination for the AS qualification.

The final section (Section 19) offers help, advice and examples which will assist you in preparing for each of the AS examinations. You would be wise to read and use it before the first examination and then again before the other two.

When you have completed the AS course you will need the second book in this series to carry on your studies to complete the full A level.

The format of each section

Each section is intended to be treated as a workshop and not just as a reading source. You will lose a lot of the benefit of the book if you do nothing more than read it. The activities and case studies are there to support you in your studies, use them as you work your way through each section.

Objectives

Objectives are right at the heart of all decisions that are made. We shall use the model of decision making shown in Figure 1.1 on occasions in the sections that follow. Objectives (Table 1.1) are what people or organisations intend to do, and often actions are judged by comparison with the objectives set and success in achieving them. If objectives are unclear or too ambitious they often lead to failure. If they are too easy, they will be achieved but there will be disappointment.

Objectives in this book

The objectives we have set for each section are written in terms of what we want you to achieve using that section. Please read them before starting on each section. They will give you clues as to what examiners are going to expect. We can see that from the objectives of Section 2 shown in Table 1.2. These objectives give you a good idea of the contents of the section and the

Clear	Unclear	Too ambitious?
To break even in the first year	To make a profit	To double profit each year
To increase turnover by 5% this year	To increase sales	To triple sales next year
To get a Grade B in A level Business Studies	To pass A level Business Studies	To get 100% in Business Studies A level
To take a degree in Business Studies at UMIST	To go to university	
To become an accountant	To get a job	

Table 1.1 Objectives

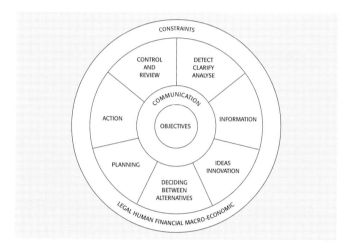

Figure 1.1 A model of decision making

On completion of this section you should be able to:

◆ understand the nature, variety and pattern of business activity through the businesses found in your area

◆ understand how businesses must meet the needs of both consumers and other stakeholders if they are to be successful

◆ explain the nature of production as added value

◆ appreciate problems associated with waste and its disposal and with various kinds of pollution

◆ understand the departments into which businesses divide as they grow

◆ appreciate some of the problems associated with the setting up of new businesses and their first year of operation

Table 1.2 Objectives for Section 2

purpose of reading it, but they are worth further study and will tell you much more.

The first objective should tell you how important to your studies is an understanding of the things that are happening in business in the area in which you live. Business is not just about what you read; it is also about what you see and what you do. Almost all aspects of the subject can be seen in your community. You will benefit from the understanding that careful observation and use of local business activity can give you.

Begin with a bird's eye view of your community. Learn from each other, your teacher and your family, some of the most important business-related features of where you live. You will find your local newspaper is an endless source of very useful information. Local television news is also very helpful from time to time. But above all keep your eyes open.

Some of the major features of a small market town could be:

◆ There is a very good railway service, which is quite unusual for small towns. What a student of Business Studies has to ask is why. The answer lies in two facts: the railway links several large towns and cities and makes the town a very good commuter town. The result is that the line is well used. There is a good demand for the service. The second is that there are few good East–West links in this railway system. So a combination of freight traffic and high passenger numbers not only keeps the service open, but has led to its improvement.

◆ There are a large number of estate agents in the town. Why? Partly because it is a good commuter area, partly because the local authority wants to concentrate new development in the towns rather than in the villages and partly because five public schools in the area have attracted people to live there.

◆ There are many fast food shops in the small town. The explanation for this is that, because of the building of a very large lake, tourists, coach parties, bird watchers, anglers and sailors are all attracted to the area.

These are but three examples of business in action. There are countless others. You must find out what is at the business heart of your community and use it to help you with your studies. See Activity 1 on page 6.

Aerial view of small town, showing railway, market, shops, housing and businesses – everything that makes up a typical community
Source: Aerofilms Ltd.

The second objective for Section 2 gets to the very heart of our subject. If you are going to be in business, you have to meet people's needs. If you do not do that in a way that satisfies them and provides a profit for you, the business will fail. There are many examples of this in small communities. You will be able to find new businesses that open and existing ones that close. Don't just observe these things happening. Keep your eyes open, read articles in the newspapers, talk to people and find out why things happen. This will tell you an enormous amount about why businesses start up, where they do and the problems they face in trying to survive. See Activity 2.

The fourth objective reminds you that businesses do not just exist on their own, doing as they please. They have to rely on others and to operate within the wishes of the community, the law of the land, the safety of customers and employees and many other constraints, which we consider throughout the book. Not all constraints stop organisations doing things. Some protect or provide opportunities for success. In one issue of a local newspaper there were about 25 items (events/news issues) which could affect local businesses in positive or negative ways. The top five of these were:

- The planning of a new large air show for the local RAF station. This will make the area known, will increase trade and will attract tourist business. It may be noisy, it may congest some of the roads. It will employ several people.
- A decision that the by-pass for the town, first considered in the 1960s, will now be built. Again, there will be more trade and income whilst it is being built, considerable temporary employment and greater freedom to travel through, park and shop in the town, once the by-pass is open. There may be some loss of passing trade and one garage may decide to re-locate.
- Plans for a new housing development and an industrial park on the site of an old brewery. Again, this will bring many opportunities for more trade and a larger market for local traders. It will also make the village in which the brewery was situated much larger. It may enable one or more of the shops in the village to survive. It may prevent the closure of the village primary school. It may alleviate the unemployment that was caused by the closure of the brewery.
- Planning application by a transport and distribution firm is turned down. Here a firm wished to locate in the town and would have brought business and employment. Permission has been refused by the local authority. This is a good example of one of the duties local authorities have on behalf of the community. The fear is that noise, traffic congestion and possible traffic dangers will be costs that are greater, between them, than the benefits.
- A medium-sized business in the town is to close. This will cause unemployment, and therefore a general loss of business in the town. It will also improve the environment because noxious smells are involved with the product this company makes.

To explore this further, see Activity 3.

The fifth objective for Section 2 really underlines the idea that to be efficient we need to plan and to organise and that this organisation needs to grow in importance as an organisation, e.g. a firm gets bigger. See Activity 4.

Use these objectives to check, at the end of each section, whether or not you think you have learnt the things they say. If not, read some bits again, do some more of the work associated with the section, discuss it with your classmates and with your teacher, research in *Business Review*, on the Internet or in other written material.

Activities in each section

All the sections are meant to be frameworks for working and developing your understanding. Throughout each one, there is opportunity to show what you have learned. Activities are not meant as possible homework exercises but for self-help during reading. The Activity given as an example below is taken from Section 2 and it asks you to think about an important idea in the subject. You are not meant to attempt it now.

Activity (example)

Think about each of the following from the point of view of the organisation producing them:

- a pop concert;
- a music centre;
- a web site on the Internet;
- a second-hand car;
- how is value added?

At the centre of this task is an important concept called 'added value'. It is necessary that you read and understand that concept and that you prove to yourself that you understand by writing about it, in some examples and in discussions with your classmates. This book is based upon the idea that you will work together and learn from each other. It is not important that you do precisely the things we ask about, but it is essential that you try it with some products. Now try one or more of the following Activities.

Activities

1 Your community

Work in groups of four. Discuss your community:

   (a) What are the most striking aspects of business activity in your area?

   (b) Why do you think this is?

   (c) Have you seen or are you seeing any significant changes?

2 Hello and goodbye

Work in groups of four:

   (a) Two of you find a business that is closing down. Find out why it is closing and comment on what you discover.

   (b) Two of you find a business that is preparing to open up and find out why the owner thinks the business will be successful. Comment on what you discover.

3 Good news/bad news in your area

Take your local newspaper. Cut out all the articles you think will produce some good or bad effects for organisations or people in your community. Put them all into a pot and then draw one each out of it. Using the report you have selected:

   (a) Write a short memo on ways in which you think organisations in your town, and the people who live there, may be positively or negatively affected by the situation you have chosen.

   (b) Swap your comments with someone else.
   - See if you agree with what was written by your classmate.
   - Add to it or say why you agree/disagree with what is written.

4 Organisers please

Select one of the four activities below and discuss in your group the way it should be organised and planned. Discuss the steps you would take to ensure its success:

   - a disco for your year;
   - a school/college trip;
   - the provision or improvement of a senior common room;
   - fund raising for a school/college minibus.

Case studies in each section

Where it is useful to stop and pull ideas together you will find short cases in the sections. Some of these will simply tell a story and act as good examples for you to use. Others suggest some work for you to do arising from the case and form part of the Activities.

All our written examinations are in case study form and you need to get used to answering questions based on them. The first case study from Section 2 is a good example at this point.

The point of this case is that a firm has to know what business it is in if it is to be successful. The business here is not associated with the product, as perhaps a car dealership or a railway station might be. It is associated

Case Study – The shop on the beach

On the sea front above the beach there is a shop. Today it is busy. It sells books, but is not a bookshop; it sells buckets and spades, but is not a garden centre. In it you can buy sandwiches, tea and coffee, but it is not a restaurant. You can buy balls, comics, newspapers, swimwear and many other things. The shop is satisfying two groups of needs, those of people trying to enjoy (children) or to endure (parents) the beach and the facilities and opportunities of the seaside. At high tide and when it rains, there is no business. In the evening and in winter the shop is closed.

with a more general class of needs and what is being sold is not as important as meeting those needs. The customer wants general light reading, not a specific book, wants something to keep the child happy on the beach, not a specific toy, a snack and a drink, not a meal.

Most of the products sold must be very reasonably priced because they probably will be broken, lost or forgotten once the customers leave the beach.

You can learn general messages about business from these cases and learn how to find your own examples. Where you are asked questions, you can also develop successful styles of answering them.

Things that are important in every section
Working together
Many of the cases and Activities the book offers you suggest that you work in groups. This makes learning more complete because each one of you has different ideas, strengths and weaknesses. What you do not understand from listening or working in class or from the text you may understand from discussing it. Equally important, what you do understand you can share with others. Working together is also useful because work can be broken down into separate tasks for everyone, so that you can get much more done and broaden the area of learning. It is much more fun in any case. Whatever you do will be more successful if you can find ways of enjoying it. Teamwork of this kind is a skill in itself and you may like to bear this in mind when you are developing your key skills portfolio. However, it also carries with it responsibility as well as benefits. Your group will be contributing to your learning, but they will also be relying on you to do your bit well.

The idea that learning should be fun may seem strange, but it might do no harm to realise that a major objective for all Richard Branson's Virgin network of businesses is that those who work for them should have fun.

Language
Business Studies has its own language and every section gives you opportunity to both learn it and use it. We expect you to:
- know what terms mean.

At the moment you probably do not know the business study's meaning of words like **random**, **productivity** and **segment**. At this point that does not matter, but in an examination it could make the difference between a good grade and failure. You should, therefore, be able to:
- define them;
- explain them clearly, correctly and concisely;
- respond accurately to them if they are used in questions;
- appreciate the importance of the context in which a word or phrase is used and show this in the ways you discuss meaning and relevance in any question asked;
- use business words and phrases in your own answers correctly, confidently and as a matter of habit. The use of the right language in a correct and appropriate way not only helps to convince a reader or a listener that you know what you are saying, but it also makes the answer more to the point and usually of a higher standard.

When you come across a new word or phrase with a special meaning:
- make sure you know what it means;
- have a vocabulary book and write it up in your own words;
- check that meaning with a good dictionary of the subject and/or with your teacher, or you may find it in the glossary on page 256;
- add in an example or a way of measuring the idea.

Examples
1 For **Working capital** you might write:
'Working capital is that part of the capital of a business that is used in day-to-day transactions.' You might draw the sketch shown here to remind you. You might show how it is calculated with the formula:

CASH → STOCK → PRODUCTION → SELL → CASH

Working capital = Current assets − Current liabilities

2 For **Market segmentation** you might write:

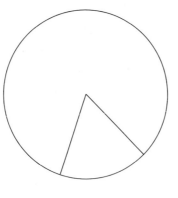

'Market segmentation is dividing a whole market up into small sections which have their own characteristics.' Methods of dividing could be by sex, by age, by occupation or by region, among others. You could use the diagram here to remind you.

- Keep looking at these words and keep the vocabulary book up to date.
- Use the words you have in there regularly in your written work.
- When you are reading and you are doubtful about the meaning of a word, check it out, try to find out the meaning for yourself first and then ask.

Always remember that a word or phrase may mean something slightly but importantly different in the context in which it is used. Examiners are most often interested in the contextual meaning and relevance of the things they ask you about. We give examples of this contextual meaning throughout the book but here is an example to make the point:

Location
  (a) 'The location of the business will be of prime importance. We must find a site in the centre of a large town.'
  (b) 'The location of the office is 34 Bridge Street. It is clearly marked on the map.'
  (c) 'I cannot locate the mineral deposits you say are there.'

All these statements are concerned with the placing of something but the differences are:

  In (a) it is about where the business might be.
  In (b) it is about where the business is.
  In (c) it is about not knowing where the deposits are.

There is both a **glossary** and an **index** at the end of this book. They will help you to research things you are uncertain about or need to find out about.

Concepts

In its simplest form a concept is an idea. Many new products start their lives as concepts in the minds of those who invent or develop them. However, we often need a word or phrase that sums up large areas of the subject in ways that will be understood by students. Mathematics and accounting are full of concepts that help to make what is happening understandable and certain.

A triangle and an equation are concepts. They help us to visualise, in the first case, any three-sided figure and, in the second, any statement that makes two things balance. See Figure 1.2.

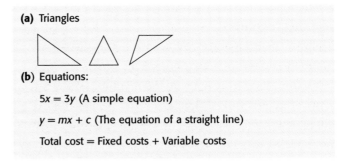

Figure 1.2 Examples of (a) triangles and (b) equations

Sometimes we have to use a word to explain a more general idea for which there is no simple or certain definition, for example:

1 It is likely that no two writers would totally agree about the meaning of the word **Motivation** and there are several different ways in which people think it should be measured. Nevertheless, the word sums up a certain group of ideas for us and enables us to think fairly consistently about them.

2 **Efficiency.** This word provides a yardstick by which we might measure the performance of a machine, a worker or a team.

In contrast, there are some concepts that are capable of precise definition:

1 A phrase like **Working capital** is an example. Go back to our earlier example and read the definition suggested for the vocabulary book.

2 **Fixed cost.** Costs that, in the short run, do not vary with output. An example of such a cost might be the cost of premises and insurance.

Summary

Each section has a summary. Its purpose is to remind you of what has been developed in that section.
It will help with location of ideas you are seeking to read about and be a useful reminder. It will never be a substitute for reading and use of the main ideas.

Studying business

What most of us see as a business is a result of a host of activities too numerous to count in many cases and involving all kinds of activity. We tend to study businesses as if they were isolated units. We look at their structure, their objectives, their internal organisation and the ways in which they work to achieve the results they want. We realise that there is a context that involves many other people and organisations, but the focus is still on a particular business or organisation for much of the time. We do much the same with the activities in the business and this is evident in Module 2, where there are sections on marketing, accounting, people and operations management. Before we break down the subject in this way we need to see the whole picture.

The picture we need to see is to be found in your community and careful study of it will tell you all you need to know about how businesses have to be aware of each other and the environment in which they work. Good management is about looking outwards and responding to, or even anticipating, changes and the ways in which they will affect business behaviour and success. Business managers must be aware of and correctly respond to the large number of influences which come from other businesses, all the stakeholders in the business and the State. The influence of the State is at three levels, that of the local authority, that of the nation and increasingly that of the European Union.

Over-to-you

The ability to answer questions should come from a combination of classroom learning, reading and practice. It could be said that the over-to-you tasks are the reason the sections are written. They certainly explain why each section has been made deliberately interactive, with things for you to do all the way through. Over-to-you tasks are likely to be used by teachers to test your understanding and skills, but they should also be used by you to ensure you are ready to go forward. There are three parts to the over-to-you tasks at the end of most sections. If you get low marks for your efforts don't just shrug your shoulders, find out why and find the time to do a better job. We all learn from experience.

Short-answer questions These are designed to test your knowledge but also to enable you to learn to give full and accurate answers very concisely. Answers would gain 2 or 3 marks on average and that means 2 or 3 minutes to give a full-mark answer. This kind of question will be common in your examinations for Modules 1 and 2. If you become skilled in answering them, you will do well. As you carry on with your studies they will still be very important in checking your subject language and subject knowledge, but will be less important in the examination.

Discover and learn It should already be clear that to be good at business studies you must be able to look away from the text books and out into the business community. This section will suggest some ways of doing that and of developing the quality and breadth of your knowledge. These exercises are also best done as a member of a group rather than on your own. In your groups you should learn to divide these tasks up and to rely on each other. This will help you to develop your skills of enquiry, observation and discussion. It will also begin to set the foundation for the coursework you may do later on.

Case study The objective of each case study is as an example of what you have been learning. Mostly they are an opportunity to use the learning derived from the section. But they also provide the opportunity to demonstrate your ability to use the information gained from the start of the course. The cases should be very similar to those you will get in the examination. It is best to undertake case studies in groups, but always to ensure that you use group discussion and research as a basis for your own answers.

Over-to-you

Read the case study below and then tackle the exercises that follow.

Case study – Business Review

To do an exhaustive survey of all the activities essential to your receipt of *Business Review* four times a year would take too long and be pointless. The main things to examine in this process include:

- ◆ Those materials, workers, capital and resources that produce the paper and the machines ready to print the magazine.
- ◆ The events and situations that occur and which someone realises will make an interesting topic for the magazine.
- ◆ The team of authors who write the articles and the editorial team who prepare them for the magazine.

- ◆ The creative team who produce the designs and the attractive layout of covers and magazine. The workers who print it.
- ◆ The management team who make business decisions like size, shape and number of pages, frequency of issues, advertisements and price.
- ◆ All the marketing, distribution and communication channels that are used at all stages of the process.
- ◆ Finally, the institutions and individuals who buy it and who, by doing so in sufficient numbers, ensure its success in business terms.

This list just breaks the surface of a closely knit set of activities that make it possible for you to pick up *Business Review* and read it.

1 Work in groups of four. Each of you should select a different product you often buy. For your product follow it through and develop its progress from its origins in the same general way as shown in the case study. Don't be too detailed.

(a) Draw a diagram to illustrate this, with short explanatory notes for each stage. Mount it on card and, where possible, display it in the classroom.

(b) Investigate where in the community you can buy this product.

(c) Explain why it is either:
- ◆ generally available in several outlets; or
- ◆ only available in one; or
- ◆ not available locally at all.

2 Where it is available in more than one outlet decide where you would buy it and explain why.

3 Where it is not available at all in your locality try to find reasons why.

2 The nature of business

On completion of this section you should be able to:

➤ understand the nature, variety and pattern of business activity through the businesses found in your area

➤ understand how businesses must meet the needs of both consumers and other stakeholders if they are to be successful

➤ explain the nature of production as added value

➤ appreciate problems associated with waste and its disposal and with various kinds of pollution

➤ understand the departments into which businesses divide as they grow

➤ appreciate some of the problems associated with the setting up of new businesses and their first year of operation

Business activity

In primitive societies there is an immense amount of work as individuals and families struggle to survive by meeting all their own needs. As society grows, the value of specialising and sharing emerges and the need to exchange things becomes apparent. Through exchange of either the skills we develop or the fruits of those skills, business activity gradually emerges.

The photograph below is of a typical town market, which is a hive of activity on Wednesdays and Saturdays. A range of businesses in addition to the market can also be found in the town. Typical businesses might include:

A typical town market which attracts many people to the town centre

A gift shop This is owned and run by a family and is typical of many businesses in the town. It sells memorabilia of the town and the area. It tells us the town is a tourist town. The shop is well located since coaches unload in the market square. It does not have a high turnover but each item it sells will have a high mark-up.

A small café Seasonal trade, especially busy in the summer and on market days. Business is largely between morning coffee and afternoon tea. The opening hours and the menu tell us this. A small business that relies on a single female owner and on part-time employees including students.

An estate agent A small office. It is one of many in the town and this suggests there is a good market for buying and selling property. A drive around would show seven large private housing estates and many villages in which there are houses for sale. A more careful study would explain why estate agents are very busy.

A small hotel Part of a national chain. The hotel can accommodate 58 people, has a restaurant with a good reputation and two bars. Trade is seasonal and the hotel barely breaks even in winter. A large hall is being built on the back. The manager sees the conference business as a good source of winter profits. The choice is either grow and prosper or close down.

Activity

Analyse your community (or a part of it) in this way. Find out what businesses there are and what customer needs they satisfy.

Consumer needs

Businesses are started up because the owners think they have found something to produce which **consumers** will want. They will stay in business if they are satisfying those needs sufficiently well to make a profit (see Case studies opposite and below).

Case study – The shop on the beach

On the front above the beach there is a shop. Today it is busy. It sells books, but is not a bookshop; it sells buckets and spades, but is not a garden centre. In it you can buy sandwiches, tea and coffee, but it is not a restaurant. You can buy balls, comics, newspapers, swimming trunks and many other things. The shop is satisfying two groups of needs, those of people trying to enjoy (children) or to endure (parents) the beach and the facilities and opportunities of the seaside. At high tide and when it rains, there is no business. In the evening and in winter the shop is closed.

Case study – Selling televisions

Do customers just want a television set? Will any set do? If the answers to these questions are 'Yes' then the shop will offer little choice for a straight sale. Think of three different customers:

Sharon Has never had a television set. She can't afford to spend much but is wary of second-hand sets and needs helpful advice.

Simon and Kate They have been married ten years and already have two colour sets. They have a high disposable income and watch television a lot. They have no children. Why do you think they are buying together? How will this influence the attempt to sell? What might they be looking for?

Mary Mary is a Head of Business Studies and is looking for three sets for classroom use. What might Mary be seeking?

There are no right answers and the purpose is only to set you thinking about consumers satisfying needs rather than just buying products. Products like television sets are sold as packages. The simplest package is a basic set for cash, taken away by the customer. More complex packages include insurance, delivery, aerials, rent or buy decisions, HP or cash decisions, and add-on products like video recorders, digital receivers and teletext. Mary might even want a discount. Selling televisions is much more than stocking a range of them in the shop. What the customer needs must be diagnosed and anticipated. It would be a mistake to assume that customer needs are all product orientated or that the business which offers a host of different packages will necessarily be successful.

Think of these two situations:

The dead hotel A potential customer needing a room for the night rang a hotel he had often stayed at. No reply. He tried again. No reply. He phoned another hotel and made the booking.

The missing product Customer: 'I need two pairs of shoes. You only seem to have up to size 11 on the shelf.' Assistant: 'Yeah! We don't bother with larger sizes. We can't sell them.'

In both cases the business has lost a sale and probably a customer. In both cases the customer's dissatisfaction may be spread to other potential customers. Part of satisfying customer needs is to give good and helpful service.

The needs of owners

Being in business is a two-way process. To succeed, the business must satisfy sufficient customers and persuade them that they want to come back. To stay in business, it must satisfy the needs of the owners. The cost of setting up most small businesses is very high and commonly requires reliance on other people's money. These people may be family and friends or there may be a loan from the bank. In almost all cases there is very little left and the risk that the owner and others may have taken is often high. All borrowed money has to be returned, usually by agreed dates, and it has to be paid for in the form of interest. Even using your own money has a cost since it could be earning interest in a safe investment. The business owner has to earn enough to make these payments regularly, to earn a wage on which to live and to earn some profit that makes the risks taken worthwhile. In fact, ownership normally implies several **stakeholders** and the interest in the success of the business that each of them will have. Do not confuse stakeholders with **shareholders**. The distinction is as follows:

Shareholders The term implies that the business is a public or private limited company and that ownership has been divided into shares owned by a few or by many owners of shares.

Stakeholders People who have an interest in the organisation. Clearly owners, whether they be shareholders or not, will have an interest, but lenders, employees, customers are among those who have a stake of some kind in the business and so are stakeholders.

Owners do not expect to make good profits, or even to earn good wages, immediately; they do not expect to pay off all borrowed money by the end of year one, but they realise the importance of **cash flow** and the need to pay bills as they come in. Many of the businesses that fail do so because their forward planning and market research has not been good enough; because they have not anticipated the ease with which cash will flow outwards at the start or the sluggishness with which it flows inwards. Even profitable young businesses have failed because they could not compete with cash-flow problems.

Adding value

Goods and services are bought because consumers see value in the purchase. They think they have value for money. There is no absolute measure of value. Many purchases are habitual and their value is not often questioned. Watch a shopper in a supermarket. Many of the purchases are made quickly and with little or no thought. In these instances shoppers have little need to think about value. But watch those same shoppers when buying durable consumer goods or deciding on a holiday. Now they will shop around. They will consider many alternatives, will look in several shops or catalogues, will take a long time to decide and will seek as much information as possible. They may seek to bargain with the providers. Unless producers can add value through what they do, they will not sell very successfully. All businesses start with a range of **inputs**. Typically these will be:

Natural resources These include resources such as land, coal, oil, fish, and there is concern that many of these are being exhausted. Buildings and machinery are physical assets.

Capital The assets through which business is done or the cash that makes it possible. All businesses need capital. For a shop, needs are small compared with those required to build and run an oil refinery.

People Often said to be the most important asset of a business. People think and act for themselves. This can be a great strength or a source of weakness. Some people provide unskilled work in situations where the machines do most of the producing; others, skilled work where training, experience and care are vital; and some craft work, where a particular talent is paramount.

Activities

1 Think about each of the following from the point of view of the organisation producing each of them:

   (a) a pop concert;   (c) a web site on the Internet;

   (b) a music centre;   (d) a second-hand car.

   What inputs were probably used to produce these for you? Which ones may have been most important? How might value added be measured in each case?

2 Read the following case study and then, working in small groups, discuss value from the point of view of both the producers and the purchasers of the desks.

Case study – Value for money?

Anna and Dyfed both need a desk. Anna is a busy computer analyst and has a very full social and sporting life. She sees this as a simple problem, goes to a furniture shop with a reasonable choice and selects a desk she likes. The firm agrees to deliver and the cost to Anna is £780. Anna would have been prepared to spend £850. Dyfed is a young teacher in Newport, South Wales and his budget for the desk is £350. He looks in several shopping catalogues and on the Internet and eventually selects one that will be delivered at a total cost to him of £290. When it comes it is a flat pack with instructions for assembly, which Dyfed cannot understand. He seeks the help of three young friends and eventually the desk is assembled and everything seems to be in the right place.

Managerial work requires attitudes to others that motivate them, as well as effective leadership styles.

These inputs will vary in nature and importance from one situation to another. Their unit value can be calculated and represents the minimum value that must be associated with the good or service produced. The business will only flourish if the end value is significantly greater than the value of the inputs and customers are prepared to buy at that price.

- From the producer's point of view **value added** is measured by the difference between the cost of inputs and the net revenue from output.
- From the consumer's point of view, value added is measured by the difference between the price charged and the price the consumer would have paid otherwise. The producer measures the consumer's perception of value by the number who return to buy again, by the number of buyers who become customers.

What is produced?

Some businesses produce only goods, e.g. farming, mining, construction and manufacture, although services will be associated with them. Others are service providers and people often think that there is no production in a bus ride or in borrowing money. Of course there is, since the term production includes all activity that adds value. The kinds of goods you might find on a shopping expedition include:

Single-use goods All food, drink, football matches, one-day business studies conferences and many other products can only be used once. Some you use regularly, others are infrequently used; some may be recycled.

Multiple-use goods Not normally consumed in one go but not expected to last for any length of time. These include a box of matches, a packet of sweets, a weekly season ticket.

Durable consumer goods Expected to last a long time and often the subject of guarantees and maintenance agreements to ensure that they do. Cars, domestic appliances, carpets and houses are examples.

Investment goods All organisations have to buy things in order to work effectively. Investment goods are so called because of the way they are used and not for what they are. Businesses will buy machinery to make things and vans or lorries to deliver. They will also buy the goods consumers buy, but for investment purposes. You may buy grapes to eat, while the vintner will buy them to make wine. For home use you may buy sugar, but the bakery will buy it to make bread and cakes. You will buy peas for the home but the factory will buy them straight from the farmer to can, freeze or dry.

Services These are produced for both the consumer and the producer and have become important in our economy. We want utilities like gas and electricity, government-provided services like defence and law and order, convenience services like the delivery of newspapers, the post and milk, communication services like the telephone, fax, email and the Internet. Most of these services are also available to business and industry. Services like the police, roads, libraries and transport are public, but many services are private and personal. Services are a specifically produced good requiring providers to use inputs, to add value and to market them to potential buyers. They are not to be confused with 'service', which is an essential ingredient in providing any good or service to any buyer.

Activity

Working in pairs or groups, analyse the service provision in your locality and decide:

(a) What services seem to be over-provided?

(b) Can you think of an explanation for this?

(c) What services seem to be unavailable or in short supply?

(d) Can you think of an explanation for this?

Unwanted production

Not everything that is produced is valuable. Less desirable 'productions' include:

Waste materials Whilst every effort can and should be made to recycle these materials, this is not always possible. The production of waste has led to laws designed to protect the community and to require socially acceptable practices from producers. Waste has given rise to many businesses that make their profits from the collection, recycling or disposal of waste.

Waste products These arise from some defect in the production process or from over-ordering, which leaves products which are past their sell-by date.

Noise There is some protection from noise within businesses through the Health and Safety at Work Act. Noise often affects the community. Planning permission is required for firms that emit excessive noise. They need careful location.

Waste material collected, sorted and put into bundles ready for recycling

Pollution The law attempts to control pollution, but emissions from buses and lorries are often difficult to control. Sometimes the pollution is a smell, e.g. from a glue factory or from an abattoir. Sometimes objections are to things like the smell from a fish and chip shop or to the litter such shops are thought to cause.

All of these external factors are considered in greater depth in Section 6.

Business on the inside

The smallest business has no employees and there are many like that, particularly in service industries such as plumbing, gardening and window cleaning. In such businesses there is no scope for specialisation, although owners may well organise and plan to be as effective as possible. Often there is hidden support in the unpaid help the family give. A window cleaner may have his wife answering the telephone, taking bookings and doing the VAT returns. Remarkably, he will not think of her as part of the business, just as 'giving him a hand'. There is much help of this kind that supports many businesses. Once a business grows beyond this point there is scope for **specialisation**:

◆ A team of two who decorate houses divide the tasks into lower work done by the older man and 'up the ladder work' done by the younger person.

◆ A small gardening company devoted to garden makeovers, works with a team of three. Primarily, one of them plans and directs, one does the water features and the third does all the other construction work.

Specialisation isolates particular types of work and seeks to ensure that these are undertaken by the worker with the greatest skill in completing them. In the example of the windowcleaner the unpaid wife is really doing all of the 'office work'. In fact, the windowcleaner now employs two other people, has taken on more rounds and each of the three has their own round. Specialisation in large firms tends to occur first by operations within a function. An example of this is when law partners divide the work so that one partner does all the conveyancing, one all the work associated with wills, one all the other civil work and one all the criminal work. Once a firm gets bigger, it tends to organise by function and a common pattern is:

Personnel Some personnel departments are quite small, while others are large and subdivide even further into recruitment, training, payments and training functions.

Activities

1 Look around your local community. How might waste and pollution be a problem in your area? What steps are taken to control them?

2 Read the case study below and then tackle the exercises that follow.

Case study – Corridge plc

Corridge plc is a rapidly growing waste disposal firm.

It has applied for permission to set up a waste disposal site in a disused quarry 6 miles from your town and 2 miles from a small village. The site would also be a depot from which 40 lorries would operate. No toxic or nuclear waste would be disposed of on the site, but the waste would be exclusively industrial. When fully operational the firm would employ 90 people, most of whom would be recruited locally.

(a) Why should the firm have to apply for planning permission and why should the local authority be able to say no?

(b) Discuss the issues involved and consult local opinion. Make it clear that this is not an actual proposal. Decide whether the firm should be given permission.

Not everyone thinks a specialist department is necessary. In some organisations each department does its own personnel work. This makes implementing common policies and practices for the whole organisation rather difficult.

Marketing Marketing has become increasingly important. It can no longer be assumed that a good product will market itself. Markets have to be found, targeted and then served. This is a continuous process as new uses for products and new products come on to the market and as consumers seek to satisfy a widening range of needs. For an increasing range of goods the market is worldwide. Although ecommerce has yet to make a real impact, it will not be long before many goods and services are sold over the Internet. Marketing also has its specialist divisions to meet these changing needs.

Production This used to be considered the core of the firm. Now most firms must produce what they can sell and must be flexible. They must become more efficient in a fast-moving world, where modern technology can be crucial to success. In effect, the modern production department has a much greater market focus. The approach is increasingly set on such targets as continuous improvement (Kaizan), just-in-time stockholding policies, total quality management and lean production. Lean production is an attitude of mind, which changes approaches to all aspects of production.

Finance and accounts First, the department must order all information about costs and revenues that concern the firm. This will be used to inform and to report to the stakeholders. Second, it must control. The department usually produces the plans (budgets) and assists in allocation. It is also expected to control practices and procedures and to ensure that they are common throughout the firm. The money the firm uses and collects is not its own. It belongs to the stakeholders and it must be properly and honestly accounted for. Finally, the department is at the centre of planning and forecasting. In general, things will not be done unless the firm can see that the benefits of an action will outweigh its costs. Many of the factors (but not all of them) will involve the inflow or outflow of money.

All of these functions exist in any organisation, whether or not there is a specialist person or department. The two case studies in the Activity demonstrate this.

Activity

Read the case studies below and then tackle the exercises that follow.

Case study – All Saints Church

Personnel There are three levels of personnel: the vicar and his team of curates, who are paid a salary by the Diocese; the organist, the parish secretary and the verger, who receive a salary from All Saints Parish Church funds; and a large volunteer group, who receive expenses only and often nothing at all. The Vicar is the equivalent of a managing director.

Marketing Whilst it may be surprising, the church markets extensively. It markets regularly among its members and collectively through 'Churches Together', which represents all denominations in the town. It promotes special services and activities. Part of its marketing is in regular visits by the clergy and part in their distinctive dress. It tends to employ no specialists. Everyone is involved in the marketing process and one of its focal points is the monthly magazine.

Production The obvious products are the regular services offered on Sundays and on special occasions. However, special needs are met by services for baptisms, marriages and funerals, by visits to hospitals and other caring institutions, by participating in the education provision in local schools and by day-care facilities offered to those who need them.

Finance The parish to maintain its building and grounds and to pay its share for the administration of the diocese, salaries and pensions has working capital requirements. It gets most of its revenue from voluntary giving and from bequests. It earns fees for some specially provided services and it holds a massive calendar of fund-raising events to support itself and its purposes in the community. It is controlled through a network of committees, the core of which is the Parochial Church Council (PCC), an elected body. Budgeting is difficult because most expenditure is either fixed or determined by the Diocese and income is always uncertain. The church barely breaks even and, since annual expenditure is tending to rise faster than annual income, the need to find additional sources of income is an acute one.

Case study – Home Farm

This is a local business, which changed its focus dramatically over the ten year period (Table 2.1). The owners have been forced by the Common Agricultural Policy of the EU and by the changing fortunes of agriculture to seek other markets, to service the markets in more cost-effective ways and to organise what they do in a very much more 'managed' way.

Personnel The farm was a family partnership until it broadened its market base by converting its outbuildings into holiday accommodation in 1998. At that time it formed a private limited company. This was partly to raise more capital, but largely to obtain limited liability status. The six members of the family are on the Board, together with two other directors. It employs eight others full time. One of these runs the Home Farm office. It also employs additional casual labour at lambing and harvest times and for the holiday months. These are usually students. It has a 'pick your own' approach to the marketing of fruit and some vegetables. Family members are salaried and workers are paid an hourly wage.

Marketing There is a varied approach to marketing, which depends on the products concerned. With arable and meat products most marketing is by contract with an industrial user. With fruit and vegetables some marketing is through 'pick you own' and some through the farm shop. These are advertised on local radio, in local papers and through on-site promotion. Some marketing is through a local 'farmers' market' established recently. A registered camp and caravan site is marketed through the specialist press and bed-and-breakfast facilities through the Regional Tourist Board. Milk is collected daily. The holiday part of the business has been carried out through an agency agreement with 'Country Holidays' a holiday letting firm. However, they now get a large number of regular returners and have decided that this and word of mouth promotion will be sufficient from now on.

Production Most of the staff work on the traditional farm products, but there are three people who work on the holiday side. One is full time and the other two work only between April and October. Farming activities are capital intensive, but holiday activities are labour intensive. The directors are considering the potential for moving into organic food production, but this will be a long-term objective since it takes about five years to ensure that the land is free of non-organic substances.

Finance The farming and the holiday accounts are kept separate through the formation of a private limited company, which manages the tourist business and the farm business as separate units. Financial control is difficult because of the seasonal aspect of most of the work. Only chicken, egg and milk production are continuous, all the rest have a seasonal cycle. Most of the revenue comes in from May to September. Good management is necessary to avoid cash-flow problems in the winter months. The farm relies heavily on bank finance during this period. In the last ten years most of the profits have been ploughed back into the changes which have taken place. The capital of the firm was increased by the company formation and there is no long-term borrowing.

1990	Four members of the family worked on a mixed farm. No other activities.
1992	A farm shop was opened to sell farm-produced fruit, vegetables and eggs. As the shop grew, a wider range of produce was bought in.
1993	A camping and caravan site was developed using some under-used hectares close to the road. This has been extended and developed each year since.
1994	Beef farming was discontinued and pig and poultry farming increased. New, local markets were found for an increasing volume of produce.
1996	'Pick your own' developed for soft and hard fruit and for some vegetables.
1998	Four outbuildings were converted for bed and breakfast and holiday cottage lets. Staff were taken on to run these and the camping and caravan site. Marketing was through a national holiday-cottage chain.
1999	Camping and caravan site extended. All animal husbandry except poultry and pigs discontinued. Both of these converted to free range and vegetable production to organic methods. Regular attendance at a farmers' market.

Table 2.1 Home Farm: calendar of change

(a) Choose a large retail business and a manufacturing business known to you and analyse them in the same way.

(b) Find a business in your area that is either (i) relocating or (ii) closing down and try to discover why this is happening.

Business start-up

What persuades people to set up in business? Most of them start small and many because of the personal objectives of the sole owner who wants to be the boss. What has deterred many has been lack of capital and many businesses can be traced to winnings, inheritances and redundancy payments. All that the 'entrepreneurs' lacked was the financial opportunity. Something like 400,000 new businesses are started every year and every major bank has extensive literature and service and support departments devoted to business start-up.

The difficulties of small businesses

Suppose you want to set up a small business. You have been a well-respected chef for some years and you think you can go it alone. What are the issues you must face if you are to have a hope of being successful?

- Is there a market sufficient to sustain the business and provide a reasonable living for the owner? Many businesses do not research well enough and are satisfied by a few positive indications from well-meaning friends. Without real evidence it is impossible to plan. Without a plan it is difficult to persuade those whose financial support you need, to provide it.
- Under what conditions will the potential consumers actually buy? What is your unique selling point (USP)? What is going to be different about your menu and your venue?
- Is there likely to be a long-term market? Will your restaurant survive beyond the curiosity visits?
- What kind of business ought you to start? Most start as sole owners or as partnerships. The risks of unlimited liability can be massive. Is it wiser to be a private limited company? It is often thought that a limited company is more creditworthy than a sole trader or a partnership.
- Are you going to buy an existing restaurant or set up a new one?
- The business name is a vital marketing tool and your own name may not have the impact of a more imaginative approach. Names like 'The Happy Eater' and 'The Lunch Box' carry an initial marketing boost. It is difficult to change a name because of the goodwill attached to it. You may

Case study – New businesses

Discover the new businesses that have set up in your area in the last two years. Try to discover why the owners began the business.

Among the reasons you may discover are:

- An opportunity to turn a hobby into a business. In one town there is a motor cycle shop and workshop started by a speedway rider after he retired from the sport.
- To develop a market for a product. One of our shops is a bakery specialising in making and decorating speciality cakes. The owner had been doing this from home for years but demand grew and premises were needed.
- The wish has always been there and now the capital is available. The common source is redundancy payments because the owner of the capital is also unemployed. This often happens with older workers for whom job prospects are bleak. The electrician, the windowcleaner and the plumber in one area all came from redundancy when the local steel works rationalised and greatly reduced its workforce.
- Belief in greater rewards from self-employment. Often, people doing this do not understand the management aspects or the risks of being self-employed and their businesses are short lived. Two take-away food businesses and one florist in one locality failed for these reasons, within a year of starting.
- The desire for independence. There comes a time in most peoples' careers when they are fed up with taking orders. They want to be their own boss. One of these now runs a very successful small café, having previously driven a mobile ice cream van. He was fed up with driving around all day and being under pressure to achieve high weekly targets.
- The desire to leave something for the family. Many sole-owner shops are really family businesses because every one in the family plays some part in their success. They often close when family individuals no longer want to be so closely tied or do not want to carry on the business.

have a unique selling point that can be summed up in the name or its associated logo. Names like 'Kwik Save', 'Prontoprint' and 'Rapid Results' were all designed to promote a feature of the business. One owner chose the name 'Alpha' because it would come high in an alphabetical list of businesses in the same trade.

♦ You are in business. You could not afford a High Street location so nobody knows about you. You have to get the message across and almost certainly on a limited budget. Which market are you going to be in? The lunch trade is a different market from the evening trade. How can it be targeted? You must target it as well and as often as you can. Many businesses have failed because their owners thought they could not afford to advertise.

♦ Setting the right prices is crucial. Many have failed because they set low prices to attract custom and then lost it all when prices had to rise. Giving value for money is much more important than being cheap. In the restaurant business quality of service, range of menu, comfort and environment are often more important.

♦ Choosing an effective location. A sandwich bar will need to be convenient; a speciality restaurant can be almost anywhere; car-parking facilities may be necessary.

♦ What are your objectives? If these are too ambitious or if you have not really worked any out and are just going to drift along, the business risks will be far greater and you are more likely to fail.

♦ Finance. It is difficult for organisations to acquire credit support before a trading reputation has been established. Inadequate financing, cash-flow problems, failure to keep good records and to plan for cash needs are, between them, major reasons for failure.

Over-to-you

1 Discuss the advantages and disadvantages of buying an existing business. Decide what you would do and why. Compare notes and reasons with other groups.

2 Working in groups, think about the needs of your community. What business do you think might be successful? Use the above checklist and other ideas you think are important. Work out a business plan for such a business.

Short-answer questions

1 What is meant by the term 'stakeholder'? Give two examples of internal and two examples of external stakeholders.

2 Mary (see the Case study about selling television sets) is seeking a 'discount'. Explain what this is and why Mary thinks she is entitled to a discount.

3 Explain why the trader might be prepared to give Mary a trade discount.

4 Explain the process of 'adding value'. How would you measure added value if you ran:
   (a) a fish and chip shop?
   (b) a bus service?

5 Explain what is meant by the term 'capital' in the context of owning a business.

6 Explain why it is that the same good may be either a consumer good or an investment good.

7 Explain what the activities of (a) a personnel department and (b) a finance department might be.

8 Explain what is meant by the term 'unique selling point' (USP) and give an example of one for either a business or a product known to you.

9 What problems are commonly faced by new businesses?

10 What would you consider were the necessary factors that would make it likely that a new business would succeed?

Discover and learn

1 Choose a consumer durable good priced at more than £100. Discover where, in your locality, it can be bought and how many ways there are of buying it. Think about the associated services and consumer advantages. Decide where you would buy it and explain why.

2 What have you learnt about the importance of identifying and satisfying consumer needs from the exercise in the previous question?

Case study – Railway preservation society look to the future

A railway preservation society has been running a small section of track, which passes from one major town to another and through three rural stations. The members of the society have worked as amateurs for many years, raising enough from summer holiday rides and from memorabilia to keep their hobby going. They think that now is the time to turn the hobby into a business. They know that substantially more income will have to be created and that the summer tourists and memorabilia sales will be nothing like enough. They are in the initial stages of planning for development.

3 Read the case study opposite and then advise the society concerning:
   (a) The difficulties associated with turning their hobby into a business.
   (b) Possible market opportunities they could investigate in order to make the business pay.
   (c) Particular things you think might be important in view of the nature of their intended business.

Summary

In this section we have recognised that:

● Business activity has a particular nature and various features.

● Your locality can be used to understand the great variety of organisational activity and what these organisations contribute in context.

● Good business satisfies consumer needs and also meets the needs of its stakeholders.

● All businesses seek to add value and, because they succeed in this, they are producers, regardless of whether they produce a good or a service, or of whether their market is a consumer good or an industrial one.

● To achieve this they must use resources effectively. Consumers are constantly looking for value for money, which is a complex of many things.

● The production process leads to many different kinds of waste and pollution. Society must find ways of dealing with this problem.

● All businesses must be organised and, as they grow, the organisation becomes more complex with the opportunity for specialisation.

● Work is departmentalised to keep it focused and controlled.

● All businesses have to start somewhere and will face problems and difficulties, particularly in the first year.

Key words

Definitions of Key words can be found in the Glossary on page 236

capital	noise
cash flow	production
consumers	services
finance and accounts	shareholders
inputs	specialisation
investment goods	stakeholders
marketing	value added
natural resources	waste

3 Classification of businesses

➤ explain the ways in which businesses within the economy are classified

➤ classify any business appropriately

➤ consider ways in which the size of a business can be measured and difficulties in doing this

➤ explain the different ways in which a business may be legally structured

➤ explain the advantages and disadvantages of different legal forms

➤ distinguish between public and private ownership

➤ discuss the issues arising from public and private ownership

Introduction

Classifying things helps us to understand them but classifications are rarely discrete and this is certainly true when we think of businesses. In this chapter we look at some ways of classifying business but realise that many businesses do so many things and in such a variety of different ways that they make classification very difficult.

Classification by nature of activity

Business is possible because one group of people has the skills and resources to make things and make them available to others. This would be a waste of time if nobody actually wanted them. Here we can see two groups that are essential to business activity:

◆ those who grow the food, build the furniture, provide the power, make the cars;

◆ those who seek to buy the products because they have the ability and willingness to do so.

You want your newspapers and post delivered and you want a whole range of other services, such as hairdressing, banking and legal services. Business and industry want services too, including financial support, delivery services, maintenance and repair. Most of these services we want as individuals, but there is another group that we want collectively. These include road and transport links, education, defence and law and order. This produces two more groups:

◆ those who provide the personal and private services that individual businesses and individual people need;

◆ those who provide the public services we all need.

The government itself provides some of the latter through organisations that it develops and creates, e.g. the armed forces and the police force. Others it contracts out to private firms, e.g. road building. Some are jointly provided by state and private organisations, e.g. education. Firms which provide our essential services, such as water, telephone and electricity are called utilities and are run by private business but are subject to firm control by public bodies, such as OFWAT which oversees the supply of water.

This classification is not very helpful but it does serve to remind us of two things:

◆ that production without likely consumers is a waste of time;

◆ that the services we use are as much production as the goods we buy.

Classification by level of activity

Within the economy there are three levels of activity, each of which takes businesses closer to the consumer.

Primary activity Takes all the natural resources and makes them more useful to consumers. In Section 2 we called this process adding value. Fish are of little (economic) value in the sea and timber is not available until the trees are cut down. Little of food value would grow without agriculture and the mineral resources we need have to be mined. All of these are primary activities using the resources that nature provides.

Secondary activity Takes the materials provided by primary industry and processes them so that some of the more complex needs of society are met. Food is processed both to give variety and to provide more effective storage. Minerals are processed to provide energy or to enable construction. It is through these manufacturing activities that cars and computers come on the market.

Tertiary activity Provides all the services private, personal and public, that industry and consumers demand.

Again these are not completely separate categories. There is much that is manufactured found in modern agricultural and fishing methods. There are many firms operating at all three levels of activity. However, the classification is a useful one and changes in the relative importance of each type of activity tell us much about the way the economy is changing.

Classification by size

In the Activity opposite you will classify the businesses by size. You could use the terms large, medium and small. How did you decide what a particular firm was? If we consider the three businesses in Table 3.1, which one is the biggest? How can we decide?

Factor	Hotelier A	Hotelier B	Hotelier C
Number of hotels	1	10	15
Capacity	700 rooms	600 rooms	600 rooms
	900 people	1,000 people	1,100 people
Employees	350	140	90
Turnover per annum	£2 million	£1.5 million	£1.5 million
Net profit	£100,000	£200,000	£400,000
Capital employed	£14 million	£7 million	£6 million

Table 3.1 Problem of defining size

In this example we see the problem of defining size. Hotelier C has the most number of hotels but they are

Activity

Go to the map of economic activity in your area that you built up in working through Section 2. From that information classify the businesses in your area in accordance with Table 3.2. To qualify for entry into your table there must be a firm, or a branch of it, located in your area. For example, every office and most houses will have a telephone, but that does not qualify unless there is a telephone company in your area. On the other hand, a railway station would qualify.

Level of activity	Example	Number/Size
Primary agriculture	Farming	
Primary/Others	Forestry/Fishing	
Secondary/Construction	Builders	
Secondary/Others	Manufacture	
Tertiary private services	Banks/Doctors	
Tertiary public	Gas/Water/Electricity	
Total		

Table 3.2 Example of levels of activity in your local area

(a) What do you conclude about the nature of economic activity in your area?

(b) Has it changed significantly in the last five years?

quite small. Firm A has only one hotel, but has more rooms than either of the others. Firm A has by far the largest capital employed but makes a much smaller net profit. With all these problems how can we measure size?

At the extremes there are no problems. We all accept that a multinational is a very large business, even though its establishment in a particular area may be quite small. We also know that the majority of businesses are very small. This is probably true of your area. It is also true that most businesses start small and then grow.

Potential measures of size
Number of workers

This is the simplest measure and it is clear that shops with just the owner or the family are small. Perhaps it is more obvious that a firm employing many people is large since labour is not a cheap resource. But there are problems. How do you measure part-time employment? How about firms in which the labour force is self-employed? How about the firms that employ few people because they are very highly capitalised?

Example There are two breweries in the same town. One is traditional, making 200,000 gallons of beer a week and employing 88 people in the processes involved. The other is totally automated, produces 1,000,000 gallons a week and employs eight people.

Capital employed

Where this is high the firm is likely to be large, provided the capital is being used efficiently, but it may not be large for the industry it is in. There are, of course, many industries where the scope for capital intensity is low and the measure would not be a helpful one. This is true of many of the personal service industries.

Turnover

In most instances, if turnover is large the firm is large. However, there are businesses in which small scale is associated with high turnover. Financial services and working precious stones and precious metals are examples.

Balance sheet values

One of the values shown in a balance sheet is the net worth of the business and this may well be a good measure of size. This too, may be misleading with some industries in which quite small-scale activity is associated with a high net worth.

Market share

Market share is a relative term. If a firm has a high market share, then it must be among the leaders in its field and hence comparatively large. However, when total markets are small, the measure will not indicate a particularly large firm.

Share values

Firms with large shareholdings are almost certainly large. The problem lies in the potential for organisations that are not companies to be large. In the days when most of our utilities were in public hands they were large, but had no shareholders at all. The Post Office is still like that, although attempts have been made to privatise it. Many government bodies are very large.

National networks

There are many businesses in which the size of the technical unit can be small but which, overall, are large. In the hotel business, there are many chains with small or moderate-sized hotels and the same is true with retail chains. The business here is not the individual outlet but the whole network. What is large by this criterion? Each unit may be so small that it cannot really enjoy economies of scale. How many of them should there be to qualify as large – 10, 15, 25?

Unit costs

The value of being large is related to the unit costs at which the firm can produce. If a firm has low unit costs, it is certainly efficient but is it large?

Impact on the community

In many small towns one or perhaps two employers dominate. When those firms are going through difficult times, so also does the town, its people and its businesses, which all rely on the prosperity of the dominating business for their livelihood. A current example is Tiverton with John Heathcote and another example used to be Corby with British Steel. In both instances these firms are considered large on other measures.

How to measure

We are really no nearer a conclusion and the best way to make the choice is probably to test a firm on more than one of the above criteria and accept that it is large or small if three criteria point to the same conclusion. The Bolton Commission, established in 1968 to consider this problem, recommended two criteria should be sufficient to determine size.

Legal structure
Sole traders

This is the most common form of business, although many only last a short period of time and others grow and change their structure. Sole traders, however, account for a relatively small proportion of annual business turnover. All sole traders have **unlimited liability**, which means that the owner's personal possessions and property can be taken to pay the debts of the business. They also run, in most instances, on limited capital and find it difficult to acquire more and to grow. Examples of this type of business are small construction, retailing, farming, personal services, finance and catering. Advantages and disadvantages of this business structure are given in Table 3.3.

Advantages	Disadvantages
Less legal restriction	Unlimited liability
Personal; complete control	Poor profits often
Keeps profits	Long hours
Choose work patterns	No scope for specialisation
Relationships more personal	Difficult to raise additional capital
	Lack of continuity

Table 3.3 Sole traders

Partnerships

Most commonly found in professional services, retailing, small construction, and in catering and financial services. A partnership is an agreement between two or more people to work together. At least one of the partners, and it can be all of them, must take unlimited liability for the business. Partners who do not do this can only offer their money to the business and can take no part in decision making or management. For this reason they are called limited partners. Partnership requires mutual trust to work, since one partner can bind all the others by action taken. Advantages and disadvantages of this business structure are given in Table 3.4.

Advantages	Disadvantages
Possible to specialise	Unlimited liability
Shared decision-making	Shared profits
Increased capital	No continuity
Greater market opportunity	Bound by actions of the partner(s)
Tight control	Capital not easy to raise

Table 3.4 Partnerships

The dangers of unlimited liability

Business is about taking risks and, if the risk of failure is high or the cost of failure may be financial ruin, few will take those risks. Yet, change and development come because people are prepared to take risks. Partnerships and sole traders will rarely grow to a great size if liability remains unlimited. An economy that wishes to grow and develop needs a form of business structure in which there is a limit to the risk taken and in which the business begins to take responsibility, rather than the people who own it. The other big business risk that sole traders and partnerships face is that the business has no life beyond that of the people involved; there is a lack of continuity. Finding a way out of this problem required the development of three legal principles:

- **legal personality;**
- **limited liability;**
- **continuity.**

Legal personality

You are a person and as one you have all kinds of legal rights. Those rights grow as you reach certain ages and are complete by the age of 18 unless you are subjected to legal restrictions by circumstances such as being an alien (i.e. not a citizen of the country in which you live), not being of sound mind or being in prison. You can make contracts and you can take responsibility for the credit you receive. You can enter into business agreements and it is to you personally that people will come if they seek redress. You can use the law against people who break their agreements and in turn the law can be used against you. Nobody else is responsible for you. All of this, of course, assumes that you are 18.

How much easier it would be if a business had these rights and responsibilities. Provided the business becomes a company, registers as a co-operative or is a public corporation, it does achieve these rights. It acquires legal personality. This means that in all possible ways the business is treated as if it were a person and all transactions and agreements are pursued in its name. This does not take all responsibility away from those who are its owners or managers. They must still act responsibly and in accordance with the approved objectives of the business, and within the law.

Limited liability

The ownership of companies is divided up into small units (shares), usually but not always of one pound (£1) in face value. People can buy these shares and hence become part owners of the business. In the main these shares are owned in blocks and in some instances one person or organisation has absolute control by virtue of owning more than 50% of the shares. People who own large blocks often become directors of the business.

The only liability a shareholder has is for the amount paid for the shares. Nobody can make any further claim against shareholders. Liability is limited to the shareholding. Thus people are prepared to provide the necessary finance for very much larger firms.

Continuity

When sole owners die or when partners leave a business, the business ceases to exist. For a sole owner the value of the business passes into their estate and may well continue in the family if it can be inherited intact and the beneficiary wishes it to continue. A partnership can regroup around different people, but continuity is not guaranteed. In a company all that happens is that ownership, through the inheritance of shares, carries on and there is no break.

Private limited companies

The protection that comes from being a company is, therefore, substantial and it can be obtained by small firms, the owner(s) of which will create a private limited company. It is the word 'Limited' or 'Ltd' that tells us that a business has adopted this form. It has limited liability for its owners, legal personality and continuity, but the shareholders own their shares privately, meaning that they cannot sell them or advertise them publicly and can only sell them at all with the agreement of the other shareholders. Usually these shares are owned by family, friends or employees. They know each other and often the previous sole owner still has a controlling interest. The structure is adopted for its protection and for the possibilities of further capital for growth that are opened up. The capital to which the company has access is still small but significantly greater than that for unincorporated firms. The shares are usually owned by a small number of people and someone, usually the original owner, has overall control. Since the capital is owned in shares, the firm has continuity and the shares can be passed down from one generation to the next. The fact of incorporation does impose certain legal formalities. These are primarily designed to protect various stakeholders because the liability of the shareholders is limited. Examples of this type of business are found in retailing, computer services, financial services, small and medium manufacture and small construction. The advantages and disadvantages are given in Table 3.5.

Advantages	Disadvantages
Limited liability	Capital acquisition limited
Legal personality	Legal constraints
Continuity	Difficult to sell shares
Tight control	
Easier capital acquisition	Greater status

Table 3.5 Private limited (Ltd) company

Many of the Activities and cases in the sections on accounting and finance focus on this issue of small private limited companies, looking at whether they should change their structure to pursue a new objective. Any one of these will help in understanding the issues involved in company structure.

Public limited companies (plc)

These are not always large but virtually all the giants of the business world have adopted this form. They can be recognised by plc or inc. at the end of their business name. They have all the advantages of private status plus the quotation of their share values and the public marketing of them through the Stock Exchange. Because ownership is more divided and because it is divorced from control, the law, through the Companies Acts, places even more detailed controls on the way a plc must be run and on the matters that must be reported to the shareholders. Examples are highly capitalised industries, multinationals and high-risk developments. Advantages and disadvantages of this business structure are given in Table 3.6.

Advantages	Disadvantages
Limited liability	Legal formalities
Legal personality	Cost of incorporation
Continuity	Shares subject to fluctuation
Ease of share buying and selling	Legal requirements
Ease of capital acquisition	Subject to possible takeover battles

Table 3.6 Public limited companies (plc) or (inc.)

Activity

Give yourselves a present of £1,000 (or more if you wish) and discuss the share values you see in the financial sections of a daily newspaper. Select a range of them at the prices quoted. Monitor the prices on a weekly basis and decide when to sell and buy something else. Keep this exercise going for six months. Discuss and try to find reasons for your results at the end.

Alternatively, there are several national competitions, one of which is 'Beat The Boss'. This competition has a much broader business base than simply buying shares.

The formalities of incorporating

As soon as you form a company, ownership and control is divided and risk is shared with those who become stakeholders in the business. For these reasons, companies, like people, need birth certificates and the State needs a device through which it can protect the weaker parties in this situation. The documents the directors must complete are:

Memorandum of Association This shows the agreement to form a company and the objectives it will pursue. It also indicates the maximum share capital the company seeks authorisation for and registers a head office through which the business can be contacted.

Articles of Association The day-to-day constitution of the company, which covers the firm's operating arrangements in relationships with its stakeholders, for example the way meetings will be conducted and how voting will be carried out. The document is a more sophisticated form of the kind of formal document that a cricket or tennis club would call its constitution.

As is always the case, there are fees attached to this procedure and when all is in order a Certificate of Incorporation is issued. Private companies can be open for business from this point on but public ones need to show they can raise the capital first and from that point they are issued with a certificate to commence business.

Some interesting exceptions

For some people the risks of business are large and they will incorporate purely to limit liability. A number of 'pop groups' have done this because their business is not just music but, if they are successful, all the memorabilia and spin-off trading that takes place.

Individual people can do this and become known as **corporations sole**. For example, in the church, a Diocese must always have a Bishop to lead it, but would lack continuity every time a Bishop died or retired. This problem is solved by incorporation, which makes each Bishop a corporation sole.

Some small non-trading organisations also need a means to ensure that the finances of the organisation will not dry up with nobody responsible. They can incorporate by guarantee. This means that, in the event of difficulty the directors and shareholders guarantee a certain sum of money. They do not buy any shares at the time of incorporation. A local cricket club may have this kind of structure.

All three of these types of organisation have one thing in common. They need the security or continuity given to them by company status, but they do not need capital.

Co-operative societies

Whenever this term is used, the local retail co-operative probably comes to mind. To most people that is just another supermarket, but its legal structure is different. Its purpose is to serve the interest of the members and its profits are shared with them. The organisation does have shares but there is little purpose, for ordinary members, in having more than one share since all members have equal voting rights. In the older form all members participated in the running of the business, but in the modern form the business is managed professionally.

In fact co-operation is much more common than that. It sometimes happens through special contracts

Activity

Read the case study below and then tackle the exercises that follow.

Case study – Hobson's Garage

Ron Hobson has been in business for many years owning a small garage in a Devon village. He has two sons and a daughter and they want to be involved in his business. It isn't big enough to support more than one family and all Ron's children are married, living elsewhere in the village. Many of the village car owners buy fuel from Ron but there is little return in that and specialist garages are taking more and more of Ron's repair work. Ron is thinking of several ways of expanding:

♦ Philip, one of his sons, is licensed to drive buses and taxis. So Ron thinks there might be prospects in providing a taxi service.

♦ The local bus service has been withdrawn and workers who need to get to Tiverton, Exeter or Crediton now find it difficult. There is a possibility of running services or of tendering for contracts for special factory and school journeys.

♦ The village has only had one shop for many years and now this is closing down. The garage is in the centre of town and there is plenty of space and one spare building. Ron wonders about the possibility of opening a shop and knows that his daughter Stephanie and her husband Iain would be interested in running it.

Ron knows that, unless he takes some action, his present business will not survive. He also wants to retain control of his business and pass it on to his children. He has very little money saved and each of the possible ways of expanding will require capital. Early in his life Ron had real difficulties over debts in his family and under no circumstances will he consider borrowing.

(a) Suppose that Ron can only afford to choose one of the possible ways of expanding. Which would you suggest and why?

(b) Make and justify an assumption about how much capital the firm will need.

(c) Advise Ron on ways in which it might be obtained.

(d) How might possible ways of finding the capital also help Ron to 'keep things in the family'.

between the members and is called a **joint venture**. A good example of this was the production of *Concorde*. Joint ventures are often set up by farmers, who co-operate to buy and use expensive farm machinery, such as combined harvesters. In buy-out situations, particularly where the new owners are the members of the workforce, the resulting structure is often a co-operative.

There are many examples of housing associations that work on this principle. They permit people who wish to own their own homes, but do not have enough capital, to come into the property market.

Concorde is the only operational supersonic transport aircraft. It was developed as a joint Anglo-French venture when it was realised that neither country alone could fund the project. The Concorde project would probably have never been started had it not been for hopelessly optimistic initial estimates of development cost. As the true costs escalated, and the British economy faltered, the British Government attempted to pull out, but this was strongly resisted by France. The Government was forced to scrap its advanced military aircraft the TSR2 instead. Initial entry of Concorde into service was hampered by American resistance on the pretext of the high noise levels. As a consequence it was some time before flights to New York were permitted. The aircraft now returns an operating profit, but the development costs will never be recovered. Subsequent studies for a replacement have so far always foundered on the inability of manufacturers to demonstrate a positive return on investment.
Source: This photo appears with kind permission of Dick Barnard.

Public corporations

The two uses of the word 'public' often cause confusion, but public corporations are very different from public companies. Public corporations are owned by institutions such as insurance companies and pension funds and also by private individuals through the shares they buy. Each public corporation is subject to the provisions of its own Act of Parliament and its modes of management determined within the Act. Responsibility for the running of the corporation lies with a government minister. There used to be many public corporations, but the majority have now been privatised. Examples that still exist are the BBC, ITV and the Post Office.

The importance of classifying businesses

There is a mass of detail associated with the way firms are classified and this is specially true when they are classified by legal structure. It is not this detail that is of interest to us in Business Studies. We are interested in what firms want to do (their objectives), the context in which they do it (their environment) and the efficiency with which the activities are undertaken. It is in each of these senses that the features of a business may be of importance.

A firm may well start small, it may be locked into one limited form of business activity and, in most instances, it will be a sole trader. Many of the successful ones will want to grow. Some will do so by increasing activity gradually over time, some will do so by acquisition and merger, some will do so by moving into other, usually related, fields of activity. All will need more capital for these purposes and few will gain it entirely from their own resources or from the profits of the business. They will need to seek another structure. Here is where our real interest lies. How do firms change from one structure to another, how do they decide what form will be best suited to their environment and their needs?

Over-to-you

Table 3.7 shows the statistics for a small town:

(a) Calculate the actual and percentage unemployed for each year.

(b) Which level has declined most in recent years? Explain your answer.

(c) What might have been the effect of such a decline?

(d) How has the relative position of the three sectors changed over time?

(e) How might these changes be explained?

(f) Compare the changes you have noticed in this case with ones that have occurred in your area.

Year	1995	1996	1997	1998
Total population available for work	34,500	34,650	35,700	33,600
Percentage in: Primary employment	3.0	3.0	2.9	2.5
Secondary employment	37.0	35.0	33.0	27.6
Tertiary employment	56.3	57.2	59.6	60.4
Unemployed (actual)				
Unemployed (percentage)				

Table 3.7 Statistics for a small town

Short-answer questions

1 Into what three levels of activity may businesses be divided?

2 Distinguish between private and public consumer services.

3 Why do some owners wish to keep their businesses small?

4 Distinguish between ownership and control.

5 Why is this distinction important?

6 Limited liability seems unfair. Why is it necessary?

7 Explain how legal personality and continuity help businesses to operate efficiently.

8 Why is Manchester United a plc?

9 Explain what is meant by privatisation.

10 Explain why there is no point in owning more than one share in a retail co-operative.

Discover and learn

1 Using the classification primary, secondary and tertiary, analyse business in your area.

(a) How important is each level relative to the others?

(b) What changes have been noticed in the last ten years?

(c) What explanations can you offer for these changes?

2 Select one large firm in your area:

(a) Has it grown or declined in recent years?

(b) How do you explain the change or the fact that there has not been one?

(c) Comment on its legal structure.

(d) What might be the impact on the community if it closed down?

3 Explain the structure and ownership of each of the following in your area:

(a) the local hospital;

(b) the library;

(c) the bus service;

(d) a charity shop;

(e) a church.

4 Work as a small group of three or four; each choose a different sole trader and discover what the owners objectives:

(a) were when the business was opened or taken over;

(b) are now.

Discuss your findings with other members of your group. What conclusions do you draw about the objectives of sole traders? Compare your findings.

Summary

In this section we have recognised that:

● There is no perfect way of classifying business but it helps to try so that the pattern of business is clearer. We can learn much about our own local area from the patterns of business it contains.

● We can classify businesses on various different bases.

● The classification can be based on the nature of the activity, e.g. consuming and producing.

● It can be based on the level of activity from primary through to secondary.

● It can be based on the the size of the business, from the micro business through to the very large and the public company.

● It can be based on the legal structure, from sole trader through to public limited company.

● It can be based on the distinction between private and public enterprise.

● There are other classifications largely based on the financial and capital structure of the firm. These measures will be discussed further in Sections 10 to 13 where finance and accounting are considered.

Key words

Definitions of Key words can be found in the Glossary on page 236.

corporation sole	primary activity
joint venture	secondary activity
legal personality	tertiary activity
limited liability	unlimited liability

4 Organisations and their objectives

On completion of this section you should be able to:

➤ understand the nature and purpose of objectives

➤ state, explain and comment on the objectives an organisation is likely to have

➤ understand the patterns of objectives an organisation may develop and show awareness of ways in which priorities may change and conflicts may develop

➤ show understanding of the elements of SWOT analysis and how this technique may be used in diagnosis

➤ understand how objectives influence business behaviour and business decisions

➤ name and explain the role of different stakeholders in business and comment upon the objectives they may have and the way these are likely to influence business behaviour and decisions

➤ comment upon the objectives of an organisation in a given situation

Introduction

Every activity in which we take part has an outcome. When that outcome is planned and worked for we can see an objective, a strategy to achieve it and a result.

Objective To attend a meeting in Scarborough tomorrow at 9.30 a.m.

Research Check on times of trains from home. This reveals that you cannot arrive in Scarborough before 10.15.

Strategy Find and book a hotel room for tonight, so as to arrive at the meeting place in plenty of time. Catch train this evening.

Not everything we do is planned. Some things happen by accident, some are a surprise and some things we do on impulse, but the most important things are carefully thought about and, for each, we begin by deciding the objective.

The objectives of an organisation

Objectives are right at the centre of everything a business does (see Figure 4.1). This is a decision wheel that emphasises the fact that the process of making decisions and putting them into practice is a continuous one. Two things are right at the centre and influence every stage. At the heart is objectives and surrounding it communication.

Three objectives are commonly associated with all organisations:

◆ survival;

◆ **profit**;

◆ **growth**.

Survival

Surviving only becomes important as an objective when an organisation is threatened. The rest of the time it will be an objective that makes people a little cautious and prevents them doing things that are likely to put the business in danger. Not all organisations look for long-term survival. Many committees are formed to complete

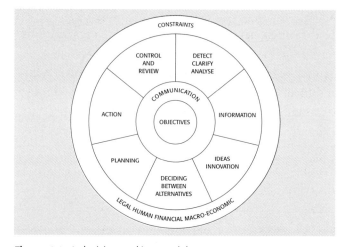

Figure 4.1 A decision-making model

Activity

1   Explain what your objective might be in each of the following situations:

(a) You have to decide what to do after A levels are over.

(b) It is your birthday and you have £500 to spend.

(c) You have been asked to organise a disco at the end of term.

For each of these outcomes you could have several potential objectives; decide between them explaining the basis of your decision.

2   Read the case study below and then answer the questions that follow.

Case study – Tea time

When two friends decided to open a teashop last year, they thought that the increasing number of visitors to town, and the greater frequency with which coach excursions were stopping in the town for short breaks, would provide a ready market for their 'home-made' produce. In a way they were right and business seemed brisk on most days of the week, although dependence on the weather was obviously a problem. Neither had any business experience and they had not undertaken any research to back up their belief in a favourable outcome. Pricing had been based on what they thought people would pay and had erred on the side of 'not being too expensive'. Many of their bills over the first six months were a surprise to them and within eight months, with the lower income of the winter, they had an overdraft and no real prospect of reducing it for three months or so.

This teashop serves traditional cream teas as well as a range of light meals, cakes and ice cream

(a) How would some careful thinking about objectives, before they started on the venture, have helped them to work more efficiently?

(b) What should their objectives be from this point on and how might they pursue them?

a given task, such as organising a school disco or researching a new market segment. Some organisations have a life that is time limited: the life of a Parliament cannot be extended beyond five years. Some people find it difficult to take risks, although survival is vital for an organisation some risks need to be taken.

Profit

Profit is a word we must always use precisely. Get into the habit of putting an adjective in front of the word profit. On its own the word means very little. You should be familiar with the definitions in Table 4.1.

Most organisations must make a profit. Some, like local authorities and leisure centres, seek only to break

Gross profit The profit from the firm's activity before any of the expenses and provisions involved in running the business have been deducted.

Net profit Profit after provisions and expenses have been deducted. Net profit may be considered before or after tax and interest on money borrowed have been deducted.

Disposable profit That part of the profit of the firm which is available to distribute to owners. The amount disposed of to sole traders and partners is called drawings and that given out to shareholders is called dividends.

Retained profit That part of the profit which is retained in the business to provide necessary additional capital.

Table 4.1 Definitions of types of profit

even, whilst others seek to maximise profits. In between these two extremes are organisations in which the aim is to make enough profit. A profit objective is often expressed in terms of a target return on capital employed. This is an idea we shall return to when considering balance sheets. Sufficient profit will provide:

- the working capital with which the activities of the organisation can continue;
- finance for growth and development which reduces the need for external funding;
- a reward for the owners without which the risks of business would not be accepted by anyone.

Suppose a new venture requires the investment of £30,000 and the firm expects a return on capital employed of 20%. Then the net profit on the venture must be at least £6,000.

Owners of small firms are very often content to make a reasonable profit. Their real objective is more the satisfaction of working for themselves than with making the largest possible profit. As firms get bigger there are more stakeholders in their success and more interests to satisfy. The urge for bigger profits often comes from this.

Growth

It is possible to grow in one or more of many measurable ways. Some organisations see growth as desirable. After all isn't a bigger business better than a smaller one? Isn't

Tesco more successful than a small local shop? Others see growth as necessary, arguing that, unless a business grows, it will decline and that it is impossible to stand still.

Is growth always the right objective? Can a business or an organisation get too big? Are there not situations in which small is not only beautiful but is also more efficient and more successful?

- What might happen in your school/college if growth continued for too long?
- Do you think you would be as well taught in a class of over 50?
- Might there be greater cost than benefit if the number of students doubled?
- Would the speed of growth make any difference?
- Would the nature or direction of the growth matter?

In one school the head master pledges that A-level classes will be no larger than 12 students and lower-school classes no larger than 25. Think of the marketing aspect of this. For many, growth is an objective, but it has to be pursued with care. Too-rapid growth can threaten survival. Growth attempts that are badly timed can lead to disaster. Look around your community; you will see examples of very successful growth and you will see examples of businesses that flourished for a little while and then were either absorbed or closed because growth did not work.

Activities

1 From your local community choose:
  (a) one example of a firm that has grown successfully over the years;
  (b) one example of a firm that has stayed the same successfully;
  (c) one example of a firm that grew (or tried to) and failed;
  Try to find a good explanation for each of these three situations.

2 Read the case study below and then discuss possible reasons why Andrew so nearly lost his business.

Case study – The ambitious son

John Hinman ran a small local butcher's shop and had made a satisfactory living for many years. When he was 60, he retired and handed the business over to his son, Andrew, who was very ambitious and determined to make the business 'more successful'. Within six months he had opened a second branch in a town 12 miles away and another on a large housing estate in the same town. Total business grew by about 10% in the first year and by a further 12% in the second. However, by the end of that second year Andrew had a large overdraft about which the bank was very concerned and he owed a lot of money to suppliers. His attempt to grow threatened his survival. His father helped Andrew out of his difficulty but only on the condition that the two new branches were sold. That was several years ago and now Andrew runs a successful single branch shop.

Other objectives

The three objectives we have considered are thought to be the most important objectives of most organisations. However, those who manage or control organisations often have other objectives. These may be long or short term. Some examples follow:

- An important objective of all organisations in the public sector is to operate in the interests of the consumer. The Inland Revenue and the Benefits Office seek to ensure that people make the claims to which they are entitled.
- Charity organisations and shops seek to maximise profits, but only so that the causes they support receive greater benefits.
- Increasingly, businesses are showing concern for the environment and adopting codes of practice that follow 'ethical' lines. However, many have argued that this is because such behaviour is now profitable. There is really nothing new about this approach. Many of the industrialists of the nineteenth century showed far greater concern for the welfare of their workers than conventional practice of the time required.
- Owners of small businesses are often more interested in their business as a way of life than they are in profit or growth. The ability to hand over a successful business to the next generation may be more important than annual net profit.

The importance of a business culture in setting objectives

Think about groups to which you belong. Within your school or college there may be many: the place itself, the classes you are in, the activities, organisations or informal groups of which you are a member. The people involved in each of these groups will have attitudes to what they do as members. There will be rules, expected patterns of behaviour, expectations of each other, past experiences and perceptions. Someone will be leading the group and will have a particular style of doing so. Your feelings about that leadership style may be positive or negative. All of these things, and many more, make up the culture of the group and it is within this culture that objectives will be set.

The same is true of organisations. The culture of the whole business will influence the objectives set, the plans that are worked out to achieve them and whether they are achieved. For example:

- A skilled craftworker may be most concerned with the quality and beauty of the work done. The result may be that the product is very costly and has to be sold at a price that nobody is prepared to pay. The worker has to learn to produce at the level of quality that the market is prepared to pay for. The objective here was to make something good and beautiful. It should have been to make something the consumer is prepared to buy.
- The business you work for has set an objective to achieve a 30% return on capital employed. This is thought to be a realistic objective, but the leadership style of your boss is poor, the work of people in your group is poor and the target is not reached.

To have set objectives is not enough; they have to be realistic and possible within the culture of the organisation. As the second example shows, the culture may well prevent achievement of a realistic objective.

Conflicts between objectives

There is no constant order in which objectives are considered and pursued. The priority that an organisation attaches to a given objective will vary from one situation to another. In the first year of business a firm will be most anxious to survive, will have no ideas of growth and may be happy to aim for break-even. But, in most cases, break-even cannot be a long-term objective. As a firm becomes more successful, attention may well turn to greater profit and even to growth.

Businesses change their objectives over time. Indeed, those refusing to do so often go out of business. Reasons to change might include:

- Circumstances have changed.
- The original objective was not well thought out or was too ambitious.
- A new opportunity has arisen.
- Competition has endangered survival.
- Consumer attitudes, needs, perceptions or buying habits have changed.

Objectives can only be changed if the culture of the organisation permits it. Continuous change is no more desirable that being inflexible. To anticipate the need for change and to be able to make successful changes, organisations must monitor what is happening and have an agreed procedure for making changes so that people will accept them, understand them and make them work.

Communicating objectives

Go back and have another look at Figure 4.1. Surrounding the objectives that are at the hub of the wheel is the word 'communication'. To communicate objectives is essential. How does anyone know what is to be done unless someone has explained? But it is not enough to tell people about the objectives. Suppose you were working as a member of one of several production teams and one of the messages you were given said: 'We must reach a net profit target of 30% on capital employed.' That might well be the target and it may well be achievable, but what does it mean? The chances are that you will ignore it because you do not understand it. It is certain that achieving the objective is important and that you are expected to play your part in making that possible, but what is your part, what do you have to do? Obviously the objective has to be communicated in a better way. What might that better way be?

Figure 4.2 illustrates one way in which an objective may be translated as it goes down the hierarchy of a business so that it is understood and can be acted upon at all levels. Now you and your team know what you must do – produce 20 units per shift/per hour. You may

not want to do it; you may not think it is possible, but you know what is expected. This suggests another aspect of good communication. The business needs your team to produce 20 units per shift/per day. It must find a way of ensuring that you do. Good communication does not just tell you about things in ways you understand; it gets from you the response that is needed.

Objectives and time

Time span is a vital element of many objectives. A management team may know that its ultimate goal is market leadership but that may be too far into the future to be an objective for the present. The planning has to be broken down into a series of objectives which will reach that goal. It is difficult to respond to something which must be achieved in five or even ten years time but wise to plan towards it.

Example

Objective: Market leadership in a stated segment of the market.

This is far too vague, distant and unattainable but the following might be achieved:

Year One: To penetrate the market and establish sales of 10,000.
Year Two: To achieve a 10% market share.
Year Three: To ensure growth in market share to 25%.
Year Four: To become market leader.

These more precise, and directed targets are likely to be more feasible and each year there is a specified objective against which to measure progress. Strategy and/or tactics can then be modified to keep the firm on course for its overall four-year objectives. In establishing these objectives a firm may well work backwards from the eventual goal to establish the intermediate ones. To know where you want to be and then to work backwards towards the steps that must be taken to get to the ultimate goal is sensible planning. This kind of time span planning is often necessary within the strategy to achieve a short-term objective. Table 4.2 shows an example from *Business Review*: it works backwards from the known publication date and hence sets firm targets for all those involved.

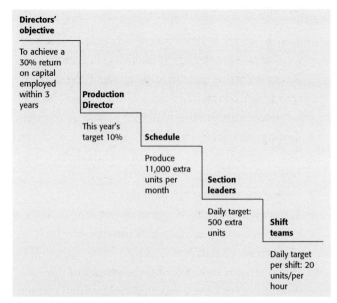

Figure 4.2 Interpreting objectives

Activity

Apply this kind of analysis to your own life and the long- or medium-term objectives that you may have. This could well begin with a stated objective to achieve a good AS grade in Business Studies.

Objectives and strategy

In effect what Table 4.2 shows is a strategy to ensure the achievement of an objective. *Business Review* is published four times a year and the stages of planning to ensure publication on the date specified and the availability of the magazine to you, are more detailed than the stages shown above. The whole process will begin with a planning meeting, probably annually, at which the editors review the recent issues and decide on the kind of material which would be appropriate for the next volume of four issues. This must be balanced so that each issue comes fresh and worth reading. There will be some features which are common to every issue and others which are part of a series for one volume. The magazine will then be filled with individual articles which the editors think you will benefit from. For some of these the authors will be known and for others authors may have to be commissioned. Occasionally the editors will receive articles from writers who would like to be given space in the magazine and these will be carefully considered and a decision made.

The magazine has a defined market and the editors must ensure that this market is satisfied. If the known market is not given value for money then the magazine will fail. Editorial policy establishes what the magazine should look like and contain in order to meet the needs of the market, and careful editing will ensure the required standards are reached.

In due course the editor will have put together the features and articles needed for the coming issue. The following ideas will have been part of the strategic thinking to this point:

- Have I ensured that all the articles are edited in a way which reflects the objectives and style of the magazine and that they represent a balanced coverage of issues to which the readers will respond positively?
- Have I ensured that the ideas in the articles are clearly expressed and likely to be of interest and value to most of the readers?
- Have I ensured that the issues are accurately expressed in terms of the specifications for which they are written?
- Does the issue provide a reasonable balance of articles?

These are just some of the strategic ideas which underpin success and there will be similar ones which determine the way in which the magazine is illustrated, the design of the cover and the order in which it is put together. These are the responsibility of the publishing editor.

From the above you can see the ways in which objectives are planned for, and reached, and you should gather that the following things are true of successful strategy:

- It is designed to achieve a stated objective. Any elements which do not do this must be removed.
- It is necessary to monitor it wherever possible so as to ensure that the objective will be achieved. Remedial action or reconsideration of the objective may be necessary.
- To ensure success flexibility and planned ways of dealing with problems should, as far as possible, be built into the system.
- In the majority of cases time will play an important part in the whole process.
- There must be some elements of the approach which define the strategy and which will be adhered to. In the case of our example there will be general publication decisions, such as four issues a year at known times, and editorial decisions which form the policy.

Publication date	September	10th
Copies complete	August	12th
Film to printer	August	1st
Final corrections	July	3rd
Page proofs to editor	June	25th
Galley corrections	May	27th
Galleys to editor	May	12th
Copy at publishers	April	1st
Copy to editor	March	1st

Table 4.2 *Business Review* publishing schedule for an issue

- ◆ Several groups of people are normally involved. In a business these will usually be the managers and the departments of the organisation. In our example they are the original authors, the editors, the publishing team, the printers and the distributors.
- ◆ At the end of it all the position will be reviewed. Much of this will be on the basis of 'in house' information, but if the strategy was designed to produce a product or a service the response of the market, largely judged by its buying behaviour, will be crucial evidence.
- ◆ The result of the review will possibly be some modifications to the way things are done next time. We all learn from experience and the successful business puts this learning to good effect.

There is a very close link between the objectives of an organisation and the strategies it adopts. Indeed the starting point of all strategy is the objective. Without a known, clear and measurable objective no coherent strategy is possible. Without an effective and well-executed strategy any objective, however good, is unlikely to be achieved.

Objectives around the firm

The setting of the objectives we have been considering takes place at the top. For larger firms, objectives must then be set for all the various areas of operation. The absolute requirement is that objectives set for a section of an organisation will not conflict either with those of other sections or with those of the organisation as a whole.

Marketing objectives

For a business, success means that consumer needs have been identified, targeted and satisfied at a profit. Initially a firm will be satisfied to break into a market and the objective will be a successful launch. Thereafter, the objective will change to one expressed in terms of volume of sales, sales revenue or market share. Over a period the firm will seek at least to maintain its position or to obtain a steady growth. Before realistic objectives can be set, the firm must know where it is (**market standing**) and what the possibilities are (**market potential**) Then the objective set must be a specific target in relation to time and to segment(s) of the market. Next, it can be translated into targets for each member of the sales team. In setting such an objective the marketing department should be aware of the quantities and qualities the production department is capable of delivering and intends to deliver.

A firm could be product orientated. If it is, it is simply producing at the most efficient levels of production and leaving it to the marketing department to maximise revenue from that product.

The danger in this situation is that the product does not meet the needs of the consumer and the goods cannot be sold in sufficient quantity or will produce too low a level of profit. It is wiser for modern business to be market orientated. With this approach the firm first identifies all the characteristics of consumer needs and then produces to satisfy them. The attitude changes from 'sell what you have produced' to 'produce what you know you can sell'.

Activities

1 Think about the part-time job that you have or about one you might have taken on. What might be the best way of communicating to you what you need to do to help achieve a return on capital employed of 25%.

2 Read the case study below and then answer the questions that follow.

Case study – Confused negotiation at Broland Plastics plc

Broland is a small company located on an industrial estate outside a city in the north west of England. The following conversation took place between a union representative (UR) and the managing director (MD). Tuesday afternoon. 2.30 p.m. (The union representative had been waiting since 1.30 p.m., the agreed time of the meeting.)

MD We must get down to detailed discussion of our production plans right away.

UR Certainly, there is no time to waste. We have worked things out and I know what our objectives are. If you know your objectives, perhaps we can get somewhere.

MD Our new plant is larger than we intended at first. The market is growing and we think we can sell enough to keep the plant going at 90% capacity. That gives us some room for growth. I will have targets for each shift for you by tomorrow and we should be able to put them into operation from Monday.

UR Just a minute! We should take things one at a time. Conditions of work are not good enough to make a start possible on Monday. I came to discuss pay and conditions, hours of work and training.

MD Look! It's very important to get production started.

UR All the more reason for you to state what your intentions are and what you are going to offer. We must come to a working agreement; the workers are not going to be ignored.

MD You do realise that without products to sell we can't pay or employ anyone. We can make improvements in time.

UR We certainly expect that. The heating and lighting are poor and dangerous. The sanitary facilities are below standard, especially for the women. Health and safety procedures are not always followed and there are no canteen facilities. It is impossible to reach any targets in these conditions.

MD I guarantee that these problems will be sorted within three months of working for the new targets.

UR Now what about rates of pay? Our figures are based on a 40-hour week, differentials for night-shift working, keeping to national agreements and bonuses for exceeding the targets.

MD National agreements, of course, and we have a bonus scheme to propose but we expect a 44-hour week.

UR We expect that every employee will be trained or re-trained as an insurance against change.

MD It's not that simple.

UR Are you implying you will not fulfil your obligations to train, as required by law?

MD The Act is not really appropriate for small firms like us.

UR So! No training, poor or illegal facilities and a 44-hour week. I don't think we are talking the same language... (walks out)

(a) What do you think were the objectives of:
   ◆ the managing director?
   ◆ the union representative?

(b) What do you think has been achieved by this meeting?

(c) How would you suggest the situation might be saved?

Activity

Read the case study below and then answer the questions that follow.

Case study – What customer needs are we satisfying?

Burfield Plastics plc is a medium-sized firm that produces a wide range of plastic moulded products. This case concerns one of those products. The product was a moulded plastic indoor dustbin in a range of colours with good handles and a tightly fitted lid. Production and sales were steady for many years until, in one year, the demand jumped. The firm sold 500,000 more bins than it had budgeted to sell and had difficulty in meeting the demand. It put in an extra production line and for the next eighteen months this was more than justified. Then, as quickly as sales had risen, they suddenly returned to the steady figures of two years earlier. The firm was faced with excess capacity and no apparent way of using it. It was in danger of losing more from the idle capacity that must now be maintained than it had gained from the extra sales.

(a) What might explain the extra sales the firm enjoyed?
(b) What did they apparently fail to do?
(c) What could they do now?

Research and development

This is not just about new products, or even new ways of producing them. Satisfying consumer needs is much wider than that. In Section 2 we discussed the idea that consumers buy different packages of services that surround the product. Research and development may be about the characteristics of the market or about all the consumer services that might make a sale more likely and build regular buying habits around the product. Change is a rapid and continuous fact in the business environment. Good and constant research and development is the lifeblood of adapting successfully to that change.

Human resource management

Annual reports to shareholders commonly stress that people are a firm's most important resource. Modern approaches to personnel management see people less as individuals and more as members of a team empowered to take responsibility and make significant contributions to achievements. The culture of the business is centred much more on people and on their integration into all stages of business activity. This being so, objectives relating to recruitment, induction, training and human resource management now assume an importance they did not have in the past. The law plays an active part in ensuring that personnel objectives are set. It requires businesses to adopt equal opportunity policies and to make provision for the effective employment of people who are disadvantaged. It requires an approach to all aspects of employment and this protects the interests of the employees. Central to all of the objectives that might be set is an overall workforce plan.

To provide a consistently excellent standard of service forms the basis of this company moto
Source: Select Appointments plc.

Social responsibility

Businesses have responsibility to their stakeholders. How much wider than that does social responsibility go? In many of the things a firm does, particularly if it is a large one, it produces good and bad effects for groups not really considered its stakeholders:

- A firm that produces waste may dump it far away from the community in which it is located or may spill into the sea or a river.
- A firm that makes people redundant will reduce disposable income throughout the community and be likely to cause further unemployment.
- Some firms cause problems of noise and air pollution.
- Some firms tend to cause litter.
- Some firms have little regard for the environment, whilst others make a point of emphasising their environmental concerns and policies.
- Some firms behave in ways that would be considered unethical whilst others have a strictly applied code of ethical conduct.

What firms will do about issues like this depends upon a number of things, many of which are part of their culture. Among those things are:

- the beliefs and opinions of the management and the leadership style they adopt;
- the social conditions prevailing at the time and in the locality;
- the costs and benefits the firm associates with a given line of action;
- the strength of pressure groups and pressure organisations;
- political decisions and procedures put in place by government;
- the prevailing law at local, national and EU level.

Stakeholders and their objectives

The larger a business gets, the more stakeholders it has. All of them have at least one vital relationship with the business and objectives that will not always be in harmony with the objectives of the firm. This often changes the firm's priorities or creates conflicts with which the firm must deal.

Owners

At its simplest level ownership involves one person, who is probably the sole or major decision-maker within the firm. Ownership and control are fully integrated. This should mean that there are no conflicts, but this is not necessarily true. Sole owners often have ambitions to grow, about which they are impatient or for which they have insufficient evidence. Pursuit of growth can then lead to failure to survive. In the early years they often lack the expertise to pursue a realistic objective. The case study concerning the ambitious son earlier in this section is a good example of these problems.

A first step in growth may be to find a partner. While the liability is still unlimited, there is now another interest in the business and its success. The partner may not have the same objectives as the original sole owner but will have the authority to commit the firm. Here there is a clear need for organisation and planning to ensure that both or all partners are pulling in the same direction for the same or very similar reasons.

It is when a firm moves into limited liability status that ownership and control begin to move apart. Ownership is divided into small units called shares and it is the shareholders who own the business collectively. In a private limited (Ltd) company this is less of a break. The owners are often the controllers because shares are divided between members of a family or between a group who work together in managing the business. Control is usually firm in that one of the owners has a controlling interest. Where this is not the case, scope for conflict exists between the managing group, who wish to pursue business-centred objectives, and the owning group, who wish to see a good dividend. The controllers may want to plough profits back into the business, whilst the owners may want a better return. The controllers may see a need to raise more capital externally, whilst the owners may be anxious to maintain their position.

When the firm has reached public company (plc) status, ownership and control are effectively divided. Apart from those who own large blocks of shares and are probably directors, shareholders have a very weak voice. Their interests are still the same, but they have less power to defend them. The group is a widespread one and, even collectively, the shareholders find it difficult to have an influence on the firm's activities. Unlike shareholders in a private limited company, who must seek the approval of their fellow owners, they can attempt to sell their shares and invest elsewhere. The objectives of the Board are always certain to be different from those of some of the shareholders and the only meeting to discuss these issues is the general one. At this meeting, if sufficient support is there, one or more of the directors can be voted off the Board. Collective opinion may convince the Board to change its objectives or its priorities or to find different methods of pursuing them.

The State intervenes to protect the interests of shareholders by requiring a registration procedure before a company can commence business. This also includes a 'constitution', which sets out the objectives of the company (Memorandum of Association) and the rules under which it will work (Articles of Association). Audited annual accounts are required and there are regulations as to what these must contain. If directors operate outside this framework, shareholders can use the courts to bring them back in line.

Most of our national utility services were owned by the State, but have now been privatised. To keep them under control and following appropriate objectives in the interest of the consumer, the State has set up monitoring groups, which can and do intervene. Keep your eye on the newspapers to see what OFTEL and OFWAT are saying to British Telecom and the private water authorities.

The State uses the same kind of controlling body in dealing with organisations it controls and most of you will have come face to face with members of OFSTED, who try to ensure standards in education.

Where an organisation is either part of State provision or is still in State control, it will have different objectives from those common in private business and different priorities in pursuing them. There are strong reasons for retaining some activities within the control of the State. These are usually related to the need for such industries to be large and potentially monopolistic or to ensure that the interests of either the nation as a whole (defence and law and order) or the interests of all consumers (the Post Office) are maintained. Such industries are still expected to break even in the long run. Beyond that, consumer and public interests should be the main objective. The State tries to promote this approach even within industries that are now in private hands:

- Many rural bus services are run by the bus companies, but are heavily subsidised by the local authorities whose communities are served by the buses.
- Even in large city areas like Manchester and the West Midlands, some rail services are supported by the local authorities.
- Many dramatic societies are given support by local authorities to enable small communities to receive their services.
- Many of the country's great orchestras are in financial difficulty and have been given additional support, provided they pursue objectives including musical education.

Employees

The people who are employed by an organisation will have very different objectives. Some may simply be working for the money they earn. This is generally true of student employees working at weekends and some evenings. Some will have a much broader interest in the job and see themselves as seeking promotion within it. Some may have an interest in the profits of the business through productivity bonuses or through shares they hold. Some may have found objectives through things other than the work. This could be working for the union or just a friendship group. Some will have managerial responsibility and through that a wide range of objectives.

In some instances a person's overwhelming objective may be to keep a job that they believe is under threat. In many instances employees will unite to protect their interests and to pursue their own objectives. This is the purpose of unions and the Broland Plastics case (page 00) illustrates this. Have another look at the objectives of workers, which are being represented by the union representative in that situation. The objectives of employees are so diverse, particularly in some instances those of management and other workers, that collective action is difficult. Those who often find themselves in a very difficult position are workers who are not members of a union that is in dispute with the management.

Some time ago, the drivers and conductors of Devon General (a bus company) were in dispute with the management over one-person operation. A student working there was recommended to join a union if he wished to keep his holiday job with the firm. Now he could not be required to join, but relations with workmates would not be very good if he did not join.

Customers

Here you have to think about those who *might* be customers as well as those who are. It is the aim of every business to create customers, i.e. people who come back to purchase on a reasonably regular basis. Most business is done through regular customers. The objective of a customer is to get value for money. Most often the customer knows what he or she wants and where to get it and recent history has shown that the customer has power. This power has been exercised positively in ensuring recycling, the provision of organic foods, better provision for vegetarians and better labelling. It has led to Sunday opening and to 24-hour shopping. Negatively, it has led to goods being withdrawn from sale; the ban by some supermarkets on French goods during the beef crisis was a typical example. Collectively, consumers have more power through specialist agencies like the Consumers' Association and through consumer programmes like 'We Can Work It Out' and 'Watchdog'. In highly competitive fields, such as food and general sales in supermarkets, consumers have, by their actions, led to the closure of many small shops and led supermarkets to fight for their custom. Every day brings a new way in which this fight is pursued:

- *Price wars*: low-price strategies at Asda; price match promises by John Lewis; 'two for the price of one' offers by Somerfield.
- *Loyalty Cards*: Tesco linked with cheaper in-store purchasing; Co-op linked with dividend on selected purchases, Somerfield linked with Argos purchases and Sainsburys linked with Air Miles.
- *Delivery services*: in one area both of local supermarkets have introduced them.
- *Increased facilities*: bag-packing services, more tills, a restaurant, a mother and baby room.
- *Longer opening hours*: 24-hour opening or late night opening; Sunday opening.

The State offers considerable support to the consumer through the law and such acts as the Consumer Credit Act, the Fair Trading Act and the Food Safety Act. This is usually enforced through local agencies such as the Trading Standards Office. Much depends on what the consumer wants. Using the rights conveyed by law will often put things right but without much benefit to the consumer. An individual, whose goodwill is too precious to lose, might get a better result by direct contact with the firm. However, in this country, when things go wrong, most customers seem to take their custom elsewhere for a while and grumble to their friends. This may, of course, have a powerful effect; bad news often travels fast.

Suppliers

The main interests among this group are to retain or increase the business, to make a satisfactory profit on the business and to be paid as promptly as possible. Their views of the purchaser will be in pursuit of these objectives. They tend to avoid giving credit to unknown organisations or those with poor financial reputations. Sometimes, particularly when sources of supply are easy to find, suppliers have to put up with long credit periods in order to retain the business. Sometimes the supplier can dictate terms, because there are few reliable sources of supply or it is costly to change from one supplier to another. There are certain brands that customers expect to see on the shelves and if they are absent the store may lose business. Suppliers sometimes negotiate contracts that ensure further business.

If the suppliers of, for example, a photocopier, sells the customer a maintenance contract, this will ensure that, at least in three years, the customer will have the machine repaired by them and will buy paper and toner from them. On the other hand, many supermarkets have contracts with suppliers that specify the day and time when goods will be delivered, often as strictly as 9.00 a.m. on Thursday morning.

Lenders and creditors

A creditor of an organisation is owed money for goods or services supplied. His/her objectives are to protect their own cash-flow position, to ensure they get their money in full as quickly as possible and to keep the customers' subsequent business. It is often a difficult position to be in. Often they may not want to give credit, but have to do so in order to get business. Often they would like to push for payment, but this may risk losing later business. Cash-and-carry businesses avoid this issue by not giving credit, while most businesses minimise the risk by requiring credit references or making credit enquiries. Some, particularly those who finance on hire purchase, franchise the debt to specialist finance houses; some give inducements like 5% off for prompt payment. Creditors who feel that the position of a firm is precarious and fear they will not get their money back can often exert pressure and may even force a firm into liquidation or a sole trader into bankruptcy. However, they do not always get their money back.

Loans may be short or long term. Business relies heavily on borrowing and the objectives of the lender are to carry on doing business of that kind, to get the sum lent back when it is due and to receive the interest when that is due. In most cases these objectives will not conflict with those of the business, but, when they do, lenders may enforce the agreement and this too can lead to the closure of the business.

Community

A community develops objectives in relation to the activities of a firm when it sees cost or benefit to the locality resulting from the intentions of the business. Sometimes these objectives are focused through the local authority, as when business and industrial parks are developed and incentives offered to move to an area. It is also through local authorities that firms and intending firms must apply both for change of use permission and for planning permission. Sometimes the community will be organised by a single individual and pressure groups will develop to make a point. In one locality in recent years pressure groups have attempted to influence:

- the construction of a reservoir;
- the path of a by-pass round the town;
- parking charges;
- the building and location of a new supermarket;
- the retention and development of railway services;
- the location and waste disposal activity of a local business;
- a proposal to close the local hospital.

On some of these issues the community, with the aid of the media, has won, on others some concessions have been granted. For example, the local hospital has not been closed, but its maternity facilities have been withdrawn. The railway services have been retained and significantly improved. Even when the objectives of the community are not achieved, the fact of pursuing them reminds both the local authority and firms intending to take action that there is an interest in what they do. Those interests may have to be built into an action taken or into the way of doing it.

Table 4.3 gives a summary of stakeholder objectives.

Changing objectives

An organisation must continually review its objectives and progress towards their achievement if it is to retain or improve its position in a dynamic business world. The actions of competitors, changes in technology, actions by government and the changing pattern of consumer tastes and preferences are among the many things that may change and influence the objectives that a business can and should pursue. Every day is really a new starting position and ongoing analysis of where the organisation is and where it can go is essential. Tesco

have responded positively to ecommerce by ensuring that 90% of its UK customer base will be able to shop on the internet by the end of the year 2000.

SWOT analysis

SWOT is an acronym for Strengths, Weaknesses, Opportunities and Threats (see Table 4.4) and is normally associated with marketing, but it can be used to analyse any position by reflecting on the internal and external factors relating to it. It is an audit of the position now:

Internally It discovers and analyses the strengths and weaknesses of the organisation with a view to using the strengths to greater effect and minimising the negative effects that weaknesses might have.

Externally It identifies the opportunities that may be grasped and ways of grasping them. It also identifies the threats posed by the variables outside the firm. These must be anticipated and action taken to avoid damage.

TESCO WIDENS NET FOR DIRECT SALES

Tesco is to treble the number of stores from which it runs Internet shopping in an attempt to push sales by Tesco Direct through the £300 million level by the end of the year.

Terry Leahy, chief executive, yesterday said that the company will be delivering Internet orders from 300 stores within nine months to cover 90 per cent of the UK population.

The sales figure is 20 per cent more than the City had expected and helped Tesco shares to jump 6 per cent yesterday, as the company reported pre-tax profits of £955 million (£881 million) for the year to February 26.

The company has now set up Tesco.com as a separate, wholly owned company in which it will invest £35 million this year. Tesco said that this may eventually be floated.

Its international stores generated £50 million of profits, on £2 billion of sales.

Source: Fraser Nelson, *The Times,* 12 April 2000 (adapted).

Stakeholder	Objectives	Power
Sole owner	Survival, profit, independence	Very limited
Partner	Survival, profit, growth	Limited, depends on agreement
Shareholder in private limited company	Survival, independence, return on capital	Limited but one may have overall control
Shareholder in plc	Continued good dividends	Can sell but little power unless holding is large enough
Employees	Job security, job satisfaction, good wages, promotion	Little unless skilled, except through unions and the law
Customers	Satisfaction of , needsgood service, convenience	Through pressure groups and the law
Suppliers	To retain customer, to be paid on time	Varies with market conditions
Lenders	To be paid on time, continue business, receive interest	Depends on amount and nature of the lender
Creditors	To retain business, to be paid in full on time	Often depends on size and the relationship with debtor
Community	To maintain quality of life; objectives often vary within the community	Through pressure group or the law; can be strong
The State, local authorities, the national government, the EU	To maintain the economy, act in the interest of various groups	Very powerful but often act through persuasion and support; action at one level must not conflict with that at a higher one
	To pursue its own priorities through constraints upon and support for business decision and activities	Direct action, fiscal and monetary policy and the enactment and enforcement of new laws are the normal methods. Much is done through financial support. The Directives of the EU are increasingly important, and the devolved governing bodies of London, Scotland, Wales and Northern Ireland will increasingly have an impact.

Table 4.3 A summary of stakeholder objectives

Strengths Internal	Weaknesses Internal
Good efficient equipment	Equipment is old and there is more sophisticated equipment available
Good well-trained workforce	All three workers are soon to retire
Steady market	Market is loyal but very few new customers in last 18 months
Location well known	Poor location
Good reputation for high-quality work	Prices are not competitive
No cash-flow problems	Sole trader. No scope for further finance

Threats External	Opportunities External
Larger firms with lower unit costs and improved technology	Overall demand is rising
Many more potential customers providing their own facilities	Quality segment increasing very rapidly
Rising unit costs if costs continue to rise and customer base declines	Potential for entry into the repair and maintenance market
Compulsory purchase	Agency work for larger firms
Failure to survive in the long term	Entry into the market for consumables
New and expensive technology in a field change is rapid and replacement expensive. Continuous training needs are also difficult to meet	Possibility of merger with a local firm. This could enable a larger technical unit and therefore economies of scale which would decrease unit costs, broaden the range of services and make the firm more competitive.

Table 4.4 Norton Photocopiers – a SWOT analysis

Over-to-you

1 Taking into account all or most of the points outlined in Table 4.4, analyse the present position of Norton Photocopiers and suggest:

   (a) what its short-term objectives should be;

   (b) what its long-term objectives should be.

2 Read the case study below and then tackle the exercises that follow.

Case study – Middletown High School

Middletown High School is a school for 1,000 pupils aged 11–19. It is due to accept its first pupils in a year's time. The Governing Body, the Head and the senior staff have been appointed and they have a year to plan so that the school will operate effectively. The Head wants to set out the objectives of the school as a framework for how the school should work. Some of his colleagues think this is an impractical waste of time, but he produces his ideas for the second meeting of the group. His paper began with what he called a **mission statement**, which was:

'To search for excellence, to provide for maximum development of the individual and to equip all students for the world of to-morrow'

The Deputy Head argued that objectives should now be set in four areas and that she considered these to be:

- The operational structure of the school. By this she meant divisions of the school into upper, middle and lower, into year groups and into classes, the subjects that would be offered and how these should be grouped.
- New ideas. By this she meant the extent to which the school should venture beyond the traditional subject areas. For example, the school's catchment area is multicultural so what languages should be taught and what social and religious education should be offered? Which of the 'modern' subjects should be offered in the Upper School and what examinations should be possible?
- Staffing. What should be the number of teaching staff, support staff and others. What should the job descriptions and the roles be?
- Administration. What support systems should be in place to ensure the effective marketing of the school and its efficient relationships with staff, students, parents and the community? How should relationships with feeder schools, with business and industry and with higher education be developed?

The Deputy Head stressed that the ideas she presented merely scratched at the surface of the things that needed to be done. She suggested that four groups be formed and that in each group there should be at least one member of the Governing Body and at least one senior teacher. Each group should develop the objectives and outline a strategy for one of the four areas. The Head accepted this and suggested that they should all meet again in a fortnight.

(a) Summarise the advantages to be gained from setting out objectives for the school in this way.

(b) Using your school or college as a basis for comparison, comment upon any areas of school activity that you think may be:

   - under provided for; or
   - under provided for in the above framework.

(c) Choose any one of the four areas and comment on the objectives from the point of view of:

   - a prospective student;
   - a prospective parent;
   - a potential employer of students from the school.

Short-answer questions

1 Explain why objectives are a crucial part of good business practice.

2 What do you understand by the term 'culture of the organisation'?

3 What part does culture play in the setting of objectives?

4 Why is conflict between objectives likely to occur?

5 In what ways would you expect the objectives of a state run firm to differ from those of private business?

6 List the stakeholders in the activities of a business and explain what their objectives are.

7 Why should a firm take notice of the objectives of the local community?

8 Explain the main features of SWOT analysis.

9 Use SWOT analysis to analyse your strengths and weaknesses.

10 What do you see as the main threats and opportunities in the pursuit of your objectives?

Discover and learn

1 Consider your own objectives.
 (a) How well are they formed?
 (b) In what ways do they influence what you do?
 (c) Are they realistic?
 (d) What are you doing in order to achieve them?
 (e) How might a modification of your actions improve the position?

2 Choose any one of the local public services (Police, Fire Service, Ambulance). Discover what their objectives are. How have those objectives changed in recent years?

3 By any method you think appropriate discover the extent to which one of your local supermarkets is aware of customer objectives and responds to them.

4 Choose any sole trader, discover what the owner's objectives are and the extent to which he or she thinks they have been achieved.

Summary

In this section we have recognised that:

● The objectives of a business are central to all its activities.

● The main ones will be survival, profit and growth but priorities between these will depend on the situation.

● The culture of the organisation will play a big part in the formulation of objectives.

● A business will establish objectives for all departments that are in harmony with the overall objectives.

● Stakeholders will have their objectives and these may sometimes conflict with the interests of the firm.

● No firm can afford to ignore the objectives of its stakeholders.

● Business is in a dynamic environment and must constantly review its position.

● SWOT analysis is one technique which might be helpful in this context.

Key words

Definitions of Key words can be found in the Glossary on page 236.

growth
human resource management
lenders
market potential
market standing
profit
research and development
social responsibility
suppliers
SWOT analysis

5 Responding to external economic influences

On completion of this section you should be able to:

➤ understand the nature of a market and its role in influencing business behaviour

➤ show how demand and supply interact in the market and how business might respond

➤ show how the market allocates resources

➤ discuss the effects of competition on business behaviour

➤ understand the importance of the rate of interest

➤ understand the influences of exchange rates on business behaviour

➤ show how changes in interest rates and exchange rates may influence business behaviour

➤ understand the nature of taxation, both direct and indirect, and show its influences on business behaviour

➤ show how, and consider possible reasons why, the level of business and economic activity changes

➤ show understanding of all economic influences on business behaviour

Introduction

However hard a business may try to be independent, it is surrounded by pressures and constraints that influence the way in which it can work and which change the consequences of many of the decisions made. The business world is dynamic and within it there are conflicting interests. In Section 4 the objectives of the business and its stakeholders were discussed. Here we concentrate on economic influences on business decisions.

Our view of these influences is not that of the economist. This section uses economic ideas, but it is not about economics. Try to put yourself in the position of business owners and managers observing the things that are happening and constantly trying to predict the effect on their businesses. This section is not really theoretical; it is about a manufacturer of washing machines in Newcastle, a travel agent in Nottingham, a farmer in Norfolk or an importer in Cardiff, all trying to decide what action they need to take in the light of their interpretation of the things they see.

Building up the picture

Figure 5.1 presents a picture of the forces and relationships that businesses have to work with, some of which concern the internal stakeholders, the owners, the managers and the workforce. We considered those in Section 4.

Others are outside the business. Managers have to anticipate and work within many external influences and we consider these by working through the activity based on Figure 5.1.

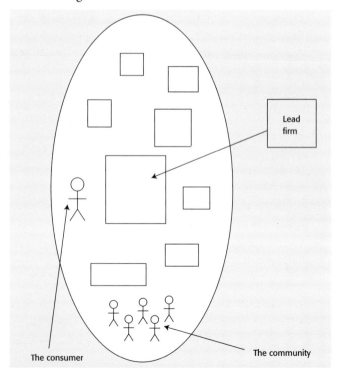

Figure 5.1 The environment of business

Activities

Copy Figure 5.1, making it bigger than it is. The rectangles represent a business and there are a multitude of those in the economy. Our diagram shows seven of them, as well as a stick person, representing the consumer, and a group of stick people, representing the community. Think of the big rectangle in the middle as the business we are interested in.

1 Between the large rectangle and one of the others draw an arrow:

This represents the supplier relationship. Ensuring that the business gets the supplies it wants when it wants them, where it wants them and within the right specifications is essential to a successful business. Yet there are many things that can go wrong and disturb this relationship. In some situations the supplier will be able to dictate terms and in others it is the purchaser who has the upper hand.

2 Select another small rectangle and draw an arrow in the other direction between it and our business:

This represents the buyer relationship. For some businesses this relationship is with other businesses and we call it **industrial marketing**. The machines, raw materials and vans that a firm buys are examples of goods being sold in the industrial market.

3 Draw another arrow to the stick person representing consumers. For many firms, such as retailers, caterers, hotels and hairdressers, the market is the consumer one. It is often the changing tastes and habits of consumers that upset even the best managerial decisions of a business. Many markets are at best uncertain; the pop and fashion markets are good examples.

4 The fact that a business offers goods for sale is no guarantee of selling them. Not only do they have to meet the needs of potential consumers, but they have to beat off potential competition. Firms adopt an almost endless range of strategies to keep their goods in the eye of the potential buyer and to ensure purchase. This relationship is one of **competition**.

Draw a fence around our business to show that it has to defend itself from other businesses. But competition is not as simple as it seems. See the Case study 'Who are Petra's competitors?' (p. 49).

5 Each of those supplier and buyer relationship is really a two-way one because many suppliers are **creditors** of the firm and many buyers are **debtors**. So, make those arrows two-way ones.

Few businesses can get by without offering and accepting some sort of credit. Most of us work on credit because we are paid at the end of a week or a month. Houses, cars, domestic electric appliances are expensive items and are largely bought on credit. Small short-term expenditure is often undertaken through Mastercard, Visa or various store cards.

Observation of consumer purchasing in a supermarket revealed that, in a sample of 200 customers:

◆ 22% of purchases for more than £10 were for cash;
◆ 48% were by debit cards;
◆ 30% were by credit card.

Most trading transactions, particularly between traders who are known to each other, take place on credit. The problems arise when the credit gets too big; both firms and individuals have cash-flow difficulties. Credit is a form of short-term lending, but many businesses have to engage in borrowing beyond this. The overdraft is variable and short term, but bank loans and debentures are examples of longer-term borrowing. The expectation is that businesses will pay the interest when due and return the capital of the loan when agreed, but it is not always as simple as that and a new range of difficulties may lead the business to change its objectives or its methods. In extreme cases the company becomes **insolvent** or the owner of an unincorporated business becomes bankrupt.

The influence of the state

The oval shape around the businesses in Figure 5.1 represents the State, but we really need three circles, so draw two more either inside or around the outside of the one that is there. The three outside shapes, from the inside outwards represent:

◆ the local authority;
◆ the nation state;
◆ world relationships.

The local authority

Much that is important to a business happens through the local authority. In many instances the business is only where it is because planning permission has been granted. In some instances, the location has been provided in the form of business parks and industrial sites. All businesses pay business rates and all are subject to the law, which is often administered through the local authority.

In some instances the local authority is a buyer using the services of local businesses, just like any other consumer, or placing industrial contracts such as those to build and repair roads or to collect refuse.

In other cases, the local authority is a competitor. Local bus routes are a common example. Some authorities offer support, for example, to uneconomic

bus and rail routes. In some areas local villages, which had not seen buses before, are now on bus routes into town supplied by a local carrier but paid for by the local authority. Another example is education. The authority is the main supplier of education but competes with independent schools.

The nation state

The nation state is the main constrainer and supporter of business. Like the local authority, it is a business playing leading roles in such areas as defence, law and order and the Post Office. In these ways and as an employer of the Civil Service, it is the biggest employer in the land.

It supports business through its policies, it charges them through the taxation system and uses its budgets as a way of directing and constraining business life. Its main tools in having an all-embracing influence are the annual budget and the law of the land. It has its own objectives and, in pursuit of those, it significantly affects the environment in which businesses operate and the success of their decisions.

World relationships

These are really on two levels and you could put in a fourth oval shape to make this clear.

The most immediate of the two shapes is the European Union. We may not have clarified our exact relationship with the EU and the reality of particular business relationships may well be very different from the political stance. However, the role of the EU in the United Kingdom and of the United Kingdom in Europe cannot be denied. Directives from Europe and rulings of the European Court change the way we work, the markets that are available to us and the results of our decisions. Agriculture and fishing are two industries in which this is very evident. Transport has been changed and all industries are being affected by issues such as the age of retirement, the rights of part-time workers and the number of hours employees should work. The issue over beef has had an impact that is far wider than the effect on farmers, drastic though that is.

Wider agreements are ones like those made through the group of seven countries (G7) and trading agreements like the General Agreement on Tariffs and Trade (now the World Trade Organisation). But other things are vital too, like the general level of economic and business activity in the world, the effects of political decisions and disturbances and changes in exchange rates

This is the general framework within which businesses have to work. It is a framework within which much is unpredictable and some things are sudden. It is an environment in which continual awareness and flexibility are absolute requirements.

The market

To be successful, a business must identify a market or a market segment, satisfy the needs of the consumers in that market and do so at a reasonable profit. This will happen in a context where competitors are always juggling for market share, the state is intervening and the consumer is constantly making different decisions about what is wanted. Meanwhile, ways of producing things will be changing and new or better products will be continually entering the market.

The term 'market' simply means the coming together of buyers and sellers. This is often a place like the local markets at which many consumer goods can be bought. Some of these, like the market in Leicester, are world famous and large, while some are small, local markets open only on one or two days of the week. However, many marketing activities take place without a particular place and this kind of market is increasing rapidly with the development of ecommerce on the Internet. Here buyer and seller never meet, the seller provides, while the buyer surfs the net and makes a decision. Some markets, like that for shipping, for

precious metals and for shares, are specialist; others like local supermarkets will sell anything they think will provide a profit. The two aspects of the market are:

Supply Hopeful sellers making goods and services available on the market and trying to persuade people to buy. When there is too much on the market there is a glut and when there is too little there is a **shortage**.

Demand The extent to which people are prepared to buy. Being a buyer means having sufficient disposable income available, or the preparedness to buy on credit, and being prepared to buy when a product or service is offered and at the price asked.

Factors that determine supply
Price

The object of making things available for purchase is usually profit. Most goods offered for sale have already been produced and the cost of producing them is known. It follows that, the higher the available price, the more people will offer for sale. A supply schedule might look something like Table 5.1.

Potatoes being a staple food commodity, we would not expect the price range within which they are offered to be very wide. If there is a shortage, the price may go well above this range, but if potatoes are priced too high we would expect that people would buy less of them, switching to other vegetables, rice or bread. We can express the reaction to price in the form of a graph (Figure 5.2).

Activity

Read the case study below and then answer the questions that follow.

Case study – Who are Petra's competitors?

Petra runs a very successful catering business in central London. She works from two premises she bought near Russell Square in London. In one she provides for those who need breakfasts, light lunches and snacks and also has a very busy sandwich bar. Petra opens for business at 6.00 a.m. and closes at 5.00 p.m.

In the premises next door she opens at 6.00 p.m. and closes at about 12.30 a.m. Here you can have a superb evening meal with a speciality range of Italian dishes to supplement the English menu. She also caters well and imaginatively for vegetarian customers.

She employs a staff of 23 to run the business. Six of these are in the common kitchen, which services both parts of the business; two are managers who are in charge when Petra is not there; two are wine waiters; two are cleaners; two are kitchen assistants; the rest are waiters and counter workers.

(a) Why has Petra separated off the two sides of her business?
(b) With whom does Petra compete?

Price per kilo	Quantity on offer (1,000 kilos)
12p	200
13p	220
14p	260
15p	320
16p	500

Table 5.1 A supply schedule: potatoes

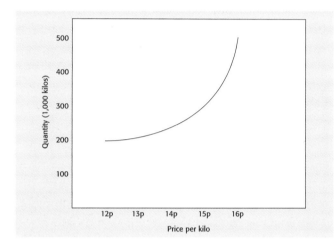

Figure 5.2 The supply of potatoes

Costs of producing

The lower the total cost of producing a unit of a product, the lower the price at which a firm can enter the market. If a farmer can produce at 10p a kilo, the market can be entered at the lowest price shown in the schedule. The higher the actual price, the greater will be the producer's profit margin. Any action that can lower costs of production without reducing quality will persuade suppliers to enter the market. Supermarkets can buy at much lower costs per unit than small shops; hence their stock is much more extensive and their prices lower. New technology often lowers costs of production and makes supply at a lower price possible.

Production methods

To produce a car to customer specifications and without mass production methods is very costly. This can be seen in the cost of producing Aston Martin cars. It is the application of mass production methods to standard designs that makes cars available to most consumers.

The new Aston Martin DB7

Product flexibility

Where it is possible to respond easily to changes in the market, such a change will occur. For example, a change in the price of many publicly quoted shares will often produce an immediate response. Other responses take longer. In agriculture a fall in the demand for sweetcorn might persuade farmers to switch to another product, but it will take a full season for the change to be felt. On the other hand, a news-vendor on the streets of London can vary the number of papers available on a daily basis.

Government action

The biggest supply shift would come as a result of a government ban on a product. This might not take the product out of the market, but it would remove it from the local market. Quotas placed on milk production and on fish catches are examples. A government may subsidise in order to increase supply, as it does with branch railway lines. A government may interfere, through organisations like OFWAT and OFTEL, in the prices that water companies and telephone service providers can charge

Legislation is also a government weapon. Through laws like the Sale of Goods Act the State ensures that goods are fit for the purpose for which they sold. Through health and safety legislation it governs the conditions in which goods can be produced. This may well affect the quantity of goods that can be produced and the cost of each unit. The budgetary policy of the government may also affect costs of production and the prices of goods. Increases in the rate of interest may reduce investment, whilst an increase in VAT is likely to be passed on to the consumer.

Political decisions may also influence supply. A good example is the EU ban on British beef, our own ban on beef on the bone and, even after the EU had lifted the ban, the refusal of the French to accept the beef. Regulations controlling the conditions under which motor fuel can be sold to the public have closed down a number of small rural petrol stations.

The weather

The weather has its most noticeable effects on supply in the transport industry and in agriculture, but extreme forms of weather can close down any source of supply.

The climate and seasonality influence the supply of many products. Several coastal hotels in the UK close down in the winter season, whereas in parts of Europe winter conditions have the opposite effect.

Forecasts

Supply is often managed so as to get the best return. Agriculture is a good example. Suppliers try to ensure that there is a steady supply of fruit and vegetables from around the world. The producers on the Scilly Isles try to get spring flowers on to the market as early as possible in the spring and all producers of flowers focus supply on special occasions like Mother's Day and Easter. The greetings card industry does its best to develop reasons for buying cards, but its main push is Christmas. The toy industry has a similar focus on the Christmas market. Forecast demand for millennium entertainment persuaded providers to inflate their prices, but many consumers rebelled against that and stayed at home.

The objectives of the firm

Most businesses try to increase the return from their efforts. This sometimes leads to marketing and promotional campaigns that temporarily increase the amount supplied. Early in the marketing of new products supply may be kept at a minimum in order to ensure the enjoyment of higher prices by the producer. In the production of novels, the issue of paperback versions is deliberately delayed to ensure a good market for the hardback versions. The world markets for diamonds and gold are carefully controlled by the suppliers to maintain prices.

Promotion and the focus on unique selling points (USP)

Firms can work hard to persuade customers to make a purchase and to distinguish their products from those of competitors.

People will not buy things that do not satisfy a need. The art of being successful includes that of correctly predicting what consumers will want and how and when they will want it. Failure to forecast accurately can be very costly, as when McDonalds made a two for the price of one offer and totally failed to appreciate how much this would increase the demand for the product.

The nature of demand

Demand is a positive attempt to be in the market. It is not sufficient to merely want a good; we must also be able and willing to buy it at the price asked. We defined a supply schedule for potatoes in Table 5.1. In Table 5.2 a demand schedule has been added. It is, as you would expect, showing that as price falls there is a demand for more potatoes. Supply and demand are the two forces in the market that have to be equal if we are to avoid either glut or shortage. In this simplified schedule you can see **equilibrium** at a glance, when the price is 14p per kilo. This we can plot on a graph, as shown in Figure 5.3.

Price per kilo	Supply (1,000 kilos)	Demand (1,000 kilos)
12p	200	500
13p	220	320
14p	260	260
15p	320	220
16p	500	200

Table 5.2 Demand and supply schedules

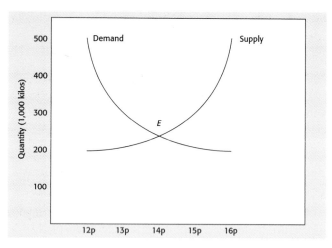

Figure 5.3 Supply and demand curves for potatoes

Factors that affect demand

Price

Are there any things that you would buy without even considering price? Maybe some 'one off' good or activity that you have been determined to be involved in or to purchase. Even in that case you would spend so much of your disposable income that something else you normally buy would have to be given up. Prices affect the likelihood of buying a particular good, the amount of it we purchase in a given time and/or the pattern of our demand. If someone wants to see England play Australia in a test match at Lords, or would like to enjoy an expensive holiday abroad or their purchase their own house, they may be able to spread the expenditure through some form of credit or borrowing, but the effect is always the same: if they cannot command more income, they will have to change their pattern of spending so that the expensive item can be paid for.

Changes in prices of other goods

There are different situations here:

◆ Changes in prices of goods that we are committed to consume. These might be electricity, gas or water. An increase may lead to personal economy drives to try and keep the amount paid the same, even though the price has gone up, or it will lead to a decrease in disposable income and a change in the pattern of our expenditure or saving.

◆ Changes in the prices of brands of goods that we buy. For most products brand loyalty is not very great and most people will switch to a cheaper brand for as long as that is possible.

◆ Changes in the prices of close substitutes. One general magazine may be much like another; you may be equally content with tea or coffee or with one kind of soft drink rather than another. You may be prepared to desert your favourite fast food shop for another where prices have not gone up.

◆ Complementary goods are those that tend to be bought together and therefore changes in the price of one may cause a change in the demand for the other. If the price of cars goes up sufficiently to deter demand, then the consumption of petrol or diesel will fall. For many, if the price of bacon went up it might cause a fall in the demand for eggs or a rise in the demand for sausages. A rise in the price of any computer hardware will cause a fall in the consumption of associated software.

Activity

Think of the price of something quite expensive that you are intending to buy and then map out the changes in your spending patterns that this is likely to mean.

Income

We have to look at income in several different ways. It usually comes from work and the total amount earned is **gross income**. From this must come some unavoidable deductions, such as national insurance payments and taxation. These are usually taken away by the employer and leave us with **net income**. As we get older, we tend to acquire more and more commitments that use up our income and must be paid for regularly. These would include, for example, rent or a mortgage on the place we live in; electricity, gas and other regular bills; and items bought on credit. For some people this list is long and for others quite short. After all these payments have been accounted for, we arrive at **disposable income**. This is the income that can freely be used, but much of this may still be required for habitual expenditures such as food and clothing for ourselves and a family. The greater the real disposable income is, the more freedom there is to choose. Some people might choose to save some or all of this or might take the opportunity to buy the things they could not otherwise afford. Changes in ordinary income tend to come in small amounts so they lead to gradual changes in lifestyle, but windfall changes like winning the lottery or receiving an inheritance of some value may have substantial effects. Few of us know what we would really do with a sudden change in income and experience shows that the often stated, 'it won't change my life' just isn't true.

Some changes in disposable income are outside our control. Here are some examples, there are many more:

♦ for home buyers with a mortgage a change in the rate of interest or for those who rent their home an increase or decrease in the rent they have to pay;

♦ a change in either national (income) tax or in local tax (council tax);

♦ an increase in pay or an unexpected promotion;

♦ redundancy, sickness or injury.

Some of these we can provide for by savings or by insurance. If we do insure ourselves well or save significant amounts, we are reducing our present disposable income to provide for the future.

Activity

Assume you have acquired additional money in some way. Think seriously about ways in which you would use that money and compare notes with other members of the class:

(a) What would you be likely to do if it was £100?

(b) How about £1,000?

(c) How about £10,000?

Tastes, fashions and customs

In the marketing of some goods and services, these factors are crucial. The two obvious examples are the fashion industry and the pop music industry, but there are other examples. A new toy, for adults or children, tends to have a short hectic life and then often disappears from use. Cinema attendances dropped with the advent of television, but attendances are growing again now. The mobile phone has become a product that some hate and everyone else wants because of the convenience it offers. Customs tend to affect the availability of products and their prices at different times of the year. Cards at Christmas, fireworks before 5 November and flowers for Mothering Sunday are all examples. The custom of giving presents on religious festivals and on birthdays and anniversaries adds to the demand for a wide range of products.

Population changes

Our population changes in several different ways, all of which affect the pattern of demand.

The age distribution What people need depends on their age. We have an ageing population, so demand for health care, for social services and other products chiefly associated with the elderly may be expected to rise. Over recent years the demand for school places has fallen, but this is now changing again.

The ethnic pattern of the population Race and culture affect demand patterns. This is most evident in food provision, clothing requirements, religious observance and education. In some areas, such as parts of London, Leicester and Bradford we can see the way retailers and schools have both reacted to these changing needs.

Other population characteristics What shops stock is a very good indicator of what people need. The range of clothing found in predominantly rural areas, such as Devon and Norfolk, is significantly different from what will be found in Oxford Street, London. Many people require specific things for work and, in areas where a particular kind of occupation predominates or particular pursuits are evident, there are features of this in the demand and therefore in the supply. A small market town will not necessarily have a good bookshop but you would expect more than one in a university town. A country town near the moors is likely to provoke more demand for climbing, walking and camping equipment, a tourist town is likely to mean greater demand for catering facilities and a seaside town more demand for holiday accommodation. A large city will mean more demand for taxis and entertainment. The demand for a car is almost universal now, but the need is probably greater in remote areas.

Changes in lifestyle

Many changes in lifestyle have come about over the past few decades. For example, because of reduced grants, most students look for part-time jobs. Many more women seek work outside the home. Lifestyle changes bring about changes in patterns of demand, some of which are as a result of increased purchasing power; for example more people take at least one holiday a year, sometimes abroad. This is reflected in the increased number of travel agents and holiday brochures. The tendency for people to own their own home is greater than ever, particularly in Britain.

Advertising

That advertising affects our choices is undeniable. It will probably rarely persuade us to buy things we really do not need, but it is instrumental in promoting new products and new services, and it may well affect our brand choices and our purchase decisions between close alternatives. It may well influence where and when we buy things. Similarly, promotion within a shop may well persuade us to buy the occasional product on impulse.

The law

The law has an impact on our behaviour in various ways. For example most people probably wear motor cycle helmets only because the law requires it. Most cyclists do not wear them. The law imposes age limits on the sale of alcohol, on cigarettes; an age limit applies to a driving licence; a passport and sometimes a visa are necessary for foreign travel.

Activity

Think of three unusual things that you or a relative have bought recently:

(a) Try to analyse the factors that led to the purchasing of those goods or services.

(b) What conclusions, if any, do you draw about influences on your buying patterns?

The interaction of supply and demand

Let us consider Figure 5.3 again. The graph shows the interaction of supply and demand and one point E at which supply and demand are equal. Here everyone who wants to buy at that price can do so and everyone who wants to supply will do so. This is the **equilibrium point** and is unlikely to be reached. A large number of suppliers all making independent decisions about what to supply and a larger number of customers all deciding to purchase are unlikely to bring about such a precise position. What matters is what happens if the position is different.

Situation 1 Demand is greater than supply (Figure 5.4). There will be a shortage, so some people will be prepared to pay more and the price will rise until enough people have withdrawn from the market in the short term. In the longer term the higher price will bring more supplies onto the market and this will bring the price back down.

Situation 2 Supply is greater than demand. If supplies can be withdrawn from the market and stored then that is what will happen. If not, there is a glut and suppliers will reduce prices until the product is sold. This may lead to greater demand and force the price back up towards equilibrium (Figure 5.5).

In other words, equilibrium is the market position around which activity and price tend to fluctuate. These natural market forces come into play when the market is able to operate freely, but this is not always the case. Some reasons for the market not operating freely are considered in the following sections.

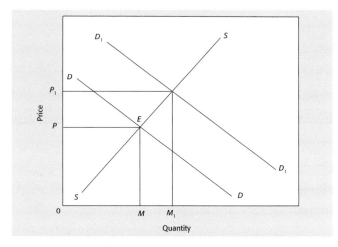

Figure 5.4 Demand is greater than supply

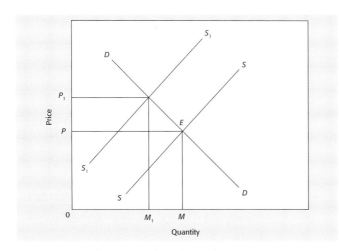

Figure 5.5 Supply is greater than demand

Supply fixed

There are only a limited number of tickets for a concert or a football match. If the number wanting to go is less than this, there are no problems, except for the organisers whose income is lower than they might have expected. But if demand is higher, the price will rise unless it is fixed. If it is fixed, as it usually is, it will lead to an unofficial **black market** in tickets (Figure 5.6).

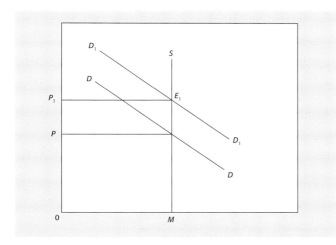

Figure 5.6 Fixed supply, but demand increases. Tickets will exchange on the 'black market' at P_1

When pop concerts are held at Wembly tickets are hard to get and must be bought well in advance. A ticket costing £24 can sometimes be sold outside the grounds for over £100.

Demand fixed

For an event at Peterborough Cathedral, tickets were limited to two per person. This can happen through rationing. In times of great shortage, rationing is applied to a wide range of essential goods. Your grandparents will remember ration books. Time sharing is an increasingly common way of going on holiday, but if at any time you want to exchange your holiday for one of the popular resorts you can find yourself waiting up to four years.

Legislation

The EU banned British beef and this led to demands that Britain should retaliate. The effect on suppliers and on customer choice was significant. From time to time we make laws that restrict demand. For example, a restriction on credit purchasing would substantially cut the demand for durable consumer goods. However, there is little evidence to suggest that the ban on TV cigarette advertising has reduced smoking.

Unexpected factors

In the case of food products this could include the weather, which often creates shortages of basic foods. Strikes may make either production or distribution difficult and political action in other parts of the world may restrict choice. One of our major problems in the world economy is the inability to find effective distribution methods so that we have food 'mountains' and 'lakes' in the EU and desperate shortages in other parts of the world.

Activity

In the text, changes that occur when demand or supply is excessive have been shown. There are two other possibilities. Map out what happens when:
   (a) supply falls below demand;
   (b) demand falls below the supply.
At this stage we have looked only at the forces that determine both demand and supply . We have not considered what happens when the whole pattern of demand or supply changes and more is demanded or supplied at the same price. This produces new curves and new equilibrium points. Neither have we considered what determines the rate of change of supply or demand in response to things like prices, income or advertising. All of these are considerations in Part 2.

Allocation of resources

There are times when the free market system does not work very well and we have to find means like the law or price control or rationing to try to ensure that distribution is as fair as it can be and that things do not simply go to those with very high disposable incomes.

This is not just a matter of ensuring a fair distribution of consumer goods, but of guaranteeing the most efficient distribution of all our resources. In the labour market we need to find ways of ensuring that there are sufficient supplies of the skilled and trained personnel we need. In part this is a matter of general education, e.g. ensuring that we are computer literate and have all the key skills needed. In part it is a matter of attracting into specific careers those we need with the skills we need. We must have efficient and imaginative management, good teachers in sufficient numbers, enough people in the health service and enough craft persons and skilled engineers. Getting this right is not easy and it is unlikely to happen unless we can control market forces or make an input into them that will have the desired effect.

This is not simply wages and salaries; it is often things like suitable remuneration in long training processes, conditions of work, status in society and prospects for promotion. In all of these situations, clear objectives have to be set and followed through and we have to decide that the costs of meeting the objective will be met.

The impact of competition

What is competition? It is other sources of supply of the same good or service to which a potential consumer can go, but it is more than that. Think of the case study of Petra's cafe on which you spent some time earlier in this section. With whom does Petra compete? Petra is satisfying a range of needs. We can examine some of them.

◆ In providing breakfast Petra is competing with many other cafes doing the same in a fairly small local area, with breakfasts brought from or eaten at home, with catering businesses on the way to work or on the train and with a decision by potential customers to forget breakfast altogether. To gain business Petra will need to be good in terms of what and how she cooks, to offer this at reasonable prices and to give good service, because time is short.

◆ In providing take-away sandwiches Petra is competing with many of the same buying opportunities, with business canteens, with pubs and with other quick sources of a meal at lunch time. To compete successfully she has to use good-quality materials, provide a wide range of sandwiches or baguettes, pack them well and give speedy friendly service.

◆ In the evenings Petra caters to an entirely different market. Here the needs that are being satisfied are much broader. There are many ways in which people can spend the disposable income that a meal in the restaurant will take. Now, Petra is competing with all ways of using that amount of income. A night at a disco or in the pub, a trip to the cinema or the theatre, eating at home and saving the money for something else and many other uses. The consumer is looking for a good meal, probably one that would not be cooked at home, a good atmosphere, attentive service, additional things like wine and a good night out.

So, deciding who our competitors really are and devising a good strategy is not as easy as it seems. The first step is to analyse the needs that are being satisfied and the relative importance of each of them in attracting customers. Like most businesses, Petra is not in one market but in several.

Competition and its effects

You may think that the obvious way to compete is to cut prices, but this is not always possible because firms need a sufficient margin on the things they sell in order to survive. Sometimes cutting prices would have the opposite effect. If the suppliers of Aston Martin or Rolls Royce cars tried to compete through price, people would think the cars were less desirable, that lower prices meant either loss of status or that inferior materials were being used.

Activity

Read the short case study below and then tackle the exercises opposite.

Case study – Great Western Railway

Great Western Railway runs trains that cover the area from Paddington in London to the counties of Devon and Cornwall and parts of Wales. It offers transport seven days a week and for most days from very early in the morning to very late at night. It also offers some overnight services. At certain times of the day it is very busy and on certain days of the week, like Saturdays in the summer, it is busy and runs additional trains. It carries passengers throughout the day. The needs it satisfies are clearly different for different groups of passengers.

The table below shows some times and distances to help you.

Start	Destination	Distance	Time taken
Exeter	London	176 miles	2 hours, 37 mins
Reading	London	36 miles	29 mins
Paignton	Exeter	29 miles	46 mins
London	Penzance	305 miles	5 hours
Exeter	Exmouth	11 miles	30 mins

(a) What kind of consumer needs are likely to be satisfied by each of the following trains:
- the 05.55 from Exeter to Paddington, particularly on a Monday;
- the 08.02 from Reading to London Monday to Friday;
- the 08.00 stopping train from Paignton to Exeter;
- the 09.41 from Paignton to Exeter;
- the 10.35 from London to Penzance on a summer Saturday;
- the 18.00 from Reading to London;
- any train from Exeter to Exmouth on a summer day;
- evening trains from Exeter to Exmouth in the winter.

Note that the last two categories of train are run by Wales and the West Trains.

(b) What is the competition for each of these services? Explain your decision.

(c) How do you think the providers should compete?

Great Western Trains.
Source: Photographer Roy Nash

If small shops tried to compete with supermarkets through price, they would make losses rather than profits. The smaller a business is, the greater the number of competing products in the market, while the closer alternative suppliers are to each other, the more difficult price competition is. Firms try to improve their chances of competing through price by differentiating their products, by trying to find **unique selling points** (USPs) for their products and by various point-of-sale promotion strategies.

Activity

Read the case study below and then tackle the exercises that follow.

Case Study – Competition

Non-price competition is simply any way of competing with other firms that does not involve price. A visit to a superstore will give you a good idea of what these methods might be. They range from customer services through additional services to loyalty cards. Competition among providers of holiday packages is very keen at the moment and this is reflected in:

- facilities in the packages to allow holidaymakers to arrive at the end of their journey by coach, rail or air;
- feeder services from as many points as possible;
- tour packages within the holiday itself;
- services provided on the coach;
- extension packages for second weeks;
- free insurance or free child places;
- tempting discounts for second, third and fourth holidays a year.

Competition is a fact of business life for most producers. The need to find ways of survival is there, even for the very large. This is well demonstrated by:

- the fight between the big superstores for market share;
- the number of small businessess that fail because they cannot compete;
- small businesses that succeed because they find a small market niche which they can satisfy but which does not tempt the bigger organisations;
- many small shops, which survive because of where they are, i.e. on an outlying housing estate or in a small village;

- businesses that are prepared to go to the customer; we buy our milk, newspapers, fish and fresh vegetables from suppliers who are prepared to come to us;
- businesses that cut out stages in the process of distribution, e.g. farmers who sell at the farm gate, go to farmers' markets or sell through 'pick your own' are doing this;
- businesses that deliberately appeal to consumers who have high disposable incomes, e.g. the elite car market, the five-star hotel and shops like Harrods;.
- businesses that go to the other end of the market, e.g. market stalls where products can be cheap because there are fewer overheads, shops like Kwik Save and others where all the frills are cut out so as to sell a limited range of goods at much lower prices.

Where there is no, or little, competition, there is the danger of much higher prices. There is the possibility that customers will be exploited. This is one of the arguments for keeping industries like the utilities and the transport suppliers under state control. At the moment we have a halfway situation, where these goods and services are privately provided but the State appoints watchdogs to act on behalf of consumer interests.

Competition does vary and the extent of competition is a major factor influencing business behaviour. Competition is said to be in the interest of the consumer, but if its effect is to close businesses and to reduce choice that is not necessarily good. There are many villages without shops, post offices and other amenities because those who would provide them cannot survive.

Working in groups of four to six, choose one advertisement. Look at it or watch it closely.

(a) What part of the market is the firm aiming at? Make sure you have evidence for your view on this.
(b) What do the advertisement designers think is the USP that this product has?
(c) Make a collective and supported judgement of the success of the advertisements.

The rate of interest

The rate of interest is a cost. It is the cost we pay for using other people's money. For individuals it is a drain on their disposable income and for businesses it is a cost to them of investing. Without interest charges, borrowing, which is essential to our culture and its development, would not happen and growth and development would be very much slower. The market today is flooded with offers to borrow money. An individual may get two or three offers to take out loans ranging from £500 to £30,000, every week. Some of the rates of interest are very high indeed and only the desperate will borrow at those rates. On the other hand, you can also find offers to sell on credit at either delayed interest or at no interest at all. These offers are common in the furniture and the new-car market. The base rate for borrowing money is set by the Monetary Committee of the Bank of England. Until 1997 it used to be decided by the Treasury. Borrowing at that rate is unlikely and all other rates are usually higher. Given that the rate is an expense, we can usually live with once it has become a part of expenditure. The problem comes with changes in that rate.

Why should the rate change?

In some circumstances a fixed rate can be negotiated and this would be common for short-term borrowing or for long-term borrowing like debentures (read Section 2 if you are not sure what debentures are). In other instances, interest rates rise and fall in response to changes in the base rate. Base-rate changes are usually small and may be supposed to have little effect. However, changes are as important for the impression they convey as they are for the difference they make.

A rise in rates

Suppose your mortgage rate goes up by 0.5% and therefore your monthly mortgage payment by £30, then you have £30 less to spend per month than you had before. If similar interest payments occur for credit cards, bank charges and other flexible-interest loans, then disposable income could fall by a total of £50 or more per month. This will cause a fall in savings or a cutback in demand for goods. This kind of effect will hit different people to variable extents, but the overall fall in the level of purchases will be considerable, just because the money is not there. The effect is increased because anyone who was thinking of buying a car, a washing machine or any

other durable consumer good on credit may well decide to delay that purchase and anyone who was thinking of buying a house is even more likely to delay purchase. The level of business activity will fall significantly.

A business will be conscious of two things when this interest rise occurs. The first will be that its own cost of borrowing, particularly on bank loans and overdrafts, is going to rise. The decision-makers will be more inclined to push debtors to pay and yet to delay their own payments if they can. They will be less inclined to invest, partly because the cost of doing so will have risen and partly because they anticipate that demand for goods and services may fall off. So investment activity will also fall off. The combined increase in costs and expectation of a fall in demand will lead to attempts to reduce the wage bill, through cutting out overtime, reducing hours of work or even redundancies. All of these will reduce disposable income and this begins to have further effects on the level of activity. For those with larger disposable incomes it is likely that the rewards for savings will rise and they may be persuaded to save a larger proportion of their income rather than spend it. This too may reduce the level of activity.

Businesses will seek other outlets for their products to maintain turnover, employment and profits. This will be in markets overseas. They may also sell on lower margins rather than lose sales. Bargains may tempt consumers not to delay purchasing certain items.

It is probable that the rise in the rate was originally designed to bring about precisely this effect, because the projection is that the economy is starting to run too fast and needs to be slowed down. This is the sense in which the level of interest is a tool in managing the economy.

A fall in rates

When interest rates fall the general movement downwards tends to be less speedy and any positive change in attitude is often more difficult to bring about, but otherwise the changes are the opposite of the ones outlined above.

Activity

Trace the likely effects of a fall in interest rates on a business arising from:

(a) changes in its costs and potential costs;

(b) changes in consumer buying decisions.

Exchange rates

If you want to trade with French customers they will want to pay in Euros and you may want sterling. This requires currency exchange. The rate at which one currency exchanges against another depends on world trade in each one. Suppose you are trading with a customer in France and that customer is paying in Euros.

You agree to sell 100 units to the customer at	£25 a unit
Total cost in sterling	£2,500
The rate of exchange is	1 Euro = £0.58
Cost to French customer	4.310.3 Euros
But suppose the Euro falls against sterling to	1 Euro = £0.50
Cost to the French customer now	5,000 Euros
You gain 690 Euros which is	£345

Activities

1 Calculate the loss to you if you had agreed to be paid in Euros and at the time the rate of exchange was 1 Euro = £0.50 but before payment was due the Euro appreciated against sterling to 1 Europe is £0.65

2 Use the results of your calculations to explain why many exporters are in difficulty when the pound is strong in foreign markets.

3 Explain the likely effects if the value of holidays taken in Germany by British nationals was to increase by 25% whilst the value of holidays taken by Germans in the UK remain unchanged.

Exchange rates and the rate of interest

If the rate of interest is higher in the UK than it is in other countries lenders will move their money towards the UK. This will reduce the general supply of sterling and cause its price in terms of other currencies to rise. Large fluctuations can cause real problems.

The government can and does intervene to influence the external value of sterling. When the international value of sterling is too low the government will buy other currencies thus releasing sterling and causing its value to fall. They work the other way when the value is too high. Individual movements will go on all the time

as a result of trading, tourism and buying and selling in currencies. What matters is the overall effect at any one time.

Further effects of exchange rate changes on business

When the value of sterling falls:

- ◆ Imports are dearer and may be reduced.
- ◆ Overseas holidays are more expensive and may be reduced whilst the overseas tourist is more attracted to the UK.
- ◆ If demand for overseas products remains high disposable income will be reduced and demand for other products will fall.
- ◆ Demand for home country holiday accommodation is likely to rise.
- ◆ Manufacturers will look for cheaper, possibly home-produced, raw materials.
- ◆ If they cannot find them the prices of many home-produced goods are likely to rise.
- ◆ Many exports will be easier and producers may be attracted to sell abroad.

The effects of a rise in the value of sterling will be the opposite of this. But these are probabilities rather than certainties. Factors other than price will always be taken into account. There will be contracts which the parties to them will have to honour and there will be loyalties which may not change. Governments will want to avoid instability because of the uncertainty it brings and to do this they may well use interest rates as a weapon.

The government budget

The government does generate some income from the things that it does but most of what it needs comes through the budget which is normally introduced once a year in April. First they must decide how they need to spend money in the coming year and then how it is to be raised. This takes money out of the pockets of consumers and businesses (or puts it in) and thus affects what we do. Governments have many purposes including:

- ◆ to raise the money needed for the year;
- ◆ to affect the balance of disposable income by determining who it is taken from and in what ways;

Gordon Brown
Source: Popperfoto Reuters.

It has become common practice to signal some changes so that they are announced in one budget and are put into effect in the next. This is because it is sometimes necessary and often wise to take time over some changes and to give warning that they are to be made. Recently signalled changes were to remove the TV licence fee for those over 75, to maintain the winter heating allowance at £100 and to allocate taxes in cigarettes and tobacco to the National Health Service. You should listen to the budget when it is given in the Spring and discuss the effects of the changes it makes.

Taxation

For people the two main taxes are **Income tax** and **VAT**. We all make significant additional contributions through things like National Health contributions and TV licences. Table 5.3 lists some of our payments and the way in which we pay them.

For most people who have a regular job, income tax is calculated on a monthly or weekly basis and deducted straight from earnings before we receive them. National Insurance is dealt with in the same way. Each income earner tells the Inland Revenue about earnings and about allowances which are claimed on an annual tax return. The deductions and the code number on which they are based can be seen on a payslip. If you have one study it carefully and make sure that you know what each statement on it is telling you.

◆ to decide who will benefit from expenditure, to what extent and in what ways;

◆ to manage the economy towards the achievement of a stated objective;

◆ to keep the economy under control and to minimise or reverse any unwanted changes;

◆ to send signals to business, industry, consumers, overseas governments and traders, intended to influence their attitudes and behaviour.

Type of payment	Frequency	How	Fixed or variable
Car licence	Year or half year	From take home pay	Fixed annually
TV licence	Year	From take home pay	Fixed annually
National insurance	Per week/month	From gross pay	Varies with gross pay
Income tax	Per week/month/year	From gross pay	Varies with gross pay
VAT	Most things we buy	Through purchases	Fixed at 17.5%
Customs duty	On imports	At port or airport	Fixed
Excise duty	On car fuel/tobacco	Through purchases	Fixed annually

Table 5.3 Examples of regular payments to government agencies

The effects of taxation on business

Corporation tax or profits tax

This is levied on profits and hence reduces the dividend or drawings that owners can take out of the business or the profit that can be retained for use in the business. Either way an increase has the potential to reduce the level of activity because consumer spending power or business investing capability has been reduced. The extent to which activity reduces will depend also on the effect the reductions have on the attitude of the business and the income earners. The same tax change will occur for all businesses unless the Chancellor is selective in terms of applying it. Many consumers will have their buying power reduced. Some firms, particularly those that sell non-essential goods, may have their earnings reduced.

Import duties

The objective in imposing these duties or increasing them is to change buying habits. Purchasers are discouraged from buying the taxed goods and encouraged to buy cheaper alternatives. These may still come from abroad or they may be either made by the supplying firm or bought in from home producers. If the firm continues buying what are now more expensive imports, this will increase costs and either increase the price or decrease profits.

Excise duties

The major duty of this kind is on alcohol and tobacco products. In most budgets there is an increase in these duties, which make a substantial contribution to government revenue. A change usually deters expenditure in the short term, but the long-term effect is very much less. Businesses must decide the extent to which they will bear the burden of this tax themselves or pass it on in price rises to the consumer. To the extent that it dampens down trade it reduces business incomes and profits. If there was little competition in the market, consumers would bear the whole burden of tax increases. However, if competition is very fierce, decisions about margins are often revised to gain a competitive edge.

Value Added Tax (VAT)

This is the major tax on purchasing and, for most products, is fixed at 17.5% This is subject to change in the annual budget. From the consumer's point of view an increase raises prices and discourages expenditure. Once it is imposed and if it remains unchanged for some time, consumers get used to it and its effect is noticed less. There is no real incentive to change purchasing behaviour if the rate is common to all goods. Governments can decide the goods upon which it is levied, such as no VAT on food and on children's clothing. Firms must pay the tax to the State, but do not have to pass it on to the customer.

Income tax

This is generally thought of as the major tax we all pay because it comes in a significant lump sum from income. In practice, most of us are likely to spend more on VAT than we pay in income tax. There are three ways in which the State can influence the effect of income tax and direct it at or away from defined groups of people:

Allowances and reliefs In calculating taxable income we have to deduct income that is not subject to tax because we have been able to claim allowances.

Levels of income below which tax is not paid Below a certain level of income (depending on how many allowances you can claim) you will not have to pay income tax. If the government raises the tax threshold more people will not have to pay income tax.

By changing taxation bands and other variables the State influences the disposable income we have.

Activities

1 Obtain a copy of the most recent statement of taxation bands, rates and allowances. Using them calculate the amount a single person earning £38,000 a year and entitled only to the personal allowance, might expect to pay in a year.

2 Explain, for the benefit of someone who does not understand, why these taxes are raised and why different people will pay different amounts.

The overall effect of changes in income tax on business comes through the resulting changes in disposable income. However, it is not a simple effect because it depends on who bears the burden. If an increase in income tax falls on those with high incomes (i.e. through the higher rate or through moving that threshold downwards), then the effect may be small.

This is partly because those who earn sufficient to pay the top rates are not a very large number and partly because they are less inclined to change their expenditure habits unless the change is very substantial. If the change releases or removes income from people having average or below-average incomes, the effect is normally more substantial and more immediate. When these incomes are reduced, the greatest changes will be found in businesses selling durable consumer goods and non-essential goods, the purchase of which can be delayed. Sales of cars, washing machines and holidays may be affected. There will, of course, also be a reduction in the tendency to invest in those industries and employment may be reduced. In effect, the economy will be slowed down.

But this is only one side of the story. What happens will also be influenced by the things that the Chancellor does with the additional income collected. There will be a reduction in income from VAT and there may be increased unemployment and family support costs, so it will not all be a gain for the Treasury. The increased revenue can be used positively (i.e. put back into the economy through pensions, benefits and investment programmes) and, in as far as it is, it will create employment and expenditure. The net effect will be to dampen down some industries and to stimulate others. There may be other effects which influence the balance of payments and the rate of exchange. For example, there may be a greater tendency to take holidays or short breaks in this country rather than go abroad.

There is no certainty about these changes. If there were, the Chancellor's job would be much simpler. What examiners look for is your ability to think about these things and produce well-argued, logical responses.

The level of activity

Several references have been made in this section to the level of economic activity, to dampening it down and to stimulating it, to the role of the government in controlling or manipulating it. No economy stands still; nor does it grow steadily. It is rather like a roller coaster with movements up and down, which are sometimes sudden and violent, as they are in periods of great depression followed by growth out of it. The objective of government is to keep fluctuations as small as possible so as to provide an environment in which it is

easy to plan and to forecast, easy to take risks and effectively manage them. Figure 5.7 shows the cyclic pattern that economies tend to follow.

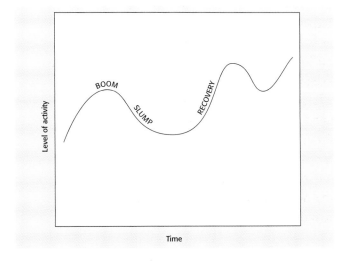

Figure 5.7 The business cycle

In times of decline we would expect to see that:
- The number of new businesses is smaller.
- The rate of failure of businesses has increased.
- The disposable income of many people is lower.
- Unemployment is high and rising.
- Investment by business is falling.
- The profit margins of most businesses are falling.
- Merger and takeover activity is rising.
- There is government action to stimulate the economy.
- There is concentration on survival and a reduction of risk-taking activity.
- Firms and consumers are stretching credit to the limit.
- Firms are increasing credit control and debt recovery activity.
- There is increased reliance on short-term financing.
- There are reductions in stock levels.
- There is increased competitive activity.
- Profit margins are reduced.
- Firms will be searching for other markets.
- Firms will be cutting back and keeping to safe market segments.
- There are continuous searches for cost-reducing methods.

Indicators of growth would include:

◆ a rise in consumer spending;
◆ a fall in unemployment;
◆ greater activity in the housing market;
◆ new businesses starting up;
◆ government action to manage growth;
◆ increases in reported profits;
◆ greater activity in the holiday and leisure industries.

There are firms such as pawnbrokers and money lenders that tend to thrive in times of low growth, but firms in general tend to suffer. In times of steady growth we can expect to see changes such as the following:

◆ The atmosphere in which activity takes place gradually changes from one of uncertainty and a concentration on survival to one of optimism and confidence. Regular reporters from both sides of industry, from government and from economic agencies will be making positive predictions.

◆ Consumer spending will broaden out into the non-essential purchases, which have been neglected for a while. The quantity of goods bought on credit will begin to rise and people will again be seeking to buy houses.

◆ Demand can only rise if suppliers can make the goods available. Businesses will see the opportunity for greater profits and will increase supply as much as is possible in the short term. In the longer term they will invest in new machinery, in technology and in research and development, all of which provide stimulus to further growth.

◆ Some firms will seize the opportunity to expand. This could require more staff or more overtime, relocation and greater capitalisation, all of which will stimulate further activity.

◆ Business is about taking carefully controlled risks and, in an atmosphere of growth and confidence, risk taking will seem more attractive.

But:

◆ If some of the risks are unwise, it will produce failure and this can flatten growth.

◆ If the speed of growth is too rapid, it will simply raise prices and therefore discourage investment and reduce disposable income.

◆ If the government sees growth to be too rapid, it will take action to control it and dampen activity down, perhaps by raising the rate of interest.

◆ In an atmosphere of confidence and greater prosperity organised labour can be expected to seek better rewards. If these remain within increased productivity there will be no problem, but if they rise above that level they will raise unit costs and therefore prices.

Over-to-you

Short-answer questions

1 Who are (a) the internal and (b) the external stakeholders in a company?

2 Giving examples, show how the objectives and interests of stakeholders may conflict.

3 Why should (a) local authorities, (b) our government and (c) the EU intervene in the activities of business? Give examples.

4 'The market is a process.' Show what this means.

5 If supply is never expected to be equal to demand, why is equilibrium important?

6 Distinguish between gross, net and disposable incomes.

7 State one way, as a consumer, that you feel the law (a) supports you and (b) constrains you. Explain your view.

8 Explain one way in which market forces tend to fail.

9 Explain why a strong pound may be disadvantageous to businesses.

10 With the aid of a diagram comment on the stages of the business cycle.

Discover and learn

1 Go into any supermarket and discover the ways in which they compete.
   (a) Discover which of those ways are known to customers.
   (b) Discover how consumers react to them.
   (c) On the basis of your research, what advice would you offer to the managing team?

2 Find out how small shops are trying to compete.

3 Choose one firm in each case and find out how each of the following have influenced its activities and decision-making:

(a) The Sale of Goods Act.

(b) The Food Safety Act.

(c) The Health and Safety at Work Act.

(d) Employment legislation.

4 Choose any one firm and find out how the following affect the running and success of the business:

(a) exchange rates;

(b) interest rates;

(c) taxation.

5 Discover from the local council:

(a) If it has a business or industrial estate and why the estate is there. If the council does not have such an estate, why is that?

(b) Examples of ways in which it:

◆ supports business in its area;

◆ constrains business in its area.

(c) What part it plays directly in the local economy.

(d) Goods and services it supplies for consumers.

6 Look around your area. Find examples of ways in which membership of the EU is influencing business activity in the area.

7 Look around your area, using the indicators given in this section and any others you think are useful. Decide whether, on local evidence alone, we are in a period of growth or a period of decline. Provide and analyse sufficient evidence to support your case. Compare your findings with those of others.

8 Read the case study below and then tackle the exercises that follow.

Case study – Frobishers Engineering plc

The firm makes components for domestic electric appliances. It came to your area in 1985 and has gradually grown so that it now employs 300 shop floor workers, 85 workers involved in packing and distributing its products and 43 in administration. For the past four years it has found it increasingly difficult to compete with overseas competition, both from the EU and from Japan. Part of this difficulty has arisen from the strength of the pound (£) and part from its reliance on fairly old production methods. The firm is part of a multinational group with its headquarters in the United States. The directors have decided to close the factory in your area and to build a larger more capital-intensive factory in another part of the UK.

(a) What factors do you consider might have attracted the firm to your area? (In answering this question, assume that they are coming now.)

(b) Why might fluctuating exchange rates have caused problems for the company?

(c) Trace the effects that the closure of the firm might have on the local economy.

(d) How might you expect to get support for your local economy from government at all levels in this situation?

Summary

In this section we have recognised that:

- Businesses operate in a dynamic and often uncertain environment and the stage on which they perform is now the world.

- Most markets are worldwide and changes wherever they occur will have effects on what businesses can do and how they should do them.

- Market forces determine much of what happens, but they are not always the best way of distributing resources or of ensuring fairness and stability. These are among the reasons why the State intervenes to manage and control the economy using the main weapons of the Budget, the legal system and the rate of interest.

- Despite the intervention of government at local, national and EU level, the level of activity changes in a cyclic fashion, significantly changing the ways in which businesses behave.

- In all of this the 'feel good factor' is often as important as any changes which occur. If consumers or businesses are not confident, little can be done that will have any assurance of success.

- On the other hand, if the stakeholders in our economy are too confident and want to move too quickly, this can overheat the economy and send the cycle downwards again.

- Both exchange rates, and the budgetary decisions made by the government, have significant effects on personal and business decisions.

Key words

Definitions of Key words can be found in the Glossary on page 236.

black economy	import duties
competition	income tax
corporation tax	industrial marketing
creditors	insolvency
debtors	net income
demand	shortage
disposable income	supply
equilibrium point	taxation
exchange rates	unique selling point (USP)
excise duties	value added tax (VAT)
gross income	

6 Responding to other external influences

On completion of this section you should be able to:

➤ exemplify and explain social and cultural factors that constrain business

➤ demonstrate understanding of the ways in which stakeholder interests may combine or conflict in influencing business decisions

➤ show how businesses try to balance the needs of all stakeholders

➤ explain the purpose and impact of the laws which constrain decisions in the main aspects of business behaviour

➤ explain how moral and ethical restraints can influence the way business decisions are taken

➤ understand the impact of environmental issues on business

➤ show how the political relationships and activities of the state influence business actions

➤ explain the role of technology and the opportunities and threats it creates in different business situations, explain how business reacts to all the constraints within which it must work

Introduction

In Section 5 we looked at the ways in which economic constraints might influence business behaviour and at the ways in which businesses might react to them. In this section we extend the discussion to consider the constraints shown in Table 6.1.

◆ Social constraints:	The effects people have
◆ Legal constraints:	The State working through the law
◆ Environmental:	Our world and its changing nature
◆ Ethical constraints:	The moral code by which we live
◆ Political constraints:	The effects of government behaviour
◆ Technological:	The change we create

Table 6.1 Constraints on business behaviour

The conflicting pressures and influences that make up the business environment are bound to offer opportunities to some firms and pose threats for others. In some cases they will support and in others they will frustrate or prevent. Effective response is therefore a key to success. The business management cannot afford to ignore what is happening; in fact, most of the time managers must reach out, discover and interpret. Only by doing this can they plan ahead or modify existing plans in the light of changing circumstances.

The working population

Figures on the UK population are collected every ten years in the census. Every household is legally bound to return the census form correctly completed. The first year of each decade is chosen. The main features suggested by the last census that would be of significance in business have been updated by the publication of other data collected from a variety of sources.

Mid-term estimates by the local council in one area make it clear that population has risen by about 17.4% since the last census. This is a big change and by far the greatest contributor to this increase is people who have moved into the area from big towns. From *Social Trends*, which is an annual publication to be found in all public reference libraries, we can gather the general features of changes that will affect the labour market and the pattern of demand.

Table 6.2 shows that approximately 75% of people of working age are economically active. The economically inactive include those who have retired early, those who choose not to work outside the home and those who are unable to work. Working patterns have changed considerably in the period. One of the biggest changes has been in part-time employment, which has increased by 30.95% in the period.

	1986	1998
Full Time	16.6	17.4
Part Time	4.2	5.5
Self-employed	2.7	3.1
Other[1]	0.4	0.3
Total	23.9	26.2
Unemployed	3.1	1.7
Economically active[2]	27.0	27.9
Inactive[3]	7.5	7.9
Working population	34.5	35.8

Table 6.2 UK population of working age by employment (figures in millions)
Notes: 1. Examples: Government training schemes, unpaid family workers. 2. Includes the unemployed available for work. 3. Those who could but do not seek work.
Source: Office for National Statistics.

Activities

1 What other changes in the pattern of work can you see in table 6.2?
2 Comment on the significance of this evidence.
3 Compare your findings with those of other groups in the class.
4 Use either the Internet or the reference library as a source and obtain the most recent figures you can. Comment on any significant changes you see and try to explain them.

One of the features of change concerns the role of women and this is shown in Table 6.3, together with a forecast of the positions expected in 2001 and 2011. One of the things we can see from Table 6.3 is that the role of women is changing. The number of women in work or actively seeking it has risen by 2.4% between 1991 and 1997 and is projected to rise by a further 11% on the 1997 figure. The number of economically active men has declined, probably as a result of the increasingly common practice of early retirement, between 1991 and 1997. However, this trend is projected to reverse between 2000 and 2011. This is because we have an increasingly ageing population.

The pattern for young people entering the labour market is also changing. The ageing population is partly a consequence of falling birth rates and hence there are

fewer teenagers available to enter the labour market. This fall is made greater by an increasing number who are continuing full-time education after the age of 16. The larger number of younger women in the labour market reflects the tendency for women to postpone their families until later in life.

		Age 16-24	25-44	45-54	55-59	60-64	65+
1991	M	3.1	8.1	3.0	1.1	0.8	0.3
1991	F	2.6	6.1	2.4	0.8	0.3	0.2
1997	M	2.4	8.1	3.4	1.1	0.7	0.3
1997	F	2.0	6.4	2.9	0.8	0.4	0.2
2001	M	2.4	8.2	3.4	1.3	0.7	0.3
2001	F	2.1	6.4	3.0	0.9	0.4	0.2
2011	M	2.8	7.3	3.9	1.3	0.9	0.3
2011	F	2.3	6.2	3.6	1.0	0.7	0.2

Table 6.3 UK labour force by gender and age (figures in millions)

The *Family and Working Life Survey* (1994-1995, Office of National Statistics) offers a range of reasons why part-time employment is rising and why women tend to seek it more than men. These include:

◆ Only a quarter of men working part time do not want a full-time job, whilst more than three-quarters of the women only wanted part-time employment.
◆ The main reasons for women in part-time employment were child related. Women said that either they wished to be with their children or they regarded their children as too young to permit a return to full-time work.
◆ A significant number have more than one part-time job. More women than men have second jobs.
◆ More than half of those who have second jobs are putting together two or more part-time jobs.

Some effects on business of patterns of work

The effects of part-time working, job sharing and early retirement are that many people have more time for leisure and this is seen in increased activity in the leisure industry and in the holiday industry. The holiday industry in particular now targets those it calls the 'empty nesters', older people whose children have now left home, and the 54+ group, which includes many who have retired early and who seek more regular holidays and short breaks. The success of SAGA is an indicator of this. Part-time working, particularly among students, increases disposable income and there is now a significant sector of business that targets the income they earn. Among the leaders are fast-food shops, music retailers, fashion clothing shops and the holiday and leisure industry.

The effects of women showing a greater tendency to seek employment include:

◆ a much greater tendency for firms to meet the requirements of the equal opportunity legislation and to offer employment to women;

◆ a considerable increase in families with two or more cars;

◆ the building of houses either with parking space for more than one car or with double garages;

◆ an increase in child-care facilities and in the numbers employed in the child-care industry;

◆ an increase in the tendency for firms and educational institutions to provide child-care and crèche facilities;

◆ an increase in the disposable income of many families and therefore changing patterns of demand;

◆ significant changes in shopping habits; consumers now want 24-hour shopping, convenience foods, pre-packed foods and one-stop shopping;

◆ an increase in the number of people working in the domestic services industry;

◆ an increase in sales of domestic electric appliances.

Time spent at work is also changing. In part this will be a reaction to the EU Working Time Directive. This Directive requires employers to ensure that employees do not work more than an average of 48 hours a week against their will. Nevertheless, more than 30% of all men are at work for more than 48 hours, as are 7% of women. The Directive is not universally applicable and owners and self-employed people are excluded. It is not a requirement and still permits willing overtime. Nevertheless, the trend is towards longer working hours. Table 6.4 illustrates that trend.

Hours worked per week	
1986	42.6
1990	43.7
1998	44.0

Table 6.4 Increasing average working hours per week (UK)
Source: Labour Force Survey. Office for National Statistics.

Occupational patterns

The kinds of things people do have also changed over the years. The comparison given in Table 6.5 represents a trend that has been going on for some years.

Occupation	Males 1991	1998	Females 1991	1998
Managers and administrators	16	19	8	11
Professional	10	11	8	9
Associate professional and technical	8	9	10	11
Clerical and secretarial	8	8	29	26
Craft and related	21	17	4	2
Personal and protective services	7	8	14	17
Selling	6	5	12	12
Plant and machinery operatives	15	15	5	4
Other occupations	8	8	10	8
All employees (millions)	11.8	12.2	10.1	10.6

Table 6.5 UK employees by gender and occupation (percentages)

Activities

1 Use the table to comment on the main changes in occupational structure.

2 Compare your findings with those of other groups and discuss possible reasons and effects.

3 Obtain more recent information of the same kind and try to explain any differences you observe.

The environment of work

The environment in which businesses work has changed. Among the changes are:

◆ the continuing decline in Britain's manufacturing activities;

- the increasing role of the tertiary sector;
- the change, due to technology, in the nature of many tasks both on the shop floor and in the office; in the years to come the Internet will have as big an impact;
- the development of the EU, which has meant that the focus of both work and the marketplace is now the whole of Europe and in some instances the world;
- an increasing body of Euro-law to which British businesses are subject.

Table 6.5 still shows gender differences. Women are far more likely than men to be engaged in clerical and secretarial jobs and in nursing. The craft jobs, although they are rapidly declining, are still largely the preserve of men. The progress of women towards management roles is significant, with a 10% increase from 30% to 33%.

Other evidence shows that the number of males engaged in manufacture between 1981 and 1998 fell from a third to a quarter, whilst the percentage in distribution rose from 16% to 20% and that in financial services from 10% to 16%. Self-employment has increased in significance. Table 6.6 shows the top five self-employment areas for both men and women in 1998.

Male	Percentage employed	Female	Percentage employed
Construction	27	Distribution	23
Distribution	18	Public administration	22
Financial services	18	Financial services	17
Manufacturing	8	Manufacturing	8
Transport	8	Agriculture and fishing	5
Agriculture and fishing	8		

Table 6.6 Self-employment 1998

Notes: Distribution includes hotels and restaurants; 21% of all women work in 'other services', as compared with 8% of men. The total number of self-employed people is 3.3 million, of whom 2.4 million are male.

Legal influences

The law intervenes in what business does more and more. There is much more legislation from Westminster and, additionally, there is more direction from Europe.

You do not have to know the detail of this body of law or even the names and dates of Acts of Parliament. In effect what is needed is:

- an understanding of why the law intervenes;
- an ability to explain where intervention takes place;
- the effects on business decisions of complying with the law;
- the consequences for the various stakeholders.

Why intervention?

All business activity has at least two parties involved and interested in or affected by the outcome of that activity. In most situations one of the parties is much stronger than the other and the law intervenes to protect the weaker party. Thus:

- In the raising of finance, shareholders who are not directors are in a much weaker position than those who are, particularly where one or two shareholders have a controlling interest.
- In recruitment the applicant is usually in a much weaker position than the employer.
- In employment the employee is usually in a much weaker position than the manager or the owner.
- The customer is in a much weaker position than the supplier in most cases.

In all of these situations there is law to protect the weaker party:

- Once an organisation incorporates and becomes a private or public limited company, accounts must be audited and specific information must be publicly available. There has to be an annual general meeting and the Memorandum of Association prevents the company from acting outside its declared objectives.
- In recruitment most organisations must be equal-opportunity employers at all stages of the recruitment, selection and training process. This relates to discrimination in respect of age, sex, race, creed, culture and disability.
- In employment the law protects the employee from unfair dismissal and provides a procedure through which employees can go to protect their rights. In the work situation the employee is also protected with respect to health and safety. It is the responsibility of the employer to provide a safe place of work and healthy conditions of work. This protection also applies to people visiting the place of work.

◆ The general principle of buying things is that you are presumed to want to buy what you do in fact buy. However, there is a large body of legislation that protects consumers in certain situations.

How does the law work?

Interesting as legal principles and practices are, they are not part of this syllabus. However, it does help to know where the law comes from

The nation state

Most of our law comes from Acts of Parliament and is administered through either a specialist body of people created for the purpose or through the courts. Much of the law that applies to business is **civil**. That means that it lays down what the rights and responsibilities of the parties to a situation are and leaves it to them to take an issue to the courts or to a tribunal if one of the parties wishes to do so. In civil law we are not dealing with crimes but with a breakdown in a relationship and an attempt either to put things right or to obtain compensation for one of the parties.

Some law is administered through specially created bodies given the right to intervene in what businesses do. The utility services like gas, water, electricity and the telephone services are constrained by '**watchdog bodies**' called OFTEL, OFWAT and so on. They have intervened to ensure improved quality of services and to control prices. OFSTED may well be better known to you since they have the duty to ensure standards in education. Some bodies like this operate at local level. The trading standards officer is particularly concerned about matters relating to the sale of goods and the conditions within which goods and services are offered. That officer operates at local-authority level. The local authority itself is responsible for the general control of business activity in its area. On the one hand, it may offer support and develop business parks; on the other, it may give or refuse planning permission for new business developments in its area. Finally, the local authority has duties of its own, which it must perform in the community. It can franchise these to private businesses if it wants to. It can run activities itself: education, libraries and transport are examples. It can give direct support to business that is considered necessary for the welfare of the community. It is on this basis that many local bus and train services are run.

Activities

1 Find out what your local authority is called and where its offices are.
2 Find out what officials it has who control what businesses do and protect your interests.
3 Find out what planning permission is. You may find that bank or local-authority literature will help with this.
4 Find out what your local authority does directly in the community.

The State now shares some of its responsibilities and controls with a wide range of organisations. These include:

◆ newly created centres of government and decision-making for Scotland, Wales and Northern Ireland (although the Northern Ireland Assembly has subsequently been suspended);
◆ the European Community;
◆ treaty arrangements and international agreements like the World Trade Organisation (WTO).

Of these, the one with greatest effect on us is the European Community, which continues to grow rapidly. There is almost endless controversy about the role of the EU, the monetary system and our membership of it. The situation changes almost daily and you will need to keep up with the changes as they occur. Increasingly, the EU is important to us as a market, as a competitor within our markets and as a law-making body whose directives apply to our businesses. Businesses such as farming and fishing are particularly tightly controlled by EU directives, but the rest of business and industry is also subject to an increasing number of directives, particularly ones that affect the rights of workers.

Some law, like place of work legislation, has been a concern of government for centuries. Nowadays, it is far more complete. Health and safety provisions apply not only to the obvious working situations but also to institutions like schools and churches, as well as to leisure and entertainment complexes. What happens in the marketplace has also been a long-standing concern, with consumer protection extending to goods that are fit for the purpose for which they are bought and to circumstances in which consumers buy on credit. Other law has arisen in response to changing circumstances and to emerging concerns. The Food Safety Act is a case in point. It controls the manufacture of all things that relate to food, the processing of food and its sale. In any café or restaurant now you will see at least one certificate of food hygiene displayed and you will see the extensive use of protective clothing. At both European and state levels, directives and legislation about the sale of beef and beef products are only just being reconsidered and removed. These things show that government bodies can react quickly to worrying situations and also have long-standing areas of concern for particular situations. The protection of shareholders is contained within the Companies Acts and attempts to ensure a framework of true, fair and public reporting is in place.

Some legal changes are in pursuit of government objectives. The best example is the annual Finance Act, which sets out the framework of taxation for each year. It contains all the changes that the Chancellor has made in the Budget. The Act usually contains measures of support either for all business or for selected ones. It affects decisions like investment and business growth or decline. The changes that are directed at individuals will affect disposable income and often the price of goods on which different taxes have been levied. An objective of government in 1999 was to establish a minimum wage, which was established at that time at £3.60 an hour.

The State takes the view that some situations are of very great social importance and cannot be left simply to the parties themselves. The implications of some behaviour are so extensive that the criminal law is involved. Businesses cannot be permitted to defraud customers, employees or shareholders. Practices that would expose people to injury or real danger and situations in which things are done with reckless negligence must all have a penalty under the law. It is important to prevent these situations and to ensure that there is a general awareness of social disapproval.

Two sides to rights

Most people remember their rights. In fact, when examiners ask about rights and responsibilities at work, they find that answers are long on rights but very short on responsibilities. An employee has rights at work but also has a duty to give a fair day's work, to keep the secrets of the employer in so far as they relate to the business, to work safely and to wear and use all safety clothing and equipment. Every right that anyone has can only be ensured because that right is someone else's responsibility. We shall return to this when we consider ethics.

Law in action

In this sub-section, through examples of situations involving the law we will see how it influences business behaviour. These examples show the extent and operation of the law. You can think of many of your own examples, especially where you are involved in buying something, going on a journey or doing a part-time job. Even at school or college the law has a lot to say about what goes on.

Activities

Read the case study below and tackle the exercises that follow.

Case study – Branstead Components plc

Philip Branstead set up a small light engineering business on a business park run by the local authority outside a small town in Devon. After three years he went into partnership with another small business and they relocated to Somerset. The business has grown and a public limited company was formed in 1998.

The business produces components for the domestic electric appliance industry and, apart from some small business for self-employed repair people, there are only seven large customers.

The firm needs to expand on site and to extend the factory into an adjoining field. This was discussed at a recent Board meeting. The following points were made:

◆ There are some concerns relating to finding the right staff.
◆ The layout of the factory does not give much scope for expansion.
◆ Additional capital will be needed. A share issue may be necessary.

◆ The coming budget will increase taxes.

◆ Employment prospects are good since unemployment is high and wages could be kept low. The difficulty will be finding skilled labour.

◆ Increasing the numbers employed might make it necessary to provide for refreshments and possibly lunches.

◆ Transport will need to be supplied for many new workers.

◆ There is a dispute with two workers sacked last week and one of the charge hands is leaving to have a baby.

The discussion continued...

This is only an extract but it provides an example of how understanding of the effect of the law on business decisions can be worked out. Within the case there are many examples of situations where what the firm does is covered by the law. Consider some of them.

1 *Branstead Components plc*. The firm started as a sole ownership business. Philip was supported by a local authority business park. Here, the authority is fulfilling a duty to act in the best interest of the community and its economy. If Philip had set-up elsewhere he would have needed planning permission. In the early days Philip would have been running the risks of unlimited liability. Later he formed first a partnership, and then a plc. A partnership still has unlimited liability and there has to be an agreement between the partners. Forming a plc really brought the law into operation. The company had to have a memorandum and articles of association; it had to state clear objectives and keep to them; in getting the finance a prospectus had to show

a true and fair view of the prospects of the business. Properly audited accounts had be made public.

2 *Finding the right staff*. Here there are implications that the recruitment and selection processes will be conducted fairly with equal opportunity for all. It is not sufficient that the interviews are fair since it is possible to exclude people by what is said in advertisements and by where and when they are displayed.

3 *The layout of the factory*. The intention is that the firm is going to grow and therefore there is the possible danger of overcrowding and lack of space, which could contravene the provisions of the health and safety legislation, and could cause accidents. It could make movement around the factory floor difficult and hence increase the risks to personnel.

4 *The coming budget will increase taxes*. This would happen through the Finance Act. If taxes on businesses are increased, this could reduce the profits of the business. This would mean less to pay out in dividends and less available to plough back into the business. It might lead to a greater amount borrowed or to increased prices. If VAT is increased, this would increase prices, or it might be absorbed by the business, increasing their costs and reducing profits. If the increase is in personal taxation, this will reduce disposable income. The firm makes components for domestic electric appliances, which are consumer durables. Buying this kind of good is often delayed when disposable income falls. The overall effect of such changes might be to convince the firm that now is not a good time to expand the business. The firm might react to a falling home market by seeking new markets overseas.

(a) Some of the features of the above case that involve the law have not been considered in the examples. Trace the legal point involved and the possible effects in each of the following:

◆ raising additional capital by share issue;

◆ keeping wages low;

◆ providing refreshments and possibly lunches;

◆ providing transport for many of our new workers;

◆ resolving a dispute with two workers sacked last week;

◆ replacing the charge hand who is leaving to have a baby.

(b) Work in groups. Each member of the group should choose another case or a business article from a newspaper. Go through it identifying the legal issues involved.

◆ Exchange your article and list with one of the group and work through the one you now have.

◆ Do you agree with the issues selected or do you want to cut some out or add some in?

◆ Now comment on the issues and their possible effects on business or personal behaviour.

Ethical issues

These are very close to the legal ones we have been discussing. It could be said that law is about the things that society has decided we must do but might try not to do, whilst ethics is about those things we ought to do in the opinion of society generally. People may differ about what they think is ethical, but would normally recognise behaviour that they considered unethical. Some examples may help.

For employers

- It is unethical to sell goods that are known to be faulty. In some situations the law would take over, e.g. goods past their sell-by date and those known to have been stolen.
- It is unethical to let someone work for so long without rest that they may no longer be able to do a job, e.g. doctors and nurses in hospital. Again, through the Working Hours Directive the EU has stepped in to limit this. However the Directive does not apply to every situation and would not apply if the worker was willing.
- It is unethical to run the business in ways that damage the environment. The law does demand environmentally friendly behaviour in many instances. Businesses can ignore the law and pay the price.

For employees

- Employees are paid to give a fair day's work. Ethics would suggest that they should not be deliberately absent without good reason. It could be argued it is less unethical to be absent from work if you are then not paid than if you are paid a salary and would still be paid.
- It is unethical to use the employer's time and resources for your own private purposes unless this has been agreed. If this amounted to stealing from the employer, there would be redress through the courts or by dismissal.
- It is unethical to steal the employer's clients and do business with them on your own private account. An example might be a garage mechanic who worked for customers he had persuaded away from his employer.

For customers

- If you are given more change than you are entitled to at the checkout, on the bus or anywhere else, technically this is stealing. Since the change giver does not know it has happened, it is your responsibility to give it back.
- If you jump the queue at the checkout or anywhere else, you could argue that it is up to other people to make sure that you don't queue jump. However, this is deliberately relying on other people to let you bully them.
- Here is a more difficult one. If you know that something wrong is taking place, should you speak out? There is a growing belief that you should.
- You could simply take a dangerous toy, or a contaminated pie, back to the shop and probably benefit from the shop's goodwill. But what if that same business continues to sell the dangerous toy or the contaminated pie? Someone could be injured or die.
- If you don't tell your employer that a worker is smoking in a dangerous situation in which smoking is banned lives, jobs and valuable equipment and products could be lost.

Business and ethics

Ethical behaviour is not always easy. One of the responsibilities of business managers is to make a profit, either to plough back into further growth or to distribute to the owners. Without that profit, owners would not have taken the risks involved in business. How far, then, should they pursue the ethical interests of others if doing so means that profits are lower than they would otherwise be? It could be that money spent on ethical behaviour would so reduce the profitability of business that jobs were lost.

All this is not to suggest that businesses should not behave ethically, but only to demonstrate that the conflicting needs of stakeholders do not make the decision clear cut. However, there is increasing evidence that more and more businesses are concerned about ethics and want to behave ethically. Examples include:

- Not trading with others whose practices appear to be unethical. Not trading with firms that supply arms is an example.

◆ Not stocking goods of which there is disapproval.

◆ Stocking products that are healthier, that are recycled or that show a greater concern for human welfare.

◆ Only investing in firms that have a good ethical or environmental reputation.

◆ Engaging in business practices that show concern for the environment, keep the streets clean and free of litter, etc.

This is likely to develop further if the benefits to a business of behaving ethically become more obvious and become greater than the costs. The law does much to ensure certain minimum standards and the test of an ethical business is that it is not behaving in a socially responsible way because the law says so, but takes that responsibility beyond the extent and letter of the law. The benefits of doing so might include the following:

◆ Recruitment of staff may be easier. A firm that has a reputation for ethical behaviour is likely to attract people with high ideals.

◆ For the same reasons, there will be greater likelihood of retaining staff. We would expect to see lower labour turnover, which reduces costs.

The success of Body Shop is based on its reputation for ethical behaviour

◆ If employees want to work for a firm, they are already a long way towards being motivated to work well.

◆ Sales may grow. There is increasing evidence that, where there is a genuine choice for them, consumers are more likely to patronise and be loyal to firms that behave ethically. The success of Body Shop is based on this belief.

Activities

1 Debate 'Should firms behave ethically?' Work in groups of four or six. Half the group should prepare a case for ethical behaviour, while the other half of the group prepare the case against ethical behaviour. Debate the issues and come to a conclusion. Groups should get together and pool the different conclusions.

2 Read the case study below and answer the questions that follow.

Case study – Burnside Double Glazing Ltd

Burnside Double Glazing is a small firm trying to survive in this market. Its main product is the fitting of doors, windows and double glazing. It also fits new facia boards and carries out cavity-wall insulation. Its methods of selling are by cold calling on the telephone and by direct visits to potential customers. The techniques are high-pressure ones that attempt to make sales immediately, promising massive reductions for immediate acceptance and making claims for the product that cannot be substantiated. The sales teams always work in pairs (one man and one woman).

Suppose a team has just visited your house:

(a) What is your view of the ethics of this method of selling?

(b) How does the law protect consumers in this situation?

Environmental issues

The environment in which a business operates will impact on its operations in many different ways. This is not just the physical environment, but everything that influences decisions and actions. Some pressures we have already considered in this section and in Section 5. Among those we have not considered are:

- government objectives;
- the level of employment;
- global activity;
- business and the physical environment.

Government objectives

We have seen how important objectives are in all aspects of business discussed so far. It is also clear from Section 5 and this section that government has a central role in how the economy is managed and the support and constraint of businesses within that economy. It should not be surprising, then, that governments have objectives. Here we are concerned with the objectives that all governments may be expected to have rather than with those that have a party-political purpose. It is in pursuit of its objectives that the State takes the action it does. Chief among them are:

Economic growth This is what determines the extent to which standards of living can at least remain stable and possibly rise. Too rapid growth will lead to inflation and to other problems. The State will be looking for steady and balanced growth. Even the economy of this small country does not grow in a balanced way. We have seen good growth in London and the South East, often balanced by poor growth or even decline in the regions. Growth always means change and it is not possible for every firm or every industry to grow. There has been considerable growth in the tertiary sector and decline in manufacture and primary industry. Governments may deliberately seek to foster and encourage growth in some areas of our economy and to dampen it in others.

Price stability In the modern world this means keeping a curb on inflation and this has been a major issue of policy. In order to make the objective more stable and to make work towards it both long term and free of party politics, in 1998 control over the rate of interest was passed from the Treasury to a Monetary Policy Committee chaired by the Governor of the Bank of England. He has been given a target of 2.5% inflation.

Stable exchange rates The rate at which our currency exchanges against the major currencies of the world is crucial to the success of British firms in the world markets. In 1999 and early 2000 our currency has been too strong in foreign markets, which makes it difficult

for our firms to export, although this has advantages for importers and for everybody taking holidays abroad.

Reducing the level of unemployment A high level of unemployment means that there is a big burden on the social services as well as a reputation of poor performance for the government. Increasing employment is largely associated with growth, but much modern growth is not labour intensive and does not solve the problem. Job sharing, increasing part-time work and the growth of the tertiary sector all help with reduction in unemployment. The level of unemployment varies enormously from one region to another and governments often implement policies that attempt to attract industry to the unemployment black spots.

Greater equality of income It is neither possible nor wise to aim for absolute equality of income, but there are some major imbalances. Governments often use income-tax levels and allowances to promote greater equality. One measure that was designed to move towards greater equality was the introduction of a minimum wage, which applies to most but not all wage earners.

Managing the economy Market forces do not always operate efficiently or smoothly. The result is that the State has to intervene to keep the economy on course. It does so through the Budget, through monetary policy changes and through direct intervention measures. The danger of this intervention is that timing may be poor or that the adjustment may be too little or too much. The only evidence available is forecasts and they are often inaccurate.

The level of employment

The number of people in work varies substantially and is difficult to measure with any degree of accuracy. The occupation and unemployment statistics were shown in Table 6.2, which is repeated here.

There are several reasons why people may be unemployed:

Inactive People are not seeking work, in many instances because they cannot through disabilities of one kind or another. There is a small group who could seek work but have no intention of doing so. The biggest element in this group is housewives who have no desire or intention to work outside the home in gainful employment.

	1986	1998
Full Time	16.6	17.4
Part Time	4.2	5.5
Self-employed	2.7	3.1
Other[1]	0.4	0.3
Total	23.9	26.2
Unemployed	3.1	1.7
Economically active[2]	27.0	27.9
Inactive[3]	7.5	7.9
Working population	34.5	35.8

Table 6.2 Population of working age by employment (figures in millions)
Notes: 1. Examples: Government training schemes, unpaid family workers. 2. Includes the unemployed available for work. 3. Those who could but do not seek work.
Source: Office for National Statistics.

Seasonally unemployed There are more jobs on the market at different seasons of the year. In the summer this includes substantially greater employment in the leisure and tourist industries and in agriculture. In the winter there are small pockets of increase, like that associated with Christmas

Unemployment associated with change This happens when people move and is more acute when families move from situations in which all are employed to places elsewhere in the country where only one person is employed. Because the others will be actively seeking work, this kind of unemployment is often short term. Improved communication of job vacancies would reduce this problem.

Structural unemployment This comes about because of the demands of the economy for labour change. In this country fewer workers are now needed in mining, in heavy manufacture and in farming. This kind of change often produces balancing increases elsewhere. Examples would be in financial services, computer technology and in the personal service industries. But much of the change in this country has led to high unemployment in the regions and a steady increase in jobs in London and the South East.

Technological unemployment This has been one of the most dramatic creators of unemployment and has particularly affected middle management as computers have replaced people and chains of command in business have become much flatter. Certain manufacturing

industries have also been affected in this way as computer-aided design and computer-aided manufacturing have become more common.

Demand-related unemployment This is often called cyclical unemployment and comes about because the level of economic activity changes. This is maximised right at the bottom of the business cycle. Extreme periods of depression are rare now, but the economy does fluctuate, as seen in the cycle Figure 6.1. It is a central objective of government to so manage the economy that extreme fluctuations do not occur.

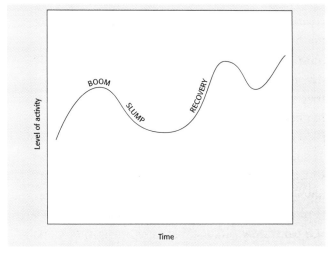

Figure 6.1 The business cycle

Business and unemployment

There are firms that lose and firms that benefit in any situation. There are benefits for business in unemployment, but on balance it reduces the level of activity and drives many businesses out of existence. The real damage of unemployment comes from:

Falling sales The obvious effect of unemployment is that disposable income falls and the greatest effect is on non-essential products and services. Firms producing leisure goods, durable consumer goods and non-essential services suffer most.

Falling profits These come partly from falling sales and partly from cuts in margins in an attempt to maintain sales.

Search for new markets This may be a broader product range in the home market, but it is more likely to be new markets abroad where disposable income may be higher.

Increased unemployment One of the highest costs for most businesses is labour costs. Firms will lay off staff or reduce hours in order to cut this cost when revenue is falling.

Lower investment Times of high unemployment are not the best for growth and development, so firms will be less inclined to take investment opportunities.

Personnel People who leave are less likely to be replaced and this may require greater flexibility of retained staff and some new training so that they can take on the responsibilities and skills of leavers.

Creditors Businesses will try to extend their own payments to firms that supply them with services and resources.

Debtors Businesses will try to be more careful in taking on new debtors and will be pushing existing ones for payment or selling the debt to factors in a search to maintain cash flow. Debts from both business and industry are likely to be more difficult to collect and may have to be 'written off'.

Increased costs These may include retraining, greater marketing costs and redundancy payments.

Bankruptcies and liquidations These could be because of falling trade or extreme cash-flow problems. They could occur because creditors have 'pulled the plug'. Many businesses operate on a very thin line between failure and survival and the failure rate can be very high at these times.

Activity

What happens when a country recovers from a slump is very much a mirror image of the above changes. Outline the likely effects on businesses as a recovery develops.

Global activity

Increasingly, in response to improvements in transport, carriage conditions and quality packing, through the medium of such communication devices as the telephone, fax machine and Internet, the world has become a very small place and almost a single market. Large firms have become multinationals and have the ability to produce and sell worldwide. Brand names like McDonalds, Coca-Cola and many others are recognised and marketed the world over. This has not only brought about an escalation in the volume of international trade, but has also created worldwide businesses for which marketing strategy focuses on the world rather than on small segments of a market. The car industry is a good example. A car may now be assembled from parts that have been made in several countries and car makers from all over the world site their manufacturing plants closer to their markets. Japanese and American cars are now sold to countries in Europe from manufacturing plants within Europe. The rapid development of these changes is largely owing to:

- Technological change: the computer first and then the spin-offs from it.
- Communication changes: the fax machine, the Internet.
- Transport: cheaper, faster and a more complete network.
- Privatisation: throughout the world governments have relinquished control of business and industry and private companies now merge on a global basis.
- World trade is freer than it was. This is largely the result of international agreements and bodies such as the World Trade Organisation.
- Consumers are less nationalistic in their trends. This has spread to a wide range of products, but can be noticed easily in our supermarkets and restaurants. It can also be seen on our roads where there is a wide variety of foreign cars.
- The industrialisation of many of the developing countries of the world. This was probably first noticed in the so-called 'tiger economies' of Asia. Although some of them have suffered a setback, the overall direction is forward.

For many businesses the effect has of this movement has been increase in the markets they serve and hence an increase in the size of the technical unit. Many more businesses have been able to reap internal economies of scale and in many industries the smaller firm has found it difficult to survive except in genuine niche markets – Aston Martin is an example – and as feeder firms producing for the larger ones.

Business and the physical environment

In one area there are all the following:

- In one part of the country there are large areas of quarried land from iron ore workings. They are all exhausted but remain as scars on the landscape; some have been recycled. There are two active RAF camps, which when they are in full swing constitute a significant noise pollution.

There is a cement factory that belches out pollutants into the atmosphere and offers the majority of its workers appallingly hot working conditions. The owners, however, have done a good job of shielding the site from all angles.

In the main street of the town, an endless stream of heavy lorries pollutes the atmosphere and makes the town dangerous for pedestrians to use.

Activities

1 Look around your community:
   ◆ How many examples of ways in which business may be damaging the environment can you see?
2 Look in the newspaper today. Find and read:
   ◆ any article about concern for the environment;
   ◆ any example of damage to the environment that is caused by business activity;
   ◆ any examples of business support for the environment.

Social costs of business activity

Not all social costs are related to what businesses do. Some result from the activities of private individuals or groups; some result from the activities of government. Nevertheless, there is growing concern for the damage that many business practices are doing to the environment and to the quality of life. Among those damages are:

Noise pollution There are many sufferers of this in areas close to our major airports but many of the causes are smaller and more local. Someone living next to a busy railway station finds the noise of constant announcements a significant burden.

Air pollution This is evident in any busy street, particularly where traffic is often at a standstill. Many factories pollute the atmosphere and many processing firms do also.

Congestion Congestion may pollute but it also has other substantial costs. The greatest cost of congestion is probably the London 'rush hour' or the M6 around Birmingham. Costs from this are in terms of valuable time and accidents as people get more and more frustrated. There will have been additional costs on a daily basis in terms of missed appointments and cancelled activities.

Physical destruction The raw materials of the world cannot be mined without destruction, There are dangers that agricultural land can be over-used and our food is polluted if chemicals are used to improve the growth of produce. Paper cannot be made in the quantities we need without felling trees. People cannot be housed without taking more and more hectares of the countryside. The list is almost endless and still growing.

Three children hold oil-covered Scater ducks shortly after rescuing them off the coast of Pendine. Thousands of birds and fish were put at risk after the oil tanker the *Sea Empress* ran aground off the coast of Wales losing over half its cargo in February 1996.
Source: Shawn Baldwan, Popperfoto/Reuter.

Water pollution There are many rivers in which fish cannot live and people dare not swim. Industrial waste of all kinds is daily poured into our rivers and into the sea. Some of that pollution is accidental rather than planned. Agriculture uses a range of chemicals on the land and there is no way they can be prevented from seeping into streams and rivers. The sea is a massive dump for waste from ships and incidents of large oil slicks from accidents at sea are common. Significant land waste is dumped in the sea and most of our beaches cannot be maintained to an acceptable standard.

Waste Modern ways of selling products in pre-packed form create an enormous amount of waste that cannot be recycled. Many production methods also create by-products or residues that cannot be used. Some of our customs create waste and litter: the daily and evening newspaper; the habit of eating in the street and on trains. An estimate of the litter left on trains in Kings Cross runs into several tons a day. As commuters come out of London at night, the waste is increased by the habit of buying evening newspapers, which are left when the passengers get off. At least paper can be recycled, but many waste products, especially those of chemical production and nuclear activity, cannot be recycled and special disposal sites have to be found.

Waste is sometimes created by inefficient systems. We waste a very large amount of water every year, partly because we are not good enough at capturing it and storing it and partly because it seeps away from our reservoirs and pipes. However, the major wastage of water is the overuse of it in many homes and businesses.

Minimising social costs

It is easy to recognise ways in which our environment is deteriorating and our resources are being depleted. It is quite another matter to find ways of controlling this that are manageable by businesses or countries and which the public will accept.

There are, however, some things that limit the problems:

Legislation This is often a blunt instrument, because laws made are not enforced. We have had legislation against litter for very many years, but that does not stop the streets around Kings Cross from being cluttered with paper waste. However, reclamation and pollution control legislation is more successful. Often the penalty is a fine and paying the fine is cheaper than changing the system. Clean-air legislation has been in force for many years and it has worked miracles in cleaning the air of London.

Taxation Effectively, this is saying that we cannot prevent the pollution but we can make you face the cost of removing it. There is a danger that any tax on business for this purpose will be passed on, at least in part, to the consumer. It is argued that high petrol and diesel taxes are designed, at least in part, to make car and lorry users pay the costs of pollution. If this were really so, tax differentials would be quite sharp between leaded and unleaded petrol and between petrol and diesel.

Specific charges If taxation is not feasible, then perhaps the pollution actually caused can be costed and then charged to the business. This sounds fair, but would be costly to administer and may still be passed on to the consumer in many cases.

Bribes Perhaps an unfair comment, but that is what grants, subsidies and tax allowances to find better methods of waste disposal are.

Traffic reduction schemes There are extreme examples, like banning cars from a town centre or complete pedestrianisation. The oldest form is the by-pass, but more inexpensive schemes include park and ride, bus lanes and cycle schemes. Cambridge tried a free cycle scheme for a while and Sheffield, Manchester and Croydon have re-introduced the tram.

Pressure There are many pressure groups whose efforts are directed towards saving the environment. Probably Greenpeace and Friends of the Earth are among the best known. There many local examples of pressure-group influences. Consumers can be very powerful through local action and through TV programmes like *We Can Work it Out* and *Watchdog*. Many of these efforts, however, are focused on righting individual consumer wrongs rather than on protecting the environment.

Conservation One method of conservation is to use wisely, and control the use of, replaceable resources. The best example is probably fishing. Fishing limits help to ensure that fish stocks are maintained. Another form of conservation is to replant. Replanting of trees on a planned basis over time is a long-term strategy, but will only solve the problem when the rate of replanting is greater than the rate of use.

Recycling Recycling is now a major industry. It occurs a lot at an industrial level, but recycling bins for paper, clothing, oil, bottles and cans are now common in every town and local authorities are beginning to collect refuse in ways that enable recycling where it is worth while.

Activity

Work in small groups. Between you, cover the local area. Undertake an audit of ways in which the environment is being abused in your area.

(a) Suggest ways in which this abuse may be removed, minimised or repaired.

(b) How should the cost of protecting the environment be met in these cases?

(c) Discover examples of pressure to protect the environment in your area. How successful is it?

Political constraints

Governments, by their actions, sometimes support and sometimes frustrate the activities of business. Some of the things a government wants to do are political in nature; they are designed to change the fabric of society. After World War II the government decided that many of the essential industries of the country should be in public control. By nationalisation, coal, transport, steel and the utilities were run as single firms controlled by government-created bodies. Subsequently that political decision was gradually reversed by a government believing in private enterprise.

On a number of occasions since 1950 there have been wars and conflicts around the world, in some of which, such as the Falklands and the Gulf War, the UK was directly involved. In others we had a part in combined United Nations involvement. Running throughout the period we have had our own problems within the nation.

Much that is done in the world is by political agreement or disagreement. One of the greatest influences on UK was, and will be, the creation of co-operative organisations in Europe, which began after World War II and is still developing through the European Union.

All of these things create and destroy businesses, determine how government spends its money, reduce or increase disposable income, change the conditions in which businesses work, create shortages and produce surpluses that it is difficult to distribute.

During the build up to the millennium, the great 'Jubilee 2000' push was to reduce or remove Third World debt, and continuing major debates are about devolution of power in this country and the exact role of the UK in the **European Union**.

Political decisions play a large part in creating the conditions within which businesses must work. Many are ongoing or predictable and businesses can plan for them or learn to work within them. But some are sudden and unexpected.

Education is an industry in a state of constant change. The pattern of education on offer depends very much on where you live. In some counties there is still selection; in some, secondary schools educate up to 16 and then students go on to either a sixth form college or a further education college. The management role of the staff and governors keeps changing and the educational qualifications towards which students work change. Surrounding all this there is a pattern of independent schools. Most of the changes described here are the result of political decisions on the structure of our education. Some of these are made at local level and others at national level.

Activity

Find out about changes in your school or college in the last ten years.

(a) Why do you think the changes were made?

(b) What effect have they had on:
  ◆ the local community?
  ◆ businesses in the community?
  ◆ students entering and leaving?

(c) Are there any changes planned for the immediate future?

(d) What do you think are the objectives of those changes?

Technology

Technology has always been a great agent for change and every age has seen its own inventions and discoveries, which have changed what we do and how we do it. Technology has changed how we get to work, who goes and when. It has changed the pattern of demand and the nature of the products that satisfy our needs. It has changed the nature and purposes of the education system and how we plan our lives. As a result of technology, most of us have a higher standard of living, are healthier and live longer. Through technology our horizons have widened from the local community in which we live to the world as a whole. Assisted by technology, the primary and secondary sectors of our economy have taken up far less of our labour and the tertiary sector has grown in importance. Change is here to stay and probably will continue to accelerate. We have to adapt to it in all areas of our lives.

Activity

Discuss the ways in which technology has changed life:

- ◆ at school or college;
- ◆ in your community;
- ◆ in individual organisations and businesses in your community;
- ◆ in the things you can buy locally;
- ◆ in the way one person known to you does his/her job;
- ◆ in any other way you think is obvious or important in your community;
- ◆ in your personal life as compared with someone your age 10 years ago.

You may find that your relations, the library and old photographs can be of help to you.

Over-to-you

Short-answer questions

1 State two situations in which the state intervenes in each of the following:
   (a) the transport industry;
   (b) the employment of workers;
   (c) the protection of the environment.
2 For each of the examples you chose explain why the state intervenes.
3 Why should a firm develop an attitude of public responsibility?
4 Explain to an individual what personal action could be taken in each of the following circumstances:
   (a) a packet of salad bought locally contains a slug;
   (b) the telephone company has overcharged for its services.
5 State and argue one objective you would expect to be pursued by:
   (a) your local authority;
   (b) the national government.
6 State three reasons why you think part-time work has become more common in this country.
7 What is the amount of the current minimum wage?
8 Look around your school or college:
   (a) State and explain three things that you consider are done to ensure your health and safety at work.
   (b) State and argue for one thing that could be done to make your school or college safer or more healthy.
9 Suppose you are a small shareholder in a large business. Why should the law offer you any protection?

Discover and learn

1 Work in groups. Choose a different business each. Find out how the business is affected by each of the constraints discussed in the Sections 5 and 6.
   (a) In what ways and for what reasons is the business limited by what you have discovered?
   (b) In what ways and for what reasons is the business supported?
   (c) Explain any similarities and any differences you have discovered.
2 What evidence can you find in your community of action taken by the local authority. Explain what you have discovered and explain why it is happening.
3 What evidence is there in the local community of the effects of membership of the European Union?

4 If there is debate in the local community about an issue relating to the environment in which business operates:

(a) Explain both sides of the issue.

(b) Debate the issue.

(c) Explain what may happen if your conclusions are correct. Keep to issues that will influence the pattern and behaviour of local business.

5 Read the case study below and then answer the questions that follow.

Case study – Berrymans shop

In a small village there is a typical village shop that sells everything and does not look as if it has changed very much in a generation. For the married couple who have run it for more than 60 years it is more a way of life than a business. If it were analysed, it would be seen to be making a loss. Every change that has been imposed on the business has been stoutly resisted. You would see no 'new-fangled' products in the shop, decimalisation was resisted for a very long time and now the resistance is to conversion to the metric system. Most of the support they get is sympathetic purchasing from the locals and this is slowly falling away. The shop will probably close in a year or two anyway because of the age of the owners, but they are threatening to close rather than change to metric.

This case shows an extreme example of resistance to change.

(a) Why do you think people commonly resist change?

(b) Should we make people more accepting of change?

(c) How can we do it?

6 Read the case study below and then tackle the exercises that follow.

Case study – Brotherton Construction plc

The country is just recovering from a period of very low activity in which credit restrictions have greatly reduced the number of houses that Brotherton has built and this has forced some redundancies. With the lifting of these restrictions and the lowering of the rate of interest, Brotherton is already seeing signs of renewed life in the demand for houses. The company has decided it must employ some new workers, but the management are divided between part-time and full-time employment. They are also divided about the pay to be offered. They agree that an hourly rate will be better, with no guaranteed working week and a rate of £3.40 an hour.

They have decided to advertise at the local job centre and by word of mouth and to see what applications they get. John Brotherton says he wants the equivalent of eight full-time men and will want to promote one of the existing men to gang manager in charge of the new recruits. To accommodate the expansion, the firm will need to expand the existing yard or to open a new one in the area. Most of the Board are in favour of a second yard at the other side of town. The problem will be finding a site with good access for the heavy vehicles they use and capable of tight security.

(a) Explain the constraints that may be placed on the firm with respect to:
   ◆ their intended employment policy;
   ◆ the location and use of a new site.

(b) What role might be played in this situation by:
   ◆ the local authority?
   ◆ the State?
   ◆ local people?

(c) Why might the lowering of the rate on interest stimulate the purchasing of houses?

(d) If possible, visit a local building site. From observations and enquiry explain, with examples, how health and safety are assured on site.

(e) What would you expect Brotherton to do to ensure health and safety for the new recruits?

Summary

In this section and the previous one we have recognised that:

- Business is affected by the environment within which it operates. In Section 5 we were concerned with the economic aspects of that environment and in this section the focus has been on all the other constraints within which business activity takes place. There has been a strong emphasis on the local community from which you can draw rich examples of the dynamics of business behaviour.

- The different forces for change are:

Social constraints:	The effects people have.
Legal constraints:	The State working through the law.
Environmental constraints:	Our world and its changing nature.
Ethical constraints:	The moral code by which we live.
Political constraints:	The effects of government behaviour.
Technological:	The change we create.

- Although these constraints have been considered separately, they are interactive, with many of the things that organisations do being a response to the perceived total effect of these constraints, rather than a consequence of any one of them.

Key words

Definitions of Key words can be found in the Glossary on page 236.

civil law	occupational patterns
conservation	price stability
economic growth	recycling
environment	social costs
ethics	unemployment
European Union	watchdog bodies
legislation	

7 Business finance

On completion of this section you should be able to:

➤ understand why business activity requires finance

➤ understand the objectives of those who provide finance and become stakeholders in the organisation

➤ show critical understanding of the different sources of business finance and evaluate their appropriateness in different circumstances

➤ analyse the factors managers will consider before deciding on the most appropriate methods of finance

➤ understand the rights and responsibilities of the providers of finance

➤ be able to consider the provision of finance from the point of view of both the organisation and actual or potential stakeholders

Why business activity requires finance

Finance is required for many business activities. Here is a list of just some of the main circumstances in which businesses will require finance:

◆ Setting up a business will require cash injections from the owner(s) to purchase essential capital equipment and, possibly, premises.

◆ All businesses will have a need to finance their working capital – the day-to-day finance needed to pay bills and expenses and to build up stocks.

◆ When businesses expand, further finance will be needed to increase the capital assets held by the firm – and, often, expansion will involve higher working capital needs.

◆ Expansion can be by taking over other businesses. Finance is then needed to buy out the owners of the other firm.

◆ Special situations will often lead to a need for greater finance. For example, a decline in sales, possibly as a result of economic recession, could lead to cash needs to keep the business stable, or a large customer could fail to pay for goods and finance is quickly needed to pay for essential expenses.

◆ Apart from purchasing fixed assets, finance is often used to pay for research and development into new products or to invest in new marketing strategies, such as opening up overseas markets.

Activities

1 Using the list of reasons why businesses require finance, identify:

(a) two situations that are likely to need long-term finance (more than five years);

(b) two situations that might require only short-term finance.

In each case, explain your answer.

2 Sheila and her friend Alison have decided to run their own mobile hairdressing business using the training they have received at college and the experience they both gained working for three years for a local hairdresser. Investigate, locally, the equipment and working stock they will need. From this, estimate the capital they will need to set up the business and survive the first year.

Some of these situations will need investment in the business for many years – or even permanently. Other cases will need only short-term funding – this is usually defined as being for around one year or less. Some finance requirements of the business are for between one and five years and this is referred to as medium-term finance.

The list, given, above of reasons why businesses need finance is not complete – you could probably add to it yourself. The important point to note about this list is that all of these situations are rather different. In practice, this means that no one source or type of finance is likely to be suitable in all cases. Managers will have to decide which type and source of finance is best in each case. Before we are able to assist in this type of decision-making, it is necessary to be aware of all of the many sources of finance available to businesses in an advanced economy.

Where does finance come from?

This section deals initially with sources of finance for limited companies – and then considers sole traders and partnerships. Companies are able to raise finance from a wide range of sources. It is useful to classify these into:

Internal Money raised from the business's own assets or from profits left in the business (ploughed-back profits)
External Money raised from sources outside of the business.

Another classification is also often made, as was seen above, that of short-, medium- and long-term finance; this distinction is made clearer by considering Figure 7.1.

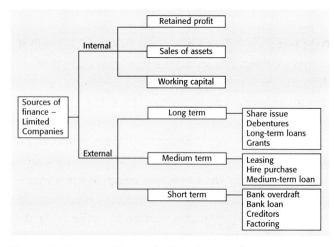

Figure 7.1 Sources of finance for limited companies

Internal sources of finance
Profits retained in the business

If a company is trading profitably, some of these profits will be taken in tax by the government (corporation tax) and some is nearly always paid out to the owners or shareholders (dividends). If any profit remains, this is kept (retained) in the business and becomes a source of finance for future activities. Clearly, a newly formed company or one trading at a loss will not have access to this source of finance. For other companies in the UK, retained profits are a very significant source of funds for expansion. Once invested back into the business, these retained profits will not be paid out to shareholders, so they represent a permanent source of finance.

Sale of assets

Established companies often find that they have assets that are no longer fully employed. These could be sold to raise cash. In addition, some businesses will sell assets that they still intend to use but which they do not need to *own*. In these cases, the assets might be sold to a leasing specialist and leased back by the company. In 1999, Somerfield, the grocery retail company, announced the sale of 50 of its stores to raise finance for investing in other areas of the business.

Reductions in working capital

When businesses increase stock levels or sell goods on credit to customers (debtors) they use a source of finance. When companies reduce these assets – by reducing their working capital – capital is released, which acts as a source of finance for other uses. There are risks with cutting down on working capital, however. As will be seen in Section 15, cutting back on current assets by selling stocks or reducing debts owed to the business may reduce the firm's liquidity – its ability to pay short-term debts – to risky levels.

Internal sources of finance – an evaluation

This type of capital has no direct cost to the business, although, if assets are leased back once sold, there will be leasing charges. Internal finance does not increase the liabilities or debts of the business.

However, it is not available for all companies, for example, newly formed ones or unprofitable ones with few 'spare' assets. Solely depending on internal sources of finance for expansion can slow down business growth as the pace of development will be limited by the annual profits or the value of assets to be sold. Thus, rapidly expanding companies are often dependent on external sources for much of their finance.

Activities

1 In each of the following cases, explain briefly why internal sources of finance might be unavailable or inadequate:

(a) a new business venture between two partners;

(b) the rapid expansion of a business, which requires expenditure several times greater than current profits;

(c) the purchase of additional stocks by a retailer just before Christmas.

2 Sheila and Alison have worked out what they need to start their hairdressing business and it is clear that they will need some financial support. Sheila thinks that her parents would help but Alison is anxious to stand on our own feet. She has heard that the Department of Trade and Industry might help them. Contact the Department of Trade and Industry and find out details of the Loan Guarantee Scheme. How could this assist a newly created business?

External sources of finance

Short-term sources

There are three main sources of short-term external finance:

- bank overdrafts;
- trade credit;
- debt factoring.

Bank overdrafts A bank overdraft is the most 'flexible' of all sources of finance. This means that the amount raised can vary from day to day, depending on the particular needs of the business. The bank allows the business to 'overdraw' its account at the bank by writing cheques to a greater value than the balance in the account. This overdrawn amount should always be agreed in advance and always has a limit beyond which the firm should not go. Businesses may need to increase the overdraft for short periods of time if customers do not pay as quickly as expected or if a large delivery of

stocks has to be paid for. This form of finance often carries high interest charges. In addition, if a bank becomes concerned about the stability of one of its customers it can 'call in' the overdraft and force the firm to pay it back. This, in extreme cases, can lead to business failure.

Many rural branches of this bank have closed down creating redundancies and inconvenience for local residents

Trade credit By delaying the payment of bills for goods or services received, a business is, in effect, obtaining finance. Its suppliers, or creditors, are providing goods and services without receiving immediate payment and this is as good as 'lending money'. The downside to these periods of credit is that they are not 'free' – discounts for quick payment and supplier confidence are often lost if the business takes too long to pay its suppliers.

Debt factoring When a business sells goods on credit it creates a debtor. The longer the time allowed to this debtor to pay up, the more finance the business has to find to carry on trading. One option, if it is commercially unwise to insist on cash payments, is to sell these debts to a debt factor. In this way immediate cash is obtained, but not for the full amount of the debt. This is because the debt-factoring company's profits are made by discounting the debts and not paying their full value. When full payment is received from the original customer, the debt factor makes a profit. Smaller firms who sell goods on hire purchase often sell the debt to credit loan firms, so that the credit agreement is never with the shop but with the specialist provider.

Sources of medium-term finance

There are two main sources of medium-term external finance:

◆ hire purchase and leasing;
◆ medium-term bank loan.

Hire purchase and leasing These methods are often used to obtain fixed assets with a medium life span – one to five years. Hire purchase is a form of credit for purchasing an asset over a period of time. This avoids making a large initial cash payment to buy the asset.

Leasing involves a contract with a leasing company to acquire, but not necessarily to purchase, assets over the medium term. A periodic payment is made over the life of the agreement, but the business does not have to purchase the asset at the end. This agreement allows the firm to avoid cash purchase of the asset. The risk of unreliable or outdated equipment is reduced as the leasing company will repair and update as part of the agreement. Neither hire purchase nor leasing is a cheap option, but they do improve the short-term cash flow position of a company compared to outright purchase of an asset for cash.

Medium-term bank loan This will have the same advantages and disadvantages as long-term loans referred to below.

Long-term finance

The two main choices here are **debt** or **equity finance**. Debt finance increases the liabilities of a company. Debt finance can be raised in two main ways:

◆ long-term loans from banks;
◆ debentures (also known as loan stock or corporate bonds).

Long-term loans from banks These may be offered at either a variable or a fixed interest rate. Fixed rates provide more certainty, but they can turn out to be expensive if the loan is agreed at a time of high interest rates. Companies borrowing from banks will often have to provide security or collateral for the loan; this means the right to sell an asset, if the company cannot repay the debt, is given to the bank. Businesses with few assets

to act as security may find it difficult to obtain loans – or may be asked to pay higher rates of interest. Alternatively, a small business can apply to the Department of Trade and Industry for the loan to be part of the 'guaranteed loan scheme'. Banks will be more willing to lend if a company has been successful in this application because it gives the bank security of repayment.

Debentures A company wishing to raise funds will issue or sell these to interested investors. The company agrees to pay a fixed rate of interest each year for the life of the debenture, which is often 25 years. The buyers may resell to other investors if they do not wish to wait until maturity before getting their original investment back. Debentures are often secured on a particular asset, which means that the investors have the right, if the company ceases trading, to sell that particular asset to gain repayment. When this is part of the agreement, the debentures are known as mortgage debentures. Debentures can be a very important source of long-term finance – in the British Telecom 1999 accounts the total value of issued loan stock amounted to £3,000 million.

Sale of shares – equity finance All limited companies issue shares when they are first formed. The capital raised will be used to purchase essential assets. Section 5 explained the essential differences between private and public limited companies. Both of these organisations are able to sell further shares – up to the limit of their authorised share capital – in order to raise additional *permanent* finance. This capital never has to be repaid unless the company is completely wound up as a result of ceasing to trade.

Private limited companies can sell further shares to existing shareholders. This has the advantage of not changing the control or ownership of the company – as long as all shareholders buy shares in the same proportion to those already owned. Owners of a private limited company can also decide to 'go public' and obtain the necessary authority to sell shares to the wider public. This would obviously have the potential to raise much more capital than from just the existing shareholders. This can be done in two ways:

◆ Obtain a listing on the Alternative Investment Market (AIM), which is that part of the **Stock Exchange** concerned with smaller companies that want to raise only limited amounts of additional capital. The strict requirements for a full Stock Exchange listing are relaxed.

◆ Apply for a full listing on the Stock Exchange by satisfying the criteria of (a) selling at least £50,000 worth of shares and (b) having a satisfactory trading record to give investors some confidence in the security of their investment. This sale of shares can be undertaken in two main ways:

– Public issue by prospectus: this advertises the company and its share sale to the public and invites them to apply for the new shares. This is expensive as the prospectus has to be prepared and issued. The share issue is often underwritten or guaranteed by a merchant bank, which charges for its services.

– Arranging a placing of shares with institutional investors without the expense of a full public issue.

Once a company has gained plc status it is still possible for it to raise further capital by selling additional shares. This is often done by means of a rights issue of shares. Existing shareholders are given the right to buy additional shares at a discounted price. By not introducing new shareholders, the ownership of the business does not change and, by avoiding expensive merchant bank and advisors' fees, the company raises capital relatively cheaply.

Activities

1 Study the three cases below and then tackle the following exercises.

Case study – Dominos goes to market

In 1999 Dominos Pizza Group floated on the alternative investment market by selling £2.5 million worth of shares. Stephen Hemsley, the finance director, stated that the extra capital would be used to open ten more non-franchised stores over the next ten years.

Case study – Peacocks to go public

In November 1999 Peacocks, the discount clothing and houseware retailer, issued its prospectus to the public. The company is going public to raise £42 million (after expenses) to fund further expansion and to repay outstanding debt. The managing director believes that there are great benefits in replacing debt finance with equity or share finance.

Case study – Euro Disney launches new park rights issue

On 10 November 1999, Euro Disney, the operator of Disneyland Paris, announced a rights issue to help finance a second theme park. This will be built in Paris and is due to open in 2002. The rights issue is expected to raise £147 million. The new park will cost three times this amount; the remainder of the finance will be borrowed.

(a) Why do you think Domino's Pizza Group decided to join AIM rather than the full Stock Exchange?

(b) Peacocks decided to issue shares by prospectus to the general public. Why do you think this method of selling shares was selected?

(c) What did the managing director of Peacocks mean when he said that there were advantages in selling shares to repay debt? What are the advantages of repaying debts?

(d) Why do you think Euro Disney decided to use a rights issue of shares?

(e) Much of the money for the new park will be borrowed. Why might Euro Disney have decided not to raise all of the capital from the sale of shares?

2 Work in pairs. Study the financial pages of a quality newspaper each day for one month. Track the share price of a public limited company of your choice for this period. Make sure your choice is different from the other choices in the class. Plot the share price changes on a graph and read any comments that might relate to these changes in the newspaper.

(a) Try to identify and comment upon at least three reasons for the changes in the share price over this period.

(b) Would these share price changes you have identified make it easier or more difficult for this company to raise finance by the sale of further shares?

(c) Compare your findings with the findings of other pairs in the class. Are there any general conclusions you can draw?

Debt or equity capital – an evaluation Which method of long-term finance should a company choose? There is no easy answer to this question. And, as seen above, some businesses will use both debt and equity finance for very large projects. Debt finance has the following advantages:

◆ As no shares are sold, the ownership of the company does not change or is not 'diluted' by the issue of additional shares.

◆ Loans will be repaid eventually, so there is no permanent increase in the liabilities of the business.

◆ Lenders have no voting rights at the annual general meetings.

◆ Interest charges are an expense of the business and are paid out before corporation tax is deducted, while dividends on shares have to be paid from profits after tax.

◆ The gearing of the company increases and this gives shareholders the chance of higher returns in the future. This point is dealt with more fully in Section 15.

Equity capital has the following advantages:

◆ It never has to be repaid; it is permanent capital.

◆ Dividends do not have to paid every year; in contrast, interest on loans must be paid when demanded by the lender.

Other sources of long-term finance

Grants There are many agencies that are prepared, under certain circumstances, to grant funds to businesses. The two major sources in the UK are the central government and the European Union. Usually, grants from these two bodies are given to small businesses or those expanding in developing regions of the country. Grants often come with 'strings attached', such as location and the number of jobs to be created, but if these conditions are met grants do not have to be repaid.

Venture capital Small companies that are not listed on the Stock Exchange – 'unquoted companies' – can gain long-term investment funds from venture capitalists. These are specialist organisations, or sometimes, wealthy individuals, who are prepared to lend risk capital to, or purchase shares in, small to medium-sized businesses that might find it difficult to raise capital from other sources. This could be because of the new technology that the company is dealing in, with which other providers of finance are not prepared to get involved. Venture capitalists take great risks and could lose all of their money – but the rewards can be great. The value of certain 'high tech' businesses has grown rapidly and many were financed, at least in part, by venture capitalists.

Factors influencing choice

The decisions taken by managers to obtain finance from a particular source are influenced by many factors: This is shown in Table 7.1.

Time – this will be determined by the use to which the capital will be put	The longer the period over which the financing will be needed, the more likely it will be that longer-term sources of capital will be used
Amount	The greater the amount of capital to be raised, the more likely it will be that either a share issue will be needed or that a combination of equity and debt will be used
Control	If the owners/shareholders do not wish to alter the ownership structure of the business, then either debt finance or a rights issue will be appropriate
Cost	This includes the actual cost of raising the finance, e.g. a public issue of shares by prospectus, and the cost of servicing the finance, e.g. rates of interest; these costs, and others, will have to be assessed before a final decision can be taken
The current financial position of the business, e.g. value of assets available for collateral and the gearing of the business	The greater the proportion of loans to capital employed in the business, the less likely it is that further loans would be advisable
The legal status of the business	Apart from the significance of the distinction between private and public limited companies, the exact form of business ownership will determine the sources of finance available to a firm; it is to these other forms of business ownership that we now turn
Risk	The greater the risk associated with the use of finance, the more likely it is that speculative funding, e.g. venture capital or share capital will have to be found

Table 7.1 Factors influencing choice of finance

Finance for unincorporated businesses

Sole traders and partnerships were referred to in Section 5, so only the main distinctions between company finance and unincorporated business finance will be made now.

Unincorporated businesses – sole traders and partnerships – *cannot* raise finance from the sale of shares and are most *unlikely* to be successful in selling debentures as they are likely to be relatively unknown firms. Owners of these businesses will have access to bank overdrafts, loans and credit from suppliers. They may borrow from family and friends, use the savings and profits made by the owners and, if a sole trader wishes to do this, take on partners to inject further capital.

As was made clear in Section 5, any owner or partner in an unincorporated business runs the risk of losing all property owned if the firm fails. Lenders are often reluctant to lend to smaller businesses, which is what sole traders and partnerships tend to be, unless the owners give personal guarantees, supported by their own assets, should the business fail. Grants are available to small and newly formed businesses. One of the most significant sources is the Prince's Trust, which helps the unemployed into the world of enterprise by offering start-up grants for those with sound business plans.

Activities

1 Copy out the following table and complete it by ticking the appropriate boxes alongside each source of finance.

Sources of finance	Long-term finance	Medium-term finance	Short-term finance	Available to unincorporated businesses	Available to private limited companies	Available to public limited companies
Sale of shares to the public						
Sale of debentures						
Leasing						
Debt factoring						
Loans from family						
Take on partners						
Rights issue of shares						
Ten-year bank loan						
Bank overdraft						

2 All banks will lend money. It is their business. To do so they will check out a potential borrower to ensure that they will be repaid and that the business can make the regular interest payments that are required.

Work in groups. Each group should select a bank (different from the others) and research the borrowing potential from that bank.

(a) Find out what the bank manager would need to know before lending money to finance a new business venture.

(b) Find out what the current Bank of England lending rate is. Has this changed over the last three months, and if so, how? Will the change you have identified make it more or less likely that a business will use loan capital for expansion purposes?

Providing finance to a business creates a stakeholder relationship with that business. All stakeholders have certain rights, responsibilities and objectives, but these will differ between the various sources of finance. This is made clear in Table 7.2, which looks at the three main providers of company finance.

	Rights	Responsibilities	Objectives
Shareholders	Part ownership of the company in proportion to the number of shares owned To attend the AGM and vote, e.g. on election of directors To receive dividend as recommended by the Board To receive a share of the capital if the business is wound up after all debts have been paid	The capital invested cannot be claimed back from the company except when it ceases trading	To received an annual return on investment in shares – the dividend To receive capital growth through an increase in share price Possibly, to influence company policy through pressure at the AGM
Banks	To receive interest payments as laid down in the loan or overdraft agreement To be repaid before shareholders if the company is 'wound up'	To check on business viability before loan or overdraft is agreed; this is both a responsibility to the bank's shareholders and to the business – advice to customers is an important responsibility	To make a profit from the loan. To receive repayment of capital at the end of the loan term To establish a long-term relationship, of mutual benefit, with the business
Creditors	To receive payment as agreed To be paid before shareholders in the event of the business being wound up To attend creditors meetings if the business is put into liquidation	To provide regular statements of amount owing and terms of repayment	To provide credit to encourage the business to purchase stock To establish a relationship built on trust so that credit can be offered with confidence

Table 7.2 Main financial stakeholders

Over-to-you

Short-answer questions

1 Give two reasons why a newly formed business will need finance.

2 Would research and development expenditure be likely to require short-term or long-term finance? Explain your answer briefly.

3 Suggest two ways in which a company might raise finance to pay for the take-over of another business.

4 Explain the role of a debt factor in providing finance to a business.

5 What is the distinction between internal and external finance?

6 What is meant by a company's retained profit?

7 Explain two reasons why the Board of Directors of a company might not wish to raise finance for long-term development of the business by a share issue.

8 Outline the advantages to a business of having a bank overdraft rather than taking out a bank loan.

9 Why might a business use leasing to obtain assets such as computers, rather than purchasing them outright with a loan?

10 State four factors that managers will consider before deciding on the most appropriate source of finance.

Discover and learn

1 Go back to the firm whose fortunes you followed in the case study on page 000. What is its position now? What reasons can you offer for any changes? Do you think it would be more or less likely to find additional funds now if it needed them?

2   Read the case study below and tackle the exercises that follow.

Case study – Sharma Taxis

Joe Sharma started his taxi business with just one vehicle. He purchased this vehicle out of his own savings. Initially, he ran his business as a sole trader, but after two years of operation he took on a partner, who had injected further capital into the firm. This had been used to purchase other vehicles and a small garage where maintenance was carried out. The business continued to expand. Joe and his partner decided to convert into a private limited company and shares were sold to business associates, family and employees of the firm. The capital raised from this conversion was used to start a small road haulage department with two vans. As the fleet of vehicles was growing, substantial stocks of spare parts were held to avoid cars and vans being off the road for any longer than was necessary following a breakdown. Regular clients of the firm were offered credit terms of up to two months.

Joe has heard of another taxi business being sold by the owners. It has a fleet of prestige cars and substantial premises. The Board of the limited company agreed to put a bid in for this business. They agreed that it should be partly financed by floating the company on the alternative investment market with a view to obtaining a full Stock Exchange listing if further expansion was envisaged. The alternative had been to obtain a substantial long-term loan, but the directors were concerned about the chances of an increase in interest rates and preferred the share issue plus the use of some retained profits to buy out the other business. The bid for this firm was successful. The most recent development has been the decision to completely update the computer facilities at the head office. This should lead to efficient scheduling of vehicle use and an update of the accounting and invoicing system. This will allow much speedier sending out of bills to customers.

(a)   Identify the stages of this business's development where additional finance was required.

(b)   At each of the stages you have identified, explain what type of finance was needed.

(c)   In your opinion, how could the increase in spare parts and debtors of the business have been financed?

(d)   Examine the decision by the directors to float the company on the AIM.

(e)   If the company were to expand further, evaluate the case for and against financing this expansion with a long-term loan.

Summary

In this section we have recognised that:

- The choice of the most suitable source of finance is a crucial one for all businesses.

- If managers are not aware of all available sources or if they do not consider all of the relevant factors before making the choice, then their business could suffer from inappropriate and costly capital. This finance could prove to be too expensive, too short term or involve serious disadvantages over business ownership and control, which the owners would be most concerned about.

- Inadequate finance can lead to business failure.

- Selecting inappropriate sources of finance can reduce business profits or liquidity or increase the degree of risk to unacceptable levels.

- There are many different types and providers of finance.

- There is a range of factors that managers should take into account before taking the important decision as to which type of financing to use.

Key words

Definitions of Key words can be found in the Glossary on page 236.

Alternative Investment Market (AIM)
bank overdraft
debentures
equity
factoring
grants
hire purchase
leasing
loans
retained profit
Stock Exchange

Part 2

Business decisions and business behaviour

8 The market: definition and structure

What is marketing?

There are many ways of defining **marketing**. Some of them are more complicated and long-winded than others. P. Kotler (*Marketing Management*, Prentice Hall, 1977) described marketing as 'a human activity directed at satisfying needs and wants through exchange processes'. Here, he is emphasising the importance of exchange, i.e. payment.

Marketing has also been described as a complete system of business activities designed to plan, promote and distribute goods and services to target markets, where they are desired and/or needed. Note the difference between needs and wants/desires. A need is something that is necessary to existence. It fulfils the achievement of physiological needs: the basic requirements for sustaining life, such as food, water, warmth, clothing and shelter. A want is something that a consumer would like to have, but is not necessary for survival, such as ice cream or a trip to an amusement park.

To put it simply, marketing is best described as discovering what the potential consumers want and then supplying it (at a profit).

'At a profit' is in parentheses because profit is usually, but not always, one of the main objectives of a business. In certain state-owned, or charitable, organisations, it may be that the aim is still to find out what the consumers want and then to supply it, but making a profit may not be an essential part of the equation.

The role and importance of marketing

All organisations market themselves. They may not do so intentionally, but simply by producing goods and services and by dealing with customers, they are involved in marketing. If this is the case, then it is better that firms should have a carefully planned marketing strategy rather than a slapdash approach. For a number of years, it was assumed that marketing was only really important for firms dealing in **fast-moving consumer goods** (FMCGs), but now it is realised that it is also essential for firms dealing in services and manufacturing. Indeed, organisations such as charities, hospitals, art galleries and even universities are now marketing themselves fairly aggressively.

Marketing is of extreme importance, since it covers many of the functions of management. Design, production, pricing, promotion and distribution are key areas in almost all organisations and they are all under the umbrella or influence of marketing.

Marketing in the UK and Europe has only really grown in importance since the end of the 1950s. The main reason for this rise in the importance of marketing is that, before this time, people did not have the **disposable income** available to demand a large range of products. Since the recovery following World War II, **demand** has grown and many businesses have arisen to satisfy that demand. Also, as incomes have risen, people have satisfied many of their product needs and now demand a far greater number of services than they once did. This accounts for the greater **supply** of restaurants, travel agents and leisure facilities.

The demand for more products and services has led to the emergence of a great number of businesses and brands. In addition, in the UK, there is now more competition from abroad, especially from Europe, following membership of the EU. This increased competition has made marketing all the more important to firms if they wish to survive.

With the improvements in average incomes, fashion has become more important and people's tastes tend to change more frequently. Lifestyles have altered and demands have changed. For example, there is now a whole health and fitness industry, with products ranging from aerobics classes to vitamin tablets. These changes in tastes, fashion and lifestyles are another reason why marketing has become so much more important in recent times.

In the time period we are considering, there have been exceedingly rapid changes in technology. So many products that are now taken for granted were not available 30 years ago, such as mobile telephones, personal computers and CD players. These new and improved products have had to be marketed and now, of course, consumers expect new advances in technology and improvements in products at all times and it is up to the marketers to provide and sell the products. Fear of obsolescence is a much greater worry these days than in times gone by.

To summarise, the role of marketing is immense. It involves all areas of an organisation and successful companies are those that know what their customers really want and then set about supplying it.

Market orientation and product orientation

Marketing focuses on consumer needs and wants and, in modern-day management, it is the consumer who drives product development and production more than the product developer. This is known as a market- or consumer-orientated approach. On the whole, the days of developing a product and then finding a market, a product-orientated approach, are disappearing. However, this still happens to an extent and there are a number of approaches that put the consumer, or market, last:

◆ Product-orientated businesses invent and develop products in the belief that they will then find consumers to purchase them. They believe that they know what the customers want and that if they produce a product of good enough quality, then it will be purchased. This sort of pure research and development is becoming rarer, but there will always be a place for it to some extent. Firms in certain industries, such as pharmaceuticals and electronics, have to operate in this way to survive. The industries are so innovative that to stand still is to risk going out of business.

◆ Production-orientated businesses concentrate their efforts on efficiently producing high-quality, relatively cost-efficient products. The belief is that the products will find a market if the price is relatively low and the product is of a high enough quality. Although production-orientated firms are not as prevalent as other types, they do exist, especially in areas where quality, or safety, are of great importance, such as bottled-water plants or the making of crash helmets.

◆ Sales-orientated businesses tend to produce a product and then concentrate upon different selling techniques and skills, so that they can then clear their supplies. It is argued that some pyramid selling firms work in exactly this fashion.

Activities

1 What is marketing? How do you account for the increase in the importance of marketing in the last 40 years?

2 Attempt to identify five products that have evolved in the last 25 years. Select one of the products and attempt to discover as much as you can about its early marketing.

3 Use your own school or college if you wish and work in groups of four to six. It has become increasingly necessary for all educational establishments to market themselves and what they do. Examine the ways in which your selected school or college markets itself and comment on the success of this. Discuss, in your groups, the strengths and weaknesses of the marketing effort and suggest ways in which the marketing effort could be made more effective.

All of the above approaches take little notice of the consumer and are much more interested in product production and selling techniques.

Market-orientated firms put the consumer/customer first. The business will attempt to produce what the consumers want, rather than try to sell them a product that they do not really want to buy. Market orientation is the most common form of marketing these days and the reasons for it were very well described by Robert Heller, in his book *The Supermarketers*. He said,

> It's quite misguided to pursue the technology-push policy – a delusion with much industrial blood on its hands. The myth goes that if you make a better mousetrap the world will beat a path to your door. It has been disproved again and again, never more comprehensively than by the total defeat of competitors who had genuinely stolen technological marches on IBM in mainframe computers ... Despite all such evidence, many allegedly marketing orientated companies still operate on the mousetrap principle: improve the product, they think, and technology push will create the sales.

In fact, success and survival in business depend upon the whole marketing process, which will be covered in this and the next two sections. Finding out what the consumer wants and then supplying it at a profit requires the following:

◆ carrying out effective market research and identifying the target groups;
◆ designing the product;
◆ assessing the reaction of consumers to both the product and the packaging;
◆ calculating a suitable price, related to costs of production and what consumers are willing to pay;
◆ deciding upon a suitable promotional strategy;
◆ organising the distribution system that will be used to get the product to the market.

Marketing objectives

Objectives are what we attempt, or wish, to achieve. As should always be the case, the **marketing objectives** of a

Activities

1 Explain the difference between production-orientated marketing and consumer-orientated marketing.
2 Go to your local shops and identify two products that you think were invented and then marketed and two products you feel were the result of market research and then development and marketing. Explain why you think the individual products were marketed in the way they were.
3 Try to identify products that might be production orientated and sales orientated.

business should relate to the hierarchy of objectives that the enterprise has. The hierarchy of objectives is:
◆ mission statement;
◆ long-term objectives;
◆ short-term objectives;
◆ departmental objectives;
◆ set strategy;
◆ set tactics.

The marketing objectives should come under the heading of departmental objectives and they should reflect the aims of the whole organisation and attempt to aid the achievement of the objectives above them in the hierarchy. The marketing objectives are the outcomes that an organisation is trying to attain through its marketing.

The long- and short-term objectives of the business will have an influence on the marketing objectives. For example, if a firm is attempting to maximise profits, then the emphasis of the marketing strategy will reflect this. In the same way, if a firm is attempting to enter a market and gain a sizeable market share, then its marketing objectives will be different from the previous example.

It is fair to say that whatever the greater aims of an organisation, its marketing objectives will normally be achieved through an appropriate blending of marketing variables. These make up the marketing mix and are discussed fully in Section 10. Marketing objectives would normally involve six aspects and we can look at each of these in turn.

Market segmentation

The marketing objectives of a business ought to include an analysis of which market segments the firm wishes to operate in and which market segments they might aim for in the future. It is unusual for a firm to be large enough to attempt to satisfy all of a market, unless the market is a relatively small, usually specialist, one. Because of this, firms usually identify their prime market segments and one of their objectives would be to enter those segments. Thus, a shoe company may decide to aim at the sports shoe and leisure wear segments of the shoe market. They may hope, in time, to move into the work boots segment.

Market share

Once markets, or market segments, have been identified, then firms will normally set objectives relating to the amount of market share that they might hope to gain. Thus, the shoe firm above might set themselves a target of achieving 5% of the sports shoe market and 10% of the leisure shoe market within a period of three years. Obviously, if these market-share objectives are achieved, then new ones emerge. The firm will have to decide whether to attempt to maintain its share, increase the share or move into a new market.

Product development and product range

Firms must set objectives relating to the type, and range of products or services that they wish to develop. This will give them specific areas upon which to focus. In the beginning, our shoe firm might decide to try to develop three different styles of sports shoe and a range of beach shoes. In some ways, the more specific the **product development**, the more the market is being segmented.

Price versus quality analysis

Objectives may be set balancing the quality of the product against the price for which it can be sold. Quality will obviously have an effect upon cost and this, in turn, affects price. Put the other way around, the price that a business thinks it can get for a product may put a restraint on costs and quality. For example, an objective of the shoe firm may be to make the best quality pair of training shoes that can be sold below a price of £30. No-one would pretend that they would be the best shoes on the market, but the point would be that they were the best quality available at that price.

Range of trainers for sale in a typical shoe shop

Sales performance, revenue and profit

Marketing objectives may be set relating to sales (in either volume or revenue terms), revenue gained from specific products or profit gained from particular products.

Distribution strategy

Objectives may be set in terms of how well distributed, or 'placed', the product is going to be. A large pharmaceutical firm may aim to have its products in every chemist shop in the country within a space of two years, or a coffee shop chain may aim to have an outlet in every town with a population over 20,000 in the South East of England.

Segmenting the market

Market segmentation is a vital element of marketing. It is customer orientated and is thus consistent with the concept of marketing. It occurs when the total demand in a market is analysed, so that specific sets of buyers, with distinct characteristics, can be identified.

Once this has been done, then it is possible to design products and services that will apply directly to specific market segments. After this, it is possible to design marketing plans that will then aim the specific products directly at the segments chosen. The act of market segmentation enables organisations to:
   ◆ define their markets accurately;
   ◆ position various products and brands in the right market area;

- identify gaps in the market that might be successfully filled;
- make more efficient use of marketing resources.

There are three commonly used bases for segmenting markets. The first of these categories is **geographic**. Consumer tastes may vary between different geographical areas and so it may be appropriate to offer different products and to market them in alternative ways in each area. For example, large national breweries offer different brands of beer to different areas of the country, even though they could offer a single brand. They will also promote the products in different ways, because they realise that there are regional differences in attitudes and consumers' tastes.

The second basis for segmentation is **demographic**, i.e. relating to the science of population statistics. This is the most commonly used basis for segmentation and is usually based upon such factors as sex, age, income or ethnic background. For example, manufacturers of washing powders will aim different brands of their products at different ages of consumers. Some brands, such as Bold, will be aimed at the younger end of the market and others, such as Daz, will be aimed at slightly older customers. The promotional strategy for each product is then devised to appeal specifically to the targeted market segments.

The third basis is **psychographic**, which in turn can be split into three main areas: social class, personality characteristics and lifestyles. There are a number of ways of defining social class. One of the most common is to split the population into upper class, upper middle class, lower middle class, upper lower class and lower lower class. These classes are sometimes classified by letters. An individual's social class will have a great influence upon his or her purchasing patterns in many product categories.

In theory, personality characteristics should be very influential. One would expect an aggressive person to have different purchasing patterns from a timid person. The same could be said for impulsive people as opposed to very cautious people. In reality, such personality characteristics are very difficult to identify specifically and to measure accurately. However, many firms especially in their advertising, still do, attempt to appeal to consumers who have particular personality traits. Thus, we see products aimed at outgoing young people who wish to pursue all sorts of relatively dangerous outdoor activities, such as sky-diving or bungee-jumping. Even though it is not possible to measure the market segment accurately, the seller knows that it is there, believes that it is large and is aiming at it. Lifestyle is a very broad term and often overlaps with personality characteristics. Lifestyles tend to relate to activities undertaken, interests and opinions, rather than personality traits.

There are a number of advantages to segmenting the market:

- It enables the division of the market into distinct areas at which the product can be more specifically aimed.
- Small firms, which could not compete in the whole market, are able to concentrate on one or two smaller segments.
- It is possible to design and produce goods and services that are specifically matched to the demand of a more distinct group of consumers.

There are, however, a number of disadvantages. First, there are higher production costs, because it is obviously more expensive to produce a range of products, all aimed at different market segments, than it is to produce a single product aimed at all potential customers. The second disadvantage relates to this point as well. If there is a range of products on offer, then there will be a need for higher levels of stockholding, which will have obvious cost implications. Finally, promotional costs will rise as different strategies are required for different markets and administration costs will also increase as many more products are produced and marketed.

Market growth and market share

The term 'market' is difficult to define. Basically, a market is a group of consumers who have a need to satisfy, money available and the willingness to spend that money. There are two main types of market, consumer markets and industrial markets.

Consumer markets are where the products or services are bought for personal consumption, whereas in industrial markets products or services are for use in manufacture or business, or for resale to other customers.

Market growth is the percentage increase in the size of a whole market. It may be measured in terms of volume, i.e. units sold, or value, i.e. revenue generated. For example, if total sales in a market for sports shoes rose from 24 million pairs at an average price of £32 to 26 million pairs at an average price of £36, then market growth can be measured in the following two ways:

◆ By volume – the market has risen from 24 million to 26 million, which is an increase of 2 million or 7.69%.

◆ By value – the revenue has risen from £768 million to £936 million, which is an increase of £168 million or 21.87%.

Market share is the percentage of sales that a single firm has in one market. Again, this might be measured in terms of volume or value. Thus, a firm that sold sports shoes in the above market and had sales of 3.5 million pairs and revenue of £140 million in the second year might measure its market share in the following two ways:

◆ By volume – the firm sells 3.5 million pairs of shoes in a market of 26 million, which is a market share of 13.46%.

◆ By value – the firm has sales of £140 million in a market of £936 million, which is a market share of 14.96%.

A market with a high growth rate is obviously one that organisations would wish to be involved in. In the same way, individual firms would wish to have a high market share. This may give a number of advantages, such as a price-setting position in the market and the ability to gain from economies of scale.

There are a number of problems associated with the measurement of market share and market growth. The main one is obvious and can be seen above. It is highly likely that when market growth and/or market share are measured in terms of volume and value, different figures will be obtained, as we have seen in our example. It is thus difficult to make comparisons between firms. For example, there may be a firm in the car industry that specialises in selling high volumes of cars at relatively cheap prices. The firm's market share, if measured in terms of volume, would be high and yet the share measured in terms of value may not necessarily be so large.

Activities

1 What is the hierarchy of objectives and where would marketing objectives fit in?

2 In what areas would marketing objectives normally be set?

3 What is market segmentation? Why might a firm wish to segment a market?

4 What is the difference between market growth and market share?

5 How may market share be measured?

6 Go to the web site of a large company, for example Unilever, and try to identify the market segments that the company targets and which products it is aiming at which segments. Attempt to gather information on both the growth of the various market segments over time and also on the market share that the firm enjoys in each market segment.

Over-to-you

Short-answer questions

1 What is a market?

2 Explain briefly why marketing is necessary.

3 Why is it best for a firm to be consumer orientated?

4 State two situations in which you might expect a firm to be product orientated.

5 State three possible marketing objectives and suggest situations in which each might be found.

6 What is market segmentation? Why is it done?

7 State and give examples of three ways in which a market may be segmented.

8 Explain what market share is and draw a diagram to illustrate it.

9 Choose a particular product and suggest a way in which that market may be segmented. Explain your choice.

10 Explain why a business may not be interested in market growth.

Discover and learn

1 Take two or three newsagents in your area. How do they compete with each other?

2 Work in a group. Consider the restaurants in your area. In each case:

(a) What segments of the market is each in?

(b) What segments have each avoided?

(c) Explain your findings.

3 Consider the market for any product you choose. Of the outlets in your area, where would you buy that product and why? Do you all agree? If not, why not?

4 Read the case study below and tackle the exercises that follow.

Case study – Tubular Chairs Ltd

Brian Carnes was a strong character and he was determined to set up his own business and not to work for anyone else. In the mid-1970s, he was finishing his marketing degree in Birmingham and he was looking around for a market niche that might suit him. His girlfriend, Jean, was studying furniture design at the Art College and she and Brian used to spend a lot of time going around the local stores looking at various types of furniture. In doing this, Brian began to take an interest in tubular furniture, i.e. furniture made from tubular steel with upholstery attached. In conversation with Jean and people in the stores, he decided that the construction methods were not too complicated and that the mark-up must be reasonable.

On leaving university in July 1974, Brian founded Tubular Chairs in his home town of Stoke-on-Trent. Brian was funded by his father, who invested money from his own wholesale vegetable business, and by the bank, which lent Brian the rest of the necessary capital through a loan that Brian's father guaranteed. In return for his support, Brian's father received a 25% stake in the firm. Jean also moved to Stoke-on-Trent and began to design the furniture that the firm would sell. Having invested money herself, she also received a 25% share in the firm.

In the early days, the firm grew at a startling, and sometimes alarming, rate. After an initial period of acting as a middleman and simply buying in chairs produced elsewhere and then selling them on, it began to produce and sell Jean's designs.

The marketing policy was all-important in those early days. Jean was designing basic, colourful furniture, which was sturdy, reasonably long lasting and capable of simple and quick production. The furniture was sold at low prices, with a small profit margin, in order to gain high market share. It was sold through large cut-price furniture warehouse chains, which undertook to promote the furniture under their own brand names. The economic climate at the time was difficult, so cheap but reasonably attractive furniture was popular. In no time at all, Brian found that the combination of the

firm's market penetration pricing policy and the attention given to below-the-line promotion methods was a great success. By 1980, Tubular Chairs was the market leader in the field and the factory in Stoke was producing large quantities of a wide range of tubular-steel furniture.

Sadly, the good times did not last for the firm. As the 1980s progressed, their type of furniture went out of fashion and sales fell dramatically. The economic boom of the mid-1980s did not mix well with the image of the furniture that the firm was producing. Indeed, the firm was only kept going by its foreign sales, which remained fairly constant throughout the period. Most of these sales were in France and Germany, where the style of furniture remained popular. Brian tried to increase this part of their market and he had some success in selling to Spain and Portugal.

As the 1990s have progressed, the firm has just managed to keep its head above water. In January 1996, in a desperate attempt to change the pattern of things, Brian brought in a firm of management consultants headed by Val Richards, an old university friend. Over a period of three months, Val and her team studied the firm and the markets in which it operated and then produced a report on the situation and recommendations for the future survival of the firm. A shortened form of the report is given below.

Main points of the report on Tubular Chairs Ltd
Prepared by Val Richards and based upon information relating to the period 1/1/1990 to 31/12/1995.

A. Aim
To identify the current market situation facing Tubular Chairs and to make recommendations for the future.

B. The current situation
The total UK market for tubular design chairs has fallen significantly over the last ten years and the sales of Tubular Chairs Ltd have fallen rapidly in the same period.

Tubular Chairs, once the market leader, has now lost that position to a firm based in Taiwan. The Taiwanese firm has successfully managed to copy the existing range offered by Tubular Chairs and to supply them at a lower price. Consumer research indicates that tastes in furniture have changed markedly in the UK and that people now prefer to spend more on their furniture in the belief that it will last longer and be a saving in the long run. Tubular furniture is now considered to be more suited to the garden than the sitting room.

The market in the European Union does not yet seem to have gone into decline and, indeed, there has been market growth of 10% between 1990 and 1995. This market, which accounted for 30% of the total sales of Tubular Chairs in 1990, accounted for 40% in 1995.

C. Recommendations

The firm should consider each of the following:

1 A more aggressive pricing policy in order to compete with the Taiwanese competitor, cutting prices and using the economies of scale from the increased output to reduce costs and maintain a profit.
2 Designing a new range of chairs, improving the quality of the materials used in production and aiming at a higher-income segment of the market.
3 Diversification into the production of other types of furniture, such as garden furniture, picnic furniture and camping accessories.

4 Investigating the possibility of expanding its operations in the European Union.
5 Investigating the potential market in the former Communist Bloc countries, such as Poland or Hungary.

In April 1996, a meeting was held between Brian, his father, Jean and Val Richards to discuss the report and to make decisions regarding the future direction of the firm. Brian's father could not see what all the fuss was about and he felt that although times were not good, they were still making a reasonable return on their investment. He suggested that they should leave well alone and carry on as they were. Jean, as one would expect, liked the idea of designing a new range of products and was sure that she could produce something that would appeal and so she was in favour of recommendations 2 and 3 in Val Richards' report. Brian also felt that their products were a little old-fashioned, but he equally felt that there were other markets for them abroad, if they could only get into them. He favoured a combination of recommendations 1, 4 and 5. After much discussion, Brian went away to consider the future of the firm.

(a) Describe how Brian might go about segmenting his market.
(b) Explain the difference between the terms market growth and market share.
(c) Use the following data referring to the UK market, in the context of the case:

Year	Total market sales (1,000s)	Tubular Chairs Ltd sales (1,000s)
1990	200	90
1993	180	85
1995	150	52.5

♦ Calculate the total market sales of Tubular Chairs in the UK and the European Union in 1995.

♦ Calculate the percentage change in the market share of Tubular Chairs, in the UK market, over the period 1990 to 1995.

(d) Using your figures from question 3 and any other relevant data, evaluate the current market position of Tubular Chairs.
(e) Outline Tubular Chairs current pricing policy as revealed in the case, and suggest ways in which it might be 'more aggressive'.
(f) What might be the benefits and the costs associated with diversification into other types of furniture?
(g) Attempt a SWOT analysis of Tubular Chairs and use it to discuss the possibility of entering markets in continental Europe.

Summary

In this section we have recognised that:

● Marketing is of great importance to an organisation.

● The role of marketing is important and it involves all aspects of an organisation's functions.

● Marketing may be aimed at consumers or it may be product, production or sales based.

● Most marketing today is consumer (market-) orientated.

● It is vital to set marketing objectives and to ensure that they fit in with the overall objectives of the organisation.

● Where necessary, markets should be segmented and the marketers should concentrate upon suitable segments for their products.

● Market growth is desirable for all organisations within a market and the higher a market share that an organisation can achieve, the stronger will its position be.

Key words

Definitions of Key words can be found in the Glossary on page 236.

FMCGs (fast-moving
    consumer goods)
market segmentation

marketing objectives
psychographic

9 Market research

On completion of this section you should be able to:

➤ define marketing research and market research and differentiate between the two

➤ distinguish between primary and secondary research

➤ understand some of the different sources of data

➤ understand methods of data collection

➤ understand the importance of sampling

➤ understand sampling methods

➤ discuss research methods and their appropriateness in given circumstances

➤ devise a survey strategy to achieve a given objective

➤ use the data as a base for information gathering appropriate to your project

Marketing research and market research

Market research is the process of discovering relevant primary and secondary information about the demand for a good or service in a specific market.

Marketing research is a much broader and wider-ranging process, which involves the analysis of every single aspect of the marketing sequence. Marketing research involves discovering consumer reaction to many areas of the marketing process. Thus, it might include market research, product development and testing, pricing, promotional aspects, distribution and selling theory and the evaluation of competition.

The terms market research and marketing research are often used to mean the same thing, but this is obviously not the case. In effect, market research is a part of marketing research. However, market research is of great importance and it would be foolish for an organisation to make decisions with no knowledge of the demand factors in their particular market.

Successful market research enables organisations to reduce the risk of making a mistake, when introducing new products. However, there is no guarantee that market research will lead to success. In the two most famous cases of fairly recent years, Clive Sinclair was told that the C5 would be a success and Sony were told that the Walkman would never sell! This just goes to show that market research is not infallible.

Desk research and field research

The world is full of data. Data are the total amount of knowledge available in the world. They are all the facts, figures, opinions and views that exist. Information is a different thing and is far more focused. Information is data that are especially relevant to a given question, or a specific problem that has to be solved, or a decision that has to be made. For example, the fact that it is 105 miles from London to Birmingham is a piece of data. However, as soon as someone is trying to decide whether they can cycle from London to Birmingham in a day, this piece of data becomes relevant and so is information that will help to answer the question and make the decision.

There are a number of different methods of market research that are used to gather required information. They can be classified into two main groups, desk research and field research.

Desk research uses information which is already there. It is cheap to use such information though it may not be directly relevant. Some of this information will be available internally. Examples would be accounting records, internal reports and feedback from customers. Other information can be found externally and the government is a rich source of it as are specialist magazines. By far the most extensive source is the

Internet through which information about almost anything is instantly available.

Field research tends to be the collection of what is known as primary information. This is information that has been directly collected by the researchers themselves and so it should be suited specifically to the use of the collectors. The main drawback is that it tends to be more expensive to collect.

Information can also be classified in another way, qualitative and quantitative:

◆ **Qualitative information** contains no measurable quantities. It tends to be based upon opinion, for example, 'I thought that the evening was too expensive.' It is especially useful if the person giving the opinion is well known to the questioner.

◆ **Quantitative information** contains measured, or estimated, numerical values. For example, 'The evening cost us £75.' The numerical value offered does not have to be exact, as in this example. An estimate is acceptable.

Neither type of information is better than the other; it really depends upon the situation and the people supplying the information. Ideally, a combination of quantitative and qualitative information enables organisations to make the most reliable decisions.

Methods of collecting primary information

There are a number of methods for collecting primary information and these should be considered at this point.

Observation

This method usually involves the use of a trained market researcher watching the behaviour patterns of consumers, either via direct observation or by use of a hidden camera. For example, this method is used in supermarkets to track the routes that customers take through the shops, the products and shelves that attract the most attention, the effectiveness of promotional activities and the amount of time taken in making purchasing decisions.

The great advantage of observation is that it records how people really behave rather than how they say they behave. However, it is an expensive method of gaining information and it only provides a limited amount of information to the researchers. Also, it records what people are doing, rather than the reasons as to why they are doing it. Explanations for the observed actions will still depend upon the views of the researchers who are analysing the viewed or recorded behaviour.

Experiments

This involves the establishment of a controlled experiment that is supposed to represent a real market situation. Obviously, it will not be possible to make the situation exactly real, but the closer the better. The reason for using experimentation is that the small-scale experiment should give information that will lead to the eventual success of the intended large-scale project.

The main use of experimentation in marketing has been in test marketing. Firms establish a control market, where things remain normal, and a test market, where

Activities

1 Explain the difference between marketing research and market research.

2 Explain the advantages and disadvantages of using desk research.

3 Join together with two or three other members of your business studies group and select a product that interests you. Your job is now to discover as much about the market for that product as you can. You should do the following:

(a) Identify the areas of marketing research that you will need to consider, e.g. product, prices, packaging, promotion and distribution.

(b) Research those areas using whatever secondary information you can find.

alterations are made to different marketing factors. They may then be able to judge the success of the marketing changes by comparing the results in the two markets. For example, a firm may have been producing breakfast cereals for a number of years and be considering changing the packaging. They could leave things as they are in one city and try out a number of different ideas in others. In this way, by looking at results, the firm may be able to judge what is the most effective form of packaging. The hope is that if the only marketing variable that has changed is the packaging, then the change must be the reason for the relative changes in sales.

Obviously, the main weaknesses of experimentation of this type are the selection of the control and test markets and then controlling the variables. It is important that the control and test markets are very similar and this is not very easy to ensure. Also, there may be variables in the different markets that are beyond the control of the organisation involved. Any differences in the markets or changes in uncontrollable variables will distort the results of the experiment.

Surveys (including questionnaires)

A survey normally takes place when a **sampling** of the members of a given market is carried out in order to find the views of that sample. These views are then taken as being representative of the views of the market as a whole. It is possible to ask the whole market, but this would probably be too expensive.

People are surveyed on how often they use some of the facilities provided by a local council

The choice of a survey method will depend upon:
- the available budget for the task;
- the time available;
- the accuracy of the result required;
- the types of people to be surveyed and the people conducting the survey;
- the geographical spread over which the survey is to take place.

There are a number of ways that surveys can be conducted in order to gain primary information:

Personal interviews   This is a commonly used method, where an interviewer obtains information from individuals face-to-face. The interviewer may be working from a pre-set questionnaire or the interview may be completely unstructured. The pre-set questionnaire makes it easier to collate the information, but the unstructured interview allows the interviewer to follow any interesting directions that the interview might take. The advantages of this survey method are that the interviewer can deal with any problems or misunderstandings that might arise and can also often tell when incorrect information is being given on purpose. However, there are disadvantages of cost and also of possible interviewer bias.

Postal surveys   In this case, letters and questionnaires are sent to members of a chosen sample group, each of whom is asked to fill in the questionnaire and return it by post. The inclusion of a pre-paid reply envelope is very important. Completion is often further encouraged by the offer of a small gift or entry into a competition, when replies have been received. Postal surveys have many advantages. They can cover a wide geographical sampling area and they are relatively inexpensive. There is no danger of interviewer bias and the respondents have time to consider their answers. However, there are also disadvantages involved. Although they seem to be cheap, postal surveys may be expensive if the response rate is very low, because then the real cost per reply goes up. Also, there is no supervision of the people filling in the questionnaires and you cannot be sure that they have been filled in properly or by the people who were meant to complete them. In addition, the questionnaires tend to be short, so not that much information can be collected, and the whole process takes a long time to complete because of the nature of the method being employed.

Telephone surveys In this case, an interview is carried out over the telephone. The respondent is usually asked a set of questions from a pre-written questionnaire. The replies are normally put straight onto a computer and so analysis of the responses is relatively easy and quick. The advantages of this method are that it is relatively low cost, can cover a wide geographical area and a large number of interviews can be conducted in a relatively short time. Obviously, this method is restricted to those who have telephones and so there is an element of built-in bias. However, these days, most people have access to a telephone and so the bias is not too great. More of a problem is the fact that the majority of the public view telephone surveys with some distrust, because they think that the interviewers may be trying to sell something. The advent of 'tele-sales' has made the job of the telephone surveyor much more difficult.

Panel surveys A panel is a group of consumers, who are normally used on a regular basis in order to conduct research into a specific market or across a wide range of markets. The use of a panel allows the researcher to consider the views of the same group of people over a reasonable period of time. Some panels are put together for a strictly limited period of time, but others may continue for many years. There are advantages to be gained by using panels. First, it is possible to discover trends, because the information is collected over time and the same panel members are used. These trends may then be analysed and acted upon. Second, the panel members tend to be more truthful than the average respondent, because they obviously want to be on the panel. The main disadvantages tend to concern the actual panel members. There is bound to be a loss of panel members over time, for a wide variety of reasons, and this will obviously affect the balance of the panel. In addition, if people are panel members for a long period of time, it may affect their views and attitudes and lead to responses that are not typical.

There are a number of different types of panel that may be considered, but we can simply concentrate on the main three. First, there are consumer product testing panels. This is where consumers are asked to try out various products and then to give their views upon them. Second, there are consumer purchasing panels. Here, the consumers report regularly upon their own purchasing patterns, purchasing intentions and views on products. The information is normally collected by postal questionnaires, although sometimes the panel members are asked to keep a diary or are interviewed at regular intervals. The third type of panel is the audience panel. In this case, a representative panel of viewers and listeners to TV and radio is set up. Their responses to programmes and advertising are then monitored and used by a variety of organisations.

Questionnaires

Questionnaires are an essential part of the market research process and it is important that they are constructed as well as they can be. Questionnaires are normally split into four distinct sections. First, there is the preamble section, where the purpose of the questionnaire is explained to the respondent and any factors relating to anonymity or incentives for completion are described. Second, there are the classification questions, which will enable the analysts to tell what sort of person the respondent is, e.g. sex, age, income bracket, etc. The third section consists of information questions, where the main research questions are asked. The final section should be a short statement of thanks for completing the questionnaire, plus any necessary information for its return.

The individual questions should not be:
- too long;
- overly complicated;
- too mathematical;
- ambiguous;
- offensive;
- reliant on memory.

The above description of a questionnaire is an example of a structured questionnaire, where the questions are set out in a specific order and must be followed. There are also unstructured questionnaires, where there is a selection of questions from which the interviewer may choose. These sorts of questionnaires give much more leeway to the interviewer, but they are harder to analyse when the results have been obtained.

The importance of sampling and sampling methods

In a perfect world, information would be collected from every individual in any given market that was being researched. However, in reality, this is not possible.

Researchers would not attempt to interview all women between 16 and 40 in the UK in order to find their views on perfume. It would simply be an impossible task. Instead, the researchers will select a sample of women they hope will be representative of the whole group, or population, as it is known.

It is imperative that the sample is large enough to be able to give statistically valid results and that it is as representative of the population as possible. If this is the case, then the views of the sample respondents can be used to make predictions about how the whole population feels.

Those involved in market research have two options when it comes to sampling:

Random or probability samples   In these types of samples, every member of the population has an equal chance of being chosen as a member of the sample.

Non-random or non-probability samples   Here, every member of the population does not have an equal chance of being chosen as a member of the sample, because the sample is chosen by the researchers, who may be biased.

It is necessary to look at different sampling methods in more detail and it is easiest to classify them as we have done above.

Random or probability samples

There are several sampling methods that come under this heading:

Simple random sampling   This is where the sample is drawn at random, usually from a list of names or numbers and, these days, the process is normally carried out by a computer or by using a computer-generated list of random numbers. It is a reasonable method to use when there is no difference between the views of the members of the population. However, if the population consists of distinct strata, then it is not an appropriate method.

Systematic sampling   This is where a set numerical formulae is used to choose the sample, for example every tenth or twentieth person is selected. Again, if the population consists of distinct strata, then it is not really a very appropriate method.

Stratified sampling   A sample is taken, at random, from specified strata of the whole population. Thus, a producer of sports shoes may feel that the majority of

customers are between 10 and 35 years of age and so will only sample people from that stratum of the population. The success and accuracy of this method will depend upon how relevant the chosen stratification criteria are. In cases where it is not clear, the usual strata of age, sex and geographical position are most commonly used. This is a relatively expensive method but, if the strata are correctly identified, it is usually the most accurate.

Cluster sampling   In this case, the population is separated into a number of distinct clusters and then one, or a number, of the clusters is selected at random. Examples of clusters might be blocks of flats on a large estate or villages of a certain size. Once a cluster has been chosen, then it may be sampled by strata and so it is possible to have a random, stratified, cluster sample.

Non-random or non-probability samples

There are two main methods that are used under this heading:

Quota sampling   This is the most commonly used sampling method. The interviewers choose the respondents by checking to see that they fulfil certain pre-agreed criteria, relevant to the population being researched. For example, the interviewer may be asked to obtain the opinions of 50 women, 30 of whom are married and 20 of whom are not. In addition, the women may need to be working full time and be between the ages of 20 and 40. This is a relatively cheap method of sampling, because specific people do not have to be visited. However, there is a lot of scope for interviewer bias, because certain interviewers may find some types of people to be intimidating and so may not approach them, and will in this way introduce their own bias.

Convenience sampling   In this case, the interviewer selects any convenient place, where large groups of people might congregate, as the location for conducting the interviews. Obviously, this makes the sample quicker and cheaper to conduct, but bias may be introduced by the fact that everyone is from the same location. An example of this might be interviews carried out in large shopping centres or in queues for the cinema.

Over-to-you

Short-answer questions

1 Distinguish between primary and secondary information.

2 Explain the circumstances in which you would use secondary research.

3 State three different ways of collecting primary data.

4 What are the advantages and disadvantages of each of these methods.

5 What are the strengths and weaknesses of telephone surveys?

6 Explain what a consumer panel is and the circumstances in which one might be used.

7 What is an open question and when might it be useful?

8 Why is it that most questions in a project enquiry should be closed ones?

9 Why are small samples dangerous?

Discover and learn

1 As a group choose a headline from your local newspaper.
   (a) Agree on questions (not more than three) that you can ask to test the general public's awareness of that issue.
   (b) Each member of the group go and ask ten people those questions.
   (c) Bring back your findings and collate them.
   (d) What do you conclude from your collective findings?

2 (a) Go and research the price of tomatoes in all the shops in which you can find them.

(b) Decide how you can display the data you have collected in a way that would convey most information to the reader.

(c) From your research:
   ◆ What is the range?
   ◆ What is the arithmetic mean?
   ◆ What is the median price?
   ◆ Is there a modal price?
   Which one of these descriptive data would you choose to represent the price of tomatoes? Explain your answer?

3 Suppose you needed to research the market for a new bus service in some part of your area. What secondary data would you seek to use and how would it be of assistance to you?

Case study – Tubular Chairs Ltd

Using the case study at the end of Section 8 (pp. 102), answer the following questions:

1 Discuss the market research methods that Val Richards and her team might have employed to find the information given in the *Current Situation* section of the report.

2 What sampling methods might Val Richards and her team have adopted to gain the consumer research information in the report?

Summary

In this section we have recognised that:

● Market research is not the same as marketing research, it is a sub-set of it.

● Information is relevant data and may be categorised as primary, secondary, quantitative or qualitative.

● Information may be collected by field or desk research.

● Primary information can be collected by observation, experimentation and surveys.

● Questionnaires are usually involved when surveys are being carried out.

● Because it is usually impossible to interview a whole population, or market, some form of sampling usually takes place.

● It is important that the sample is large enough to be significant and that it is representative of the population as a whole.

● Samples may be random or non-random.

Key words

Definitions of Key words can be found in the Glossary on page 236.

observation	quota
probability samples	random samples
qualitative information	sampling
quantitative information	surveys
questionnaires	

10 Market planning

On completion of this section you should be able to:

➤ define the marketing mix
➤ understand the requirements of a good product
➤ define and discuss the product life cycle
➤ understand and explain how products can be positioned through the use of portfolio models
➤ understand the influences upon price of different pricing strategies
➤ understand the factors that influence the level of demand
➤ define, calculate and interpret price elasticity of demand
➤ identify and explain different promotional methods
➤ understand and discuss the appropriateness of different promotional strategies
➤ understand different distribution channels and strategies
➤ understand the importance of a strategic approach to marketing
➤ formulate and justify marketing strategies in different situations

The marketing mix

The **marketing mix** is the combination of variables that has to be taken into account when formulating a marketing strategy. Different management theorists will name different variables, but the most common variables are known as the '4 Ps':

◆ product;
◆ price;
◆ promotion;
◆ place.

Some would add packaging as an extra 'P' and others would separate publicity from promotion. However, most still stick with the original variables. In simple words, a marketing mix involves a combination of supplying a product at a price that consumers will pay, making sure that the consumers know that the product exists through promotion and ensuring that the consumers will have easy access to the products through an efficient distribution system.

It is important that the different elements of the mix do not clash and that a firm has a mix that suits its own particular needs. There is no ideal marketing mix, the emphasis upon each element of the mix will vary from firm to firm.

Some firms will emphasise especially the actual product that they are producing. These will tend to be firms who produce high-quality goods that are often technically advanced. Here, they will emphasise quality and will not be so interested in price. If firms make products that are common, have many competitors and are relatively simple, then they will not be so likely to emphasise the product, but will put more emphasis upon price and promotion.

Firms supplying manufacturers with equipment will stress the quality and appropriateness of the product, assuring them that the machinery on offer is the best for the job. In many industries, it is impossible for firms to ignore the marketing mixes of their rivals. Many firms will match the style and content of the marketing mixes of their competitors. A good example of this would be the high-street banks in the UK, such as Lloyds, Barclays, HSBC and the National Westminster Banks.

In the end, all firms are looking to find a 'Unique Selling Point' (USP) somewhere in the marketing mix. This is the point that, in the eyes of the consumers, sets their product apart from its rivals.

The product

A product can be defined as anything that can fulfil a consumer's needs or wants. It may be a good, i.e. tangible, or a service, i.e. intangible. It is sometimes thought to be the most fundamental and important element of the marketing mix, since, if a product does not fulfil the needs or wants of a consumer, then that consumer will not buy the product.

Product development is an important area for any business. In order to be a 'good' product, an item needs to satisfy three major requirements:

- The product should be able to fulfil the function for which it is intended. If a product does not do what it is meant to do, then consumers will not buy it. No-one wants a basketball that does not bounce or a chair that collapses when people sit on it. When considering this, the developers of products should be aware of all of the tasks that consumers might expect product to fulfil. People use screwdrivers for a number of tasks, not just inserting and removing screws. Amongst other things, they may use them to open paint tins, mix paint and punch holes in thin wood and metal. They would expect a reasonable screwdriver to be able to perform these functions and so the designers will have to ensure that they do.
- The product should be as aesthetically pleasing as can be expected for the price. If possible, products should look good, but this will obviously depend upon the product in question. People do not expect a cheap ruler to look aesthetically pleasing, but they would expect it from a sports car or a pair of earrings. Products that are basic and functional do not normally have to be very visually appealing, but luxury products usually are.
- The product needs to be capable of economic production. There is no point in making a product so well that it is functionally perfect and aesthetically wonderful, but so costly to make that the price that would have to be charged to make a profit would not be one that consumers would be willing to pay.

In addition to these three requirements, a firm will also have to consider any legal requirements that might be placed upon their product. Furthermore, in this more enlightened age, firms may also take into account environmental factors that may be encountered by the production process or by the disposal of the product when it has been consumed.

It will be up to the product developers to strike a balance between the above five factors. This balance will normally be decided upon having considered the results of any market research that has been undertaken.

Activities

1 What are the elements of the marketing mix? Use illustrations to show how each different element may be the most important in specific markets.
2 What are the five requirements for a good product?
3 Identify ten different products and, for each one, attempt to rank in order of importance the five requirements for a good product. Explain your reasoning.

The product life cycle

The **product life cycle** looks at the different stages that a normal product will go through in its life, from development to decline and eventual failure. It shows the product's life, over time, measured in terms of sales revenue or, more often, profit. A typical product life cycle is shown in Figure 10.1.

As we can see from the figure, the first stage is that of development, and here we would expect costs and no

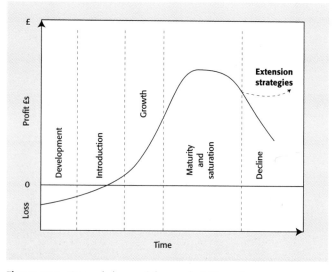

Figure 10.1 General shape of the product life cycle

revenue, since there would be no sales. Thus, the product would be making a loss. The second stage is introduction and the product may be introduced to the whole market or, more likely, it may be tried out on a test market. This is a smaller, normally regional market, which has the same characteristics as the main market. It is thought that, if the product flourishes here, it will do the same in the main market. It must be said that it is normally at this stage that the majority of new products, a figure as high as 75%, fail. If the introduction goes well, then the product may move into profit at the end of this stage, but promotional costs are high and so any profit is unlikely to be great.

If the product is successful, it then moves into the growth stage and we will find that sales are increasing, as is market share. It may be that there is marked market growth as well, but this will eventually slow down as the market becomes stable. In this stage, promotional expenditure is still fairly high, but sales are ever increasing and so profits rise. Eventually though, as the market growth slows down, the product enters the maturity and saturation stage, where it has a high market share in a stable market. This makes it a valuable source of funds and profits, since promotional costs are not too high (because the product is well known) and the sales revenue is high and constant. However, for most products, but not all, demand will eventually begin to diminish and the product will move into the decline stage. Sales will fall and profits will do the same. The firm will have to decide whether to cease production and sales of the product or whether to attempt to prolong the life of the product through extension strategies.

Extension strategies are such ploys as:

- redesigning the product in order to make it attractive again, such as altering the design of a watch to include an alarm function;
- redesigning the packaging in some way, such as making Apple Mac computers coloured;
- developing add-on products, such as the male companion doll Ken, which was added to the Barbie range to try to increase sales of Barbie.

The actual shape of the product life cycle will not always, or even often, be like the one that we have just seen. The shape of the curve and the lengths of the stages will vary from product to product.

Product portfolio

The **product portfolio** of a firm is sometimes called its product mix. It is the range of products that a firm produces and it is imperative that a firm has a balanced portfolio. Very few firms will be able to survive over time with only one product. As we have seen from the product life cycle, almost all products will eventually go into decline and so firms should have products in all stages of the product life cycle. In this way, the successful products, in the maturity stage, can be used to fund new products that the firm wishes to develop and introduce to the market.

In Figure 10.2 we can see a balanced product portfolio of three goods. However, many firms will have a much larger product mix, consisting of many different products. A good example of this would be ice-cream manufacturers, such as Walls, who produce many different ice-creams and are always adding new products to their range.

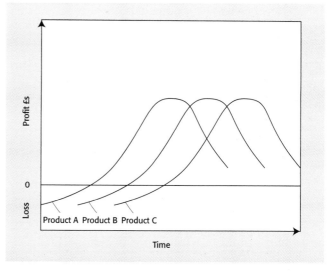

Figure 10.2 Product portfolio

Activity

1. Explain the difference between a product life cycle and a product portfolio.
2. What are the main stages of a product life cycle?
3. How might a firm extend the life of a product?
4. Select a large firm, such as Lever Brothers or Virgin, and attempt to identify the products in their product portfolio. Explain where you think each product is in its product life cycle.

New product development

As we saw in the product life cycle, new products need a period of development before they are launched onto the market. If a firm is going to have a reasonable and balanced portfolio of products, then it is essential that it develops new products to replace those that become obsolete and to widen the product mix. New products may be completely new or they may be an adaptation of an already existing product. In either case, the process of product development may vary greatly in the time taken to reach the production stage. For some pharmaceutical products, product development may take 15 years or more. However, this is seen to be worth while, because the possible financial rewards are massive. What would be the selling price of a cure for AIDS? In other cases, such as making children's toys, the process may be six to nine months. It is interesting that car firms are attempting to reduce drastically their product development times and some of the Japanese firms are now working on a period of 18 months, as opposed to five years in the 1980s. New product development relies on:

Identifying new product niches   This is usually carried out by a mixture of market research and technological prediction. Markets are identified and the consumers are asked what sorts of products they would like to see. In addition, experts in the markets try to foresee what technological breakthroughs might occur in the market, or might be possible to create. In this way, ideas for new products are generated.

Once the idea of the product has been decided upon, it is necessary to assess whether the product will actually be desirable to the market and whether it will be able to be sold for a profit. Market desirability has normally been indicated in the original market research and so it is usually only necessary to estimate costs and possible revenues in order to predict the profitability factor. This is often carried out by the building of a prototype.

Developing the product   Sometimes, the new products are developed after market research or technological prediction has identified a possible winning product. Occasionally, new products occur as an offshoot of pure research. The most famous example of this is when Teflon, which is used for non-stick frying pans, was discovered as an offshoot of the US space research programme.

When products are developed following research and prediction, the process of development is known as

An Israeli high-tech company developing a sunscreen using a material most people would not dream of rubbing on their bodies, glass. Jerusalem-based Sol-Gel Technologies said it has developed a way to encapsulate sunscreen solutions in tiny glass bubbles that can be incorporated into a smooth non-penetrating lotion. In this photo a lab technician inspects the prototype production process in the company's laboratory in the science campus of the Hebrew University of Jerusalem.
Source: Popperfoto.

applied research. It is at this stage that the prototype product is developed into the marketable final product. In doing this, it is important that the designers take notice of the requirements for a 'good' product that we considered earlier in this chapter.

Piloting and test marketing the product   Once the product has been developed, the firm will normally try it out on a small scale. This will involve producing a relatively small number of the products and then attempting to sell them in a test market, which is representative of the main market that is being targeted. This process should show whether the product can be produced economically and also whether there is a market for it. If the piloting and test marketing of the product is a success, only then will the product be released on the wider market.

Products fail at all stages of the product development process, but if a product reaches the full production stage, there is still no guarantee that it will be a success. There are many reasons why a product may reach the wider market and then fail. Some of them are as follows:

- Competitors release a product that the consumers prefer.
- Changes in technology leave the product dated.
- Tastes change and the product is quickly obsolete.
- The market research was not accurate.

- The costs of production were greater than predicted.
- The product could not fulfil its main functions.
- The pricing estimate was wrong.
- The promotion was not effective and so not successful.
- There were problems of distribution and consumers could not gain access to the product in sufficient quantities.

There are so many possible causes of failure that it is almost miraculous that products succeed at all.

Activities

1 What are the phases involved in the development of a new product?
2 Why do firms produce new products, if so many products fail?

Product positioning

Product positioning places a product in the market in terms of its rivals. It identifies where a product stands in terms of the major characteristics that consumers expect products in that market to have. The first step to take, when positioning a product, is to discover the main qualities that consumers expect from this type of product. This is best shown by an example. Assume that a firm is trying to position a product in the sliced wholemeal bread market. The main expected qualities are discovered by means of market research and it is discovered that they are price and variety of nutrients.

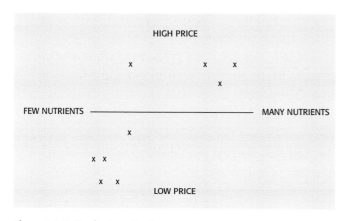

HIGH PRICE

FEW NUTRIENTS —————————————— MANY NUTRIENTS

LOW PRICE

Figure 10.3 Product positioning map

Once the main desired qualities have been identified, then a 'map' can be drawn like the one in Figure 10.3. The existing products in the market are placed on the map and it is then studied in order to decide where the firm's new product should be positioned.

In this case, we can see that there are two main groups of products. There are those that are high in both price and variety of nutrients and those that are low in both qualities. There seems to be little in between.

The firm must now decide where it will place its own product. There are a number of possibilities. First, the firm could aim for a gap in the market. This may be rather risky but, if it pays off, then there may be the chance of substantial profits. A second option is to position the product in with others. In this way, the firm is producing a similar product and hoping for some of the existing market share. This is a less risky option than trying to fill a gap, but the potential profits will usually be much lower.

Firms will sometimes identify more than just two qualities and may position their product against a number of different factors. They may also aim to reposition an existing product by altering it so that it will then occupy a different point on the positioning map. An example of this may be making a product more exclusive and moving it up market or making a product more available and moving it towards the mass market.

Market positioning

In just the same way that a product can hold a certain position in a market, so can a firm. There are a number of different market positions that firms may occupy.

Market leader

This is a firm that is regarded as the main producer in the market. Invariably, the firm will have the largest market share and will normally be a 'price setter', i.e. it will dictate the prices for the market and the market followers will adopt those prices or very similar ones. The market leader will be keen to achieve market growth and may be attempting to drive other firms out of the market. However, in large markets, the small firms often do work that the market leader does not want and the market leader will tolerate them so long as they toe the line.

Market challenger

This is normally the second largest firm in the market, or a new firm that has high aspirations. The aim of the market challenger is to become the market leader. Markets that have a leader and a challenger tend to be very competitive and price wars may well take place as the challenger attempts to gain market share. Supermarkets are a good example and the fight between Tesco and Sainsbury is a constant one.

Market follower

This is a firm in the market that is actually satisfied to simply maintain market share and to follow the market leader. These markets tend to be less competitive in terms of pricing and most competition takes the form of non-price promotion.

Niche marketer

This is a firm that simply concentrates on a specialist, discrete, area of the market, such as a publisher that specialises in publishing only children's books. Niche marketing will be successful if the niche is large enough to be profitable, but too small to be of interest to the larger firms in the market.

Activities

1 Select three different products, identify their main rivals and then attempt to plot a positioning map for each product. Justify your decisions.
2 Select three individual firms, in different industries, and then attempt to position the firms in their separate markets. Explain your positioning.

Price and demand

Price is the amount of money that a consumer is prepared to pay for a good or service. In a wider sense, it is the money value of a good, service, asset or factor input. There are a number of approaches to pricing.

Demand-based pricing

This is where the firm attempts to charge what the market will bear and to gain the highest price that will still clear the amount supplied. In order to undertake demand-based pricing, it is necessary to understand the concepts of the demand curve and price elasticity of demand.

The demand curve is based upon the simple idea that people will buy more at a lower price than they will at a

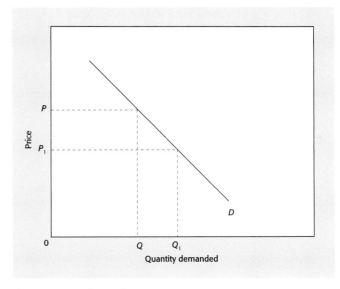

Figure 10.4 A demand curve

higher one. Although this is not always true, it does apply in the majority of cases. A typical demand curve is shown in Figure 10.4.

As we can see, when the price falls from P to P_1, demand rises from Q to Q_1. Thus, it is obvious that price is one of the most important determinants of demand. Demand will also be influenced by:

- the prices of substitute goods, e.g. buses instead of taxies;
- the prices of complementary goods, e.g. eggs and bacon;
- the level of people's incomes;
- the changing tastes of consumers;
- the overall size of the population;
- government policies;
- the distribution of income among the population.

In reality, firms find it very difficult, if not impossible, to draw their demand curves. They actually only have an idea of how demand changes over a very small range of prices. However, if they can understand price elasticity of demand, they can make predictions about what is going to happen to their total sales revenue when they alter their prices.

Price elasticity of demand is a measure of the responsiveness of demand to changes in price. When the price of a product rises, demand will fall, but the question is 'by how much?'. If it changes little, then the firm will be happy and total revenue will rise. We say that the price elasticity of demand is inelastic. If it changes a lot, then the firm will be unhappy, since total

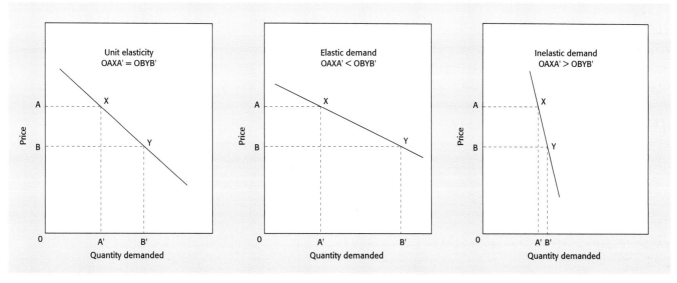

Figure 10.5 Varying elasticities of demand

revenue will actually fall. We say that the price elasticity of demand is elastic. If price and quantity change by the same percentage, then the total revenue will be unchanged and we say that elasticity is unitary (equal to one). The relative levels of price elasticity of demand are shown in Figure 10.5.

The degree of elasticity is normally measured by using the following equation :

Price elasticity of demand (PED)

$$= \frac{\text{Percentage change in quantity demanded}}{\text{Percentage change in price}}$$

The value of PED is normally negative, because a fall in price normally produces a rise in demand. This movement in the opposite direction is called an inverse relationship but it is usual to ignore the negative sign since it is only the extent of change that matters. Table 10.1 shows how different values for PED are classified.

Value of PED	Classification	Explanation
Zero	Perfectly inelastic demand	The same amount is demanded, no matter what the price. In reality, there is no product that would have this sort of PED.
Between 0 and 1	Inelastic demand	The percentage change in demand is less than the percentage change in price. If a firm faces this sort of demand, it can raise the price, not lose much demand and increase sales revenue. However, this cannot keep happening. As the price continues to rise, demand will become more elastic.
Unitary	Unit elasticity	The percentage change in demand is equal and opposite to the percentage change in price, so any price change will lead to an equal change in demand and the total sales revenue will remain constant. When PED = 1, sales revenue will be maximised.
Between 1 and infinity (∞)	Elastic demand	The percentage change in demand is greater than the percentage change in price. If a firm faces this sort of demand, then it can lower the price, pick up a lot more demand and increase sales revenue.
Infinity (∞)	Perfectly elastic demand	An infinitely large amount is demanded at one price and then demand falls to zero if the price is raised, even by the smallest amount. In reality, there is no product that would have this sort of PED.

Table 10.1 The potential range of elasticity and its effects

There are a number of factors that will determine the PED of a product:

How necessary the product is   The more necessary people consider a product to be, the less they will react to price changes and the more inelastic will be their demand. If a good is considered to be a luxury, then it is likely that the demand for it will be relatively elastic.

How many competitors there are   If there are many competitors, then there are a large number of substitutes for the product and consumers will quickly switch to another brand if the price rises. Thus, the demand for the product will be relatively elastic.

The price of the product   If the price of a product is low, people will not really care as much about price increases and so demand will be relatively inelastic. However, as price continues to rise, the demand will start to become more elastic.

In an ideal world, firms will want to produce products that are necessities, with few substitutes. However, this is difficult to do for any length of time, because other firms enter the market, attracted by the inelastic demand and the profits.

Other approaches to pricing
Cost-based pricing

The basic idea is that firms will assess their costs per unit, in some way, and then add an amount on top of the calculated cost. There are a number of different methods of cost-based pricing that may be adopted:

- Mark-up pricing is usually carried out by retailers, who take the price that they pay to the producer or wholesaler for the product in question, and then just add a percentage mark up. The size of the mark up usually depends upon a combination of the strength of demand for the product, the number of other suppliers, and the age and standard life of the product. Sometimes it also depends on the tradition of the industry.

	£
Total cost of production	40
50% mark up on cost	20
Selling price	60

- Target pricing is where a company decides upon a price that will give a required rate of return at a certain level of output/sales. This is best explained by an example. If a company has costs of £200,000 when making 10,000 units of output and has an expected rate of return of 20%, then it will set its price by working out its total cost and expected return and then dividing the amount by the output.

	£
Total output costs 10,000	200,000
Required return 20%	40,000
Total return	240,000
Price per unit 240/10	24

- Full cost (or absorption cost) pricing is where the company attempts to calculate a unit cost for the product and then adds an agreed profit margin. However, it is not always easy to allocate all of the costs of a firm to a specific product, especially if the firm makes a range of products. It is especially difficult to allocate the fixed costs.

  The method differs from cost plus pricing only to the extent that a method of allocating fixed costs among the various products produced has to be found.

- Contribution cost (or marginal cost) pricing does not try to allocate the fixed costs to specific products. Instead of this, the firm calculates a unit variable cost for the product in question and then adds an extra amount that is known as a contribution to fixed costs. If enough units are sold, the total contribution will be enough to cover the fixed costs and to return a profit. For example, let us suppose that a firm produces a single product that has direct costs of £2 per unit and that the total fixed costs of the firm are £40,000 per year. The firm sets a contribution of £1 per unit and so sells the product at £3. Every unit sold makes a contribution towards the fixed costs of £1. If the firm sells 40,000 units in the year, then the fixed costs will be covered. Every unit sold over 40,000 will return a profit. Thus, if the firm sells 60,000 units, then the fixed costs will be covered and there will be £20,000 profit realised.

  Obviously, it would be good for a firm if it produced a range of products that all made a positive contribution to the fixed costs. Then, each product is 'doing its bit'. As a general rule of thumb, a product that makes a positive contribution to fixed costs should be produced so long as there is spare capacity in the firm, it does not take the place of a product with a higher contribution and there is not another option that has a higher contribution. There are many firms that have excess capacity and hence use contribution cost pricing to attract extra business which will absorb the excess capacity.

Examples are train companies, for which there is substantial excess capacity except in the morning and evening rush hours. Even then, trains tend to run rather empty in one of the two directions. Electricity and telephone companies face the same sort of situation. For fuller treatment of contribution cost pricing, see Section 11.

Competition-based pricing

This is the situation that exists where a firm will base its price upon the price set by its competitors. However, there are a number of different possible scenarios:

♦ Price leadership often exists in markets where there is one dominant firm and other firms simply charge a price based upon that set by the market leader.

♦ Some markets have a number of firms the same size, but prices are still similar in order to avoid a price war. An example of this would be the High Street banks

♦ Destroyer pricing: sometimes, firms will note the price of competitors' products and then deliberately undercut them in order to try to force them out of the market.

♦ Market pricing is where the price charged is based upon a study of the conditions that prevail in a certain market. This is sometimes also called consumer-based pricing, because, when the market is studied, it is in many ways the actions of consumers in that market that are actually being looked at. However, a study of the market is, in fact, more detailed than just looking at the responses of the consumers in the market. A number of different pricing strategies come under the heading of market-orientated pricing:

– Perceived value pricing (customer value pricing) is used in markets where demand is known to be inelastic and a price is placed upon the product that reflects its value, as perceived by the consumers in the market. The more prestigious the brand name, for example Rolex, the higher the perceived value, and so the higher the price that can be set.

– Price discrimination takes place in markets where it is possible to charge different groups of consumers different prices for the same product. An example of this would be airline firms, who charge many different rates for the same journey. Firms can price discriminate if there are different groups of consumers, with different elasticities of demand for the product, and where the firm is able to avoid resale between the groups. This is easier to do with services.

– Pioneer pricing takes place in new markets and there are normally two different approaches that may be taken. The first is penetration pricing, a relatively low price is set and strong promotion takes place in order to achieve a high volume of sales. Firms tend to adopt penetration pricing because they are attempting to gain a large market share. The second approach is market skimming, which usually occurs when a firm does not expect to have a lead in a market for a long time and so attempts to make relatively high short-term profits by charging a high price for as long as the product can hold its strong position. An example of this is pharmaceutical firms, who are given a seven-year monopoly under the Sainsbury Committee rules. They are able to charge high prices in order to recoup their considerable investments in research and to make high profits. It is not uncommon for them to lower their prices in the last year of their legal monopoly in order to hold their market share when other companies enter.

Activities

1 What is price elasticity of demand?

2 What are the weaknesses of demand-based pricing?

3 Identify different cost-based pricing methods and explain their relative strengths and weaknesses.

4 What is destroyer pricing? Is it good for consumers in the long run?

5 What are the different types of market-orientated pricing? In what sort of markets would firms pursue policies of:
   (a) penetration pricing?
   (b) market skimming?
   Use examples to explain your answers.

Promotional methods and strategies

Firms have a number of communication options, some are controllable and some are outside their control. The non-controllable methods are things such as word-of-mouth communication and independent and objective communication in magazines, such as *Which?* or *What Car?*. There are four main methods of controllable promotion used by firms and they would normally employ a combination of those methods in their promotional strategies. The four areas are advertising, sales promotion, personal selling and publicity.

Advertising

Advertising is defined as purchased, non-personal, communication using mass media. These days, it is often called 'above-the-line' promotion. Where the mass media are used, it is expensive and so is only open to larger firms.

There are three main forms of advertising. The first is product advertising, where a firm tries to inform potential customers about the existence of a certain product. Thus, we see product advertisements for Coke or Burger King. The second is institutional advertising, where the firm gives information about its activities or attempts to show itself in a good light. Information about activities may be information regarding changes in opening hours or the starting of a delivery service. Firms may show themselves in a good light by advertising the environmental or charity work that they are involved in. The third form of advertising is primary advertising, where groups of firms, or the government, get together to promote a general category of a good, such as tea or health programmes.

Sales promotion

This covers a whole range of activities that offer incentives to purchase products or features that make the products attractive to the consumer. These activities are often known as 'below-the-line' promotion. They normally come under three headings and are shown in Table 10.2.

Personal selling

This takes place when promotion is carried out on a one-to-one, face-to-face basis. The consumer has the chance to ask questions about the product and the salesperson has the opportunity to gain the trust of the consumer and to tailor each presentation to the specific customer. Personal selling may take place inside retail outlets, where sales people deal with customers, such as in department stores or car showrooms. It may also occur when salespeople go out to sell a product, such as door-to-door salespeople. Examples are Avon Cosmetics, double-glazing or company representatives (reps) who sell to other firms.

Methods of below-the-line promotion	Examples
Immediate consumer incentives – techniques that give an immediate benefit to the consumer in return for purchase.	Price reductions on packs; free samples; trial packs; bonus packs (e.g. 50% extra); premiums (e.g. two for the price of one); give aways (e.g. buy the first issue of a magazine and get the second one free); competitions with immediate prizes.
Delayed consumer incentives – techniques that give an eventual benefit to the consumer in return for purchase.	Coupons for future purchases; tokens and trading stamps; mail-in cash refunds; competitions with a specific finish date; charitable offers.
Other sales promotional methods	Point of sale (POS) displays Branding and packaging Exhibitions Sponsorships Credit facilities

Table 10.2 Sales promotion techniques

A form of selling which is one-to-one and covers an increasing range of goods is through the telephone (tele-sales). Sometimes this is 'cold calling', where the person called is selected at random. More often there is evidence to suggest that the person called might be interested. Minor house developments are often sold in this way.

The big new player on the scene is the Internet, through which anything can be bought. It is expected that the proportion of goods sold in this way will grow rapidly. Effectively it turns the market for most products into a world market.

Salespeople carry out a number of different tasks. They give advice, demonstrate products, take orders, deliver goods, collect payment for the goods, deal with complaints and provide feedback to the firm from customers. There are many advantages to be gained from personal selling, but there is one large drawback of the process: it is expensive! The cost of selection, training and paying a sales force can be very high. However, more and more these days, firms are realising the importance of having quality salespeople, especially in the retail and service-providing companies.

Publicity

This is any promotional information about a firm or its products that is not directly paid for by the firm. Publicity is usually via press releases that the firm issues to the newspapers and magazines in the hope that they will be used. However, it can also occur when celebrities 'plug' a product in a speech or interview. Publicity can be uncontrollable and very damaging, such as during the BSE crisis of the late 1990s and its long-lasting effects on the sales of British beef. Most publicity on consumer programmes, of which there are, on average, two a week, is largely negative as consumers voice their complaints about a firm or a product and the programme follows it up.

Distribution

The physical distribution of products is much more important than the consumer realises. A firm can have the best products, at the right prices, with excellent promotion, but if the products are not at the selling points when the consumers want them, the firm will soon discover how fickle the buying public can be.

Physical distribution covers the physical movement of products from producers to the eventual selling points. The costs of this are significant and, on average, can account for approximately 20% of the unit costs of a product. This is accounted for by:

- the costs of distribution facilities, such as storehouses;
- stock holding costs;
- transport costs;
- communication costs;
- costs of unitisation.

Distribution channels are the routes through which products go from the producer to the final consumer. These routes may be simple or complicated. The routes are normally expressed as two types.

Short-channel routes

These are routes where the supplier reaches the consumer either directly or through a retailer. Short-channel routes are shown in Figure 10.6.

Direct supply takes place through mail-order or telephone selling, but the rapidly growing revolution in selling is through the internet. Ecommerce is going to become the norm in the marketing of some goods and increasingly common in others (see Tesco story, page 40).

Short-channel supply through retailers is very common and there is often an interesting balance of power between the producer and the retailer. In some cases, the producer is keen to have products sold

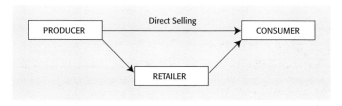

Figure 10.6 Short distribution routes

through the retailer's outlets. An example of this would be a producer of foodstuffs who would be keen to supply to Marks and Spencer. In other cases, retailers, such as garages, are keen to supply a certain product, such as BMW motor cars. The relative power will change with the circumstances of the market. In many cases, producers and retailers work together on such matters as funding, design, promotion and staff training. Obviously, it is in the interests of both parties for products to sell well.

Long-channel routes

These are routes where there is an intermediary (or intermediaries) between the producer and the eventual consumers. Possible long, channel routes are shown in Figure 10.7.

Wholesalers have two main functions, those of 'breaking bulk' and stock holding. Many retailers are too small to buy products in bulk from the suppliers and so wholesalers do it, break the large quantities down into smaller amounts and then add a profit margin, selling smaller quantities to the retailers. The small corner shop is able to buy 24 packs of washing powder from the wholesaler as opposed to the minimum order of 2,400 packs from the supplier. Wholesalers are risk takers, in that the stock could be damaged or, worse still, become obsolete or out of fashion, while they hold it.

Agents are people who have the authority to enter into a contract on behalf of the producer they represent. Agents manage the relationship between the producer and the customer. They do not take legal ownership of the products involved and simply work for a fee or a percentage of the sales value. Agents are especially employed in foreign markets, where a producer may not have contacts or outlets. Agents are common in new car sales and customary in the sale of houses.

The main disadvantage of using long channels of distribution is that all of the intermediaries will add their profit margins and so the price to the final consumer is pushed up all the time. Also, the producer becomes isolated from the market and feedback and communication will be strained.

Activities

1 Which elements of the promotional mix will be most appropriate for the following events (rank the elements in order of importance in each case and explain your reasoning):
   (a) Christmas sales at Next?
   (b) Promoting a local church fete?
   (c) Informing customers of changed opening times at the local corner shop?
   (d) A local garage changing its franchise from Peugeot to Ford?
2 Identify four actual products that each use a different distribution channel. Identify the channel used in each case and explain why this channel is used.

Marketing plans

All firms, even very small ones, should have a marketing plan. No matter how simple, it is essential that marketing is co-ordinated by means of a sensible plan. If this is not the case, then the marketing activity may not be suitable for the market in question and may have elements that conflict. A possible framework for a plan is shown in Figure 10.8. It is useful to look at each step in detail.

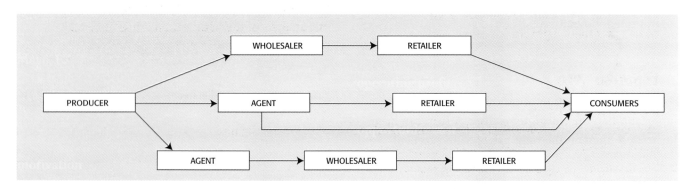

Figure 10.7 Long-channel routes involving intermediaries

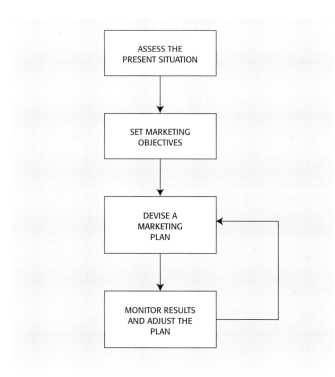

Figure 10.8 Flow diagram of the planning process

Assess the present situation

This may be carried out by looking at the internal situation in the firm and the external market in which the firm is operating. The internal investigation may be carried out by analysing accounts, interviewing employees and assessing the strengths and weaknesses of the firm as part of a SWOT analysis. The external investigation may be carried out by conducting market research, consulting experts, assessing the opportunities and threats for the firm as the remainder of the SWOT analysis and attempting to forecast where the market will go in the future.

Set marketing objectives

When that the firm has decided where it is now, it needs to ask 'What of the future'? Firms have a number of objectives that they might decide upon, such as:

- aiming for a greater market share in their existing markets;
- targeting new markets for their existing products;
- developing new products for their existing markets;
- diversifying into completely new markets;
- improving the image of the firm and its products;
- increasing profitability;
- increasing sales revenue.

The choice of objective(s) will have a great effect upon the marketing plan that needs to be adopted. When deciding upon objectives, the management of the firm will carefully weigh up risk. Some objectives will obviously carry more risks than others.

Devise a marketing plan

Now, the firm is looking at its objectives and asking the question, 'How to get there?' It is important that the plan adopted will achieve the objectives set. It will be a mixture of elements from the marketing mix and it is important that the elements do not clash. Too often, firms may decide to concentrate upon promotion, without considering how they will deal with the extra distribution pressures that may arise. A good example was the problems with McDonalds' 'Two for One' offer. In the same way, they may attempt to lower the price of a product, whilst attempting to raise its perceived consumer value.

Monitor results and adjust the plan

Once the plan has been running for an agreed time, the attainment of the required objectives should be constantly measured to ensure that the plan is operating effectively. If this is not the case, then the plan or the way of working should be adjusted to attempt to achieve the agreed objectives. In too many cases, plans are decided upon, implemented and then left to run with little analysis of their success until it is too late.

Over-to-you

Short-answer questions

1 State and explain the four variables that are usually referred to as the marketing mix.
2 Why is packaging so important in modern marketing?
3 Explain why delivering a newspaper is a product.
4 State three requirements of a 'good product'.
5 Choose any product and decide whether it is a good product.

6 Draw and label a 'product life cycle'. Explain its shape.

7 What is the usefulness of a product life cycle?

8 Explain what an extension strategy is.

9 What is a product portfolio and why is it of importance?

10 Explain how you would use the product positioning map on page 115.

Discover and learn

1 Visit the furniture shops in your town. What can you learn about the pricing strategy that each has adopted? Explain the reasons for the differences you observe.

2 Work in groups. Select a product advertisement on TV. What is the message the advert conveys? How would you judge a good advert? On the basis of your criteria, is the advert you selected a good one? Justify your answer.

3 Work in groups. Visit any supermarket or small grocery shop and each choose three products.

(a) How does the packaging of each product assist the shop?

(b) How does it attract the potential buyer?

(c) What information does it give?

(d) Discuss the quality of the total packaging effect of each of the products and evaluate the findings of the whole group.

Case study – Tubular Chairs Ltd

Using the information from the case study at the end of Section 7 (pp. 102), answer the following questions:

1 Devise an appropriate promotional strategy for Tubular Chairs Ltd.

2 Identify and explain appropriate marketing objectives for Tubular Chairs Ltd.

3 Devise a marketing strategy for Tubular Chairs Ltd.

Summary

In this section we have recognised that:

- Market planning is important.

- Most firms, whether they know it or not, employ a marketing mix.

- Products need to be developed and firms need to have a sensible portfolio of products, which are at varying stages of the product life cycle.

- Positioning of the products of a firm, and the firm itself, in the market is important.

- Firms should adopt a sensible pricing policy that supports their objectives.

- A knowledge of price elasticity of demand is especially helpful.

- Firms should adopt a mixture of promotional methods, within the budget available.

- Distribution needs to be efficient to ensure that products are available to consumers when the consumers require them.

- All firms should have a unique marketing strategy, which reflects the objectives of the firm.

Key words

Definitions of Key words can be found in the Glossary on page 236.

advertising	price elasticity of demand
competition-based pricing	(PED)
cost-based pricing	pricing
demand-based pricing	product development
distribution channels	product life cycle
market positioning	product positioning
marketing mix	promotional strategies
personal selling	sales promotion
portfolio models	

11 Using accounting and financial information

On completion of this section you should be able to:

➤ understand why accounting records are kept, which groups use them and why

➤ critically appraise the usefulness of these accounts from the point of the stakeholders

➤ understand and apply the double-entry principle of accounting to simple examples

➤ identify the different costs incurred by business activity and analyse situations in which costs are used by managers

➤ appreciate why overhead costs are sometimes apportioned and the limitations associated with this process

➤ understand the nature and purpose of contribution costing and comment critically on situations in which it might be used

Why keep accounting records?

Most people know that accounts are 'monetary records' of transactions. You probably keep simple records of your own income and expenditures – these would be basic accounts. Why do you do this? Probably because you want to know whether you are spending more than you are earning or to find out if you can afford to book that holiday you promised yourself once the 'AS' levels are over!

All businesses have to keep detailed records of purchases, sales and other transactions. Why is this? The easiest way to answer this question is to ask another one – what would happen if businesses did *not* keep accounting records? Table 11.1 lists some problems that would immediately arise and the groups who would be most affected.

None of these questions could be answered without detailed and up-to-date **accounts** being kept. We can

therefore say that accounts are financial records of business transactions, which are needed to provide essential information to groups both within and outside the organisation.

Internal and external users of accounting information

It is usual to divide the users of accounting information into internal and external users. The managers of a business are termed internal users and they will have access to much more detailed and up-to-date data than other groups. External users include the government, employees and shareholders and other stakeholders of the business. The following list gives details of all users of accounts and the reasons why they need accounting data:

Problem	Groups affected
How much did we buy from our suppliers and have they been paid yet?	Managers and suppliers (creditors)
How much profit did the business make last year?	Managers, shareholders and the tax authorities
Is the business able to repay the loan to the bank?	Managers and the bank
Did we pay wages to the workers last week?	Managers and workers

Table 11.1 Accounts and the interests of stakeholders

Business managers

- ◆ to measure the performance of the business;
- ◆ to help them take decisions, such as new investments, closing branches and launching new products;
- ◆ to control the operation of each department and division of the business;
- ◆ to set targets or budgets for the future and compare these with actual performance.

Banks

- ◆ to decide whether to lend money to the business;
- ◆ to decide whether to allow an increase in overdraft facilities;
- ◆ to decide whether to continue an overdraft facility or a loan.

Creditors, e.g. suppliers

- ◆ to see if the business is secure and liquid enough to pay off its debts;
- ◆ to decide whether the business is a good credit risk;
- ◆ to decide whether to press for payment.

Customers

- ◆ to decide whether the business is secure;
- ◆ to determine whether they will be assured of future supplies of the goods they are purchasing;
- ◆ to decide whether there will be security of spare parts and service facilities.

Government and tax authorities

- ◆ to calculate how much tax is due from the business;
- ◆ to determine whether the business is likely to expand and create more jobs;
- ◆ to decide whether the business is in danger of closing down, creating economic problems;
- ◆ to confirm that the business is staying within the law in all respects.

Investors, e.g. shareholders in the company

- ◆ to assess the value of the business and their investment in it;
- ◆ to decide whether the business is becoming more or less profitable;
- ◆ to determine what share of the profits investors are receiving;

- ◆ to decide whether the business has potential for growth;
- ◆ if they are potential investors, to compare these details with other businesses before making a decision to buy shares in a company;
- ◆ if they are actual investors, to decide whether to consider selling all or part of their holding.

Workforce

- ◆ to decide whether the business is secure enough to pay wages and salaries;
- ◆ to determine whether the business is likely to expand or be reduced in size;
- ◆ to determine whether jobs are secure;
- ◆ to find out whether, if profits are rising, a wage increase can be afforded;
- ◆ to find out how the average wage in the business compares with the salaries of directors.

Local community

- ◆ to see if the business is profitable and likely to expand;
- ◆ to determine whether the business is making losses and whether this could lead to closure;
- ◆ to decide whether there is a need to get involved and, if so, how.

Limitations of published accounts

All stakeholders in a business have a use for the published accounts of the business, but how effective are these in giving the stakeholders the information they require? It must be remembered that companies will only release the absolute minimum of accounting information. The directors do not wish sensitive data to fall into the hands of competitors or even pressure groups that could take action against their interests. The rules governing the disclosure of company accounting information are laid out in the Company Acts. Obtaining a copy of the published accounts of a plc will allow you to see what is required by law – and, just as importantly, what is not.

Issues that do not have to be publicised in a company Annual Report and Accounts include:

- ◆ details of the sales and profitability of each product or service provided;
- ◆ the research and development plans of the business;

- the precise expansion or rationalisation plans of the business;
- the performance of each department or division;
- evidence of the company's impact on the environment;
- future budgets or financial plans.

The data given are all 'past' data concerning the last financial year and this information could be several months old by the time it is published. Stakeholders are often concerned about the accuracy of the published accounts. No company can publish accounts that it knows to be deliberately and illegally misleading – these matters are checked by an independent firm of accountants known as auditors. However, accounting is not necessarily an exact 'science' and there are many areas of compiling accounts where 'judgement' is necessary. These judgements can often lead to a difference of opinion between accountants, e.g. over the precise value of unsold goods or the value of other assets, particularly 'intangible ones' (see Section 13). Where companies attempt to put a favourable gloss on their accounts, this is sometimes known as window dressing or creative accounting, because judgements are made that cast the accounts in a more favourable light. For these reasons, published accounts are a useful 'starting point' for stakeholders wishing to investigate the activities of a business, but they are by no means going to provide all of the answers.

Recording business transactions

Every time a business engages in a transaction, e.g. buying materials or selling goods to a customer, the accounting records of the business must include it. In all but the very smallest business, computer programmes specially designed for keeping accounts would be used for this task. The job would be undertaken by the business's book-keeper.

How are business transactions actually recorded?

Suppose a single purchase is made by a customer in a shop. Table 11.2 shows the details of the transaction and the records that are kept.

The double-entry principle

Can you imagine the confusion amongst the users of accounts – including 'AS/A' level students! – if every business used different methods and principles in the

Transaction:	Purchase of 1kg of sugar
Effect:	Cash receipts increased by 59p (recorded on till roll)
	Stock of sugar reduced by 1 kg (recorded by computer program)
Documents:	Customer will have a till receipt
	Owner will have sale recorded on till roll
Ledger entries:	(These may be by hand in books of account or on a computer): Sales ledger 59p
	Cash book 59p
Trial balance:	All sales collated and ledger balances totalled
	All cash receipts totalled and cash book balanced
	All other account balances totalled
	Trial balance checks the accuracy of all entries
Final accounts:	From Trial balance the final accounts for a trading period are produced

Table 11.2 Recording a transaction

recording of transactions and in the compiling of final accounts? It would, for instance, be impossible to make comparisons between business accounts if every accountant had used his or her 'own' methods and techniques. The accounting profession agrees, therefore, to keep to certain very important accounting concepts. Most of them do not concern us until later in the course, but one concept is central to most accounting and you have seen it being used in the example above. This is the principle of **double entry**. It is simple to state since there is a 'dual aspect' to every business transaction and both sides of each transaction should be recorded if the accounts are to balance. The customer who bought the bag of sugar above caused two changes in the business:

- reduction of the shop's stock of sugar;
- increase in the owner's till receipts.

Every transaction has this double effect, as shown in Table 11.3. In both cases there are two sides to the transaction. The double-entry principle requires that both sides should be recorded and, when this is done, the accounts will be accurate and will balance.

Transaction	Dual aspect of the transaction
Sale of goods for cash	Goods have left the business Cash has been received by the business
Purchase of goods by cheque	Goods received by the business Business bank balance reduced

Table 11.3 The dual aspects of transactions

Activity

Identify the dual aspect of each of these transactions writing them out in the same way as in Table 11.3:

- payment of wages in cash;
- purchase of machinery by cheque;
- purchase by a customer of a new car;
- payment by the business of its electricity bill.

Management and financial accounting

There are several different branches of accounting in the UK. Two of the most important types of accountants are financial and management accountants. In general terms, the work of **financial accountants** is to prepare the published accounts of a business. The work of **management accountants** is to prepare detailed and frequent information for internal use by the managers of the business who need financial data to control the firm and take decisions for future success. The work of these two types of accountant is summarised in Table 11.4.

What are the costs of production?

Much of the information collected and used by accountants is concerned with the costs of production. The financial costs incurred in making a product or providing a service can be identified and classified in several ways. The most important categories are:

- direct costs;
- indirect costs.

Direct costs

These costs can be clearly identified with each unit of production and they vary with the level of output. Examples are:

- One of the direct costs of a hamburger in a fast-food restaurant is the cost of the meat.
- One of the direct costs for a garage in servicing a car is the labour cost of the mechanic.
- One of the direct costs in teaching is the salary of the teacher.

The two most common direct costs are labour and materials.

Financial accounting	Management accounting
Collection of data on daily transactions Preparation of the published report and accounts of a business – balance sheet, profit and loss account and cash statement	Preparation of information for managers on any financial aspect of a business, its departments and products
Information is used by external groups	Information is only made available to managers of the business – internal users
Accounts usually prepared once or twice a year	Accounting reports and data prepared as and when required by managers and owners
Accountants are bound by the rules and concepts of the accounting profession. Company Accounts must observe the requirements of the Company Acts	No set rules – accountants will produce information in the form requested
Covers past periods of time	Can cover past time periods, but can also be concerned with the present or on projections into the future

Table 11.4 The work of financial and management accountants

Identify one direct cost from each of these business activities:

- a carpenter making a wardrobe;
- an insurance company issuing a new motor insurance policy;
- a brewery delivering beer to a hotel;
- a bank agreeing an overdraft.

Why do you think it is important to identify direct costs?

Indirect costs

These costs cannot be identified with a unit of production because they are usually associated with performing a range of tasks or producing a range of products. Indirect costs are often referred to as overheads. Examples are:

- One indirect cost of a farm is the purchase of a tractor.
- One indirect cost of a supermarket is its promotional expenditure.
- One indirect cost of running a garage is the office.
- One indirect cost of running a school is cleaning it.

How do costs relate to the level of output?

It is important for management to understand that not all costs will vary directly in line with production increases or decreases. In the short run, i.e the period in which no changes to capacity can be made, costs may be classified as being:

Fixed costs These remain fixed regardless of the level of output, e.g. rent of premises.

Variable costs These vary as output changes, e.g. direct cost of materials.

Semi-variable costs These include both a fixed and a variable element, e.g. electricity standing charge plus cost per unit used, salesperson's fixed basic wage plus a commission that varies with sales.

Problems in classifying costs

Did you find it easy to classify all of those costs? In practice, it may not be very easy or even worthwhile to classify every cost into the categories explained above.

1 Are labour costs necessarily variable, direct costs? Certainly not, because when labour is unoccupied because of lack of orders, most businesses will continue to employ and pay workers in the short run. Wages then become an overhead cost, which cannot be directly identified to any particular output. Similarly a television presenter may be employed on a fixed-contract salary, which will not be related to the amount of work done. In addition, the salaries of administration, selling and other staff are always considered to be an indirect cost, probably fixed in the short run, because these costs cannot be identified with any one of the firm's products or services.

2 Telephone charges in a busy factory could be directly allocated to each range of products made as long as an accurate and reliable record was kept of the purpose of each call. In practice, this may not be worth while and telephone charges would normally be considered as an indirect overhead expense.

Identify one indirect cost for each of these businesses:

- a building firm;
- a High Street bank;
- a TV repairer;
- a power station.

Explain why the cost is indirect in each case.

The CEGB's 2,000 MW oil-fired Pembroke power station in South Wales. The station has been built largely on reclaimed land in Pennar Gut. The main station building consists of boiler house, de-aerator bay, turbine hall and electrical annexe. There is one 700ft multi-flue chimney, a 400 kV indoor substation and a gas turbine building which has a 360ft chimney. Started in 1964 the station was officially opened on 1 June 1973.
Source: Electricity Association

Activity

The management of a small manufacturing firm is attempting to classify the costs of the business to help in future decision-making. You have been asked to assist in this exercise. Classify these costs as shown in the following table. Explain why you have classified these costs in the way you have.

Cost	Direct or indirect	Fixed, variable or semi-variable
Rent		
Management salaries		
Electricity		
Piece-rate labour		
Depreciation of equipment		
Hire of company car		
Materials used in production		
Maintenance cost of machinery		

Introduction to costing methods

Managers need to know, as accurately as possible, the cost of each product or service produced by the firm. One reason for this is the need to make a pricing decision. Go back to Section 10 and re-read the section on pricing. In fact, buyers of many products will want an estimate or a quotation before they agree to purchase; managers may also need to decide whether production should be stopped, stepped up or switched to new methods or new materials. All of these things would be foolish to think about unless accurate costings were made first. Managers also need to compare actual costs with original targets or budgets and to compare the current period with past time periods. Therefore accurate product cost information is vital and the different approaches to calculating the cost of a product or service will now be considered.

In calculating the cost of a product, both direct labour and direct materials should be easy to identify and allocate or charge to each product. For instance, the materials used in making Product X are allocated directly to the cost of that product. These are not the only costs involved, of course. Overheads, or indirect costs, cannot be allocated directly to particular units of production but must be 'shared' between all of the items produced by a business. There is more than one way of 'sharing' or apportioning these costs and therefore there may be more than one 'answer' to the question: 'How much does a product cost to produce?'

Costing methods: important concepts

Before studying the alternative costing methods, various important concepts need to be understood.

Cost centres   A cost centre is an area of responsibility, such as a department, to which costs can be charged. Examples of cost centres are:
- in a manufacturing business: products, departments, factories, particular processes or stages in the production, such as assembly, for example;
- in a hotel: the restaurant, reception, bar, room letting, and conference section, for example.

Different businesses will use different cost centres, which are appropriate to their own needs.

Profit centres   A profit centre is a section of a business in which both costs and revenues can be identified. Examples of profit centres are:
- each branch of a chain of shops;
- each department of a department store;
- in a multi-product firm, each product line.

Why do businesses use cost and profit centres?   If an organisation is divided into these centres, certain benefits are likely to be gained:
- Managers will have targets to work towards.
- These targets can help to motivate and control a business division.
- The individual performances of divisions and their managers can be assessed and compared.
- Work can be monitored and decisions made about the future.

Warehouse at Cambridge University Press
Source: Cambridge University Press.

Overheads They are usually classified into four main groups:

Production overheads These include factory rent and rates, depreciation of equipment and power.

Selling and distribution overheads These include warehouse, packing and distribution costs and salaries of sales staff.

Administration overheads These include office rent and rates, clerical and executive salaries.

Finance overheads These include the interest on loans.

Unit cost This is the average cost of producing each unit of output:

Unit cost = Total cost divided by the number of units produced.

A firm produces 20,000 desks at a total cost of £1,000,000. Unit cost is 1,000,000 divided by 20,000 = £50. Clearly, unit cost is an essential step towards pricing the desks.

Allocating costs

| Activity |

Case study – Heath Electronics Ltd

The firm produces two product ranges, a pump for central heating systems and an extractor fan. Both products pass through three process cost centres during their manufacture, although different equipment is used for each product.

The direct labour and material costs have been identified and allocated to the two products as follows:

	Pump (£'000)	Fan (£'000)
Machining department:		
Direct materials	100	150
Direct labour	40	10
Assembly department:		
Direct labour	80	40
Testing department:		
Direct labour	30	20
Total direct cost	250	220

The total overheads of the business in 1998 were:

	£'000
Rent and rates	60
Power	20
Administration	80
Depreciation	40
Total overheads	200

The management accountant has been asked for the unit cost of both products. In 1999, 50,000 pumps and 40,000 fans were produced. The accountant first uses absorption costing to arrive at a result for unit cost:

◆ Calculate specific direct labour costs for each of the pump and the fan.

◆ Calculate the total direct labour cost for both products.

◆ Express (a) the direct labour cost of the pump and (b) the direct labour cost of the fan as a percentage of the total direct labour cost.

◆ Divide the total fixed costs between the pump and the fan in proportion to the use of direct labour in producing each product.

Activity

Identify four possible cost centres within your own school or college. Discuss with the managers or heads of these cost centres the benefits and drawbacks of using this form of organisation. Check with your Bursar/College accountant the accuracy of your answer.

Full costing technique

Using this method accountants take the total overheads incurred by the organisation (£200,000) and share them on the basis of one simple rule. For example, total overheads could be divided between products and cost centres on the basis of the proportion of total direct labour costs each account for. In the case of Heath Electronics Ltd total direct labour amounts to £220,000. The pump accounts for £150,000 of this total and the fan for £70,000. They will each have to absorb the same proportion of overheads.

The full costing statement now looks like this:

	Pump (£)	Fan (£)
Direct materials	100,000	150,000
Total direct labour	150,000	70,000
Apportioned overheads	136,363	63,637
Total cost	386,363	283,637

Activities

1 Calculate the unit cost of both the pump and the fan using the full costing results.
2 Give reasons why you would or would not be satisfied with these results for decision-making, e.g. establishing market prices for the two products.
3 Draw up a new full costing statement, basing your division of the overheads on total direct costs for each of the products.
4 Recalculate the unit cost for each product on the assumption that the firm actually produces 60,000 pumps and 30,000 fans.

Full costing – an evaluation

◆ Full costing is relatively easy to calculate and understand.

◆ Full costing is particularly relevant for single-product businesses.
◆ All costs are allocated (compare with contribution costing).
◆ Full costing is a good basis for pricing decisions.

But:

◆ There is no attempt to allocate each overhead cost to cost centres on the basis of actual expenditure incurred.
◆ Arbitrary methods can lead to inconsistencies between departments and products.
◆ It is sometimes dangerous to use this cost method for making decisions because the cost figures arrived at can be misleading.
◆ If full costing is used, it is essential to allocate on the same basis over time; otherwise sensible year-on-year comparisons cannot be made.
◆ The average full cost will only be accurate if the actual level of output is equal to that used in the calculation.

Marginal costing or contribution costing approach

This approach to costing solves the problem of the appropriate sharing out of overhead costs in a different way – it does not apportion them at all! Instead, the method concentrates on two very important accounting concepts.

◆ Marginal cost is the cost of producing an extra unit. This extra cost will clearly be a direct cost. For example, if the total cost of producing 100 units is £400,000 and the total cost of producing 101 units is £400,050, the marginal cost is £50.
◆ The contribution of a product is the revenue gained from selling a product less its marginal (direct) costs. This is not the same as profit, which can only be calculated after overheads have also been deducted. For example, if that 101st unit with a marginal cost of £50 is sold for £70, it has made a contribution towards fixed costs of £20. The unit contribution is found as the difference between the sale price (£70) and the marginal cost (£50), i.e. £20.

Case study – Marginal costing/contribution statement for Oxford Printers Ltd

	Novel	Textbook
	£	£
Sales revenue	50,000	100,000
Direct materials	15,000	35,000
Direct labour	20,000	50,000
Other directly apportioned costs	10,000	5,000
Total marginal cost	45,000	90,000
Contribution	5,000	10,000

As can be seen, this statement avoids apportioning overhead costs between these two products. Overheads cannot be ignored altogether, however. They are needed to calculate the profit or loss of the business.

Total contribution for Oxford Printers Ltd = £15,000

If total overheads amounted to £12,000 then:

Profit = Contribution less overheads.

Therefore the business has made a profit of £3,000.

This link between contribution overheads and profit is a crucial one and you can see the role of contribution costing in pricing decisions if you read the pricing section in Section 7.

Activity

An electrical assembly firm produces three products. The following data (in £) is available:

Products	X	Y	Z
Unit direct costs:			
Labour	5	7	9
Materials	4	12	10
Selling price	20	30	21

Total overhead costs are £40,000

(a) Calculate the unit contribution of each product.

(b) If sales of each product are 1,000, calculate the total contribution of each product.

(c) Calculate the profit or loss made by the firm at the current output level.

Contribution costing and decision-making

Contribution costing has very important advantages over full costing when management plans to take important decisions based on cost data.

Should a firm stop making a product?

If a business makes more than one product or provides more than one service, marginal costing shows managers which product or service is making the greatest or least contribution to overheads and profit. If full costing were used instead, a manager could decide to stop producing a good that seemed to be making a loss, even though it might still be making a positive contribution. In cases such as this, ending the production of a good making a positive contribution will reduce the overall profits of the business. The following case study illustrates this point.

Should a business accept a contract or a purchase offer at below full cost?

If a firm has spare capacity or if it is trying to enter a new market segment, marginal costing assists managers in deciding whether to accept an order at below the full cost of the product or service. Hotels often offer very low rates to customers in off-peak seasons, arguing that it is better to earn a contribution from additional guests than to leave rooms empty.

If contracts are accepted or customers gained by using prices below full cost, this can, in certain circumstances, lead to an increase in the total profits of the business. There are dangers in this policy, however:

◆ Existing customers may learn of the lower prices being offered and demand similar treatment. If all goods or services being sold by a business are sold at just above marginal cost, then this could make earning a profit very unlikely.

◆ When high prices are a key feature in establishing the exclusivity of a brand, then to offer some customers lower prices could destroy a hard won image.

◆ Where there is no excess capacity, sales at contribution cost may be losing sales based on the full cost.

◆ In some circumstances lower priced goods or services may leak into the higher priced market.

In fact many businesses do use contribution-cost selling, but build in ways of ensuring that there is no leak into the higher priced market. For example, railway companies sell Saver and Supersaver tickets, but make the offers exclusive by banning their use for certain days, times or journeys. Gas and electricity companies use time bands for their cheaper priced use of energy. The following case study illustrates this principle of using marginal cost pricing in accepting new business.

Activity

Read the case study below and then tackle the exercises that follow.

Case study – Onyx Garages

The Managing Director of Onyx Garages Ltd was concerned about the profitability of the business. She had asked for cost details of the three divisions of the business – repairs, petrol sales and spare parts – together with a breakdown of sales revenue. Unaware of the differences between costing approaches, she had asked for overheads to be apportioned on full-cost principles according to labour cost. The following data had been provided:

Spanner	1998 (£000s)		
	Repairs	Petrol	Parts
Sales revenue (A)	27,000	300,000	68,000
Direct labour cost	15,000	25,000	10,000
Direct materials	5,000	180,000	35,000
Other directly			
apportioned costs	4,000	10,000	5,000
Apportioned overheads			
(total £60,000)	18,000	30,000	12,000
Total cost (B)	42,000	245,000	62,000
Profit/(Loss) (A – B)	(15,000)	55,000	6,000

Overall profit made by the business in 1999
= 55,000 + 6000 – 15,000 = £46,000.

When the Managing Director saw these details, she is quoted as saying: 'If we close down our repair division, then total annual profits will rise – they would have been £15,000 higher last year if we had shut down repairs in 1999.'

(a) As a trainee accountant working with this company you have been asked for your opinion on the figures above. Use the marginal costing method and calculate a new costing statement.

(b) Do you agree with the MD that the repairs division should be closed in order to increase overall garage profits? Justify your answer with both quantitative and qualitative reasons.

Activity

Read the case study below and then answer the questions that follow.

Case study – Bureau Office Supplies Ltd

The Marketing Director of Bureau Office Supplies Ltd was determined to gain a large order for computer desks from a major local authority. There was spare capacity on the production line as a recent contract had been cancelled at short notice. The buyer for the local authority wanted to purchase 1,000 desks at a price of £70 each. Bureau's Marketing Director knew this was a price lower than that offered to most customers. The order was being discussed at a Board meeting and the Production Manager presented the following cost data:

Computer desks full unit cost statement

Direct labour	£25
Direct materials	£30
Apportioned overheads	£30
Full unit cost	£85

The Production Manager was amazed at the willingness of the marketing department to sell the desks for £70 each. 'How can you possibly justify selling these desks at a total loss of £15,000'?', he asked.

Who has the better case? Is the Marketing Director justified in his attempt to capture this order? Is the Production Manager right to be concerned at the apparent loss the order will make?

The appropriate answer depends on the following factors:

◆ Does the order make a contribution to overheads by the price exceeding direct costs?

◆ Is there spare capacity?

◆ Can the order be accepted without further overhead expenditure?

◆ Are other orders likely?

◆ Is there another customer who is prepared to pay a higher price for these goods?

◆ Will the price of the order become known to other customers?

Activities

1 Use the marginal costing approach to reach your own conclusion on the wisdom of accepting the order discussed in the case study.

2 Prepare a brief report, containing your marginal costing statement, to the Board, together with a recommendation on whether to accept the order or not. Consider both quantitative and qualitative factors in coming to your recommendation.

Contribution costing – a summary

- ◆ Overhead costs are not allocated to cost centres, so contribution costing avoids inaccuracies and arbitrary allocations.
- ◆ Decisions about a product or department are made on the basis of contribution to overheads.
- ◆ Excess capacity is more likely to be effectively used.

But:

- ◆ By ignoring overhead costs until the final calculation of the businesses profit or loss, contribution costing does not consider that some products and departments may actually incur much higher fixed costs than others.
- ◆ Emphasises contribution in decision-making. It may lead managers to choose to maintain the production of goods just because of a positive contribution.
- ◆ As in all areas of decision making, qualitative factors may be important too, e.g. the image a product gives the business. In addition, products with a low contribution may be part of a range of goods produced by the firm and to cease producing one would reduce the appeal of the whole range.

Evaluation of the costing approaches
Full costing

Full costing can be useful for single-product firms and as a quick guideline to the costs of products. However, it does have serious flaws for multi-product businesses because the approach does not apportion overheads on a real basis. The final costing figure may, in fact, be inaccurate or misleading. Thus, full costing data could be used to make comparisons of costs calculated on the same basis over time but it should not be widely used for decision-making.

Marginal or contribution costing

Marginal or contribution costing is now the most widely used method for decision-making, because it accepts that fixed overhead costs must be paid during a particular time period, regardless of the level of production. This should help management take appropriate decisions when faced with the option, for example, of accepting a new contract or scrapping a product altogether. Marginal costing does have one potential drawback, however. If overheads are set aside for costing purposes, there is a danger that they could be overlooked altogether. This could mean that contribution is confused with profit and pricing decisions for products could ignore the fixed-cost element. Eventually overheads have to be paid for and this important fact must not be forgotten when applying the marginal costing approach.

Break-even analysis

Break-even analysis can be undertaken in two ways:

- ◆ the graphical method;
- ◆ the equation method.

The graphical method – the break-even chart The break-even chart requires a graph with the axes shown in Figure 11.1.

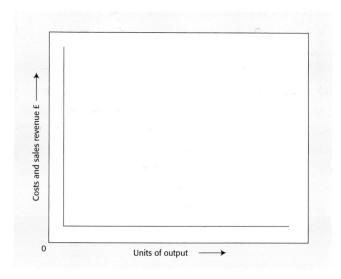

Figure 11.1 The axes for a break-even chart

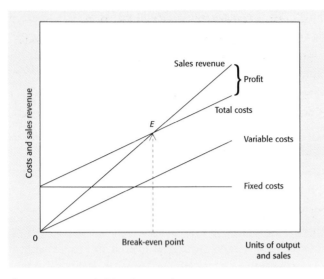

Figure 11.2 A typical break-even chart

The chart itself is usually drawn showing three pieces of information:

- fixed costs, which, in the short term, will not vary with the level of output and which must be paid whether the firm produces anything or not;
- total costs, which are the addition of fixed and variable costs; we will assume, initially at least, that variable costs vary in direct proportion to output;
- sales revenue obtained by multiplying selling price by output level.

Figure 11.2 shows a typical break-even chart. Note carefully the following points:

- The fixed-cost line is horizontal.
- The total-cost line begins at the level of fixed costs, the difference between total and fixed costs being accounted for by variable costs.
- Sales revenue starts at the origin; no sales = no revenue (0).
- The variable cost line is drawn to aid your understanding of how the chart is constructed. It is not necessary to the chart and is often omitted.

The point at which the total cost and sales revenue lines cross (E) is the break-even point. At production levels below the break-even point, the business is making a loss; at production levels above the break-even point the business is making a profit.

Margin of safety   The margin of safety is defined as the amount by which sales exceed the break-even point. This is a useful indication of how much sales could fall without the firm falling into loss. For example, if break-

even output is 400 units and current production is 600 units, the margin of safety is 200 units.

Activity

The following data relates to a single-product business.

Direct labour per unit	£12
Direct materials per unit	£18
Variable overheads per unit	£5
Fixed costs	£200,000
Selling price	£45

Maximum capacity of the factory is 30,000 units.

(a) Draw a break-even chart using this data.
(b) Show the break-even point and identify the break-even level of output.
(c) Identify from the graph the profit expected at maximum capacity.

This can be expressed as a percentage of the break-even point, for example:

Production over break-even point = 200 = 33.33%.

If a firm is producing below the point E it is in danger. This is sometimes expressed as a negative margin of safety. Hence if break-even output is 400 and the firm is producing at 350 units it has a margin of safety of −50. The minus sign simply tells us that the production level is below break-even.

The break-even equation   A formula can be used to calculate break even:

$$\frac{\text{Fixed Assets}}{\text{Contribution per Unit}}$$

If fixed costs are £200,000 and the contribution per unit of output is £50 then the break-even level of production is

$$\frac{200,000}{50} = 4,000 \text{ units}$$

This is an exact answer and therefore likely to be more accurate than many chart readings. The same method can be used if a manager wants to determine a target profit level and establish the level of output required to achieve it: Suppose the target profit is £25,000. This is treated as if it were an extra fixed cost and the calculation is

$$\frac{200,000 + £25,000}{50} \quad \frac{225,000}{50} = 4,500 \text{ units produced.}$$

Activity

Read the case study below and then tackle the exercises that follow.

Case study – Windcheater Roofracks

The sole owner of Windcheater Roofracks needs to expand output as a result of increasing demand from motor accessory shops. Current output capacity has been reached at 5,000 units per year. Each rack is sold to the retailers for £40. Production costs are:

Direct labour	£10
Direct materials	£12
Fixed costs	£54,000

The owner is considering two options for expansion:

Option 1 Extend the existing premises but keep the same method of production. This would increase fixed costs by £27,000 per year, but direct costs would remain unchanged. Capacity would be doubled.

Option 2 Purchase new machinery, which will speed up the production process and cut down on wasted materials. Fixed costs would rise by £6,000 per year, but direct costs would be reduced by £2 per unit. Output capacity would increase by 50%.

(a) Drawing the two break-even charts for these options would assist the owner in making this decision, but other issues may have to be considered as well.

- ◆ Construct break-even charts for these two options. Identify the break-even point for each.
- ◆ What is the maximum profit obtainable in each case?
- ◆ If demand next year is expected to be 7,000 units, what would be the margin of safety in both cases?
- ◆ Which option would you advise the owner to choose? Give both numerical and non-numerical reasons for your decision.

(b) The owner of Winchester Roofracks discovers that the fixed costs for option 1 will be 20% greater. Use a break-even chart to determine the new break-even point and then the equation to verify it.

(c) In option 2 the increase in fixed costs is £8,000 and the direct costs fall by £2.50 per unit:

- ◆ explain why the direct costs might fall;
- ◆ determine the new break-even point.

Break-even analysis – further uses

In addition to obtaining break-even points and margins of safety, break-even charts can also be used to demonstrate the impact of different options on the operations of a business. In this way they can assist in the decision making process. However, they must be used with some caution as indicated in the evaluation section below.

Evaluation of break-even analysis

Benefits of break-even analysis are:

- ◆ Charts are relatively easy to construct and interpret.
- ◆ It provides useful guidelines to management on break-even points, safety margins and profit/loss levels at different rates of output.
- ◆ Comparisons can be made between different options by constructing new charts to show changed circumstances. In the case study above, charts could be amended to show the possible impact on profit and break-even point of a change in the product's selling price.
- ◆ The equation produces a precise break-even result.

The limitations are:

- ◆ the assumption that costs and revenues are expressed in straight lines, which is a major drawback;
- ◆ the problem that not all costs can be reliably or consistently classified as fixed or variable costs;
- ◆ the assumption that everything produced will be sold;
- ◆ the assumption that fixed costs will remain fixed regardless of the level of output.

Activity

Explain why the assumptions that the lines in the break-even chart are straight are not realistic and will limit the usefulness of break-even analysis. Give examples to support your argument.

Over-to-you

Short-answer questions

1 List four likely users of the accounts of a plc such as Tesco.

2 Explain why these users would find the accounts useful.

3 Explain what the double-entry principle means.

4 Give three different numerical examples of the double-entry principle.

5 List three examples of fixed costs for a bakery.

6 Distinguish between direct and indirect costs.

7 How is the full cost of a product calculated?

8 How is the contribution of a product calculated?

9 Explain the difference between contribution and profit.

Discover and learn

Obtain a copy of a plc's Report and Published Accounts. You can try either writing to the head office or obtaining one via the company's Internet page. The *Financial Times* operates a company reports service, which enables you to obtain copies from several different companies at the same time.

1 Read both the Chairman's Report and the Chief Executive's Report.

How useful do you think these would be to:

(a) shareholders?

(b) future investors in the company?

(c) the workforce?

(d) competitors?

2 Read the Auditor's report. What is it telling you about the published accounts? Can the readers of the accounts be certain that these accounts are completely accurate and objective?

3 Work in small groups. Consider the setting up of a small business of your choice in your area. Discover or estimate the probable direct and indirect costs of:

(a) setting up the business;

(b) running it in the first year.

You may find that literature available from banks will be very helpful to you in this exercise.

4 Exchange your work with another group and comment upon the data you have been given. Try to be positive in your comments.

5 When your work is returned:

(a) discuss it with the other groups and ensure you know what they mean by their comments;

(b) make the changes they suggest or justify your decision not to make them.

6 Read the case studies and then tackle the exercises that follow.

Case study – Abbey Restaurant

Abbey Restaurant has a good local reputation for first-class meals at first-class prices. It has a loyal customer base, but the manager, Phil, is concerned about the disappointing number of new customers. Total revenue had fallen over the last few months and Phil believed that this was partly due to the closure of the head office of an insurance company. Job losses occurred at all levels of the organisation, especially amongst middle managers. Phil was considering introducing a new menu that would offer less variety and less complicated dishes. He considered that the new items on the menu would be cheaper to produce and he would not have to replace one of the skilled chefs, who had just given in his notice. Phil estimated that the number of customers could increase by 20% per night on average as he had noticed that a recently opened medium-price café–bar was full to bursting virtually every night.

Phil had shown the following financial data to the restaurant's accountant, who started to do some calculations before advising Phil on whether to adopt the new lower-priced menu:

Current situation:

Sales turnover per month	
(600 customers @ average of £20)	£12,000
Average variable cost per meal	£7
Overhead costs per month	
(including salaries of kitchen staff)	£7,000

Proposed new menu:

Average meal price	£14
Average variable cost per meal	£4
Overheads per month	
(including salaries of kitchen staff)	£6,000

(a) What are the maximum monthly profit figures for the two menu options?

(b) On the basis of your calculations and the financial data provided, would you advise Phil to adopt the new menu? Explain your answer.

(c) What other, non-financial factors should Phil consider before taking the final decision? Explain their significance to Phil's business.

Case study – Cosmic Cases

Cosmic Cases manufacture a range of suitcases. There are four sizes of case, ranging from a small vanity case to a large luggage case with wheels for mobility. The cases are sold mainly through department stores, either as a complete set or, more frequently, as individual items. The latest six-monthly costing statement (see below) had just been prepared, together with the sales figures for the same period. Jill Grealey, the managing director was concerned about the performance of the mid-sized case and wanted to discuss the data with the finance director.

Costing statement for 6 months ending 31/3/2000

	Vanity case	Small suitcase	Medium suitcase	Large suitcase
Total direct costs	£30,000	£35,000	£12,000	£20,000
Allocated overheads	£15,000	£12,500	£10,000	£10,000
Total costs	£45,000	£47,500	£22,000	£30,000
Total output	5,000	4,000	1,000	1,500

The selling prices to the department stores were:

Vanity case	£15	Small case	£18
Medium case	£20	Large case	£25

(a) Calculate the total revenue (price × quantity sold) for each size case.

(b) Calculate the total profit/loss made by each size case.

(c) Calculate the contribution made by each size case.

(d) Jill Grealey wanted to stop production of the mid-sized case. She said to the Finance Director: 'If we stop making this case, then our total profits will rise.' The finance director was convinced that this would be the wrong decision to make. As a management consultant, write a report to the managing director giving your recommendation for the action to be taken with the mid-sized case. You should justify your recommendation with both numerical and non-numerical factors.

Case study – Midtown Imperial Hotel

'We would be mad to accept this special request at £800 below our normal price and £300 below the cost of providing the conference facilities.'

The hotel manager, Rajesh, was annoyed that Sheila Burns, the Conference Manager of the Imperial Hotel, had even bothered to consult him about the enquiry from the Friends of General Hospital for the use of the conference suite for their annual general meeting involving 100 people. Sheila had been asked for a price to organise the Friends' AGM and had used the normal hotel practice of adding 50% to the total cost of the facility. This had been too much for the charity, so they had requested a reduction and had suggested a lower figure of £2,200. As the AGM was planned for the end of February, a very slack time for all hotels, Sheila had been tempted to take up the offer and had put it to Rajesh for his approval. She knew that many of the Friends were quite influential people with business interests and she believed that this could be to the hotel's long-term advantage.

The costing statement for the conference suite was as follows:

Variable cost per delegate including food, three drinks each and waiting staff	£15
Hotel overhead allocation per conference	£1,000

In addition, the Friends had requested some special audiovisual equipment, which the hotel would have to hire in for the day at a cost of £200

(a) Calculate the full cost of the conference for the Friends of the General Hospital

(b) Calculate the price that the hotel would normally charge for a conference of this size with the equipment requested.

(c) What would the contribution to the hotel's overheads and profit be if the conference suite were let out for £2,200?

(d) Advise the hotel manager on the advisability of accepting this special request for the use of the conference facilities. Include both quantitative and qualitative data in your answer.

Summary

In this section we have recognised that:

- There are two types of accounting, financial accounting and management accounting.

- There is a difference in both the nature and purpose of the two types of accounting and these can be explained in terms of the point of view of the stakeholders who are involved and in terms of the uses that are made of accounting data.

- There are various principles of accounting, chief of which is the concept of double entry.

- All businesses have to identify both cost and profit centres and to use costing approaches to allow determination of total costs, unit costs and the contribution that a product might make.

- Contribution costing and full costing may lead to different pricing decisions, which should be understood in the context of pricing decisions considered in Section 7.

- Break-even analysis is a forecasting tool for business.

- It can be used in either graphical or formula form.

- There are limitations on the use of break-even analysis.

Key words

Definitions of Key words can be found in the Glossary on page 236.

accounts
break-even analysis
contribution costing
direct costs
double entry
financial accounting
fixed costs
full costing

indirect costs
management accounting
marginal costing
overheads
published accounts
semi-variable costs
variable costs

12 Cash flow and budgets

➤ recognise the need to control the flow of money into and out of a business

➤ understand the importance of managing cash flow and explain why profit is not the same as cash

➤ construct, interpret and analyse cash-flow budgets

➤ demonstrate understanding of the problems caused by poor cash flow and of ways in which problems can be reduced or removed

➤ show understanding of the nature and importance of budgeting

➤ compare actual and budgeted performance by simple variance analysis and analyse the causes of such variances

Why cash flow is important to business activity

According to the Department of Trade and Industry, more business failures result from lack of cash than for any other reason. This is particularly true for new businesses. Why is cash – and in particular the flow of cash into and out of a business – so important and how can managers try to avoid cash problems developing? Consider these problems resulting from too little cash:

◆ Without sufficient cash flow a business will not be able to pay its many suppliers on time. These creditors may stop supplying goods or impose strict conditions, such as 'cash on delivery'. Discounts will be lost for prompt payment of bills. Other traders may be less prepared to deal with the firm except on a cash basis. In extreme cases, the creditors could take the company (or the business owners if not a company) to court.

◆ Wages and salaries may not be paid on time and this will cause poor motivation, absenteeism, higher labour turnover and industrial unrest.

◆ New capital assets cannot be afforded and this can reduce business efficiency.

◆ Tax bills may not be paid – government has little patience with such cases and, again, could take legal action.

The relationship between profit and cash

'If a business is profitable the firm is certain to have a cash surplus too.' This is one of the most common incorrect beliefs of students of Business Studies. Profit is not the same as cash. A profitable business may run out of cash – called insolvency – whilst a business recording a loss may have a cash surplus. How is this possible? There are several reasons why the profit or loss recorded by a business in one time period will not be the same as its cash balance. Here are two of the most frequently occurring:

◆ A business may be selling more of its output on credit than previously. Therefore, a profit is being made as the goods are being recorded as sold, but the cash payment from customers will be received at some time in the future. This period of credit may leave the firm dangerously short of cash or liquid funds.

◆ Capital expenditure is recorded on the profit and loss account under depreciation as an expense. However, only a proportion of the cost of additional capital spending will be recorded as depreciation each year, yet the total cash payment may occur in the first year.

Activity

Alex Tyrrell is an antique dealer. In June he bought five chairs for £50 cash. He sold them the same day for £30 each. He agreed that half of the money would be paid in cash and the customer would pay the rest in the following month.

(a) Calculate the profit made on the five chairs.

(b) How much cash did Alex gain from the purchase and sale of the chairs in June?

This simple example shows that profit does not equal cash.

Managing cash flow

Managing the flows of cash into and out of a business is one of the most important tasks of management. In order to do this effectively they will need to assess:

- the size and likely timing of cash flows into the business; this will largely depend on how long debtors take to pay their bills;
- the size and likely timing of payments out of the business; this will largely depend on the costs of the business and the period of credit offered by suppliers;
- whether there are sources of finance to cover periods when cash shortages could arise.

You will notice from the points above that time is of great significance to cash-flow management.

Activity

In which of these cases will the cash needs of a business be greatest:

- Materials bought and paid for with cash.
- Wages and materials paid for.
- Goods produced.
- Goods sold on credit.
- Cash received one month later.
- Goods bought for cash today.
- Goods sold for cash tomorrow.

Explain your answer.

Cash-flow forecasts: the benefits to business

A cash-flow forecast is an attempt by management to plan ahead, to prevent future liquidity problems. Cash-flow forecasts contain estimates of cash receipts and payments over the coming months – these are taken from the budgets of the business. Each month or quarter the anticipated 'cash in hand' or cash deficit (overdraft) is calculated. If an overdraft is predicted, then the firm's bankers must be warned and arrangements made for an appropriate overdraft facility. As a general rule, bank managers are much more prepared to arrange loan facilities for organisations that can demonstrate they have planned their financial needs and shown that they should be able to repay loans. This is particularly the case with new businesses. The preparation of a cash-flow forecast will show the bank manager that the owners of the new business are aware of the need to manage cash flow carefully. If there is no overdraft arrangement or if it is insufficient, then management will have to take rapid action to overcome a shortage of cash. There will always be periods of the year when large cash surpluses may build up, since most businesses have a seasonal element to their sales. Examples are:

- Many businesses expect a boost to sales in the period leading up to Christmas.
- A seaside guesthouse will be very much busier in the summer months. In fact it may close in winter.
- A florist expects high sales for 'Mother's Day' and for Easter.
- Farmers receive most of their income in summer and autumn.

Large cash balances have an opportunity cost in terms of lost interest and plans could be made to use these resources in a more profitable way, e.g. by purchasing short-term investments. Overdrafts have an even greater cost in terms of interest charges.

A typical cash flow forecast is shown in Table 12.1.

BEL Engineering Ltd

| Month | Cash flow forecast year (£000s) | | | | | |
	Jan.	Feb.	Mar.	Apr.	May	June
Receipts						
Cash sales	200	220	220	200	200	240
Payments from debtors	120	140	140	220	200	100
Other (e.g. loan received)					50	
Total cash receipts	320	360	360	420	450	340
Payments						
Materials	80	90	90	130	160	190
Labour	50	50	60	60	90	90
Rent	150			150		
Interest		25			25	
Advertising	10	10	10	10	60	10
Electricity	15			15		
Salaries	40	40	40	60	60	60
Purchase of fixed assets		100				280
Total cash payments	345	315	200	425	395	630
Net cash flow	(25)	45	160	(5)	55	(290)
Opening cash balance	25	0	45	205	200	255
Closing cash balance	0	45	205	200	255	(35)

Table 12.1 An example cash-flow analysis

Notes:
- The opening cash balance for each month is the closing cash balance for the previous month.
- Payments from debtors are cash received from debtors for goods previously sold on credit, probably in the previous month for most debtors.
- Net cash flow may be negative and this is indicated in brackets. You can see from the forecast that BEL were expecting a negative net cash flow and negative closing balance in June. What action can the management take to deal with this? The options are looked at after the next task.

Dealing with cash-flow problems

If the cash-flow forecast predicts negative cash flows and negative cash balances, managers have certain options they can consider to tackle this problem:

Reducing or delaying expenditure There may be ways in which the business can cut costs, such as reducing advertising spending or delaying the purchase of capital equipment. Clearly, these decisions would have a beneficial impact on short-term cash flow, but they might have negative effects on business performance in the longer term.

Activity

Read the case study below and then tackle the exercises that follow.

Case study – Tourist Trinkets Ltd

Tourist Trinkets Ltd owns a warehouse supplying souvenir retailers in town.

Forecast sales (£000s) are:

Jan.	Feb.	Mar.	Apr.	May	June
6	8	8	14	16	18

On past experience, 50% of sales will be cash sales. One month's credit is offered for credit sales. Stock is purchased in the month prior to sales. Sufficient stock is purchased to cover the following month's sales. The average mark-up on cost is 100%. Suppliers allow one month's credit on purchases.

Other expenses are:
- labour – £600 per month except May and June when it is expected to be £1,200;
- rent of £1,800 per half year payable in Jan. and July;
- electricity and other charges, £600 per quarter paid in Jan., Apr., July, and Oct.;
- advertising of £100 per month except June when it is budgeted to increase to £500;
- interest charges of £1,000 payable in May;
- management salaries of £2,000 per month.

Opening cash balance in January is £1,500.

In January the firm is expecting payment from its debtors of £1,000.

(a) Write a note to the manager of Tourist Trinkets Ltd. listing three benefits to the business from preparing a cash-flow forecast.

(b) Prepare a month-by-month cash budget for Tourist Trinkets Ltd for the first six months. Use the same format as that given above. If you are able to use a spreadsheet software package, prepare the cash-flow statement with it.

Rent or lease equipment rather than buying it outright This is very common with IT equipment, for example. Such moves reduce short-term cash outflows but will lead to regular, if smaller, payments in the future.

Delay the payment of bills – *extending the credit period* Suppliers may be unwilling to accept later payment –

especially from new businesses with an unknown credit history.

Get cash in more quickly from the sale of goods This could be done in a number of ways:

- Insisting on cash at the time of sale. This could lead to loss of business as in many industries it is usual to offer customers a period of time to pay for goods purchased.
- Reducing the debtor period. This could also lead customers to taking their custom to other businesses that offer extended credit terms.
- Selling the debts to a specialist institution, such as a debt factor. This option is covered in detail in Section 13.

- Using a bank overdraft. This is a flexible source of funds which – up to a predetermined limit – can be varied to meet the changing cash needs of a business. The interest rate tends to be high and it is possible for banks to recall overdrafts at very short notice if they are concerned about the future of a business. This action often leads to failure of the business.
- Obtain a short-term loan, which is less variable than an overdraft and often borrowed at lower interest rates. If there is likely to be a long-term need to increase the cash position of the business – such as during a period of rapid expansion – then a long-term loan would be appropriate.

Activity

Read the case study below and then tackle the exercises that follow.

Case study – setting up in business

Aled Jones was disappointed to hear the news that the Bank of England had announced an unexpected increase in interest rates. He had just submitted his business plan to the bank manager for approval for the business start-up loan and overdraft arrangement he would need to establish his proposed building business. The business was to specialise in building expensive conservatories. Aled had read that the Bank of England had taken the decision to prevent further increases in the inflation – the rate at which prices were rising. Aled's business plan had contained the following cash budget for the first six months of trading:

	March	April	May	June	July	August
Receipts						
Capital injection	5,000	0	0	0	0	0
Start-up loan	15,000	0	0	0	0	0
Cash sales	1,000	3,000	5,000	5,000	16,000	19,000
Payments from debtors	0	12,000	10,000	10,000	12,000	13,000
Total	21,000	15,000	15,000	15,000	28,000	32,000
Payments						
Capital expenditure	10,000	0	0	0	0	0
Labour	2,000	6,000	7,000	7,000	7,000	7,000
Materials	5,000	10,000	8,000	8,000	10,000	12,000
Overheads inc. interest	5,000	7,000	7,000	7,000	9,000	9,000
Total	22,000	23,000	22,000	22,000	26,000	28,000
Net cash flow	(1,000)	(8,000)	(7,000)	(7,000)	2,000	4,000
Opening cash balance	0	(1,000)	(9,000)	(16,000)	(23,000)	(21,000)
Closing cash balance	(1,000)	(9,000)	(16,000)	(23,000)	(21,000)	(17,000)

(a) Explain how the use of a spreadsheet would have assisted Aled in compiling his cash-flow forecast.

(b) Explain *two* ways in which the increase in interest rates could have an impact on the cash-flow statement.

(c) If inflation did rise, how would this be likely to affect the cash flow of the business?

(d) Discuss the usefulness to Aled of constructing the cash-flow statement as part of the business plan.

(e) Recommend to Aled ways in which he might reduce the negative cash flows of his business in the first six months.

◆ An established business could also sell some of its assets – such as buildings – to a leasing company and lease them back. This sale and leaseback option will give an injection of cash into the business, but will lead to continuing cash payments, which have to be allowed for in cash forecasts.

Evaluation of cash budgets

As with any judgement about the future, cash-flow forecasts need to be treated with caution. They have several significant advantages, as already noted above, but too much reliance must not be placed upon their accuracy. This would be particularly true for a new business, which was uncertain about future sales levels. Similarly, any business cash forecast could be made inaccurate by changes in the external economic environment, such as movements in interest rates or inflation at a faster rate than anticipated. For this reason, some businesses prepare optimistic and pessimistic cash budgets to reflect these possible changes. This is easy to do on spreadsheet applications and allows businesses to prepare for more than one future scenario.

Budgets and budgetary control: introduction

We all plan for the future to some degree. We plan for the long term – such as career choices – and we plan for the short term – such as how to spend the weekend. This should apply to business organisations too, although the plans of a business are likely to be expressed in financial terms. This process is known as budgeting and a budget is a detailed and financial plan for a future time period. Planning for the future is important for all organisations. If no plans are made, an organisation drifts without real direction and purpose. Managers will not be able to allocate the scarce resources of the business effectively without a plan to work towards. Employees working in an organisation without plans for future action are likely to feel demotivated, as they have no targets to work towards – or to be praised for achieving. If no targets are set, then an organisation cannot review its progress because it has no set objective to achieve.

Setting budgets and establishing plans for future actions would therefore appear to have six main purposes:

Planning Translates the objectives of the firm into intentions for achievement. It gives a sense of purpose to the workforce.

Effective allocation of resources
There will be priorities to discuss, since what can be done is always likely to be greater than resources will permit.

Alllocation to departments

Setting targets to be achieved
Research shows that most people work better if they have a realisable target at which to aim.

Co-ordination People will have to work effectively together if targets set are to be achieved.

Monitoring Plans cannot be left once in place. There is a need to check regularly that the objective is still within reach. All kinds of conditions may change and businesses cannot afford to assume that everything is fine.

Modifying If there is evidence to suggest that the objective cannot be reached, then either the plan or the way of working towards it must be changed.

Key features of budgeting

A budget is not simply a forecast, although much of the data on which it is based will come from forecasts, since we are looking into the future. Budgets are plans that organisations aim to fulfil. A forecast is a prediction of what could occur in the future given certain conditions. Budgets may be established for any part of an organisation as long as the outcome of its operation is quantifiable. Thus, there may be sales budgets, capital expenditure budgets, labour cost budgets and so on.

Co-ordination between departments when establishing budgets is essential. This should avoid departments making conflicting plans, e.g. the marketing department may be planning to increase sales by lowering prices, yet the production department may be planning to reduce output and lower the direct-labour cost budget. These targets will conflict and need to be reconciled.

Setting of budgets should be an exercise in participation. Decisions regarding budgets should be made with the subordinate managers, who will be involved in putting them into effect. Those who are to be held responsible for fulfilling a budget should be involved in setting it. This sense of 'ownership' not only helps to motivate the department concerned to achieve the targets but also leads to the establishment of more realistic targets.

The budget will be used to review the performance of a department and the managers of that department will be appraised on their effectiveness in reaching targets. Successful and unsuccessful managers can therefore be identified. These stages of involvement in constructing the budget, taking responsibility for its operation and being appraised in terms of success, are the human aspects of the process. They have a very important role to play in the motivation of staff.

How budgets are commonly prepared

Stage 1 The most important organisational objectives for the coming year are established – these will be based on:

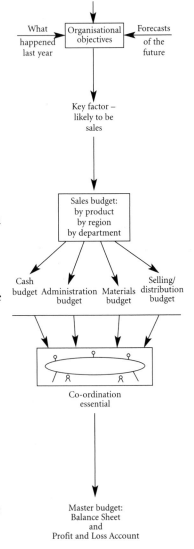

- the previous performance;
- external changes likely to affect the organisation;
- forecasts based on research.

Stage 2 The key or limiting factor that is most likely to influence the growth or success of the organisation must be identified. For most businesses this is likely to be sales. Therefore, the sales budget will be the first to be prepared. Care and accuracy are essential at this stage, because an error in the key-factor budget will

distort all other budgets as well. For example, if the sales budget proves to be inaccurate, then cash, production, labour budgets etc. will be rendered inaccurate too.

Stage 3 The sales budget is prepared.

Stage 4 The subsidiary budgets are prepared, which will now be based on the plans contained in the sales budget. These will include cash budget, administration budget, materials budget, selling and distribution budget.

Stage 5 These budgets are co-ordinated to ensure consistency. This may be undertaken by a budgetary committee with special responsibility for ensuring that budgets do not conflict with each other.

Stage 6 A master budget is prepared that contains the main details of all other budgets and concludes with a budgeted profit and loss account and balance sheet.

Stage 7 The master budget is then presented to the Board – hopefully for their approval.

Once approved, the budgets will become the operational plans of each department and cost centre within the organisation. However, the overall plan is usually too long a time period to be a stimulating target and will be broken down into short periods like a month or even a week.

Setting budgets – incremental or zero budgeting?

There are several ways in which the budget level can be set. Two of the most widely used are:

Incremental budgeting This uses last year's budget as a basis and an adjustment is made for the coming year. In many businesses that operate in highly competitive markets there may be plans to lower the cost budget for departments each year, but to raise the sales budgets. This puts increased pressure on many staff to achieve higher productivity.

Incremental budgeting does not allow for unforeseen events. Using last year's figure as a basis means that each department does not have to justify its whole budget for the coming year – only the change or 'increment'.

Zero budgeting This requires all departments and budget holders to justify their whole budget each year. This is time consuming, as a fundamental review of the work and importance of each budget-holding section is needed each year. However, it does provide added incentive for managers to defend the work of their own section. Also, changing situations can be reflected in very different budget levels each year.

Budgetary control – variance analysis

At the end of the budgeted period the actual performance of the organisation needs to be compared with the original targets and reasons for differences must be investigated. This process is known as variance analysis. A variance is the difference between budgeted and actual figures. This is an essential part of budgeting for a number of reasons:

- It measures differences from the planned performance of each department.
- It assists in analysing the causes of deviations from budget. For example, if actual profit is below budget, was this due to lower sales revenue or higher costs?
- The reasons for the deviations from the original planned levels can be used to change future budgets in order to make them more accurate. For example, if sales revenue is lower than planned as a result of market resistance to higher prices, then this knowledge could be used to help prepare future budgets.

The performance of each individual budget holding section may be appraised in an accurate and objective way.

If the variance has had the effect of increasing profit, e.g. sales revenue higher than budgeted for, then it is termed a **favourable** (or positive) **variance**. If the variance has had the effect of reducing profit, e.g. direct material costs higher than budgeted for, then it is termed an **unfavourable** or negative **variance**. These distinctions can be demonstrated by the following self-assessment task.

Activity

With the help of the tables in the case study below tackle the exercises that follow.

Case study – Oasis Cookers Ltd

Oasis Cookers Ltd – (£000s)

	Budget	Actual	Variance
Sales revenue	165,000	150,000	
less Cost of materials	80,000	70,000	
Labour cost	22,000	23,000	
Gross profit	63,000	57,000	
less Overheads	40,000	43,000	
Net profit	23,000	14,000	

(a) Calculate the variances above and indicate whether they are favourable or unfavourable variances.

(b) Suggest two possible reasons for the variance in:
- sales revenue;
- labour cost.

Department	Budget	Actual	Variance
Selling and distribution	8,000	6,000	
Administration	9,000	8,000	
Production	22,000	27,000	
Personnel	1,000	2,000	

(c) From the Oasis Cookers Ltd. overhead budget and actual results shown above, calculate the variances and indicate whether they are favourable or unfavourable.

Budgets and budgetary control – an evaluation

Setting, agreeing and controlling budgets is time consuming. Budgets can fail to reflect changing circumstances and become inflexible. Budget holders can look upon a budget as a limit up to which they can spend, whether their department needs all of the resources or not. Therefore, is the budgetary process worthwhile?

Try to think of the alternative:

◆ Without a detailed and co-ordinated set of plans for allocating money and resources of the business, who would decide 'who gets what'?

◆ Without a clear sales budget as the cornerstone of the budgetary process, how would departments know how much to produce or to spend on sales promotion or how many people to employ?

◆ Would it be possible to assess how the business had done or how well individual departments had performed without a clear series of targets with which to compare performance?

◆ Without figures to monitor progress during the budgetary period, how would it be possible to know where the business is or to suggest changes that might be made?

◆ Budgets have to be agreed and administered. This gives responsibility and a sense of direction to those delegated to work with them. These human advantages are difficult to ensure without planned money values to work with.

The arguments in favour of some form of budgetary setting and control are clear to many managers.

Over-to-you

Short-answer questions

1 Outline two reasons why businesses should prepare cash-flow forecasts.

2 Give two factors that could make a cash-flow forecast inaccurate.

3 Explain why a bank manager would be particularly concerned to see a cash-flow forecast for a new business applying for a bank loan.

4 How can sale and leaseback improve business cash flow?

5 Distinguish between a forecast and a budget.

6 What would a sales budget contain?

7 What is variance analysis?

8 List four reasons for a firm introducing a method of budgetary control.

9 What is zero budgeting?

10 What is meant by an unfavourable variance?

Discover and learn

1 Refer to the published accounts of a public limited company.

(a) Find out what the retained profits were for the last financial year (retained profits are those reinvested in the business).

(b) Find out the cash balance of the business at the end of the previous financial year and the start of the last one. By how much has the cash balance changed? Is this the same as the retained profit of the business? If not, suggest three possible reasons why the two figures are different.

2 Forecast your own cash income for the next month. Include payments from work, parents etc. Forecast your monthly cash outgoings under headings such as travel, social, clothes, etc.

(a) Are you forecasted to make a cash surplus or deficit? Record all income and expenditure over this period.

(b) Did you have a cash surplus or deficit?

(c) How different was it from your forecast?

(d) Can you identify why it was different?

3 Find out whether your school or college uses zero or incremental budgeting for departmental expenditure. Try to discover why the choice was made.

4 Read the case studies and then tackle the exercises that follow.

Case study – Gita Fashions Ltd

The bank manager had just been on the telephone to Gita. The bank was not prepared to pay a cheque she had written to her main supplier. 'Did you know that your overdraft has reached its limit of £15,000?' the bank manager had queried. 'We are only prepared to consider continuing with your overdraft arrangement if you come into the office tomorrow with a cash flow forecast for the next three months.'

Gita had never worried too much about finance as this had always been looked after by her partner. He had recently left the business, taking his share of the capital with him. Gita had used her savings to help pay him his share of the business. Now she had no idea how the business had reached such a poor cash position and she certainly could not put any more money in herself.

All that evening she looked over the accounting records of the business, including all recent sales invoices and bills for materials and other expenses. She had managed to arrive at some idea of what the business could expect over the next three months in terms of cash payments and receipts.

Sales were likely to be £12,000 for the next two months (starting in July) and 50% lower than this in the third month. Half of these sales would be for cash. Half would be on one month's credit. She had sold £8,000 on credit in June.

She estimated all overhead expenses to be £6,000 per month. Labour was likely to be £3,000 per month. Materials, paid for one month after delivery, were always one half of that month's sales. They were delivered in the same month in which the goods they were used to make were sold. Opening cash was negative – the overdraft was the opening balance for the three-monthly period.

(a) Prepare a three-month cash-flow forecast for Gita's business starting in July.
(b) Would you advise the bank manager to increase the overdraft limit?
(c) What additional information would help you to advise the bank manager?
(d) Explain to Gita how a cash-flow forecast might have helped her business avoid the problem it now faces.

Case study – Karmali Carpets plc

The Managing Director of Karmali Carpets was angry. The profits of the business had fallen for the third year running and he was determined to put all the blame on the Sales Manager, Sarah Fellows. He called her into his office to discuss the latest company results.

'The company's profits have worsened again this year and your department must take the blame – sales revenue was down from what I had expected it to be,' he grumbled. 'Why can't you manage to increase sales each year?'

Sarah expressed real surprise at this complaint. 'What do you mean sales are down? We sold more carpets this year than ever before. I know we had to increase our discounts towards the end of the year, but you are always telling us "if they come through that door, then they go home with a carpet" and we acted on that.'

'But you failed to reach your annual targets that I finalised last month.'

Sarah defended herself by saying 'Those targets were received after most of the year had gone and I never thought they were realistic anyway. I wanted to increase advertising, but you rejected my new campaign because you used the money to buy new computers for the accounts office. How can I be expected to reach your targets, when I don't believe in them myself?'

(a) From the text above, which departments in this business would be likely to benefit from a correctly managed system of budgetary control?
(b) Comment critically on the Managing Director's approach to budgeting.
(c) Write a report to the MD outlining the likely advantages to his organisation from a budgetary control system as outlined in this section. Consider the way in which you would advise him to both set and use the budgets.

Summary

In this section we have recognised that:

- Business activity needs to be planned and translated into working targets.

- Business activity needs to be controlled in ways that will ensure that actual results are likely to be in accordance with the plan.

- Business activity needs to be reviewed to check whether the actual results were in accordance with the budget. If variances are found these need to be analysed and explanations produced for them.

- Business activity needs to be modified. The effort should be to bring the activity back towards the budgeted outcome. However, in some circumstances the budget may proved to have been unrealistic and it is the budgeted outcome that will need to be changed.

- There are various techniques that are appropriate for carrying out these operations.

Key words

Definitions of Key words can be found in the Glossary on page 236.

cash-flow forecasts   unfavourable variance
favourable variance   variance analysis
incremental budgeting   zero budgeting

13 The final accounts of a business

On completion of this section you should be able to:

➤ understand what the final accounts of a business contain

➤ explain and analyse the significance of the three main final accounts – balance sheet, profit and loss account and cash-flow statement

➤ understand the importance of assessing and reducing risk

➤ understand how investments can be appraised using pay back and accounting rate of return methods

➤ understand the nature and significance of working capital

The final accounts of a business

At the end of each accounting period, usually one year, accountants will draw up the final accounts of the business. For companies, these will be included in the Annual Report and Accounts, which are sent to every shareholder. Table 13.1 gives details of the final accounts of limited companies, as these are the accounts you are most likely to come across in your studies

Profit and loss account – what it shows about a business

The profit and loss account records the revenue, costs and profit of a business over a given period of time, usually a year. There are two versions of the profit and loss account:

◆ A detailed profit and loss account can be constructed for internal use because managers will need as much information as possible.

◆ A less detailed summary will appear in the published accounts of companies. The content of this is laid down by the Company Acts and provides a minimum of information. This is because, although the shareholders would use additional information to assess the performance of their investment, the published accounts are also available to competitors and detailed data could give them a real insight into their rivals' strengths and weaknesses.

The version used in this chapter is one based on the published accounts but with additional information where this aids understanding. An example is given in Table 13.2.

The account	What it shows
The profit and loss account	The gross and net profit of the company. Details of how the net profit is split up (or appropriated) between dividends to shareholders and retained profits
The balance sheet	The net worth of the company. This is the difference between the value of what a company owns (assets) and what it owes (liabilities)
Cash-flow statement	Where cash was received from and what it was spent on

Table 13.1 Final accounts of limited companies – what they contain

Profit and loss account for Energen plc for the year ended 29 March 1999 (£m)		
	Sales turnover	3,060
(minus)	Cost of sales	(1,840)
(equals)	Gross profit	1,220
(minus)	Overheads	(580)
(equals)	Operating or net profit	640
(minus)	Interest	(80)
(equals)	Pre-tax profits	560
(minus)	Tax @ 20%	(112)
(equals)	Profit after tax	448
	Appropriation	
(minus)	Dividends to shareholders	200
(equals)	Retained profit	248

Table 13.2 Profit and loss account for Energen plc for the year ended 29 March 1999 (£m)

Definitions of terms used

Sales turnover (or sales revenue)

This is the total value of sales made during the trading period; in the example above this is during the financial year ending on 29 March 99. It is most important to understand that, as not all sales are for cash in most businesses, the sales turnover figure is *not* the same as cash received by the business. This point is covered in more detail later. The formula for calculating sales turnover is:

Sales turnover = quantity sold × price.

Therefore, if 120 items are sold at £2 each, the sales turnover is £240.

Cost of sales (or cost of goods sold)

This is the direct cost of purchasing the goods that were sold during the financial year. This figure is unlikely to be the same as the total value of goods purchased by the company during this period as items may have been added to stocks or taken from them. Only the goods used and sold during the year will be recorded in cost of sales. The formula used is:

Cost of sales = Opening stocks plus purchases minus closing stocks

This can be laid out as:

Opening stocks (at the start of the year)	£500
Purchases during the year	£2,500
Total stock	£3,000
Closing stocks (at the end of the year)	(£750)
Cost of goods sold	£2,250

Gross profit (or loss)

This is the difference between sales turnover and cost of sales. This is the final entry in the trading account section of the total profit and loss account.

Activities

1 Calculate gross profit for Cosy Corner Retailers Ltd for the financial year ending 31 March 2001. Show all of your workings.
1,500 items sold for £5 each; opening stocks were valued at £500; purchases totalled £3,000; closing stocks were £1,000.

2 Cambridge Boxes Ltd sold 3,500 units in the last financial year ending 31 December 2001. The selling price was £4. Opening stocks were 200 boxes. The business purchased 4,000 boxes during the year. All boxes cost the company £2 each.
Calculate the value of closing stocks and the company's gross profit in 2001.

Overheads

These are costs or expenses of the business that are not directly related to the number of items made or sold. These can include rent and business rates, management salaries and lighting costs.

Operating or net profit

This is the profit made, before tax and interest, but after all costs of sales and overheads have been deducted from sales turnover. This is the final entry in the profit and loss section of the total profit and loss account.

Tax

Limited companies pay corporation tax on their profits before they pay dividends or keep profits within the business.

Dividends

This is the share of the profits paid to shareholders as a return for investing in the company.

Retained profit

This is the profit left after all deductions, including dividends, have been made. This is 'ploughed back' into the company as a source of finance. These last three entries form what is known as the appropriation section of the profit and loss account. This is because it gives details of how net profits have been divided or appropriated.

Activity

Using the layout used above, construct a profit and loss account for Lancashire Traders Ltd from the following data:

Sales turnover – 5,000 items	@ £11.00
Opening stocks	£3,000
Corporation tax rate	20%
Interest paid	£1,000
Purchases	£40,000
Closing stocks	£8,000
Overhead expenses	£12,000
Dividends	£4,000

The balance sheet – what it shows about a business

The balance sheet records the net wealth of a business at one moment in time. In a company this net wealth 'belongs' to the shareholders. Table 13.3 shows an example of a balance sheet for a limited company.

Fixed assets		2,500
Current assets:		
Stocks	120	
Debtors	650	
Cash	20	
	790	
less:		
Current liabilities:		
Trade creditors	450	
Overdraft	30	
	(480)	
Net current assets		310
ASSETS EMPLOYED		2,810
FINANCED BY:		
Long-term liabilities	250	
Share capital	2,000	
Profit and loss reserves	560	
CAPITAL EMPLOYED		2,810

Table 13.3 Balance sheet for Energen Ltd as at 29.3.99 (£m)

Points to note

◆ Companies have to publish the profit and loss account and the balance sheet for the previous financial year as well in order to allow easy comparison. These have not been included in the above examples for reasons of clarity.

◆ The titles of both accounts are very important as they identify both the account and the company. Whereas the profit and loss account covers the whole financial year, the balance sheet is a statement of the estimated value of the company at one moment in time – the end of the financial year.

Definitions of terms used

Assets

These include anything of measurable value owned by the business.

Fixed assets

These are items owned by the business that are likely to be kept and used for more than one year. The most common examples are land, buildings, vehicles and machinery. These are all **tangible** assets as they have a physical existence. Businesses can also own **intangible assets** – these cannot be seen but still have value in the business. Examples are:

◆ patents;
◆ trademarks;
◆ copyrights;
◆ goodwill.

The reputation and prestige of a business that has been operating for some time also gives value to the business over and above the value of its physical assets. This is called the **goodwill** of a business and should normally only feature on a balance sheet just after it has been purchased for more than its assets are worth, or when the business is being prepared for sale. Disputes can arise between accountants about the valuation of intangible assets and there is a current debate regarding the asset value of well-known brand names. There is scope for varying the value of these and other intangibles on the balance sheet in order to give a better picture of the company's position. This is one aspect of 'window dressing' of accounts that can reduce objectivity.

Current assets

Current assets are those that are expected to be converted into cash within one year. The most common examples are stocks, debtors (customers who have bought goods on credit) and cash/bank balance.

Current liabilities

Current liabilities are debts that are likely to have to be repaid within a year. Typical current liabilities include trade creditors (suppliers who have allowed the business credit), bank overdraft and unpaid dividends and tax. Current liabilities are usually referred to as 'creditors – amounts falling due within one year'.

Net current assets

This is the difference between current assets and current liabilities. It is also known as **working capital** and is the finance tied up in the business for the day-to-day operation of the business.

Share capital and reserves

These are collectively called the **'shareholders' funds'**. They represent the capital originally paid into the business when the shareholders bought shares (share capital) or the retained profits of the business (profit and loss reserves) that the shareholders have accepted should be kept in the business. Reserves can also appear on the balance sheet if a company believes that its fixed assets have increased in value (revaluation reserve) or if it sells additional shares for more than their 'nominal' value (share premium reserve).

Capital employed

This is the total of all of the long-term finance of the business. It is the sum of share capital, reserves and long-term liabilities. These funds are used to finance the company's assets and, for this reason, assets employed always equals capital employed.

Activities

1 Copy out this table and indicate in which category the following items would appear on a company balance sheet.

	Share capital	Reserves	Long-term liabilities	Current liabilities	Current assets	Fixed assets
Company car						
Materials in the warehouse						
Four-year bank loan						
Tax owed to government						
Increase in value of company property						
Issued shares						
Cash in the bank						
Money owed to suppliers						

2 Using the layout above, construct a balance sheet for Yorkshire Logistics Ltd from the following data:

Long-term loans	£5m	Vehicles	£10m	Offices	£2m
Equipment	£1m	Stocks	£1m	Cash	£0.2m
Creditors	£2m	Unpaid tax	£1.5m	Debtors	£3m
Share capital	£6m	Reserves	£2.7m		

Assets employed

This is the total of fixed assets plus current assets less current liabilities. This is an important value, which is used in the analysis of accounts.

Long-term liabilities

These are the long-term loans owed by the business. These are due to be paid over a period of time greater than one year and include loans, commercial mortgages and debentures.

Cash-flow statement

Cash-flow statements are not examined in detail at 'AS' level Business Studies. The most important point to remember is that these statements explain to the users of accounts why the profits (or losses) made by a business are not the same as its cash flow. This surprises many students. Surely a profitable business has money in the bank? Clearly it must be true that a loss-making business is short of cash. The answer to both these questions is *not necessarily*.

Capital and revenue expenditure

What is the difference, in accounting terms, between a business purchasing a van and purchasing the fuel to fill the tank? There is expenditure involved in both cases, but one purchase is of an asset that will be kept and used by the business for several years. The petrol will be used up in the process of using the van in the day-to-day activities of the business. The purchase of the van is called **capital expenditure**; the purchase of the petrol is an example of **revenue expenditure**.

Any item bought by a business and retained for more than one year, i.e. the purchase of fixed assets, is capital expenditure. Any expenditure on assets that are used up within one year, such as stocks for resale or printer cartridges, is revenue expenditure.

Case study – M and G Taxis Ltd

M and G Taxis Ltd made a net profit of £200,000 last year. The two major shareholders, Mike and Gina Campbell, were therefore surprised to find that, at the end of the year, their business had a bank overdraft. Their accountant explained to them that out of net profit they had bought new taxis costing £50,000. In addition, the business had repaid a bank loan and several major customers had delayed paying their accounts. There had therefore been an increase in the debtors of the business; services had been supplied profitably to customers but not yet paid for. The accountant showed them the following simplified version of a cash-flow statement:

M and G Taxis Ltd cash-flow statement for the year ending 31 December 2001

Net profit	£200,000
less Increase in debtors	(£60,000)
less Purchase of new fixed assets (taxis)	(£50,000)
less Repayment of loan	(£100,000)
Net change in cash	(£10,000)

As the business had only started the year with a cash balance of £2,000, the statement above helps to explain the current bank overdraft of £8,000.

Activity

Copy out this table and complete it by writing either revenue or capital in column 2 and a brief explanation of your decision:

Expenditure	Capital or revenue spending	Reason
Purchase of computers for use in administration		
Salaries of the administration staff		
Stock bought for resale		
Maintenance costs of the building		
Extension to the existing offices		

How do accountants record these two types of spending in the accounts?

Revenue expenditure is easy to deal with. All revenue expenditure is on assets and expenses that give short-term benefit to the business – within one year. They will all be recorded in full on each year's profit and loss account and will therefore reduce that year's profits – with the exception of the unsold stocks, which will be entered under 'closing stocks'.

Capital expenditure is more complicated. Consider this situation. A removal business purchases two new trucks, which are expected to last for ten years. This is obviously capital expenditure on fixed assets. If the cost of these trucks was recorded as an expense immediately and recorded on the profit and loss account, there would be two serious disadvantages for the business:

- The trucks would not appear as fixed assets on the balance sheet because they had been recorded as an annual expense. This would lower the value of the business below its true worth – after all, the trucks will have value many years from now.
- This year's profits will be low as a result of the entire cost of the trucks being recorded straight away – and profits in later years will be higher because they do not bear any of the charge of this purchase.

How then, is capital expenditure recorded on the accounts? By a process called depreciation.

Depreciation of assets

Nearly all fixed assets will depreciate or decline in value over time. It seems reasonable, therefore, to only record the cost of each year's depreciation as a cost on each year's profit and loss account. This will overcome both of the problems referred to above:

- The assets will retain some value on the balance sheet each year until fully depreciated or sold off.
- The profits will be reduced by the amount of that year's depreciation and will not under- or over-record the performance of the business.

Depreciation may be defined as the decline in the estimated value of a fixed asset over time. Assets decline in value for two main reasons:

- normal wear and tear through usage;
- technological change, making either the asset or the product it is used to make obsolete.

Methods of calculating depreciation

Accountants are able to employ a number of different methods to calculate the annual amount of depreciation. You need to know just one of these.

The straight-line method of depreciation

The name indicates the way the depreciation is calculated, by taking away the same amount each year until all the cost of buying the asset is recovered. To do this you need to know:

- the original or historic costs of the asset;
- its estimated life expectancy;
- the estimated value of the asset at the end of its useful life with the business; this is called the asset's residual value.

Used computers and facsimile machines collected throughout Japan from major firms and private owners whose leasing terms have expired or they have been upgraded.
Source: Popperfoto

Straight-line depreciation – an evaluation

Compared to other methods of depreciation, this is easy to calculate and understand. It is very widely used by limited companies.

Look in the annual report and accounts of any plc and you will find a statement about the depreciation methods it has used. However, as with all methods, the straight-line method requires estimates to be made. Assuming that the annual depreciation charge is fixed and ignores what actually happens to the value of assets in the first year or two of life. Cars, trucks and computers, for instance, will tend to lose much more of their value in the first and second year than in subsequent years. Finally, the repairs and maintenance costs of an asset can increase with age and this will reduce the profits made by the asset. There is no recognition of this fact with straight-line depreciation. Neither is there any recognition of the very rapid pace at which modern technology tends to become obsolete.

Planning and decision making

Whilst accounting must provide the data with which to look backwards, learn from experience and modify behaviour in order to ensure that objectives are achieved, it must also enable managers to look into the future and plan. We are interested in two of the ways in which a firm may do is before making an investment which might prove unwise or unprofitable. The data for this are always present knowledge and the experience to predict, but even the best predictions are guesswork. Examples of potential investment decisions could include:

◆ a decision by a clothes manufacturer whether to extend the range of clothing offered for sale;
◆ a decision by a butcher shop whether to open a branch on a large newly built housing estate;
◆ a decision by a bus company whether to run a bus route linking local villages with the nearby town;
◆ a decision by a super market whether to open a cafe for its customers.

At the heart of all these decisions is a risk. The management in each case will want to know whether the costs will be greater than the benefits. Accounting can provide for them the financial data upon which the decision will be made and the techniques to enable the analysis to be completed. But accounting data are never sufficient, on their own, to make the decision. We return to that consideration after looking at two of the techniques for assessing an investment. The benefit of an investment does not necessarily lie in increased income, but the benefits can come from savings made or from reduced costs.

Investment appraisal – what information is necessary?

In judging the profitability or desirability of an investment project the following information will be useful:

◆ the cost of the investment, including, in the case of equipment and machinery, installation cost;
◆ the estimated life expectancy – over how many years can returns be expected from the investment;
◆ the expected net returns or net cash flows from the project. These are the expected returns from the investment, less the annual running costs of it.

The two methods we consider here are:

the payback period,
average rate of return (also known as the accounting rate of return).

Payback method

The payback period is the length of time it takes for the net cash inflows to pay back the original investment. If a project costs £2m and is expected to pay back £500,000 per year, the payback period will be four years. This can then be compared with the payback on alternative investments. A payback example is shown in Table 13.4.

Year	Annual net cash flows	Cumulative cash flows
	£	£
0	(500,000)	(500,000)
1	300,000	(200,000)
2	150,000	(50,000)
3	150,000	100,000
4	100,000	200,000

Table 13.4 Cash flows of a second investment

It is normal to refer to 'Year 0' as the time period in which the investment is made. The cash flow at this time is therefore negative – shown by a bracketed amount. What is the payback period in the example above? It occurs in the third year, but when during this year? If we assume that the cash flows are received evenly throughout the year (this may not be the case, of course) then payback will be at the end of the 4th month of the 3rd year.

How do we know this? At the end of year 2:
£50,000 is needed to pay back the remainder of the initial investment.
£150,000 is expected during year 3.
£50,000 is a third of £150,000
One third of a year is the end of month 4!
You might find it easier to use the following formula to find out which month in a particular year payback occurs:

month of payback is

$$\frac{\text{additional cash inflow needed}}{\text{annual cash flow}} \times 12$$

$$= \frac{£50,000}{150,000} \times 12$$

$$= \text{4th month}$$

Why is the payback of a project considered to be important?

Managers can compare the payback period of a particular project with other alternative projects in order to put them in rank order. Alternatively, the payback period could be compared with a 'cut-off' time period that the business may have laid down, e.g. they will not accept any project proposal which pays back after five years. There are several reasons why payback period is considered important:

◆ a business may have borrowed the finance for the investment and a long payback period will increase interest payments;
◆ even if the finance was obtained internally, the capital has an opportunity cost of other purposes for which it could be used. The speedier the payback, the quicker the capital is made available for other projects;
◆ the longer into the future before a project pays back the capital invested in it, the more uncertain the whole investment becomes. The changes in the external environment which could occur to make a project unprofitable are likely to be much greater over ten years than over two;

◆ some managers are 'risk averse' – they want to reduce risk to a minimum so a quick payback reduces uncertainties for these managers;
◆ cash flows received in the future have less real value than cash flows today, as a result of inflation. The quicker money is returned to an investing company the higher will be its real value:
> an increasing number of investments rely on modern technology and an asset which pays back over a long time or even a medium period, may be obsolete before it has paid back.

The payback method has the following advantages and disadvantages.

Advantages:
1 It is quick and easy to calculate.
2 The results are easily understood by managers.
3 The emphasis on speed of return of cash flows gives the benefits of concentrating on the more accurate short-term, forecasts of the projects profitability.
4 The result can be used to eliminate or 'screen out' projects which give returns too far into the future.
5 It is particularly useful for businesses where liquidity is of greater significance than overall profitability.

Disadvantages:
1 It does not measure the overall profitability of a project – indeed it ignores all of the cash flows after the payback period. It might be possible for an investment to give a really rapid return of capital but then to offer no other cash inflows.
2 This concentration on the short term may lead businesses to reject very profitable investments just because they take some time to repay the capital.
3 It does not consider the timing of the cash flows during the payback period.

Evaluation
The payback method is often used as a quick check on the viability of a project or as a means of comparing projects – but it is rarely used in isolation from the other investment appraisal methods. It is of greatest value in times of high inflation and when the investment has a high technological element.

Accounting rate of return

It measures the overall profitability of an investment as a percentage of the initial investment something that payback does not do. If it is possible to demonstrate that Project A returns, on average, 8% per year while Project B returns 12% per year, then the decision between the alternative investments will be an easier one to make.

Table 13.5 shows the expected cash flows from a business investment into a fleet of new fuel-efficient vehicles. The inflows for years 1–3 are the annual cost savings made. In year 4, the expected return from selling the vehicles is included.

Year	Net cash flow
0	(£5m)
1	£2m
2	£2m
3	£2m
4	£3m

Table 13.5

Calculation of ARR – the 4 steps involved:
1 Add up all of the positive cash flows.
2 Subtract the cost of the investment.
3 Divide by the life span of the investment in years £4M/4 = 1.
4 Calculate what % this figure is of the initial capital cost by this formula:

$$\frac{\text{average annual profit}}{\text{initial capital cost}} \times 100$$

Example of ARR – new vehicle fleet:

Add up all positive cash flows	= £9m
Subtract cost of investment	= £9m – £5m = £4m
Divide by life span	= £4m/4 = £1m
Calculate the % return	= $\underline{£1m} \times 100$
	£5m
	= 20%

The result indicates to the business that, on average, over the life span of the investment, it can expect an annual return of 20% on its investment. This could be compared to:
◆ the ARR on other projects,
◆ the minimum expected return set by the business – the so-called criterion rate.

In the example above, if the business refused to accept any project with less than a return of 15% the new vehicle fleet would satisfy this criterion. But if the criterion rate was 25% the investment would be rejected.

The advantages and disadvantages of the average rate of return:

Advantages:
1 It uses all of the cash flows – unlike the payback method.
2 It focuses on profitability which is the central objective of many business decisions.
3 The result is easily understood and easy to compare with other projects which may be competing for the limited investment funds available.
4 The result can be quickly assessed against the pre-determined criterion rate of the business.

Disadvantages:
1 It ignores the timing of the cash flows. This could result in two projects having similar ARR results but one could pay back much quicker than the other.
2 As all cash inflows are included, the later cash flows which are less likely to be accurate are incorporated into the calculation.
3 The time value of money is ignored. Time value of money is an important part of many decisions of this kind but we do not consider it until the A2 part of the course. If, however, you are doing a project which is about investment appraisal you might like to read about the concept called discounted cash flow in the text for the second part of the advanced level course. This is a widely used measure for appraising projects but it is best considered together with payback results. The two results then allow consideration of both profits and cash flow timings.

Activity

A manufacturing business is planning an investment programme to overcome a problem of demand exceeding capacity. It is considering two alternative projects involving new machinery. The initial outlays and future cash outflows are given below:

Year	Project X (£)	Project Y (£)
0	(50,000)	(80,000)
1	25,000	45,000
2	20,000	35,000
3	20,000	17,000
4	15,000	15,000
5	10,000	–

Project Y machinery is forecast to have a life expectancy of just four years.

(a) Calculate the payback for both projects.
(b) Explain which project should be selected if payback was the only criterion used – and why.
(c) Calculate ARR for both projects.
(d) The business has a cut-off or criterion rate of 11% for all new projects. Would either project be acceptable under this restriction?
(e) Taking both the results of payback and ARR together, which project would you advise the business to invest in, and why?
(f) What additional information would help you advise the business on the more suitable project?

Forecasting cash flows in an uncertain environment

Investment appraisal methods require cash flow forecasts. With long-term investments this can mean forecasting many years ahead and the chance of external factors upsetting forecasts become considerable. The original investment into the Channel Tunnel involved assessing returns 20 years after it was due to open – and the opening date was many years after the project began. The scope for external changes affecting the revenue forecasts – based on market research – was very great. For instance, the state of the French and UK economies influences the amount of freight and tourist traffic. Technical problems with the tunnel operations could hit revenues – as with a fire in 1997 which could not have been foreseen at the appraisal stage. The level of air fares – which have fallen dramatically since the tunnel opened – will also impact on demand levels.

These uncertainties cannot be removed but the existence of them must be constantly borne in mind by managers when considering the results of investment appraisal. The decision makers also need to be informed of the market research techniques used and the degree of confidence that can be put in the results. Manufacturers' data concerning the performance of an asset, such as machinery or a vehicle, may need to be verified so that claims of output or efficiency can be confirmed. Therefore, several factors could make the forecast of future cash flows unreliable:

- the quality of the information available;
- the degree of care with which the information is collected;
- the basis of estimates of the possible market, prices and cash inflows;
- the nature of the product or service being provided;
- the stability of the external environment;
- the activities of competitors.

Qualitative factors – investment decisions are not just about profit.

Investment appraisal techniques provide numerical data which are important in making decisions. However, no manager can afford to ignore other factors which cannot be so easily expressed in a numerate form and may have a crucial bearing on the decision. These are referred to as qualitative factors and may include:

(a) The impact on the environment and the local community. The growing concern about environmental issues is forcing businesses to consider carefully plans for developments in sensitive areas. The bad publicity stemming from the announcement of certain investment plans may dissuade managers from going ahead with the project due to the long-run impact on image and sales. An example is the dispute over rail routes to the Channel Tunnel.

(b) Closely related to this is the risk that certain projects may not receive planning permission and this would preclude continuing with the scheme. It is the duty of local planning offices to weigh up the costs and benefits of a planned undertaking and to act in the best interests of the community. Members of that community will often have a direct role through a public enquiry or may set up a pressure group to make their views known and persuade a particular outcome.

(c) The ways in which the workforce may react, particularly where any investment may lead to redundancies, to redeployment or to extensive re-training. The savings of a change may be considerable but expenses may arise from unexpected factors, such as strikes, absenteeism, lateness and other indicators of unrest and unease among the workforce.

(d) The aims and objectives of the business which must be a key consideration. The decision to close bank branches and replace them with Internet and telephone banking services involves considerable capital expenditure – as well as the potential for long-term savings. Managers may, however, be reluctant to pursue these investment policies if there is concern that the aim of giving excellent and personal customer service is being threatened. Similarly, the decision to replace large numbers of workers with labour-saving machinery may be reversed if the negative impact on industrial relations appears to be too great. An investment opportunity may prove viable on the basis of financial data but managers will think long and hard about entering a field where there is no history of success for the firm and no assurance of marketing successfully. Firms have often refused to move into new market areas because they are not familiar with them and there are spectacular examples of eventual success of a venture which initially firms rejected. Many very successful pop groups and authors can tell tales of initial rejection.

(e) Different managers are prepared to accept different degrees of risk. No amount of positive quantitative data will convince some managers, perhaps because of previous experiences, to accept a project which involves a considerable chance of failure.

Understanding of the 'other factors' involves in an investment decision is to be aware of the whole picture. Examiners expect to see this kind of awareness and expect you to be clear that investment decisions are never made on the basis of the financial data alone but by assessing all the evidence and coming to a balanced judgment.

The Channel tunnel shuttle train emerges from the tunnel opening on the French side at Sangatte on 28 April as tests continued prior to the official opening ceremony on 6 May 1993.
Source: Popperfoto Reuters.

Working capital – meaning and significance

Working capital is often described as the 'life blood' of a business. It is the finance needed for everyday expenses, such as the payment of wages and buying of stock. Without sufficient working capital a business will be illiquid. This position can be measured and analysed by using the two liquidity ratios referred to above; the results of these will be low when illiquidity is a problem.

The simple calculation of working capital is: current assets less current liabilities. You will remember from the section on the balance sheet that current assets are stocks, debtors and cash in the bank and the tills. Virtually no business could survive without these three assets, although some business owners refuse to sell any products on credit so there will be no debtors. This is very rare for businesses beyond a certain size. Where does the capital come from to purchase and hold these current assets? Most businesses will obtain some of this finance in the form of current liabilities – overdrafts and creditors are the main forms. However, it would be unwise to obtain all of the funds needed from these sources. For one thing, the liquidity ratios would be at very low levels. Another point against this approach is that it will leave no working capital for buying additional stocks or extending further credit to customers when required.

How much working capital is needed?

Sufficient working capital is essential to prevent a business from becoming illiquid and unable to pay its debts. Too high a level of working capital is a disadvantage; the opportunity cost of too much capital tied up in stocks, debtors and idle cash is the return that money could earn elsewhere in the business – invested in fixed assets perhaps. The working capital requirement for any business will depend upon the 'length' of this 'working capital cycle'. Figure 13.1 shows the simple cycle in a business that makes things, but neither seeks nor offers credit. Credit to purchasers given by the business will lengthen the time before a sale is turned into cash. Credit received by the business will lengthen the time before stock bought has to be paid for. To give more credit than is received is to increase the need for working capital. To receive more credit than is given is to reduce the need for working capital.

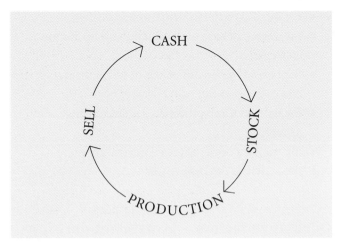

Figure 13.1 The simple working capital cycle

Managing working capital

There are business dangers from both *too much* working capital and *too little*. Working capital therefore needs to be managed. It is managed by concentrating on the four main components of the cycle:

- debtors;
- creditors;
- stock;
- cash.

Debtors

Debtors can be managed in many different ways, as follows:

- Not extending credit to customers – or extending it for shorter time periods. Will they still buy from this business? Will a major aspect of this business's marketing mix have been removed. There are dangers in this approach. Many customers now expect credit and will go elsewhere if it is not offered.

- Selling debts to specialist financial institutions acting as debt factors. These businesses will 'buy' debts from other concerns having an immediate need for cash. This will involve a cost, however, as the factors will not pay 100% of the value. They must make a profit for themselves.

- By being careful to discover whether new customers are creditworthy. This can be done by requiring references – from traders or from the bank is common – or by using the services of a credit enquiry agency.

- By offering a discount to clients who pay promptly.

Credit

Credit can be managed in two main ways, as follows:

- ◆ Increasing the range of goods and services bought on credit. If a business has a good credit rating this may be easy, but in other circumstances it is difficult. The danger is that an unpaid creditor may refuse to supply.
- ◆ Extend the period of time taken to pay. The larger a business is, the easier it is to extend the credit taken. This is often a great burden for small businesses that trade with larger ones.

Stock

Stock can be managed in the following ways:

- ◆ keeping smaller stock balances;
- ◆ using computer systems to record sales and therefore stock levels, and ordering as required;
- ◆ efficient stock control, stock use and stock handling so as to reduce losses through damage wastage and shrinkage;
- ◆ just-in-time stock ordering. There are dangers here if demand has not been forecast correctly, if there is a sudden change in demand, if suppliers are unreliable or if there are delivery difficulties.

Cash

Cash can be managed by:

- ◆ use of cash-flow forecasts, which have already been considered;
- ◆ wise use or investment of excess cash;
- ◆ planning for too little cash and provision for overdraft facilities made with the bank.

A permanent increase in working capital

When businesses expand, they generally need higher stock levels and will sell a higher value of products on credit. This increase in working capital is likely to be permanent and so long-term or permanent sources of finance will be needed, such as long-term loans or even share capital.

Activity

Read the case study below and then tackle the exercises that follow.

Case Study – Directphone Ltd

Directphone Ltd operates a direct insurance service to motorists. As part of a recent expansion programme, the finance director calculated that stocks of stationery, such as insurance certificates, would have to rise by 10% from £10,000. More motorists would be encouraged to use the company by being offered extended credit terms. This would increase debtors to an estimated £50,000 from the existing £40,000. Cash reserves to pay out for accidents would rise to £35,000 from £30,000. The only current liability was creditors (garages that had not yet been paid for accident work). This amounted to £40,000 and the director hoped to be allowed to increase this to £50,000.

(a) Calculate the proposed increase in the working capital requirements of the business resulting from the expansion.

(b) Using liquidity ratios, consider how the finance director might finance this increase in working capital.

Over-to-you

Short-answer questions

1 What does a profit and loss account show about a business?

2 What is the difference between gross and net profit?

3 What does the appropriation section of a profit and loss account contain?

4 Explain the difference between current and fixed assets.

5 What do you understand by capital employed?

6 Give two examples of capital expenditure and justify your selection.

7 What is the purpose of depreciating assets on business accounts.

8 State three limitations of using ratio analysis.

9 How can a business control credit offered?

Discover and learn

1 Consider an improvement to facilities for your school/college common room which would cost at least £5,000:

   (a) Explain why it would be a valuable addition and what the benefits would be.

   (b) Analyse all the quantifiable costs and revenues or savings.

   (c) On the basis of this data conduct a pay back and accounting rate of return analysis.

   (d) Consider all the 'other factors' which should be considered and on the basis of all the evidence, make and justify your decision.

2 Using a car magazine or a car price guide, find out the following information about a particular model of car, for example a 1.6 Ford Focus:

   (a) new price;

   (b) retail value after one year;

   (c) retail value after two years.

   Calculate the percentage decline in the value from new both one year and after two years.

   A car hire firm has ten Ford Focus cars. It keeps them for two years on average. Comment on the fact that it uses straight-line depreciation for all of its fixed assets.

3 Read the case study below and then tackle the exercises that follow.

Case study – Highfield Leisure Ltd

The following accounts refer to Highfield Leisure Ltd, which operates several amusement arcades in seaside resorts in the UK and hires out machines to pubs and clubs.

Profit and loss account for the year ending 31 March 2000

(1999 figures in parentheses. All figures in £m)

Sales turnover	320	(330)
less Cost of sales	120	(100)
Gross profit	200	(230)
Overhead expenses	150	(145)
Net profit	50	(85)
Interest	10	(5)
Pre-tax profits	40	(80)
Tax @ 50%	20	(40)
Profit after tax	20	(40)
Dividends	15	(15)
Retained profit	5	(25)

Balance sheet as at 31 March 2000

(1999 figures in parentheses. All figures in £m)

Fixed assets		80	(75)
Current assets:			
Stock	10		(15)
Debtors	25		(20)
Cash	0.5		(2)
	35.5		(37)
less:			
Current liabilities	30		(25)
Net current assets		5.5	(12)
ASSETS EMPLOYED		85.5	(87)
Financed by:			
Long-term liabilities	40		(46.5)
Share capital			
(£1 ordinary shares)	30		(30)
Reserves	15.5		(10.5)
Capital employed		85.5	(87)

   (a) Define working capital and state the present working capital of the company in the year 2000.

   (b) Stock is found to be overvalued by 20% for 2000.
      Recalculate working capital.

   (c) Using the data in any way you consider appropriate, what comments would you make about the success of this business from the point of view of:

      ◆ a trade creditor?

      ◆ a potential investor?

Summary

In this section we have recognised that:

- The final accounts of a business are its statement to stakeholders and to the world at large of the present position of the business.

- An important part of understanding final accounts is the language and concepts that are involved.

- A number of different values including ratios are used to assess companies on the basis of their accounts.

- The ratios and other calculations are an aid to decision making and not answers in themselves.

- Action that could be taken to solve problems is not always wise and there are factors, other than the numbers themselves, that are often more important.

Key words

Definitions of Key words can be found in the Glossary on page 236.

assets employed	intangible assets
balance sheet	investment appraisal
capital employed	net current assets
capital expenditure	net profit
cash-flow statement	operating profit
current assets	overheads
debtors	profit and loss account
dividends	retained profit
final accounts	revenue expenditure
fixed assets	sales turnover
goodwill	stock
gross profit	tangible assets
gross profit margin	working capital

14 Planning the workforce

On completion of this section you should be able to:

➤ show the need for organisational objectives to be met

➤ understand the importance of workforce planning

➤ consider the importance of recruitment, induction and training to an organisation

➤ understand the roles of induction and the different types of training

➤ explain why some organisations have a high labour turnover

➤ discuss workforce planning needs in given circumstances

➤ explain the nature of a contract of employment and the things it covers

➤ explain why workers may be dismissed and procedures to protect them

➤ explain work situations in which the law intervenes

The need to achieve business objectives

One of the most important ingredients of any successful organisation are the people who work for it. The extent to which the organisation's objectives are achieved will depend, to a great extent, on the effectiveness and efficiency of its employees. It is important, therefore, that managers ensure employees understand and are in sympathy with the aims of the organisation. This may not always be the case.

Consider the situation of Bill, who has been working for the same firm for the past 25 years:

◆ He has not been promoted.

◆ He is quite happy with the wages he earns.

◆ He is quite content to remain in his job until he retires.

How might Bill's objectives differ from those of the organisation?

The organisation intends to operate in the most efficient way so that it can produce the desired output at the lowest unit cost and make a profit. We could say that the objective of the firm is a reasonable return on capital employed. Bill's objective is to continue to earn a reasonable wage without causing himself any stress. Obviously there is a real problem here for a manager. How can the two different sets of objectives be brought together?

Activity

Talk to four people you know who have different types of jobs. Ask them:

(a) Why they go to work?

(b) What they see as their objectives?

(c) Consider whether or not these objectives would be appropriate to the organisation they work for.

(d) If you were their manager, or the owner of the firm, would you be happy with them?

People at work

People come to work for all kinds of reasons, ranging from the need to earn money to the need to be with other people. Managers must use their skills to provide a match between the aims of employees in coming to work and the aims of the organisation, which may range from making a profit to providing an effective and efficient service. There is a further difficulty. We live in an era of change. Businesses are dynamic and are changing because of a number of factors. Technology is changing and this may necessitate people having to adapt to new techniques or machinery, or indeed having to retrain to do a job that is completely different from the one they used to do. People are often not happy with this kind of change, and indeed may fear it. Bill, who is

A new industrial estate, now a common feature of most towns

happy simply coasting along doing the same job day after day, may be frightened by the prospect of new challenges. Therefore, managers have to be skilled in their approach if they are to avoid tension in the workplace.

Workforce planning

Good planning can help an organisation run smoothly. Lack of planning often leads to disaster. The right kind of labour is rarely easy to obtain and without an appropriate well-balanced labour force it will be very difficult to achieve the objectives of the organisation. The mix of labour needed must first be determined and then a statregy designed which will either obtain those who are needed through recruitment or by training existing staff. The workforce plan involves looking at the present workforce and the future requirements, as well as at the means by which these future requirements can be met. The organisation needs to look at all the different types of workers it requires. These will include managers, technical experts, clerical workers, skilled manual workers and semi-skilled workers or unskilled workers. Obviously the number and pattern of employees will depend on the type and size of the organisation. However, all of these people have a crucial part to play. Planning is important all the time but some

Activity

Read the case study below and then tackle the exercises that follow.

Case study – R Wilkins Ltd

R Wilkins is a small firm, which has been operating in the same town for the last 50 years. Many of the workers have been with the organisation for a long time and there has been a tradition for the sons and daughters of workers to come into the firm when they leave school. The company produces crafted wood products for a fairly small market. There has never been any real pressure exerted on the workers and there was always a casual feel to the production process. Old Mr Wilkins is about to retire and his son, who has been to Business School, is about to take over. He would like to become involved in exporting. He would also like to invest a large amount of money in new technology, such as computer-controlled lathes. However, none of the current workers have any experience of this type of technology.

(a) Outline the problems that you think Wilkins will have if he introduces this new strategy.

(b) How would you suggest he might try to introduce it with the minimum of disruption to the workforce?

(c) Explain how the objectives of the workforce and the organisation are different in this case.

factors make **workforce planning** particularly crucial. Among them are:

- People leave at all times and for a variety of reasons.
- The firm should be ready to replace them.
- This may be a time to employ different skills.
- It may be an opportunity for internal rather than external appointment.
- It may be a time to initiate or respond to change.
- Reasons for the departure need to be known and analysed.
- Technology constantly requires a revision of the workforce.
- Redundancy, retraining and/or new employment must be planned.

Redundancy and retraining need to be carefully planned as they always have the potential to cause major problems within the organisation. For example, if people feel that there is a chance of redundancy, it will cause uncertainty and unrest, may lead to industrial disputes and certainly will lead to a reduction in efficiency. Such situations often persuade workers to leave who are among those the firm would wish to retain. However, the most common aspect of workforce planning lies in the successful recruitment of new employees.

Recruitment

It is important that organisations obtain the best workforce available if they are to meet their objectives and compete successfully. As far as possible, the employees need to be chosen so that they meet exactly the needs of the organisation in order to reduce the risk of conflict between their personal objectives and the objectives of the organisation. Many organisations will be involved in recruitment fairly frequently, as they need to replace workers who die, retire, are dismissed or who move to another job. In addition to this they may need to recruit for expansion.

Work is increasingly technological with greater capital intensity and changing requirements of workers. Craft skills are less significant and the ability to use computerised equipment and work as a team is becoming more important. Organisations have to recruit for these reasons so that they will not be left behind by change.

Activity

Read the case study below and then tackle the exercises that follow.

Case study – Brendon Plastics plc

Brendon Plastics is a medium-sized firm in its industry employing 350 workers. In its community it is a large employer with a relatively high labour turnover. In one month the need to recruit new employees arose from:

- two who had retired at 65;
- one who had died;
- two who had been dismissed;
- three who had found other employment;
- the creation of a new section requiring ten staff at different levels;
- the division of two jobs, the work of which had grown.

Two of the staff in the new section will have management responsibilities and will need both qualifications and experience in plastic moulding techniques. Both the jobs that need dividing are in administration and will require experience and computing skills. All the other jobs are on the shop floor and require neither experience nor qualifications.

(a) Outline the processes that you think might be necessary for successful recruitment.
(b) Discuss ways in which the appointment of:
- shop-floor workers;
- management workers;
- administrative staff;

may need different processes.

Processes employed by firms and channels through which they will work differ from one organisation to another, but all will begin by reflecting on the consequences of a person leaving and the opportunities this offers. The organisation will wish to find the employee best suited to its needs. This is a process that requires great care because, once you have engaged someone, dissimal can be difficult.

Once the organisation has decided on the vacancy, it needs to complete a job analysis. This involves gathering together all the facts relating to the job. It may be necessary for managers to observe the job being done (provided it is not a new job!), or to ask the person who currently does the job what is involved. This is quite important, as very often managers may not fully realise what the job entails.

Once this information has been gathered, the next step in the process is to draw up a job specification. This will include items such as the basic job details, a summary and purpose of the job, who the employee will be responsible to, the conditions of employment such as salary, holidays etc., any training that will be required. It is important that the job specification is accurate, as this will determine what the prospective employee understands the job to be.

The job advertisement can then be drawn up and this must be clear so that prospective candidates are not misled. Job advertisements are normally placed in newspapers, trade journals, employment agencies, careers offices, etc. In certain cases where levels of expertise are required, they may be placed in universities or further education colleges. The cost of recruitment must not be unnecessarily high, but for many jobs, the widest possible pool of prospective employees must be reached. However, there are many jobs where applicants can be found from the contacts of existing employees or by placing a card in the window.

As soon as applications are received, then the organisation will select the ones from people they might want to interview. It is unlikely that all applicants will be interviewed, because usually there will be many more applications than can be coped with. In addition, some of the applicants may not be suitable or qualified for the job. To interview them would be a waste of time both for the organisation and the applicant. This process of selecting a small number from which the choice can be made is called short-listing. For many jobs references will be asked for so that prospective employers can have some support for, and confirmation of, the qualities and suitability of the applicant. This approach is most likely where qualifications and experience are demanded or where there is a need to protect the organisation from bogus applicants.

Applicants can then be called for interview. At interview they will be asked a number of questions to determine their suitability for the job in terms of their qualifications and experience. However, suitability of the person from the point of view of personality and ability to fit in with others with whom they will be working is

Activity

Work in groups of four. Each individual select a job. Any job will do. It could be one you do yourself or one that is done by a member of your family. If you were appointing to that job:

- ◆ What would you expect the employee to be able to do?
- ◆ What qualifications or experience do you think would be needed?
- ◆ What qualities would you look for in a potential employee?
- ◆ Draw up an advertisement based on the answers to these questions.
- ◆ Discuss your advertisement with the others and amend if you think it is necessary.
- ◆ Decide where you would advertise and why.

Activity

Employers are required to show no bias of any kind in the recruitment of employees. Discuss the four advertisements you prepared in your group. Do you think there are any unfair things in the advertisements? If so, comment upon them and change them so that they are fair and will attract the kind of people who are needed.

What do you think are the strengths and weaknesses of the advert?

also important. The type of job that is being interviewed for will clearly determine the format of the interview. What applicants sometimes forget is that an interview is a two-way opportunity. It is as important for the applicant to be satisfied that this is the right job and in the right organisation as it is for the potential employer to be satisfied. Taking a job because it is offered is one of the commonest reasons for dissatisfaction at work, for absenteeism and for rapid decisions to leave.

After the interviews have taken place, the decision will be made. Those who have been involved in the interview will discuss the various applicants as individuals, as well as how well they have answered the questions put to them. It is important that everyone on the interview panel is in general agreement as to the successful applicant(s). Some organisations provide unsuccessful applicants with feedback on the reasons why they were not appointed. This can be a very useful exercise for candidates.

Activity

Consider the following job advertisement. Do you think it is a good one? Is there anything missing? Is it legal?

JOHN BROWN LTD

Required, young man as an office employee.

No previous experience is required.

Grade C at least in GCSE English and Maths.

A neat and tidy appearance is essential.

Contact 0234 56789. Ask for Mr Smith.

Induction

The costs of recruitment are very high. No business wants to recruit more often than is necessary, so a big effort must be made to ensure that recruits stay. The first stage of this is called induction. You will remember what it was like starting at a new school with few friends. You wanted to settle as soon as possible, but there were many things you did not know. In working situations this feeling can be much worse unless the firm sets out to ensure that you fit into the culture of the organisation, know where things are, the work group of which you will be a part and what job you will have to do. All of this is undertaken in most firms through a specially provided induction programme, which sometimes lasts up to a week. It is not training for the job; it is training to be in the job, designed to make you feel part of the firm and confident that you know what to do and where to go. Time and money spent in this process may well pay dividends later as employees will settle quickly and will operate as efficiently as possible. Done well, it will reduce the expense of having to go through the recruitment process all over again and may more than pay for itself in that way.

Features of an induction programme are likely to be:

- familiarisation with the workplace and its amenities;
- introduction to important personnel;
- introduction to work mates;
- awareness of the culture, workings and objectives of the business;
- awareness of times and working practices;
- awareness of health, safety and fire drills and precautions;
- requirements when absent, ill or late.

Training

Training is an ongoing process and does not simply apply to the new entrant to the organisation. Because of continuous change in technology and processes, it is important that all staff, from shop floor to management, are trained in an ongoing fashion. Some will require training because they are being asked to do different things, being deliberately multi-skilled or being groomed for promotion. Training is expensive, but failure to train or poor training is even more expensive since it can lead to, or make worse, a number of potential problems. Among these are:

- poor quality;
- increased wastage;
- poor motivation and morale;
- absenteeism and increased labour turnover;
- lost sales and customers;
- damage and accidents.

On-the-job training

Management needs to establish who needs to be trained within the organisation, in other words, to identify the gaps. Training is only necessary because there is a gap between what a firm wants from an employee and what the employee is currently able to do. Even someone who is highly skilled may not be able to use that skill in precisely the way the employer wants. For example, someone highly skilled in computing may not be familiar with the hardware and software the firm is using or with the procedures the firm has adopted. For someone in this position training may be minimum and may be quick, but it is still essential.

Once gaps are identified and analysed, programmes can be constructed to deal with these gaps. These programmes may evolve within the company and it may be necessary to train someone to be a supervisor. Very often, people who have been good at their job are promoted to supervise others. For example, students employed to work at the checkout in a superstore are first trained by an employee who is already skilled in the job. This usually takes place outside normal hours.

However, it may be that some trainers need basic training so that they can get the best from other people. Very often the way that trainers communicate with trainees is as crucial as the task that is being learnt.

This kind of training is an example of what is known as on-the-job training and is essential where jobs must be done in a particular way and involve interpersonal skills.

1 You will certainly have seen teachers in training in your school or college and you may even have been taught by one of them. If you have, you will have noted that they are often supervised to ensure both the effectiveness of their progress and the quality of your learning,

2 You may have been to the hairdressers when a new employee is being trained. The employee can only learn by cutting hair, but this does pose a risk for the customer whose hair is being cut. The first customers are often volunteers or people who are being charged less.

On-the-job trainees are often less efficient than an experienced worker, take longer, waste more materials or make mistakes, which have to be put right. This is a natural part of the learning process.

Off-the-job training

The training of many personnel will take place off the job, particularly in the early stages. Those who have to work machines are often first taught in the training school or on reserved machines that are not used for production. Teachers spend a long time in academic and training college courses before they undertake their first teaching practice. Most organisations, nowadays, are anxious that their senior personnel, people they see with potential for promotion and managers undergo regular development programmes. These may be carried out at universities or further education colleges. It may be that there will be a formal qualification at the end.

One problem for organisations may be that they will train their personnel (often paying for the training), only to discover that those people will move to another organisation simply because they are now better trained. However, this is a risk that organisations are prepared to take. It is vital that people with responsibility are well trained and well motivated if they are to use their skills to help the organisation to meet its objectives.

Any training programme must be monitored and apparent results recorded. A debriefing for both the trainees and the trainers enables evaluation. There is always room for improvement and there are always changes in circumstances that must be taken into account.

Valuable lessons can be learnt for the future. It is wise to involve employees in the training process, not only afterwards, but also in allowing them to help decide what training they need. This gives a real sense of ownership to the process and is likely to result in a better outcome. Managers need to be aware that they may not have all the answers as far as training needs are concerned.

Labour turnover

Labour turnover is the number of people who leave an organisation in a given period of time. A rough guide can be given by expressing the number who leave as a percentage of those employed:

Employees	540
Number who left in the year	124
Labour turnover for the year	$124/540 \times 100 = 23\%$

But this not very helpful. There are many reasons why people leave organisations. Some of them are not really part of a labour turnover problem and have to be accepted. These include:

◆ those who retire at 60/65, who die or are too ill to continue;
◆ those who leave because the family is moving;
◆ those the firm has dismissed;
◆ those who were only employed short term, e.g. students.

All of these must be excluded from any analysis, although there may be something to learn from reasons why people had to be dismissed. Unexpected labour turnover is expensive and the reasons for it must be found. Only when the reasons are identified can a solution be sought.

1 If many people are leaving within a short time of being employed the reasons are likely to lie in the suitability of recruitment, in the quality of induction or in the initial training activity.

2 If the leavers are concentrated among male employees or among female employees, then the conditions of employment or of working together may be an issue.

3 If there is a high concentration within one or two departments, then the cause is likely to lie in conditions of work or in leadership style.

4 If many of the workers leaving are moving to a competitor or to a given local firm using similar skills, the answer is likely to lie in wages, in conditions of employment or in working practices.

Whatever the reason, if people are not happy in the work they are doing, they are certainly not being as efficient as they could be, and the objectives of the organisation will not be met. In addition, if people are leaving, the firm is having to recruit and train new people, and this is also very expensive. It is also important for the organisation to consider its reputation. It is certain to be the case that many employees who are moving on are not enhancing the reputation of the organisation they have left.

Activity

In small groups, discuss why you think there could be a turnover of labour within an organisation. Try to discuss a firm known to you. Perhaps you can get information from:

(a) the firm in which you work or which you yourself have left;

(b) the firm in which you are doing the Project;

(c) a friend or relative who has changed jobs.

Dismissal

There may be occasions when an employee has to be dismissed for one reason or another. It could be that the employee is unable to do the job to the standard that the organisation requires. On the other hand, it may be that the employee has broken one of the crucial conditions of employment. However, before dismissal can happen, the organisation must be seen to have done all that it can to help the employee reach the required standard or stay within conditions of employment. There should be support and, if necessary, training for the person concerned. It is important from the organisation's point of view that it does not leave itself open to allegations of **unfair dismissal**.

Sometimes employees become involved in gross misconduct, which may be stealing or some other serious offence. If this happens, the organisation can dismiss with immediate effect, without pay or notice. However, if an employee is late regularly, then the organisation must give warnings and follow the agreed disciplinary procedure before dismissal can take place. This usually involves verbal warnings followed by written warnings, before dismissal is thought to be 'fair'.

If someone is off work, because of illness, for a long period of time and it is unlikely that they will return for some time to come, then, after consulting medical experts, it may be that the employee can be dismissed or continue to be employed on lower wages in accordance with the contract of employment. The employee needs to be given full notice and full pay during the period of notice.

Whether or not a dismissal is unfair is a matter of fact to be decided by a tribunal. It is the right of every employee to claim unfair dismissal. To show that a dismissal is fair employers need to be able to show that one of the following is true and, except in the case of gross misconduct, the agreed procedures have been followed:

◆ inability to do the job in a situation where necessary and sufficient training has been given;

◆ a continuous negative attitude at work, which has affected the employees or the work of others adversely;

◆ continuous disregard of required health and safety procedures;

◆ deliberate destruction of an employer's property;

◆ continued harassment of other employees.

There are certain situations in which dismissal has been considered unfair or in breach of employment law. These include:

◆ pregnancy;

◆ a discriminatory reason, e.g. race, colour or religion;

◆ being a member of a union;

◆ a non-relevant criminal record; if the employer has previously been unaware of a criminal record, it is not a reason for dismissal unless it is central to the job, e.g. a cashier convicted of stealing from the till or a schoolteacher convicted of child abuse.

A firm cannot be required to reinstate someone who has been unfairly dismissed, but failure to do so or to employ in another capacity is likely to be reflected in the damages awarded to an employee whose case has been successful.

Redundancy

One of the most difficult situations for an organisation is when it is required to make someone redundant. If

DENIM BLUES Levi's has slashed 13,000 jobs in the past two years and closed 24 US factories and four European plants

Levi's can lay claim to being the world's biggest clothing brand but it has failed to spot what has been happening among its core 15 to 24-year-old market.

Outwitted by the vagaries of fashion, Levi's has seen its share of the key US market plunge to 17 per cent compared with 31 per cent a decade ago. It has suffered similar declines in Europe.

Throughout these troubled times rivals have been busy. VF Corporation, makers of the Wrangler and Lee brands, has increased its share of the denim market from 18 to 25 per cent share, while Gap has gone from 3 to 5 per cent.

Levi's global sales fell in 1998 to $6bn from $6.9bn the year before with worse expected for 1999. Its debts have soared to $1.8bn. It has incurred $1.3bn of restructuring costs since 1997 as it has scrambled to cut costs, shutting American and European factories and laying off workers.

Last week it had to renegotiate its borrowings with a consortium led by Bank of America with the new credit facilities secured against the company's assets, including its world famous Levi Strauss trade mark. If Levi's fails to repay $200m a year over the next two years the banks can take control of the brand name.

Source: Damian Reece, *Sunday Telegraph*, 13 February 2000

the problems of Levi Strauss (see above) are not solved they could easily result in redundancy. This can happen if a job that someone has been doing is no longer required and there is no possibility of that person being re-employed somewhere else in the organisation. Redundancy may also happen if, due to budget cuts, the firm needs to reduce its workforce. If redundancies are to take place, then set guidelines are normally followed to ensure that the correct person or people are made redundant. Often the principle is 'last in, first out'. People who feel that they have been unfairly treated can go to an Industrial Tribunal, which will consider their case and make a ruling. People who are made redundant are given redundancy payments, which will have been worked out with unions in advance and which are related to the employee's wages and the length of time employed by the firm. Many firms faced with having to lose some members of the workforce will often try to do so by natural wastage, i.e. by not replacing all or some of those who leave. Where this does not work or is insufficient, they will often pursue a policy of voluntary redundancy. However, an invitation to leave is often a high-risk strategy because those who are easily

employable elsewhere are often the ones a firm needs to keep.

The law at work

There are a number of laws that are in place to protect both the employee and the employer. These laws cover issues such as employment rights and **health and safety** issues. It would be impossible for every employee to know the law inside out, but unions will protect their members and if workers think they have a problem concerning law at work, then they should contact their union representative. The issue of **employment law** is a huge area, so we will mention briefly the more important points.

When someone starts to work for an organisation, they enter into a **contract**. This is a legally binding agreement between the employer and the employee and is designed to protect the rights of both. It is not necessary, in all cases, to issue an actual contract, but it is necessary that the employee has particulars of its main points and knowledge of where full details can be found. The main features of such a contract are shown in Table 14.1

Name of firm	Guzzlers Restaurant
Job title	Kitchen porter
Responsible to	Chef
Start work	1 Jan. 2001
Hours	15 hours per week
Pay	Hourly, 10% above minimum wage
Holidays	14 days per annum, rising to 21 days after three years
Notice	One week either side
Pension scheme	None
Trade union membership	None in business but membership recognised
Discipline	See staff handbook; copy supplied

Table 14.1 Features of a contract of employment

A contract does not have to be exchanged immediately, but, as soon as you commence work, its terms and conditions apply. That is why the date of starting work is so important. All kinds of entitlements and responsibilities begin at that time.

Employees should expect standards of safety to be good. All businesses must have a code of practice for health and safety and must conform to that code. This applies to a wide range of organisations, including schools and churches. Among the things that must be provided for at work are:

- establishing and continuously maintaining a safe and healthy work environment;

- ensuring conditions of work are safe and healthy, e.g. the temperature is reasonable or clothing to compensate is provided;
- ensuring that the space in which workers must work is sufficient for the nature of the task and the kinds of movement that are necessary;
- ensuring sufficient provisions for health, e.g. toilets and wash facilities;
- ensuring that the equipment used is safe and that the actions necessary on the part of employees to keep it safe are undertaken;
- ensuring that employees wear clothing appropriate to the product and the processes – standards of clothing and hygiene are particularly high where food or food-related products are being produced;
- ensuring habits of safety through training and the promotion of good safety habits;
- warning where hazardous areas, activities or substances are. Training to make work effective and safe in these circumstances; action to ensure unauthorised personnel do not intrude.

The law intervenes to protect the weaker party in many different situations. You will find comments about the support given by the law in all the contexts in which this is important. Nowadays, it is directives from the EU, as much as law passed in the UK, that determines how employees are protected in the work situation.

Details of the names of Acts of Parliament or of directives may be of interest, but they are not required; neither are any features of legal procedure.

Over-to-you

Read the case study below and tackle the exercises that follow.

Case study – Brankscoombe Copy Services

Branskcoombe Copy Services is expanding its business to include the servicing of office equipment. For this it will require four engineers, one office assistant and two maintenance staff. All will be expected to have driving skills and a clean licence. The engineers will be expected to have some experience in the servicing of office equipment. The engineers will have to work closely with the sales staff since they will also be expected to advise potential customers as to the most suitable equipment for their needs and to install that equipment. All staff will be expected to push for the purchase of Branskcoombe brands of software, paper and other accessories.

(a) Devise a job description for the engineers and from it a suitable advert.

(b) Explain where you would place this advert and why.

(c) The firm has no induction programme at the moment. Advise the management on a suitable induction programme for the new personnel.

(d) What training needs would you expect the firm to provide and what method(s) of training would you consider best?

Short-answer questions

1 List four objectives that an individual working for an organisation might have.
2 What is meant by a workforce plan?
3 Give four reasons why it is important that a firm does not have a high rate of labour turnover.
4 Write down a rough formula for measuring labour turnover.
5 Explain why this formula is not very helpful.
6 Explain why it is important for an organisation to have a good induction programme for its new employees.
7 Give three reasons why it might be necessary for someone to be dismissed from an organisation.
8 Explain why you think it is a good thing that there are laws relating to employment protection.
9 Explain what is meant by voluntary redundancy.
10 Why might employees try to avoid health and safety regulations?

Discover and learn

1 Work in groups. Select a business in your area and find out what kind of induction programme it runs for new employees. Compare your findings with others in your group and comment on those things that appear to be good practice.
2 Consider the induction programme for your own school or college.
   (a) Did it meet your needs?
   (b) How can it be improved? Explain your answer.
3 Talk to people you know who are in work. Find out from them what their objectives are at work. Discover the extent to which they are achieving them.
4 In what ways does the law influence the things you do at school or college and the ways in which you do them? Comment on your findings.

Summary

In this section we have recognised that:

● Individual employees will also have objectives, which may be different from those of the organisation.

● It is important for the organisation to have a plan that will consider their employment needs.

● In order to run efficiently, an organisation must be very careful in selecting its workforce.

● It also needs to carefully induct and train the workforce so that it gets the best from the men and women who work for it.

● There are employment laws that affect both the employer and the employee, both of whom have rights that need to be considered.

● Employees are the most important resource that any organisation can have.

● It does not matter how technologically advanced the machinery is or how educated the senior managers are, if the workforce are not motivated and do not have objectives that closely match those of the organisation, then efficiency will be lost.

Key words

Definitions of Key words can be found in the Glossary on page 236.

contract of employment
employment law
health and safety
induction
labour turnover
off-the-job training
on-the-job training

organisational objectives
recruitment
redundancy
training
unfair dismissal
workforce planning

15 Motivation and leadership

On completion of this section you should be able to:

➤ understand and explain the importance of motivation to business success

➤ demonstrate how motivation can reduce conflict and increase co-operation

➤ show understanding of the theories of selected writers

➤ explain and apply those theories

➤ explain different styles of management and compare them

➤ show how good leadership increases the performance of workers

What is motivation?

The workforce of any organisation is made up of individual people who go to work for different reasons. If asked, the most likely reason they would offer is to earn sufficient to meet their individual needs. Among other motives might be:

♦ Personal satisfaction is gained from the work.

♦ One gets bored doing nothing.

♦ It gives status among friends outside work.

♦ It is good to be with other people.

What matters to employers is that workers will be motivated to work in such a way that the objectives of the organisation are met as cost-effectively as possible. Employers will need to be aware of what the employees are trying to achieve, because the greatest motivation will develop if workers feel that, through working towards the objectives of the organisation, they are achieving their own. If there is a conflict of objectives the organisation will not be as efficient as it could be. Managers should be looking constantly for signs of poor motivation (see Table 15.1).

Conflicting views

In any situation people may well come into conflict with one another. This can be a very good thing if they are prepared to discuss their views with other people. If people are prepared to listen to one another, very often better solutions can be produced. It was for this reason that Mary Parker Follett (*Dynamic Administration:*

Absenteeism	Deliberate absence for which there is not a satisfactory explanation; often follows a pattern
Lateness	Often becomes habitual
Poor performance	Poor quality work; low levels of work or greater waste of materials
Accidents	Poorly motivated workers are often more careless, concentrate less on their work or distract others, and this increases accidents
Labour turnover	People leave for reasons that are not positive; even if they do not get other jobs they spend time in trying to do so
Grievances	There are more of them or there is much more grumbling within the workforce
Low response rate	Workers do not respond very well to orders or leadership and any response is often slow

Table 15.1 Some indicators of poor motivation

Activity

Work in small groups. Discuss the reasons why you think people go to work. Why may these be different depending on the kind of organisation they work for?

Discuss the different motivations to work that might exist for:

(a) a kitchen porter;

(b) someone who works on a production line;

(c) a potter who hand throws her products;

(d) the owner of a computer servicing business.

Collected Papers, Pitman, 1941) argued that conflict was not only inevitable it was desirable.

It is often the case that in organisations people do come into conflict. This may be because the objectives of an individual may be different from those of the organisation. It can be very useful for workers to talk to others in the organisation in order to minimise conflict. However, conflict can be a good thing and may be used constructively to solve problems. Listening to the views of those who operate the machines can sometimes solve production problems. Organisations can save large amounts of money in this way. Therefore, it is important for the leadership style to lend itself to this approach.

It has to be said that if people are happy at work there is much less chance of unhelpful conflict arising. Managers and leaders must have their finger on the pulse of the organisation so that potential difficulties can be spotted and, hopefully, sorted out before major problems arise.

Activity

Write down a list of all the possible causes of conflict that you can think of that might occur in an organisation. As a group compare the lists.

Discuss how managers and others could have avoided these causes of conflict in the organisation and suggest ways in which that conflict could be used positively.

Theorising about situations

The kinds of problems that exist in most organisations have been known for a very long time. Many studies have been undertaken and some of them provide helpful observations about why problems exist and how they may be tackled. Theories about human behaviour at work are simply well-researched explanations that we can apply to situations we come across.

The people behind the theories

There are many theories of motivation, but in this section we will concentrate on four of the best-known theorists. These four are in our syllabus and you need to know about their ideas. You should also read about others and feel free to use their thinking in situations you come across in your studies, or which are presented to you in your examinations.

Abraham Maslow

Maslow looked at motivation from a very broad perspective and asked the question 'why do people work?'. He then answered his own question by saying that they do so to satisfy a number of human needs, ranging from basic physiological needs like those for food, drink and survival to higher-level needs like self-expression and self-realisation. This pattern of needs is shown in Figure 15.1 and further explanation is given in Table 15.2.

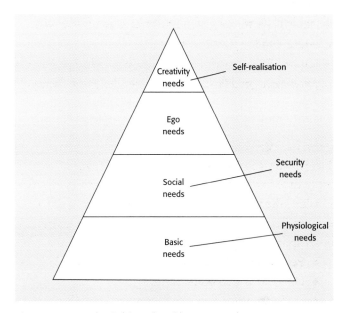

Figure 15.1 Maslow's hierarchy of human needs

Maslow argues that human needs form a pyramid because they are of a different order and that satisfaction occurs from the bottom. He also argues that, if a given need remains unsatisfied, it is likely to become the focus of attention, This is particularly true of the lower-order needs.

Needs	Examples
Physiological	Food, water, oxygen, sleep, survival.
Security, safety	Order, income predictability, steady job, freedom from fear, security
Social	Group identity, feeling of belonging
Ego	Respect, status, approval, esteem, reputation, importance, confidence
Self-realisation	Fulfil potential, develop fully, achieve greater things, success

Table 15.2 Examples of human needs

Physiological needs Most of us have never been really hungry. We have seen hunger in pictures from Africa and other parts of the world. When that kind of hunger and thirst are present, all the thoughts and actions of the human being are motivated by the need for food and where it may come from. In these circumstances we can understand that people will have no other interest and that such lower-order needs must be satisfied first. All most of us mean when we say we are hungry is that we have missed a meal. For us the physiological needs are not so much the centre of our lives. Also we are no longer dependent on work to fulfil the basic needs. Within the welfare state, when we have enforced absence from work, unemployment or sickness benefits are available to us. These will at least ensure that our basic needs are met.

Security and safety In many climates safety is mostly about shelter. In some countries it really is about safety. But what is really meant by this group of needs is that the individual needs to feel safe. This requires confidence that the job is secure, enough money to meet at least basic needs, freedom from fears of all kinds, a general confidence that all is well, and a place of safety and shelter.

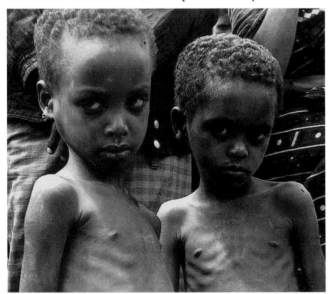

Malnourished children are paraded in the market place in the southern Ethiopian village of Haysuftu to show the extent of the famine in the area. Famine continues to stalk thousands in this region after they lost their cattle due to the lack of rains and violent inter-clan clashes.
Source: Popperfoto/Reuters.

Social needs

Once secure and safe, people can begin to look for satisfaction of needs that are associated with relationships with other people. Such needs are strong in some people and weaker in others. Some see a family including children as a central focus, whilst others are much happier on their own. Most of us want to associate with other people. We form and join groups, we make friends and we associate through clubs and societies.

Within the workforce such needs are often very important. Some people form very close bonds with those they work with and those bonds often become their main reason for going to work.

Ego needs Ego needs are not always selfish. They are about you and me as individuals. We need to express ourselves and we need to respond to others. Equally we need their response to us. For most of us it matters what other people think, whether they respect us or not and whether we are recognised as making a positive contribution somewhere.

In the work situation it is this need that spurs us on to better qualifications, promotion, leadership roles and increasing responsibilities. Not everyone is ambitious. Remember Bill, in the last section, whose only interest was to stay as he was, doing the things he had always done. Some people do avoid responsibility and would rather be led than lead. Good managers recognise these differences and try to work with them so as to maximise the effective use of the human resources available.

You achieve little but a frustrated workforce if ego needs are ignored and opportunities to develop are withheld. But it is equally disastrous to try to move the people who do not wish to change or be challenged. The way firms manage training and promotion decisions is often crucial. Some people will leave because they have not been promoted or will be increasingly unmotivated as others pass them by. Others, once they have the status and training associated with promotion, will often go off to better jobs elsewhere.

Self-realisation Most of us have potential that we wish to use. Most of us seek to be successful at something. Self-realisation is not about being talented in one of the arts, although this is the way that many people realise themselves. The well-written and well-performed play, the stimulating novel and beautifully composed and played music are all examples of self-realisation. Our history is full of examples, but this way is open to few of us. What we all seek is our own channel for achievement. It can be in a well-crafted wood working, in a well-ploughed field, in successfully bringing up a family or in playing a game to a high standard. Through these things we achieve fulfilment. Some examples are:

◆ The owner of a business, who has built it up to success and is able to pass it on to the next generation.

◆ The teacher whose ambition was to be a head and who has become one with great success.

◆ The individual who is good at a sport and who is selected to play for their country or to participate in the Olympic Games.

In effect, the person who is fulfilled is the one who sets any high target and reaches it.

Maslow helps us to understand that there is always a target, that there is always something that can motivate us and the absence of this will frustrate us. The role of the leader in the work situation is to identify those who need motivation, to discover what might motivate them and then devise a strategy to achieve it.

However, managers set out to achieve the objectives of the business and they will only seek to motivate workers in situations where those objectives are not being achieved and where there is a reasonable expectation that better motivated workers will enable the organisation to achieve objectives. For managers to do this they have to be sufficiently close to workers to know enough about them. There will, in most cases, be no general solution that will bring all workers into line. A flexible approach is always more likely to succeed than a blanket change.

Activity

Work in small groups. Discuss the main features of Maslow's hierarchy. Do you think it is a good explanation? Does it apply in all cases?

Consider your own approach to your studies. What do you learn from Maslow's theory that might be helpful to you?

Frederick Herzberg

First we must distinguish between **movement** and **motivation**. Movement is about the factors that will persuade me to go to work. Motivation is about the factors that will persuade me to work well, not because I must but because I want to. I will go to work for a variety of reasons, which have no bearing on my preparedness to work when I get there. You, too, will go to school or college or your part-time job for reasons that do not influence your desire to work and to do a good job.

Activity

Work in small groups. Each make a list, without consulting the others, of the things that make you come to school or college each day. Compare your list with other people in the group.

Now make a list of the things that do (or would) make you work well. Compare those lists

Discuss the things you have learnt from this.

Herzberg's theory is often called the two-factor theory because from his research he divided the influencing factors in the workplace into the two lists shown in Table 15.3. The motivating factors are all positive factors associated with doing the job and with the satisfaction or enjoyment that arises from this. There is a strong relationship with Maslow's ego needs and self-realisation needs. The hygiene factors are more about the conditions in which work is done, both those that are about the work environment and those that are about basic working relationships. Dissatisfied workers are more likely to be absent, to be late, to do poor work and to respond in all those ways we associate with poor motivation. Hygiene factors are those, the absence of which causes demotivation and the presence of which is expected without leading to greater motivation. They are factors that, provided they are present, will lead to movement towards work but will not persuade workers to work well.

Hygiene factors	Motivating factors
Wages	Things about the job
Conditions of work	Efforts made are recognised
Culture of the organisation	Responsibility
Relationship with bosses	Opportunity to develop
Treatment at work	Opportunity for promotion
Feelings about work and own efforts	Success
Controls and limitations	Self realisation at work
	Status

Table 15.3 Herzberg's two-factor theory

Activity

Explain why pay is not listed as a motivating factor. Do you agree with this? Give reasons for your answer.

Compare and contrast the ideas of Maslow and Herzberg.

Elton Mayo

The main thrust of Mayo's work was to show the important part that groups play in the motivation of individuals. He carried out a series of experiments, which became known as the Hawthorne Experiments. He carried these out over a five-year period and basically they involved changing the working conditions of a group of women.

Over the five years Mayo implemented a wide range of changes and discovered that, with each change, production increased. At the end of the experiment the women were returned to their original working conditions, but, surprisingly, production increased to its highest level as a result of that change. It was, therefore, obvious that the changes in the working conditions were not the cause of the improvements. The reason seemed to be that the women in the group had felt important in being singled out for the experiment.

The women (within the group) developed good relationships with each other were and they allowed to devise their own work patterns and rules. These relationships made the job a happier one and the women felt under less pressure. Mayo then decided that work satisfaction depends both upon the informal relationships between workers in a group and upon the relationships between workers and supervisors. Positive feelings of co-operation and a desire to impress will outweigh the impact of the physical surroundings, even if they are quite poor.

The significance of Mayo's work is that it shows that the group is an important factor in motivation. Individuals do not necessarily follow their own self-interest. This is fundamental if the objectives of an organisation are to be fully met. Managers need to be aware of the dynamics of a group and can then use these effectively in meeting objectives. If possible, organisations should encourage groups to become more efficient by use of training and perhaps by team-building exercises. Obviously, it is necessary for the group to be working for the organisation and not

against it, so it is important that managers do not find themselves in a situation where the group is united against them.

Groups can be formal, that is, set up by the organisation, or informal, where people meet together in the canteen, for example. People belonging to the same trade union could be a very effective group. Managers can set up formal groups, but informal groups are more difficult to control and use for the benefit of the organisation as a whole. In formal groups there is usually an appointed leader and objectives are set by the people who set up the group. In an informal group the leader usually emerges and objectives change with the membership and needs of the group.

Activity

What formal groups do you belong to in your school or college? Who set these groups up and what are their objectives?

What informal groups do you belong to? Analyse the reasons why you are in those groups. How does the role you play differ between these informal groups?

Douglas McGregor

McGregor was a social scientist, and from his experience he developed what has become known as the **Theory X** and **Theory Y** approach. What McGregor said has often been misquoted. His theories are not about motivation but about attitudes.

McGregor saw the attitudes of managers to workers as lying on a line between two extremes. His Theory X in many ways demonstrates one extreme, the traditional approach to management, which involves high levels of discipline, control, obedience and conformity. In other words, the managers tell the employees exactly what to do and when and where to do it. McGregor's Theory Y demonstrates the opposite extreme. In this he argues that managers assume that people enjoy mental effort and will actually be self-disciplined if they are committed to the objectives of the organisation.

The inference is that managers who adopt a Theory Y attitude to workers will explain and share the objectives of the organisation. Theory Y implies that people will respond to rewards, although, interestingly, McGregor says that these do not necessarily have to be monetary rewards.

McGregor also says that the majority of people have the ability to demonstrate initiative, which is not the gift of a few but of many. Managers need to be able to create situations within the work setting where subordinates can demonstrate their initiative. This would be for the general good of the organisation, as well as for the individual.

However, this view may represent a challenge to managers, who may feel threatened by a situation where they have less control and where others may be coming up with good ideas. Table 15.4 shows these two extreme attitudes.

What managers assume	
Theory X	**Theory Y**
Workers are lazy	Workers are keen
Workers need to be pushed	Will work on their own
Workers need control	Workers can be self-directing
Workers need threats and punishment	Workers respond to rewards and recognition
Workers avoid responsibility	Workers seek responsibility
Workers have no ambition or initiative	Workers are ambitious and seek to show initiative

Table 15.4 Theory X and Theory Y

In practice most managers are somewhere between those two extremes. Those close to Theory X manage in an autocratic way, whilst those closer to Theory Y are much more flexible and democratic in their approach.

It is unwise to assume that the autocratic approach is always wrong. There are people who like to be directed and controlled and there are situations in which there is little value in the democratic approach:

1 In every group of people there is likely to be at least one who prefers to be controlled and directed, likes being told what to do and when to do it. This person will often fail to achieve if deprived of the firm direction needed. Most teachers will identify at least one student like that in every group.
2 Some situations require immediate action and the unquestioning obedience of the workforce. This is true, e.g. in military situations, in the police force or the fire service.

The work of these theorists should not be seen as purely theoretical. They have much to offer managers as they seek to understand and motivate their workers. It is clear that managers need to be close to those they control if the findings of the theorists are to be applied. In today's ever-changing and often difficult organisational setting, innovative and creative management is necessary. No longer will people tolerate simply being told what to do; nor can it be assumed that they will be motivated only by money.

Activity

1 How do you like to be managed? What is best for you and why do you think that is? Are you the same in all situations? Discuss these issues within the group. What have you learnt from that discussion?
2 If organisations adopt a Theory Y approach, what do you think are the benefits and disadvantages, from the point of view of:
   (a) the workers;
   (b) the management;
   (c) the organisation as a whole.

We need to talk

All of us spend a lot of time communicating with other people. We can do this in all kinds of ways:
- by speaking to them face to face;
- by using the telephone;
- by sending faxes or emails;
- by sending letters, memos and various other pieces of paper;
- by using our body language;
- by indirect means like notice boards and other people;
- by ignoring people; this often conveys a very strong message.

It is essential that we communicate with other people, in both our business and private lives, but what is even more important is that the **communication** is effective and can be understood. How often have we got ourselves into difficult situations, simply because our message has been misunderstood or misinterpreted? This can cause real problems of frustration or even anger and a breakdown in a relationship.

Activity

Read the case study below and then tackle the task that follows.

Case study – Benson and Co.

Benson and Co. is a small clothing firm, which makes clothing principally for a major high-street store. The contract to supply the store is very valuable to the firm as it offers a ready market for the products and a good return. However, the store is very demanding in terms of delivery times and of the quality of the goods. Indeed, it sends its own quality-control expert to take random samples in the firm. Bensons' have been told that if they cannot meet delivery deadlines, the contract will not be renewed. The nature of the work is that the employees, mostly female, are each involved in one process only. They tend to operate on a very solitary basis and have little time together, except at the limited tea-break time. The employees are paid using the piece-rate system.

The management of Bensons' is concerned that production is not as good as it might be; the quality controller has noticed an increasing number of problems and morale seems to be low amongst the workers. There also seems to be an increasing rate of absenteeism. Jobs could be in danger.

You have been called into Benson and Co. as a management consultant to advise on the situation. Bearing in mind what we have been considering about motivation, write a short report giving your opinion and advice on the way forward.

More and more people have access to email and the internet and the communication doors they open
Source: ntl.

Within an organisation, the process of communication is absolutely vital if the organisation is to achieve its objectives. Poor communication can cause mistrust and suspicion amongst the employees and this can lead, at best, to a reduction in motivation and production. At worst, it leads to very poor industrial relations. It has been said that a manager in an organisation can spend as much as 80% of his working day communicating with others. It has also been suggested that 80% of all industrial problems arise or are made very much worse through poor communication. There are some very common factors that result in communication being poor:

- The words used can cause problems. This is most common when one person is using technical language that the other person does not understand. Examples are passing on accounting information or talking about computers.
- The tone of a message will often cause problems. It is not what you say but how you say it that conveys the message.
- Timing can be crucial. If someone gets a message too late, after someone else, when they are not concentrating or in poor circumstances, it can be ignored, forgotten or misunderstood.
- People's feelings and emotions can influence how a message is received. If we do not like someone or do not trust them we are likely to disbelieve what we are told. If we trust or like them, we may believe something that should not be accepted. Sometimes status gets in the way. When a boss gives a message, it is often believed and acted upon. When a subordinate gives one, it is commonly ignored.

Activities

1 Try a game of Chinese whispers in the class as a whole. Start a slightly complex message at the front and pass it towards the back by word of mouth. Relay the final message to the rest of the class.

2 Figure 15.2 shows different kinds of communication net. Try them out and discuss your conclusions.

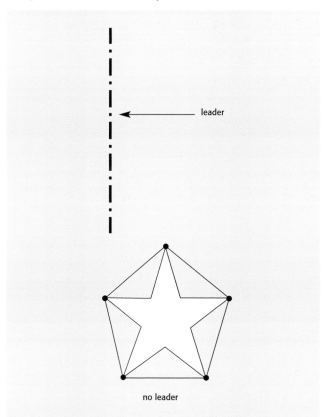

Figure 15.2 Different types of communication net

3 Choose any problem known to you from the news, local activity or what happens in your school or college. Discuss the extent to which better communication would have helped.

4 A lesson can be delivered in any one of the following ways:

(a) all talk with you listening and making notes;

(b) by using dictation;

(c) by using a case study;

(d) by using visual aids;

(e) by using a marker board or overhead projector;

(f) by brainstorm or discussion;

(g) by question and answer.

Discuss circumstances in which each of these methods might be either a good way or a bad way.

The strengths and weaknesses of communication methods are listed in Table 15.5. To get communication right we have to pay careful attention to:

- ◆ ourselves as senders and our awareness of the person to whom the message is being sent; if the receiver cannot understand or interpret the message, the communication is a waste of time;

- ◆ the nature of the message; there is no point in sending urgent messages through a slow medium, e.g. second-class post, or confidential information in a way that allows open access;

- ◆ the response we hope to get; abrupt unfeeling messages will not work where we need co-operation or want to make a sale;

- ◆ timing; sending out bills to arrive on Christmas Eve is not likely to be received kindly;

Method	Strengths	Weaknesses
Oral	Direct	Need to listen carefully
	Can be varied	Affected by noise
	Easy to understand	Passive
	Easy access	No permanent accurate record
	Can be questioned	Can be distorted
	Quick	Quickly forgotten
Written	Recorded	Often difficult to read
	More structured	No body language
	Easy to distribute	Feedback slower
	Cannot be varied	No immediate response
	Message identical	May be misinterpreted
		Costly and time consuming
Visual	More interactive	Needs close attention
	Demands attention	Sometimes too fast
	Often easier to remember	Not always clear
	Creates greater interest	Interpretations vary
Technological	Great speed	Cannot always be received
	Interactive	Relies on receiver
	Creates interest	Is expensive in hardware
	Encourages response	Not universal
	Ignores boundaries	Can be intercepted
	Good image	Diminishes personal contact

Table 15.5 Strengths and weaknesses of communication methods

Part 2 Business decisions and business behaviour

- the nature of the medium; some are not suitable for all messages; some are too costly, some are too slow, some are inappropriate for the receiver;
- the purpose of the communication; the objective is always to change someone's behaviour so that you get the response you seek; in some cases it is to encourage a purchase, in others to get into higher education or to get a job.

Motivating people

Firms have objectives and they relate to the outcomes of business activity. To achieve these outcomes they will have to motivate the workforce. The theorists give us some idea of what might motivate people and clearly effective communication is an essential feature. What methods are commonly employed?

Wages and salaries

Almost all surveys produce a strong indication that people think they are motivated by money, and up to a point we all are. Some are more money conscious than others; hence the way that people are paid tends to be the starting point. Among the most common methods are:
Time-based wages Employees are paid by the hour and the total wage they earn is determined by the total time worked. Workers may also be paid overtime rates. This could be one and a half times or twice the normal hourly rate. Overtime is voluntary, but can be a very good way of earning extra money for special times of the year, such as holidays or Christmas. No worker can be required to work overtime. At certain anti-social times, such as night working, working week-ends and bank holidays, the basic rate is likely to be increased. Time-based wages put the emphasis on quality and on taking your time over a job.
Output-based wages Employees are paid according to the output they achieve. For example, someone may be involved in a job where they pack socks into boxes. The number of boxes packed will determine how much they earn. Often, in this situation, people decide how much they want to earn during a week and work accordingly. They may have packed enough boxes in three days to earn what they regard as a sufficient wage. They will take two days off work. In most cases, managers are happy with the arrangement, because they know that, if they insisted on workers attending for five days, they

would simply slow down and not actually pack any more boxes. This type of payment is often for boring, repetitive jobs and puts the emphasis on the quantity of work done rather than on the quality.

Activity

John is in a job where he is paid by the hour. He earns £4.75 an hour. This week he has worked for 37 hours and has done 5 hours overtime at time and a half.
  Calculate his gross pay for the week.

Salary Employees are paid an annual amount of money, which is then divided into monthly payments. It is usually the case that staff, rather than manual workers, are paid in this way. In many salaried positions, it is not possible to earn overtime, any extra work done outside normal working hours is regarded as part of the job. This is true in the case of teachers and most managers. It puts the emphasis on getting the job done. It is particularly suitable when the job cannot be limited by either time or output and tends to convey status to the receiver as compared with wage earning. However, many salaries are lower than the annual amounts earned by some wage earners.
Commission This is when a percentage of a sale price is given to the employee as an incentive to sell more goods. Sales people may well be paid by a basic salary plus commission. In some cases, the basic salary is quite low and so encourages the person to sell as much as possible. It is up to the individual what the final amount earned will be. The more they sell, the more they earn. In other cases, people can be paid on a commission-only basis. Commission is often earned in professional occupations like that of the auctioneer, the estate agent and the art dealer. Estate agents and auctioneers may get commission payments from both the buyer and the seller.

Activities

1 Jennifer works in an office and earns £1,250 per month. How much does she earn per week? (Be careful. This is not as straightforward as it looks!)
2 Ahmed is a salesperson. This month he will earn a basic salary of £1,100. He has also sold goods to the value of £1,200, on which he earns a commission of 7.5%. How much will his gross payment be this month?

Profit sharing   This is meant to ensure that the workers strive to meet the objectives of the firm because they will share in the resultant profits. Such shares in profit are often described as bonuses and paid out at worker-friendly times of the year like Christmas and holidays.

Share options   These make the worker a shareholder in the business and thus give a permanent stake in the success of the business. They often have only a short-term effect because the workers sell their shares.

Productivity agreements   Often negotiated with unions. Extra payments are made when the productivity of the workforce improves to a targeted extent. Improvements in efficiency of this kind benefit all stakeholders.

Non-financial motivation

In many instances, we can use non-monetary methods of motivation. As Herzberg indicated, people are motivated by things other than pay. In jobs that do not motivate of themselves, absenteeism and lateness become common once pay has reached an acceptable level. Among the approaches most commonly used are:

Goal setting   Employees and supervisors can sit down together and negotiate achievable goals. Where this is done in a supportive climate, it can motivate people. It is important, however, that the goals have been understood and agreed by the workers. Obviously the goals that are set need to be realistic as far as the workers are concerned and yet, at the same time, they need to benefit the organisation. Honest communication is essential at the meeting where the goals are set so that there is no confusion. It is easy sometimes for people to agree to things and yet, when they consider more carefully, they realise that they have bitten off more than they can chew. This will benefit no one.

Employee participation   There are various methods of involving the employees in the running of the business. It should be noted, however, that there is a difference between employee involvement, which may only involve single workers, and employee participation, which is a principle whereby employees are seen to be an important and fundamental part of the process of management within the organisation. This process may well involve workers being on the boards of companies. When workers are involved in the decision-making

processes, and effectively in the running of the company, it is expected that they will support fully the company philosophy and strategy. Employee participation can take a number of forms:

- Financial involvement where the employees actually have a capital stake in the organisation. This may be through profit sharing or share option schemes.
- Job involvement, when employees can contribute to the way their own jobs are organised. Because they have a say in working conditions and practices, there should be fewer complaints. Also it would be expected that job satisfaction can be improved.
- Managerial involvement, when employees sit on joint decision-making committees. The most likely committee is the Health and Safety committee.

Employees feel that management is prepared to listen to them in terms of possible improvement to processes or indeed simply on more day-to-day issues. It is important in this situation that suggestions are acted upon, otherwise the basis of trust is lost. If effective employee participation is to take place, then the culture of the organisation must allow it and indeed foster it. The management style must be open and democratic and levels of trust must be high. Smaller organisations tend to lend themselves more easily to participation because discussions probably already take place as a matter of course. Larger organisations have difficulties, such as those associated with ineffective communication systems, as discussed above. It is important that comments made are passed on to senior management, even if the comments seem critical. There is a temptation for middle managers to ignore the critical comments in order to save embarrassment. However, when this happens, trust will be lost and participation will not be a success.

Job rotation   Jobs are rotated on a regular basis so that the workers can be involved with a range of operations and not simply be doing the same repetitive task day after day. This also enables workers to see how their particular function fits into the general scheme of things and how, without their contribution, the product could not be completed. A side effect of this scheme is that there can be a greater flexibility in the workforce. However, job rotation does not really work when it is just movement from one similar boring job to another. It does tend to work when it is based on multi-skilling and a genuine difference in the job being undertaken.

Job enlargement   Tasks are broadened or deepened so that employees become involved in a greater range of tasks. The result is a greater awareness of the overall process, as well as greater job satisfaction.

Job enrichment   Employees often become involved in decision-making and have much greater responsibility. The process often involves a slackening of outside supervision.

Quality circles   These are groups of employees who meet together on a regular basis to discuss issues such as the quality and level of output and safety. The groups try to devise ways of solving problems and implementing solutions. This approach has the benefit of involving the workers directly in the process of problem-solving and strategic management within their area. Undoubtedly motivation is increased as a result. There is also a greater sense of pride and achievement. There is an opportunity for the organisation to use expertise in the workforce and also the chance to see whether or not workers have potential for supervisory or management positions.

Flexible timings   This allows personnel to decide the hours they will work. It is suitable for workers with children who must be taken to school or in situations where transport is difficult and or unreliable like 'rush hours'. Generally there is a core time when workers must be in work, but choice around it. It is normal to have a limit both to the number of excess and missed hours that may be built up.

Perks and status symbols   These are most common among management and include such things as a company car, a well-furnished office, a fancy title or a parking space.

Appraisal   It may seem strange to include this as a motivator, and yet, used properly, that is exactly what it should be. Too often it is assumed that this is a method that an organisation uses to check up on employees. It has been regarded negatively and in many ways that is unfair. An effective appraisal system will be a two-way communication process where employees can discuss with their superiors their achievements over the previous period. They can then discuss ways to improve their performance. This may be an ideal way for management to discover fundamental difficulties, perhaps, in the shop floor processes. If the processes can be improved, this will be of advantage to both management and workers. Where such appraisals are genuinely two-way, it also provides valuable information on the communication and leadership skills of supervisors.

Does management style matter?

Every organisation needs effective leadership if it is to succeed. There are natural leaders. We come across them whether it is as captain of the sports team or simply the person who always seems to take the lead in a discussion group. It is important that those who manage organisations have leadership ability, whether natural or learned, that will enable them to take people with them. The leader may have very sound and well thought out objectives, but if those who are to be led will not follow, then the objectives will never be achieved.

Activity

Work in small groups. Discuss the qualities you think a good leader should have. Is anyone in your group a good leader? Give reasons. Is a leader born or can leadership be learned?

There are formal leaders within organisations who are appointed to have a managerial roles. Organisations must realise the potential of the informal leader. He or she is the person people naturally look up to and who may not have, as yet, a formal leadership responsibility. Managers should be aware of possible leaders and give them some sort of responsibility. This could be by inviting them to sit on a consultation committee within the organisation, or possibly even by having them as a worker representative on the board. The natural talents of these people need to be harnessed for the good of the organisation. In simple terms, it is better to have people with informal leadership skills working for rather than against the organisation's goals.

Leaders lead in different ways according to their natural traits and according to the situation. The main leadership styles are:

Authoritarian   This type of leader has control, avoids discussion, issues instructions, often without explanation, and is unwilling to listen to subordinates. This style can cause major problems in an organisation where people have experience in what they are doing. Workers will feel unvalued and resentment will quickly build. However, where workers are inexperienced, this style of leadership may be effective, at least in the short term. It is of course, appropriate where the luxury of discussion may not be available, e.g. in a war situation. Such a leader has much in common with the Theory X attitude to management.

Democratic   This type of leader will encourage discussion, will involve others in decision-making, will consult and generally will try to help the employees to grow in terms of performance and self-worth. This type of manager needs to be prepared to be flexible in terms of views held and must, of course, be willing to delegate responsibility. Complex problems can often be approached using this management style. There is opportunity to use the talent and experience of others. However, workers need to feel comfortable with this approach and need to feel that their views are genuinely considered. There is no point in a manager paying lip service to this approach and then proceeding with plans that have already been decided upon. Here you will recognise a Theory Y attitude.

Laissez-faire   It has been said that this type of manager is not really a manager at all. He/she will be involved only in crisis management, reacting to situations and not managing them. He/she will simply leave things alone until they go wrong. There is no sense of strategic management. In today's organisational climate, it is doubtful if this management style would succeed. Nevertheless there are situations in which the style works. In such circumstances it is known as management by exception and involves refusing to interfere in a situation or a process unless something goes wrong.

Paternalistic   This type of manager will ask for opinions, but will then persuade employees to accept his/her point of view. In a sense this is playing at democracy, but being autocratic. Again, it will not be successful with experienced staff, who will soon become frustrated and disenchanted, but it is common in small firms where the boss is seen more as the 'father' of the whole team than as a boss.

Activities

Work in small groups
(a) Consider the part-time jobs that people have. Discuss the type of management style that you think exists in the organisation you work for. Give reasons for your decisions.
(b) Outline the management style of those who teach you. How appropriate do you consider that style is:
   ◆ for them;
   ◆ for you;
   ◆ for the task they have to undertake?

The style of leadership that is adopted will depend very much on:
   ◆ the organisation and its culture;
   ◆ the subordinates (what kind of temperament do they have? are they experienced?);
   ◆ the managers themselves;
   ◆ the task that is to be performed;
   ◆ the conditions and circumstances of the task.

The most successful managers are those who can adapt their style to suit different situations, although it is true to say that people tend to display one of the styles. It may not be easy for someone who is naturally democratic to become autocratic, or the other way round. Managers can be sent on training courses to improve their management skills and to make use of theory, but it still remains true that the best managers have a feel for the job.

Activity

Which form of leadership/management style would be most appropriate in the following circumstances? You should give reasons for your answers:
   ◆ the army;
   ◆ a small computer software company that employs 12 people;
   ◆ a large engineering company where there has been a history of industrial unrest.

Theories of leadership
Trait (or qualities) theory
This theory suggests that leaders are born rather than made. People are born with certain characteristics and come from a certain background that would make them leaders

Style theory
This suggests that leaders use a different style, as indicated in the last section. This could be authoritarian, democratic, laissez-faire or paternalistic. Researchers have looked at how different styles affect performance. The findings showed that, while people tend to experience more job satisfaction when working under a democratic leader, the level of productivity is only very slightly higher.

Contingency

Fiedler is the best-known theorist here. He suggested that the style of leadership depended upon the task being done, how much power the leader had and the relationship the leader had with the workers.

Best-fit approach

Managers need to assess the situation and then adapt their leadership style to fit it.

Management by objectives

The suggestion is that managers and subordinates closely discuss the objectives that are desired and how the subordinates can contribute to the achievement of these. There are obvious benefits of this kind of approach:

- Motivation is improved. As discussed above, there is greater motivation for employees when they are involved in the process of deciding on objectives and how best they can be achieved.

- Managers are forced to plan and develop objectives. They are also forced into a process of discussion and consultation.
- The structure of the organisation will be improved as managers can see more clearly where the weaknesses and strengths lie.
- Benchmarking is provided and this helps managers to control the situation better.
- Workers are working towards realistic targets.

There are also problems with this approach:

- The approach is very time-consuming because it involves so much discussion.
- Frustration can arise when objectives cannot be met because of external factors.
- Some organisations do not lend themselves to this approach. Perhaps there has traditionally been a very strong authoritarian approach to management.
- New skills need to be developed to cope.

Over-to-you

Short-answer questions

1 Define motivation. Don't look it up until you have defined it.
2 What is the value of team working?
3 Distinguish between a formal and an informal group.
4 State five different methods of financial motivation.
5 For each of your five methods of payment, give two examples of work for which the method would be appropriate.
6 Draw Maslow's Needs diagram and explain it.
7 Why did Mayo's workers always improve with every change?
8 Leaders cannot lead without willing followers. Explain.
9 What are the advantages of a flexitime approach?
10 Explain 'Management by objectives'.

Discover and learn

1 Investigate a local organisation and determine what style of management is used. Justify your conclusions.
2 Visit a local supermarket. From your observations, do you consider the workforce is, in general, well motivated. Support your conclusions.
3 Read the case study below and tackle the exercises that follow.

Case study – Plast-flower Ltd

Plast-flower Ltd is a medium-sized firm employing 58 workers. George Wilkenson was the founder of the firm and is its current manager. He is very autocratic in his approach to running the firm. People tend not to question his decisions, but it is obvious that productivity is low. There is also resentment among the workers because they are not being consulted about anything. They believe that there is much they could contribute that would improve productivity.

George is considering retirement and selling the firm to the highest bidder. Existing managers are very keen to buy, thinking they know how to make a success of the firm.

(a) Advise them on how they might motivate the workforce.

(b) Consider ways in which resentment can be reduced.

(c) The unrest has created a number of hostile informal groups. How should the new managers react to these?

Summary

In this section we have recognised that:

- Workers need to be motivated if the organisation is to achieve its objectives.

- There are different approaches to motivation, but it is important to note that money is not the only motivator. Indeed there are situations when money will not motivate at all.

- There is a very wide range of non-monetary ways of motivating. Experience shows that these often satisfy the higher needs and hence are successful.

- Although many ways have been tried, motivating workers engaged in dull or repetitive jobs is not easy. The modern approach is increasingly towards quality circles and team working.

- There are many styles of leadership that can be used within an organisation and, in many ways, these are best used by adapting them to the situation.

- Many people have leadership potential and some of the time they may not be in positions of authority. It is important that the organisation makes use of them in both formal and informal situations.

- Leadership style will impact upon the performance of individuals and, ultimately, it is the performance of individuals that will reach the organisation's objectives.

Key words

Definitions of Key words can be found in the Glossary on page 236.

communication	McGregor
Herzberg's two-factor theory	motivation
	movement
Maslow's hierarchy of human needs	quality circles
	Taylor
Mayo	Theory X and Theory Y

16 Management and organisation

On completion of this section you should be able to:

➤ show awareness of the main functions of management
➤ describe and explain these functions
➤ understand the ways in which businesses can be organised internally
➤ define and explain the terms used in organisational structure
➤ explain the strengths and weaknesses of different structures
➤ show understanding of the limitations of charts in describing how businesses actually work
➤ describe and explain the different approaches to organisation structure
➤ outline the advantages and disadvantages of each in context
➤ choose and justify a particular structure in given circumstances

What is organisation?

All structures need organisation to make them work efficiently. This section explains how organisations are built and how they enable a business to perform more effectively. No two organisations are really the same. Each has its own history and culture. In many ways this is dictated by the traditions of the business and the objectives and attitudes of its owners and managers. Most businesses started off small with one owner completely involved in the workings of the business. The owner will have developed a view of the world, and a way of working through which the culture of the business was developed. That, in turn, will have changed with time. Out of this culture objectives and strategies for achieving them will have arisen and, to make achievement possible, a structure will have been built and modified as needed. Whatever the cultural framework, the success of the business depends on the skill with which it is managed.

What do managers do?

There are many definitions of management and much debate as to whether it is an art or a science. Certainly the role of management is to get things done as efficiently as possible and the major resource managers have is the people employed by the business. Managers or owners must first set the objectives of the business and then achieve them through the workforce. The role is usually defined through a number of tasks that manage are expected to perform. Among these are:

Setting the objectives of the business Survival, profit and growth will figure among them.

Planning Once the goals are set, a strategy for achieving them has to be developed. Managers who do little planning and simply react to situations as they arise are not normally successful. As we saw in the last section, if employees feel part of this process, they are more likely to understand and to co-operate in plans to achieve the goals that are set.

Organising The manager works with a range of inputs and has to organise both the structure through which these inputs are used and the ways in which they are combined to achieve objectives. The process is one of adding value, and organisation will make this process more effective.

Leading Workers must be influenced and motivated to achieve goals and this is the role of good leadership. It requires good team-building skills as well as a style that is effective and appropriate for the workforce recruited and for the intended outcome.

Controlling Plans may be made on the basis of realistic objectives, but circumstances constantly change. Managers must ensure that the organisation is moving in an appropriate direction. If some parts of the organisation are not doing that or some circumstance has made a change of plan essential, then the manager must be able to take appropriate action. It may be that the objective has to be redefined or it may be that plans must be changed. Only effective control will offer the opportunity to modify as desired and when desired.

Delegation: the art of management

If a business is small it will be owned and operated by one person, who will do each of the required tasks with varying degrees of skill. Some things will be very well done, whilst others will be poorly done, for none of us can do all things well. As a business grows, there is the opportunity to employ and with employment the chance to share work. The best way is to let the new person do the things you are not good at as far as this is possible. From this sharing of work some specialisation will develop and the whole job will be done with greater effect. This is the simple notion, but how effective it is will depend on the extent to which the owner/manager has learnt to delegate. The owner is still the owner with the responsibilities of the business; these cannot be passed on. Authority to do things can be delegated. For many owners and managers **delegation** is both the most necessary and the hardest thing to do.

There are three aspects of delegation:

Authority   The delegate must have the authority to undertake the tasks selected. This will come in part from ability to do the job, in part from the external trappings of the job such as an office, a title and perhaps a uniform, but largely because the superior passes it on. Authority must be clear and certain, e.g. the power to spend money and the limit on how much, the power to hire and fire. It is the passing on of authority that many superiors find most difficult.

Responsibility   The delegate will be responsible to an immediate superior. What the responsibilities are and to whom the delegate must be responsible are usually indicated in a job description. The superior will expect correct, effective and efficient use of the powers given and that the resources are used for the purposes for which they were intended.

Accountability   The boss is still accountable both in law and in fact. He/she has chosen this method of

working, has recruited and trained the delegate and has made the decision that the delegate is capable of exercising the powers given efficiently. The accountability remains firmly at the top.

Principles of good delegation

Poor delegation simply leads to poor results and often to chaos since nobody knows what is happening. Among the principles of good delegation are:

- The nature of the task(s) should be clear to both sides and to those who will work with the delegate.
- The manager must ensure, perhaps by training, that the delegate is capable and will undertake the task in ways that support the objectives of the business.
- Results expected and the timing of them should be clear and realistic. Many delegations are spoiled by expectations that are unrealistic.
- The delegate must have sufficient and known authority. This is partly personal, but authority must be supported by the system.
- Those who need to know must be informed.
- Limitations of authority should be clear.
- The manager's ultimate accountability should be clear.
- Reporting requirements should be clear.
- Sources of advice and access to them should be spelt out.

The potential limits of delegation

Delegation is not a universal solution to all problems of a business. There are limits to it and these are:

- The costs in time, money, resources and possibly poor outcome. Small firms can afford to delegate very little and autocratically led ones will be reluctant to do it. The benefits must be thought to exceed the costs.
- The need for uniformity. Different people do things in different ways and want to show their initiative and individuality. Some firms want 'organisation people' who will always work in prescribed and predictable ways. This often prevents growth and results in lost opportunities.
- The size of the organisation or task. Small firms delegate little and tasks that are either too small or too large often remain undelegated.

- The expectations of the customer. Heads of schools often find it difficult to delegate because parents expect to see them and not someone junior. Vicars often find it difficult to delegate to lay persons because people will not want to see anyone other than the vicar.
- The attitudes and philosophy of the management.
- The quality of the recruits or of the personnel training.
- In some cases there needs to be a high degree of control and this hampers the style and effectiveness of the delegate.
- The need for confidentiality.

Co-ordination

The more that work is devolved, the more it has to be co-ordinated and the greater pressure there is for working together and for good communication. However many players there are, the organisation has to work as a team to ensure the achievement of overall objectives. Among the things that often make co-ordination difficult are:

Conflicting departmental objectives A common example involves marketing and production. Marketing may push for a high level of sales and/or for short delivery dates. The production department may not be able to produce what has been promised in the time given or may have to produce at a level of output, which increases unit costs of production. On the other hand, production may want to produce at the lowest cost per unit and this may produce an output that is either too great or too small for marketing's needs. Every department works out an annual draft budget and the total of these is almost always in excess of the amount available. Here, departments have to prioritise expenditure needs and to compromise with each other in order to ensure that overall business objectives are met.

Matters of common policy Activity within large firms when it is totally centralised is very rarely effective, but some things do have to be matters of agreed common policy. Where this is not the case, problems often arise. Where it is the case, some degree of freedom is lost by each of the line departments. Common policy is most often about issues like recruitment, promotion, training and finance.

Activity

You run a small tuck shop at your school or college. You are very particular about all aspects of managing it. However, it is growing into a bigger operation and you find it is taking too much of your free time and beginning to affect your studies. You will have to find and train someone to help you.

What problems do you think you will have in doing this? What preparations will you have to make in order to carry out this task effectively? What tasks will you delegate and why? What new responsibilities will this give you and how will you carry them out?

Formal and informal organisation

A formal organisation tightly controls the things that happen within it. Activities are grouped into departments, both roles and role interaction are well defined and everybody knows exactly what they are doing and who they work with. You would expect all marketing to take place within the marketing department and that there will be little cross activity.

- Effective specialisation and division of labour should ensure that people are experts at what they do and that mistakes are rare.
- There are established procedures, which ensure that most problems are expected and dealt with in a set way.
- Communication methods are well tried and tested and work effectively.

Of course, the real world is not like that; people are variable and sometimes absent, technology breaks down and new, unknown, problems occur all the time. No organisation can be perfect; no organisation can behave with perfect predictability and efficiency.

Informal organisation defines very broad roles and allows the participants to work out what is to be done, when and by whom. Interaction is never predictable because it depends on the people involved and the circumstances. All organisations must have elements of this because informal relationships such as work groups, interest groups and friendship groups are bound to develop in any business as it grows. Informal groupings can be used very effectively to the advantage of a business. However, they can also cause major problems in that they may pursue objectives that are in conflict with those of the organisation. Table 16.1 shows the potential costs and benefits of informal groups.

Benefits	Costs
Workers have more than one focal point	Not always possible to observe
Improves the morale of the group	Difficult to monitor and control
These advantages may be capable of good use by the business	May develop objectives hostile to the objectives of the business
Communication can be easier through the identified leader who, once on side, can bring the group along	The group may be resistant to change, particularly where change will break the group up or threaten objectives; Very often groups form precisely because members want to resist a particular change
Once on side, the group can be a powerful force ensuring that business objectives are met	

Table 16.1 Potential costs and benefits of informal groups

Activities

1 Explain the difference between formal and informal groups.
2 Discuss the informal groups that exist within your school or college. In the case of each one (a) is it on balance supportive, or (b) does it make life more difficult.
3 In what ways might any one of these groups be enabled to support the objectives of the school/college?

Organisation charts

An organisation chart is a visual representation of the roles and responsibilities within a business. Because businesses are dynamic and rarely stand still, such charts can only tell part of the story. They will describe who is responsible to whom and how the chain of command from top to bottom operates. Often small operations do not draw charts, but, the larger a business, the more necessary a chart is and the more complex it becomes. Figures 16.1 and 16.2 are both examples of charts drawn in a functional way. They are very easy to read, but it is impossible to show all the complexities of an organisation on a chart like this. Some relationships will cause problems, but there will be no evidence of that on the chart. There are also many relationships that will not be indicated by the chart.

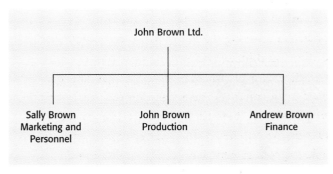

Figure 16.1 Chart for Small Firm Ltd

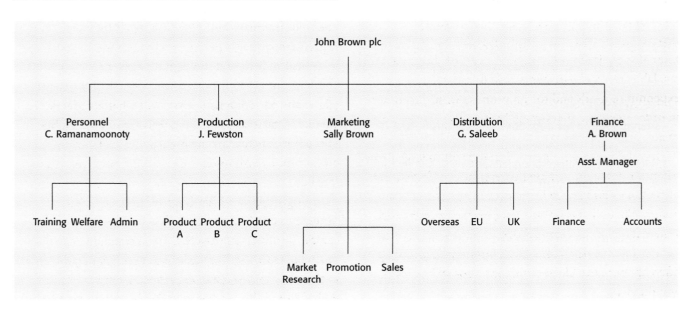

Figure 16.2 Chart for Large Firm plc

Organisation charts do contain certain elements that enable us to understand organisations and how they work more fully:

- Activities that take place within the organisation are shown. For example, it is easy to see the various departments and the main areas of work.
- The chart indicates division of labour and indicates how and when specialisation takes place. In some charts, where at least the top personnel are named, it is easy to see who is doing what.
- The official communication channels are also shown. Within an organisation there are many informal channels. They often change on a regular basis and are not always known to management.
- The chart shows who is answerable to whom. This is the chain of command. Larger organisations like that in Figure 16.2 may have a very tall structure. This in itself will cause problems. It is a long way to communicate effectively from top to bottom and from bottom to top. Smaller businesses like that in Figure 16.1 have flatter structures, which reduce communication problems. In modern organisations there is an increasing tendency to make the chart as flat as possible.
- The **span of control** individuals have is shown in the chart. This is the number of subordinates that a superior has direct responsibility for and control over. The size of span of control is often crucial.

Activity

Work in small groups. Each obtain a copy of the organisation chart of a local business. Discuss each chart using the points indicated above. What similarities and differences do you see? What do they tell you about the firms concerned?

As far as you can tell from observing the businesses, is the chart a good representation of how the firm works?

Choose another organisation known to you and try to draw its organisation chart

The firm must develop the organisation it needs. There is no such thing as a correct organisation. The chosen structure must be effective and must enable the firm to be efficient and competitive in achieving its objectives. Poor structures will fall short of this and, in addition,

are likely to lead to poor staff morale and poor communication.

We will assume that the organisation is a plc and discuss its features from the top down:

Shareholders   Not represented in the chart, but they are the owners of the business. Only the major shareholders take any part in the running of the business and they will be found, in many cases, on the Board of Directors. Shareholders can air their views at the AGM.

Board of Directors   Elected at the AGM, many of them will be there because they are holders of large blocks of shares. Some will have roles within the business, often as heads of the departments. Some will be on the Board because they add power or reputation to it. The Board determines major items of policy and sometimes ratifies major decisions.

The Managing Director   Represents the Board in the structure of the business. Sometimes called the Chief Executive. The Managing Director has overall responsibility to the Board for the operations of the business.

Heads of Departments   The standard functions are:

- marketing – which tends to be the focus of activity;
- production – working closely with marketing;
- personnel – often has responsibility across the firm;
- finance – often controls financial matters throughout the business.

There are many different names for these standard functions and some of them are subdivided. Common examples are distribution within marketing and training within personnel.

A firm may have more departments, particularly if it thinks some activities are of considerable importance. For example, a supermarket may have a customer service department and a big distributor may have a specialist transport department

The language of organisation

Understanding organisation structures is very much a matter of understanding the conceptual language that is used. Some of this has already been discussed. The main ideas are:

Authority   The right to behave in a certain way and exercise powers that have been delegated to you. It is important that people who are asked to accept responsibility are given the authority and that that authority is clear to subordinates.

Delegation   The passing on of authority and responsibility to someone else so that, through specialisation, efficiency and capability may be increased. The accountability always remains with the boss.

Hierarchy   Describes the whole organisation from top to bottom. It implies a series of levels of authority.

Chain of command   The line of authority as it passes from one level to the next. Some organisations tend to have tall charts and therefore a long chain of command, although the trend is towards flatter structures.

Span of control   The number of subordinates a superior has. Clearly there is a limit to the number a boss can efficiently control. This will depend on factors like:

- the working environment;
- the directness of control necessary;
- the pattern of work undertaken by each subordinate;
- the subordinates' skill and experience;
- the extent to which subordinates work smoothly as a team;
- the qualities and attitude of the leader;
- the leader's reputation and experience;
- the demands of the leader's own job.

The flatter an organisation, the bigger span of control is likely to be.

Centralisation   The extent to which the functions and policies of a business are in the hands of one branch, one small group or one person. If a firm allows its branches to behave as if they were separate businesses, that is decentralisation.

The extent to which there are common images (McDonalds) and common products(McDonalds), the extent to which stock ordering is centralised (many dress and shoe firms), the extent to which finance and accounting are centralised (the most likely of tasks to be treated in this way) all determine the degree of centralisation of the business. Some businesses are centralised by default because the boss finds it difficult to delegate.

Line and staff activity   All organisations that have a functional chart have lines of activity. This means the different levels of activity within a given department. In Figure 16.2 each of the departments has its own line. However, there are some functions where the help of a specialist is necessary or where a unified policy for the

McDonald's, familiar in many towns, throughout the world, has grown into the world's largest food service organisation

whole firm has to be ensured. Staff relationships occur when someone from outside who is an expert, perhaps a management consultant or a computer specialist, comes into a line to give advice. Such advice and even control are also a part of the work of members of the personnel department, whose job it may be to co-ordinate appointments, training, promotion or dismissal policies. Similarly, members of the finance department may come into another line to ensure common accounting procedures or to audit department accounts. Line and staff relationships are discussed later.

Roles   What an employee is expected to do within the business. It would have been outlined in the job description and often will change with time as an employee undertakes new tasks and responsibilities. When roles are not clearly defined, it leads to inefficiency. Sometimes an employee may have more than one role and this can lead to **role conflict** and to problems for the firm.

1 Jean Brewer is both Head Teacher of a school and a junior member of the French Department. John Duckham is head of French. Jean has to be careful not to allow her overall authority affect her departmental relationship with John and he has to develop a working relationship with her as a junior member of his department. A common problem in a school but often a difficult one.

2 John Francis is Head of a small local limited company and Jennifer Platt is a secretary in his firm. However, outside business Jennifer is Mayor of the town and leader of the Council, whilst John is a newly elected council member.

Specification Similar to role. Relates to the details of a job and its relationship to other jobs. It is the basis of recruitment, of delegation and of authority. Appraisals are often undertaken with reference to the job specification.

Problems with line and staff relationships

The line in a business involves people at differing levels but in the same activity, e.g. Production or Marketing. There are some things in which they are involved which may need skills or expertise from outside. People who come in to provide these are called staff personnel. Examples of this happening include:

- The firm will have made decisions that given activities ought to be conducted in accordance with agreed and centralised policy, for example: recruitment and training.
- Some activities are highly specialised and need experts who may not be found in the line concerned. Some of these may work for the firm as a whole and need to visit branches from time to time, for example: computer specialists, auditors from finance.
- From time to time the organisation will consult experts about broad issues that affect every department of the firm. These may relate to efficiency and need a work study expert, or to rationalisation and involve questions of redundancy.

The main problems with this approach are often ones of attitude and uncertainty about control. The Head of the department and the managing team do not like what they often consider interference in their domain. This is particularly difficult when the staff member advising about computers or auditing the books is a junior member of another line and is advising or even instructing much more senior members of the firm. Specialist skills often tend to cut across seniority and status. Often, line personnel do not see the benefits of specialist support or consultants in their midst, but they do see the cost in money and the disruption of work of their department. It often creates uncertainty and even fear when the issues are rationalisation or work study. Departmental managers have been known to be unhappy when books are being audited or when the personnel department is making decisions about how a

job should be advertised or even who should be recruited. They naturally want to have the last word in these situations.

Smaller firms have to contract out a number of services that they would like to do in house but do not have the facilities or staff for. They would simply not be cost-effective. This could apply to computer services or to market research

Activity

Case Study – Hoy and Sons

Hoy and Sons have asked you to help with some problems. Currently they employ 20 people and their main product is garden ornaments. They sell these to one retailer, who has six branches. They are unhappy with reliance on a single customer. This gives them two immediate problems:

- They need to investigate the market and find ways of penetrating it.
- They think they should use technology to cope with stock levels, ordering, invoicing and billing.

They have asked you to decide which specialist they should employ. They can't afford both. Write a short report advising them. You may wish to suggest that neither should be employed, but you must justify your advice. You will need to investigate the costs of employing either staff or agencies and consider the benefits in each case.

Other structures

The use of functional charts, such as those seen in Figures 16.1 and 16.2, is not the only approach to internal organisation, although it is the most common. Alternative approaches include:

- organisation by product;
- organisation by system;
- the matrix approach.

Organisation by product

Figure 16.3 is a diagram of the human body. What does the body produce?

- From the mind we get ideas, imagination and creativity. This 'capital of ideas' is often

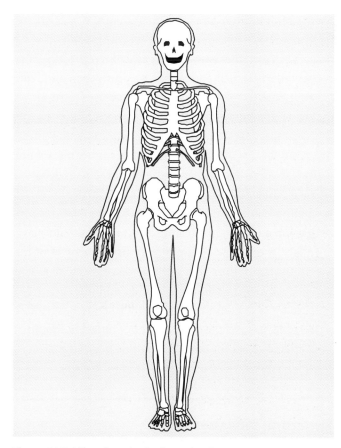

Figure 16.3 What does the body produce?

underestimated by business because it is difficult to value and will not be found in the balance sheet.

◆ From the body we get co-ordinated actions to produce products to develop and then use, as well as skills and effective communication through both speech and body language.

To do these things the body does not have a hand department, a speaking department or a production department. It calls upon all its skills and capabilities in an integrated way. Businesses can and do operate in this way, using a team to work together, blending all the necessary functions. Good examples of this are in research and development or in the launch of a new product. The product team carries out all the financing, marketing, production and personnel functions. Some firms work in this way all the time, whilst others only do it with special projects. The production of this book will be a good example of a team working together from the development of the idea through the writing, editing and printing to the final sale. Hotel chains are often large businesses and they may attempt to centralise things, but mostly they have to accept that each hotel is

a separate product with its own team and ways of working. They may, of course, centralise some things. Best Western is a group of independent hotels with separate teams in each hotel, but they work together to promote a common image and standard and to buy standard products that they all need.

Organisation by system

Again the body is a very good example. It works by a number of interlocking systems. These include:

◆ the circulatory system;
◆ the system of bones called the skeleton;
◆ the digestive system;
◆ the nervous system;
◆ the reproductive system;
◆ the waste disposal system.

Businesses may not organise as efficiently in terms of systems, but all businesses do have systems. The commonest are:

A communications system   This can be very old-fashioned and simple, going little beyond the notice board, memos, speech and the telephone. Increasingly, however, systems are more complex, but not necessarily more efficient. They use information technology, including the Internet. This puts the world, its markets and its opportunities at the fingertips of most personnel. However, it does lead to greater remoteness and problems of stress. Communication is still imperfect unless both sender and receiver can and do use it well.

A committee system   Most organisations work through committees or teams. They bring together representatives of different interests and often people at different levels. Some committees advise and others make decisions. Some are permanent and others are appointed for a given task and then disbanded. They are all formally created groups and roles within them are usually very tightly defined. Some are management committees or workers' committees and an increasing number are joint ones involving workers in management processes.

Quality circles and other team-based groups   These bring together all the workers, whatever their status within the firm to ensure the quality of the finished product by discussing, deciding and working together. This devolves responsibilities to the workforce and tends to increase motivation and morale.

The matrix approach

The matrix approach is an attempt to reduce some of the problems of communication and working together that occur with line and staff structures. It is best described as two organisations in one. The departments in the organisation still exist, but the product or project approach is added to it. If a particular contract requires skills from across departments, this will be an ideal way of tackling the problem. The structure is represented in the form of a matrix, with departments in the columns and projects in the rows. An example is given in Table 16.2. Members of each team are drawn from across departments.

If you were a member of a marketing department (column 1) and a member of a project team to launch a new book(row 3) you would be working partly in column 1 and partly in row 3, responsible both to the head of marketing and the Project leader.

There are advantages to this kind of structure. It has greater flexibility and people have the opportunity to work as members of a team, with people they would not normally work with and on tasks they would not normally be involved in. This creates new working relationships and a greater bond between members of the workforce. It also provides motivation and new challenges. From the organisation's point of view, it allows a much more integrated approach to solving problems and the opportunity to use more widely the varying skills that are in the organisation.

The difficulty with this structure is that it is more complex and can lead to problems, such as rivalry within departments and the accusation that resources are taken from a given department that would be better

used within it. From the individual's point of view there are dangers to promotion prospects within a line if a person is constantly being taken away for a project. This is particularly so if the project is medium term and real commitment to the line department has been lost in that time. It is important that teams should have the skills, temperament and training to work together and this could be a problem if the members of teams are not really known to each other at the outset. This is even worse if some do know each other and others are isolated. It will take time for good working relationships to develop and a good working bond to come into play.

In fact, most large organisations display aspects of the forms of organisation that we have discussed above. The key to good organisation is flexibility and the preparedness to adopt the structures that are best suited to the objectives of the organisation. Managers should be prepared to accept the fact that this may mean a complex pattern of structures instead of just one.

Structural weaknesses

There are great dangers in situations where, for one reason or another, the structure does not work as it should and unofficial lines of communication develop, which effectively by-pass a given person. Some of the common weaknesses are:

◆ Upward communication is slow or difficult. This is particularly difficult when the chain of command is long or when there is a lack of trust between workers and superiors. It is also difficult when managers are less than competent or their span of control is too big.

	Marketing	Production	Personnel	Training	Accounts
R and D					
Innovation					
Product A	➤ You				
Product B					
Customer service					

Table 16.2 Operational matrix

- The immediate subordinate/superior relationship is not good. Frustrated subordinates may try to by-pass the immediate boss.
- Relationships develop outside the business between people of different levels. The boss plays golf with a junior member of a department and hence offers instant access.
- A superior is inaccessible or often absent. Contact has to be made with others and new relationships are created.

Every effort has to be made to ensure that an organisation works as it should and that unofficial lines of communication are not damaging to the working relationships upon which efficiency depends. If this is difficult or impossible, thought should be given to changing the structure or the personnel. Perfection is impossible but organisations must get as close to it as is realistically possible.

Activity

Explain what is meant by a line and staff structure. How does this work in your own school or college? How are the academic line and the pastoral line interlinked? Are there any problems in this?

Discuss the organisational structure of your school or college and comment on its strengths and weaknesses.

Over-to-you

Short-answer questions

1 State and explain the functions of management.
2 Managers need to delegate as the business grows.
   What might be the problems for:
   (a) the manager delegating;
   (b) the person to whom authority is delegated;
   (c) the business.
3 What are the advantages of an organisation chart? Why is a chart imperfect?
4 What is a 'flat structure'? What are the advantages?
5 Define the term 'span of control'.
6 On what do span of control and its effectiveness depend.
7 One manager argues that span of control should be no more than five and another that it can be as high as 50. Who is right? Explain your answer.
8 Explain why managers need to be aware of the existence of informal groups.
9 What are the strengths and weaknesses of a matrix approach to structure?
10 Using the information in this section, explain what is meant by 'conflict of objectives' and how it might damage the interests of a company.

Discover and learn

1 Explore whether or not there are different structures other than functional organisation in local businesses. What are the advantages or disadvantages of the alternative structures you have found, for the organisations that use them?
2 Find out if your school or college has an organisational chart or charts? Is it an accurate reflection of what happens? Discuss and evaluate the significance of any differences you find.
3 Consider the degree of specialisation which occurs in your school or college. Is there any evidence of:
   (a) a multi-skilled approach?
   (b) a matrix approach?
   (c) role conflict?
   If you find such evidence, what do you consider to be the most significant costs and benefits for your school/college?

4 Read the case study below and answer the questions that follow.

Case study – Ahmed Ltd

Ahmed is a small private company. It employs 15 workers and is managed by Ahmed himself. The company produces computer software and has been very successful and profitable. A similar company in a nearby town is on the market and Ahmed is considering the possibility of buying it. It employs 30 people and has also been profitable. The reason for the sale is that the owner is moving to Australia to take control of a large sheep farm that has been left to her. Ahmed sees this as an opportunity to expand his capability, to widen his market and increase his profits. He is unsure of possible pitfalls associated with growth and does not know whether it is worth the hassle.

(a) What are the organisational problems of bringing two similar companies together? How can these be overcome with least hassle and pain?

(b) How might Ahmed's role change and what difficulties might he face in these changes?

(c) What structure, in broad terms, would you suggest Ahmed should consider, given that he will continue to operate from both branches.

Summary

In this section we have recognised that:

- Organisation is vital.

- Those who work within a business have to be used in conjunction with other resources to meet the aims and objectives of the business.

- People need to be organised in such a way that they know what their function is and how it fits into the rest of the organisation and that they are highly motivated to perform it well.

- Organisation charts are often used to show the internal structure visually and compactly.

- They give a good indication of chain of command, span of control and division of labour.

- Some hierarchies are tall and these tend to be large businesses. This gives rise to difficulties and such difficulties are often overcome by flattening the organisation chart or by using alternative approaches to structure, where they will work.

- Most large businesses are, in fact, a complex of different approaches.

- There is an increasing occurrence of matrix approaches, which enable workers to be multi-skilled and to work in teams.

- All approaches have their strengths and weaknesses. The real need of every organisation is to find and maintain the best fit.

Key words

Definitions of Key words can be found in the Glossary on page 236.

authority	objectives
centralisation	organisation
chain of command	organisation charts
delegation	role conflict
hierarchy	roles
matrix aproach	span of control

17 Organising production efficiently

On completion of this section you should be able to:

➤ define and differentiate production and productivity
➤ measure efficiency in a number of ways
➤ understand different approaches to production, including job, batch, flow, cell, lean and just-in-time production
➤ understand that businesses will often combine a number of production methods in one facility
➤ understand the factors that influence the scale of an operation
➤ understand economies and diseconomies of scale
➤ define and measure capacity utilisation
➤ understand capital intensity and its importance
➤ understand the factors that influence the extent of capital used in a business
➤ understand the need to optimise resource use and minimise resource wastage
➤ understand the costs of resource wastage to different stakeholders
➤ explain what is meant by an environmental audit
➤ understand the impact of legal requirements on production processes and methods

Production

Production is the measured quantity of output that a firm produces in a given period of time. Thus, if we look at the daily and weekly figures for the output of cane chairs at The World of Cane Ltd, a furniture producing firm (Table 17.1), we can see that it has two methods for measuring production, daily and weekly. Thus, we can see that the firm's production for the Friday of Week 1 was 107 chairs and that the weekly production for Week 3 was 528 chairs. Production, often called output is expressed in terms of units of the commodity being produced.

	Week 1	Week 2	Week 3	Week 4
Monday	110	115	112	108
Tuesday	106	112	109	107
Wednesday	98	95	101	99
Thursday	104	98	102	105
Friday	107	103	104	105
Weekly total	521	523	528	524

Table 17.1 Measuring output

Production is the process of combining resources, such as land, labour, capital and management, in order to produce commodities – goods and/or services. The four resources mentioned above, land, labour, capital and management, are known as the factors of production.

Land is not simply land itself, but also includes all resources grown on or found under the ground. It also includes all the resources found in the sea! Labour is the human factor and capital is described as any man-made aid to production, ranging from machinery to a simple shovel. Management is the combining factor and is there to ensure that production takes place efficiently and smoothly. Whether goods or services are being produced, it is necessary to combine the factors of production. Thus, someone producing cane chairs, as in our example, will have to combine a production unit (factory), machinery, raw materials and labour in order to manufacture the chairs. There will also be a need for people who provide support services, such as accountants and human resource workers. In the same way, someone providing a service, such as a hairdresser, will need to combine a working unit (salon), equipment and labour, as well as support services.

Production can be broken into three separate types:

◆ Primary production is the production or extraction of 'natural' materials. It is mainly in three areas, farming, fishing and mining.

◆ Secondary production is the production of manufactured, tangible, goods. It also includes the construction of buildings. The goods or buildings would be made using raw materials from the primary sector.

◆ Tertiary production is the production of intangible services. Services may be aimed at normal consumers or at businesses. These are known as direct services and commercial services respectively. Direct services are things such as taxi rides and manicures. Commercial services might be the provision and upkeep of potted plants for the offices or office cleaning services. Some services may be both direct and commercial, such as banking, insurance and legal services.

When producing, firms have to ask themselves a number of questions and make a number of decisions. The most common questions are:

◆ What product to produce? This will depend upon whether the firm is one that invents its own products and then convinces consumers that they want them or one that researches the market and produces what consumers want. This is the difference between product- and market-orientated production. In addition, obviously, the firm will have to consider the profitability of producing certain products. At the end of the day, no private company can produce in the long run without making a profit, not even Amazon.com!

◆ How to produce the product? The actual production method to be used will depend upon a number of factors, not least the type of product involved, and we will look at different production methods later in this section.

◆ Where to produce the product? The siting of the productive unit can be crucial to a firm. It will be influenced by many factors, such as proximity to the market, proximity to raw materials and suppliers, the cost of land, availability of labour and suitable infrastructure, social factors and government influence. It may also be influenced by personal factors. This is more likely with small

Primary production – dairy cattle after they have been milked.

Secondary production – Triumph production facility has been designed to be highly flexible, allowing different models, for different markets, to be assembled in sequence
Source: Triumph.

Tertiary production – hotel supplying accommodation and conference facilities

firms, which are often set up in an area because the owner lives there and has no desire to move.

◆ How big should the firm be? The scale of the productive unit will be influenced by a number of factors and these will be considered later in the section.

◆ How should production and quality be controlled? Quality is hugely important in all industries and the control of production is necessary in order to ensure that commodities are produced efficiently and to the correct standard.

◆ How should the product be distributed? Production is pointless unless the products are distributed efficiently to the customers. Different distribution channels have been explained in Section 11. It is true that one of the major problems of the modern world is still effective distribution. In parts of the world people are starving and yet we have lakes and mountains of food and an agricultural policy that, through milk quotas and 'set-aside' policies, deliberately restricts the production of food.

Productivity and efficiency

Productivity is not the same as production and the two should not be confused. Productivity can be defined as a measure of the ratio of output (production) to any of the firm's inputs, usually labour or capital. If a firm becomes more productive, then it has become more efficient, since productivity is an efficiency measure.

As has been said already, the most common measures of productivity are labour productivity and capital productivity and these will be considered in more detail. Both can be measured as output (per time period).

Labour productivity

This is measured as the quantity of labour employed (in the time period).

We can use the example from Table 17.1 to illustrate this. In Week 1, the firm produced 521 cane chairs. If we assume that they used five workers, then the weekly labour productivity is 521/5, i.e. 104.2 chairs per worker per week. In week 2, the weekly output was 523 chairs and so the labour productivity had improved to 104.6 chairs per worker per week. Because the labour productivity figure has increased, we can say that the

firm has become more efficient. However, this would be far too short a time period to be a meaningful measure.

Capital productivity

This is measured as capital employed (in the time period).

Once again, we can use the example from Table 17.1 to show this. If the 521 chairs in week 1 were produced using four machines, then the weekly capital productivity is 521/4, i.e. 130.25 chairs per machine per week.

Improvements in productivity, labour or capital, are difficult to measure accurately or to credit. It may be that an improvement in output is completely caused by more efficient, higher technology, machinery and yet the labour productivity figure will rise as well as the capital productivity figure. It is this sort of improvement in technology that has accounted for the high increases in labour productivity in many of the modern manufacturing industries over the last ten years.

Improvements in productivity usually lead to a reduction in the unit costs of production. If the cost of labour and capital inputs does not change, then any increase in output per worker and/or machine will lead to a fall in average costs.

Traditional production methods

There are a number of production methods that are available to a firm when it is considering 'How to produce the product?'. The choice of production method will depend upon a number of factors, including:

The nature of the product   Some products can only be produced in a certain way because of the type of products that they are. For example, bridges need to be produced by job production, since it would hardly be sensible to have a flow production line for bridges. Personal services like hairdressing are obviously job production

The total demand for the product   This will determine the quantity of the product required in each time period and this, in turn, will have an effect upon the choice of production method. Mass production clearly depends upon the existence of a large market.

The factors of production available This will affect the choice of method, as will the current state of technology. **The level of quality and precision required** This will also be a factor. **The size of the firm and its funding** This will be a factor because, when firms are small, they often cannot afford the more automated methods of production, even if they would be more efficient.

There are three main production methods:

◆ job production;
◆ batch production;
◆ flow production.

We will consider these in detail.

Job production

This is normally used for the production of single, one-off, products. These products are frequently large and are often unique. Thus, good examples of job production would be the Channel Tunnel or the new road bridge into Wales. However, products do not have to be large to be produced by job production. Individual wedding cakes and made-to-measure suits are also examples of job production. In order to be considered job production, each individual product has to be completed before the next product is started. Thus, at any one time, there is only one product being made.

New, smaller, firms often use job production, before they get the chance to expand. Job production enables specialised products to be produced and tends to be motivating for workers, because they produce the whole product and can take pride in it. However, this sort of production tends to be expensive, often takes a long time to complete, and is usually labour intensive. The labour force also needs to be highly skilled and this is not always easy to achieve. Aston Martin is an example of a very expensive car that is individually produced for the needs of each customer.

Batch production

Batch production involves the production of products in distinct batches, where the products in the batch go through the whole production process together. The production process involves a number of distinct stages and the defining point of batch production is that every unit in the batch must go through an individual production stage before the batch as a whole moves on to the next stage.

The most quoted example of this form of production is a baker making batches of rolls. First, the dough is mixed and kneaded. Then, after being left for a time, the dough is separated into individual amounts, the right size for rolls. After this, the rolls are baked together and then they are left to cool. When they have cooled, they are put on display in the shop and another batch can be prepared. Each roll has gone through the process with the other rolls in the batch and all the rolls have undergone each stage of the batch before going on to the next stage.

Batch production allows firms to use division of labour in their production process and it enables some gain from economies of scale. It is usually employed in industries where demand is for batches of the product. It also allows each individual batch to be specifically matched to the demand and the design and composition of batches can be easily altered. However, there are drawbacks. Batch production tends to have high levels of work-in-progress stocks at each stage of the production process and the work may well be boring and demotivating for the workers.

Batch production should not be confused with flow production. Some firms produce 'batches' of products using a flow production system, for example a soft drinks firm may bottle a batch of 20,000 cans of orange drink before resetting the line and producing a 'batch' of another drink. This is not, however, batch production. The individual items are free to move through the process without having to wait for others, so it must be flow.

Flow production

The process of flow production is used where individual products move from stage to stage of the production process as soon as they are ready, without having to wait for any other products. Flow production systems are capable of producing large quantities of output in a relatively short time and so it suits industries where the demand for the product in question is high and regular. It also suits the production of a standardised item that only requires minimal alterations. An example would be a Pepsi Cola production plant like the one in Ho Chi Minh City, Vietnam. Here, the product is standardised in that it is a can of soft drink of a standard size. The system is flow production because the cans move through the various stages independently. However, the firm can make changes to the contents of the cans and the labelling on them without having to alter the flow production system. They are capable of producing Pepsi, Sprite, and Schweppes Soda Water on the same production line.

It is essential that the flow production process be very carefully planned, so that there are no disruptions in the system. In a perfect system, the production process would be broken down so that all of the stages were of equal duration.

Flow production has a number of advantages over other types of production. Labour costs tend to be relatively low, because much of the process is mechanised and there is little physical handling of the products. The constant output rate should make the planning of inputs relatively simple and this can lead to the minimisation of input stocks through the use of just-in-time (JIT) stock control (see later in this section). Quality tends to be consistent and high and it is easy to check the quality of products at various points throughout the process. The main disadvantage is the high initial set-up cost. By definition, capital-intensive, high-technology, production lines are going to cost a great deal of money. In addition, the work involved tends to be boring and demotivating.

Recent innovations in production methods

In recent years, there have been a number of ideas that have altered thinking, to some extent, on the best way to produce products. Whilst the production systems described above are still applicable, these new ideas have widened the debate and have, in many ways, concentrated upon the human factor in production, attempting to use the expertise of the workforce and to alleviate boredom as much as possible. Some of these systems have had great success and we can consider three of the more successful ones below.

Cell production

Cell production, fully known as cellular production, is a form of flow production, but the flow production system is separated into a number of self-contained mini production units, known as cells. The idea is supposed to have started in the USSR and its aim is to create motivation and 'friendly' competition.

Each individual cell will have a leader and then, below that, a single level of hierarchy made up of manufacturers, manufacturing craftsmen and product assessors. The performance of each individual cell is measured in a number of ways against preset targets. These targets will include such things as output levels, quality, lead times and cash targets.

The cell system has led to significant improvements in worker commitment and motivation and this, in turn, has led to significant increases in productivity. Success depends upon a well-trained, multi-skilled work force. One of the most noted success stories for cell production is Lucas Industries, which introduced the system to its automotive electrical plants. Within two years, productivity had risen by 25%, the reject level had fallen by 20%, and there had been an 80% reduction in work-in-progress stocks.

Lean production and an introduction to just-in-time stock control

Lean production is a combination of a number of measures that have been developed, especially in Japan and the USA, in order to speed up, reduce waste in, and improve efficiency in, the production process. The lean production methods have been applied to all forms of production, job, batch, flow and cell.

Lean production looks at three specific areas of the production process. The first is product development, where the aim of lean production is to minimise the time taken between formulating an idea for a product and getting the product onto the market. Much of the design speed-up owes its success to the increased use of computer-aided design. Toyota has used this a great deal and is able to get a new car from the drawing board into the showroom 45% more quickly than its main rivals.

Just-in-time

The second specific area has been that of stock delivery and it is here that the use of just-in-time (JIT) stock control has made all the difference. The idea is to minimise stock levels at all stages of the production process. Stocks of all types, input, work-in-progress and final products, should be as low as possible. Supplies of inputs should be delivered exactly when they are needed. The production system should flow so that there are no idle work-in-progress stocks at any stage of production. Final goods should be produced for specific orders and so be capable of being dispatched as soon as they are produced. Obviously, this is all rather idealistic, but the nearer a firm can get to this situation, the more efficient it will be. (JIT is covered in more detail in Section 18.)

The third area of lean production relates to the production process itself and in Japan is usually connected to a **Kaizen** system. Kaizen programmes have the main aim of eliminating waste of all kinds in the production system. Most of the waste-generating ideas are gleaned from the workforce and so an educated, skilled, workforce is essential. (Kaizen programmes are also covered in more detail in Section 18.)

The scale of operations

There is no perfect size for a business and, in the UK, there are thousands and thousands of firms of all sizes. Most firms begin in a small way, quite simply because it requires less capital investment. In order to discuss the size of businesses, we need to look at the different ways that are used to measure business size. These are:

Turnover   This method values the total sales of the firm over a period of time, usually one year. The 1985 Companies Act used this method to differentiate between firms and stated that firms with a turnover of less than £1.4 million were small, those between £1.4 million and £5.75 million were medium-sized and those over £5.75 million were large.

Number of employees   This is another popular method and simply uses the number of employees directly employed by the firm to act as an indicator of size and a means of comparison. The 1985 Companies Act used this method, as well as turnover, and said that those firms that employed fewer than 50 workers were small, those that employed between 50 and 250 were medium-sized and those with over 250 employees were large. Obviously, this can be misleading, because some industries, by definition, are capital intensive and so may be very big in terms of turnover and yet small in terms of the number of people employed.

Profit   This is sometimes used, but it is not ideal. First, there may be large fluctuations from year to year and, second, small firms may make very large profits and extremely large firms may make losses.

Capital employed   This is also sometimes used and simply measures the total funds raised in the firm via equity (shareholding) and borrowing.

Stock market value   This may be used for firms that are quoted on the Stock Exchange, but it will tend to be rather variable from year to year as the share price fluctuates.

The actual size of a firm will be influenced by a number of factors and these should be considered:

The finance available   As has already been stated, most firms start small because funds are limited. In the same way, the majority stay small simply because they cannot achieve sufficient investment for growth.

The market in which the firm is working   Some markets do not have demand in sufficient quantity to support large firms. Additionally, some markets do not suit large-scale production and so will not have large-scale production units (i.e. firms). An example of this would be producers of specialist rock-climbing equipment or the makers of stamp albums. Some firms that provide services will also be small, if the demand is limited, e.g. tattoo parlours.

The objectives of the owners and management of the firm   The objectives, and the level of ambition, of both the owners and managers of a firm must have an impact on the size and potential growth of the organisation. Many people are happy to reach a certain size, often rather small, and lack the ambition to attempt to grow. Often they see the necessary risks as being too great and they are satisfied with what they have already achieved. If growth is to be attained, then much hard work, stress and risk will have to be endured and this may well not be attractive to the owners and management.

Many firms will grow over time and they do so for a number of reasons. They may grow in order to ensure survival, reduce risk and increase market share. They may also be chasing increased profits. Sometimes, firms grow simply because of the ambition and lust for power of their owners. One of the main reasons for growth is to gain cost advantages and thus to increase profitability; this will be dealt with next.

Economies of scale

As has just been said, one of the major advantages gained by increasing the scale of an organisation is the cost economies that simply stem from being larger. These are known as economies of scale and they are defined as 'any fall in unit costs that arises from an increase in the scale of the organisation'.

Economies of scale may be split into two types, internal and external. Internal economies are the unit cost reductions that arise directly from the growth of the firm itself. They have been classified into the following groups:

Commercial economies   One of these is purchasing economies, where firms are able to buy in bulk and so gain cost advantages through discounts for large orders. A good example is the ability of large retailers to buy much more cheaply than small shops. Many small shops do their best to compete in this respect by joining buying groups like Spar. Distribution economies, where large firms can take care of their own distribution and thus reduce costs would also be included under this heading. Marketing economies also fit in here. Marketing costs do not rise at the same rate as output and so unit costs fall. For example, the costs of advertising to sell 50,000 units will not be significantly increased if the firm expands to produce 80,000 units. Many fixed costs will not increase with size and so overheads can be spread over more units and unit costs will fall. This would apply to such things as administration costs and research and development costs.

Managerial economies   As businesses grow, they are able to departmentalise their management functions and there is a gain from the use of specialist employees in areas such as accounts, sales, marketing and human resource management.

Technical economies   As businesses expand, they are able to use capital, technology and techniques that are not available to smaller firms and there is often a unit-cost advantage to be gained. In small firms, the owners and managers often have to be able to turn their hands to a range of activities and cannot gain from specialisation. Computerisation does not become cost-effective until the business is at least medium-sized.

Financial economies   Because larger organisations are considered to be a safer investment, institutions that lend money tend to be more prepared to advance loans to them and will accept lower interest rates for doing so. This will be reflected in lower unit costs.

Risk-bearing economies   As firms grow, they often expand into areas that were not involved in their original activities. This is to say that they diversify. If they expand into activities that relate to their supplies of raw materials, or into the selling of their products, they will lower their costs by dealing with their own supplies and selling. This can be a significant saving. It also provides greater security if either the source of supply or the market is guaranteed.

External economies are the unit-cost advantages gained by any firm in an industry as the industry grows. External economies can be particularly large if the firms in a specific industry are mostly concentrated in one geographical area, such as the steel industry in Sheffield. Different causes of external economies of scale are:

Concentration economies   As we have said, if an industry concentrates in one area, then there are a number of advantages that can accrue. These may include:

- the emergence of a skilled local labour force;
- the development of a local tradition for the industry and specialist courses run in local educational establishments;
- suppliers and those involved with the industry moving nearer and thus reducing transport costs and improving the pool of knowledgeable advice;
- support from the local authorities, keen to see the industry stay in the area.

In such situations even the smaller firms in the industry are also able to benefit.

Information economies   As industries grow, they often set up information services that are of help to all of the firms in the industry. The tourist industry is a good example.

Diseconomies of scale

It is often argued that there is also a downside to growth and that there will be factors that will force unit costs upwards as organisations expand. These factors are known as diseconomies of scale and, whilst they are not as powerful as economies of scale, they must be taken into consideration. There are two main types:

Human diseconomies   As organisations grow, workers tend to lose a sense of belonging and feel less important. This can be very counter-productive and lead to a loss of morale and motivation, which in turn leads to inefficiency and higher unit costs.

Information diseconomies   As organisations grow, the number of levels of hierarchy increases and there is a tendency for information channels to become unwieldy. When this happens, information is often blocked or distorted and decision-making suffers. In addition, decisions take longer to make and so the firm becomes less efficient.

Capacity utilisation and capital and labour intensity

Capacity is the amount of output that a firm can produce, whilst minimising its unit costs. It is, in effect, the ideal output for a productive unit, if the unit is working efficiently. Obviously, a firm will wish to use its productive unit up to capacity, since this is usually the cost-effective level of output.

Capacity utilisation is a measure of the extent to which the maximum capacity of a productive unit is being employed. It can be measured by a simple equation:

$$\text{Capacity utilisation} = \frac{\text{Actual output}}{\text{Capacity}} \times 100$$

If a firm can achieve a high level of capacity utilisation, then it will be able to spread its fixed costs over a high level of output and so will reduce the unit cost of output. This can best be shown by an example:

Plant capacity   100,000 units per year
Actual production   60,000 units
Capacity utilisation $60,000/100,000 \times 100 = 60\%$

If the firm has fixed costs of £240,000, then the unit fixed cost is £240,000/60,000, i.e. £4 per unit. If output is increased to 80,000 units per year, then the capacity utilisation becomes 80% and the unit fixed cost falls to £3 per unit.

As can be seen, if firms can produce to capacity, then there is a definite cost advantage to be gained. However, firms can only maximise output if the demand for the product exists, if the resources are available and if they are able to use their productive resources at their most efficient level

Some production methods depend upon intensive usage of capital and others rely on high levels of labour. If a production system employs a high level of capital relative to the other factors of production, then it is said to be capital intensive. An example of this would be any large car production plant, e.g. the Ford works in Dagenham. Obviously, the set-up costs of a capital-intensive plant are usually high, so the investment can only be justified if the demand for the product being produced is high and relatively stable. Also, since capital intensity implies flow production, the product needs to be a standardised one, so that it can be produced on a production line, with minimal variations.

Some production systems do not lend themselves to the use of large amounts of capital and actually employ a high level of labour relative to the other factors of production. This type of system would be called labour intensive. Small firms are often labour intensive, as are production systems that require high levels of expertise, such as the making of top-quality cricket balls. The majority of service industries, such as insurance companies or estate agents, tend to be labour intensive.

The needs of the market may well strongly influence the level of production, particularly if that market is inclined to seasonal variation. In such circumstances normal working becomes difficult and there is a need to provide for working under or above long-term capacity levels. Often, for Christmas, firms have to do this. Means have to be found of increasing the volume of goods on the market. Typical methods of dealing with this almost always either increase unit costs or reduce profits per unit and include:

◆ working a shift pattern with up to three shifts a day;
◆ extending the working day in other ways. Shops will stay open for much longer days leading up to Christmas;
◆ the post office employs additional postmen at the same time and hotels increase their staff in high season. Most vacation employment for students is based on needs like this;
◆ working overtime which is normally at a higher rate of pay. The EU working time directive prevents such overtime being compulsory in many instances. Some industries have contingency plans for dealing with emergency situations of this kind which they can bring into operation quickly. The hospital and fire services are examples.

Dealing with the other side of the problem is not so easy. Those firms who have part-time staff may be able to react flexibly and relatively quickly to the need to reduce production levels but many do not and this leads to stockpiling and its inherent costs. This used to be a major feature of the motor industry. Many firms react to this situation by finding ways of getting rid of stock through sales and offers, some can move flexibly from the production of one line to another. In extreme situations the situation will lead to redundancies and closure of branches. The closure of a significant number of Barclay Bank branches because they no longer need the capacity of so many branches is an example. One way of coping is to stay deliberately very slim in the knowledge that it is easier to increase capacity temporarily than it is to reduce it.

Resource management, wastage and the environment

Resources are relatively scarce and have a cost. They must be used rather than wasted. For those resources which are non-renewable to be wasted – coal, oil, minerals – is a permanent loss to the economy. The greatest of these losses is in the failure to make best use of labour. One and a half million people being unemployed means the loss of 1.5 million working days every day. This is in addition to the loss of spending power, dignity and respect which being unemployed entails. Pollution also wastes because it damages and destroys and because it is often costly to remove.

Firms have become much more conscious of these issues and are demonstrating significantly more corporate responsibility about them. This is more likely to be because being 'green' is increasingly good for image and for profits.

Environmental audits

Environmental audits have become a relatively common undertaking for larger firms these days. This is where the firm carries out a review of its effect on the environment in which it operates. The review may be carried out by outside experts or undertaken internally and then verified by independent consultants. The environmental audit would normally look at such things as waste management, material usage, energy usage, efficiency of transport, compliance with legislation and impact on the surrounding countryside. Certain areas of the environmental audit can be positively beneficial for the firm. Improvements in waste management, material usage, energy usage and transport efficiency can be cost saving for a firm. However, meeting legislative requirements and ensuring that the surrounding countryside is preserved can impose costs on a firm that although necessary, are significant.

The legal aspects of production

Firms face a number of legal restrictions and requirements upon their production processes and methods. Some of them will relate to measures to minimise any pollution that may be caused in the production process, but the main laws attempt to protect the workers involved in the process and relate to health and safety.

The Health and Safety at Work Act (1974) places a legal obligation upon employers to safeguard the health, safety and welfare of their workers, whilst they are at work. The Act includes the provision and maintenance of safety equipment and clothing, the maintenance of reasonable temperatures in the workplace, the provision of breaks from work and protection against dangerous substances. Employers have to protect their employees' health and safety 'as far as it is reasonably practicable'. The more potentially dangerous the production process, the more care employers will be expected to take.

All employers have to prepare a written statement of the policy that they have adopted for the health and safety of their employees. It is up to them to ensure that the employees know what the firm's policy is. However, the law also places responsibilities upon the employees, who are obliged to act in a way that takes reasonable care of their own, and other people's, safety. The employees are obliged to obey the health and safety rules that have been set down by the organisation. If employers, or employees, fail to comply with the set rules, then legal action can be taken against them. The Health and Safety Executive is a government department that attempts to ensure that the Act is carried out in companies throughout the country. Their inspectors have the right to enter businesses and check that they are complying with the Act.

Over-to-you

Short-answer questions

1 What is meant by the term 'added value'?
2 How is added value related to the production process?
3 Explain why the term production includes services.
4 Think about your journey to school or college each day. What public services do you use? Explain your list.
5 Write down the equation for measuring each of:
   (a) labour productivity;
   (b) capital productivity;
   (c) capital utilisation.

6 Select a method of production and say why it would be the best for each of the following:

   (a) consultation with a solicitor;

   (b) manufacturing pins;

   (c) baking hot cross buns.

7 Explain what a diseconomy of scale is and give an example.

8 What is the meaning of the term 'spreading fixed costs' and what is its effect?

9 Explain why waste management is important.

10 What factors would you include in an environmental audit?

Discover and learn

1 Work in groups. Choose one firm each. Discover its methods of production. Discuss the appropriateness of those methods and comment on the findings of the whole group.

2 Work in groups. Cover as much of your area as you can. Observe ways in which the environment is being damaged and suggest realistic business solutions to the problems.

3 Are there any actual or potential examples of the advantages of concentration economies in your area? If you find them, explain why the industry selected is concentrated in your area.

4 Read the case study below and tackle the exercises that follow.

Case study – Hard Hats Ltd

Jamie Pither started up Hard Hats Ltd in 1980. It is located on the north coast of Wales, on the edge of a small village, five miles from Rhyl. Jamie rented a unit, on a recently built industrial estate, which he has since been able to purchase outright with the help of a mortgage from the bank.

In the early days, the firm only produced safety helmets for construction workers. By necessity, it was a small operation. Jamie dealt with all of the management functions and he employed two workers, one to operate the machine that produced the shells that formed the basis of the safety helmets and the other to attach the straps and cushioning parts and to pack the finished products. All parts, other than the shells, were produced elsewhere and then bought-in.

Since then, Hard Hats has grown, although it is still not a large concern. From 1985 onwards, Jamie had realised the need for diversification and had identified other areas where he could perhaps sell products that were easily capable of being produced in his existing premises. Over the period, he began to produce safety helmets for cyclists, mountain-bike enthusiasts, skate boarders, roller skaters and, most recently, in-line skaters. Indeed, it seemed that whatever the latest craze, there was a potential market for Jamie's products.

By the end of 1997, employment in the firm had expanded to 11 people, in addition to Jamie. There are now two machines for producing the various shells, each with its own highly skilled and trained operator, eight people who work as assemblers and packers, and a works manager, Howard Pedley, who is responsible for the ordering of all materials and supplies, stock control and the general running of the production floor. Jamie continues to deal with all other management functions, which are mostly marketing and accounting.

Production is organised partly on a batch-production basis and partly on an assembly-line basis. When an order is received, then a batch of the necessary style of safety shells is produced on one of the machines. The machines are computer programmable and so change-overs are relatively quick. The machines are quite reliable but, when they do break down, the firm from which they were bought repairs them. The supplier guarantees that an engineer will be on site within two hours, but production is obviously stopped on that machine whilst it is being repaired. The same firm is responsible for the regular maintenance of the machines. The machines are three years old and Jamie is considering changing them. On average, one of them breaks down once a month and production is lost for four hours. Production from each machine averages 120 units per hour and the firm usually works one shift of eight hours each day. However, if there is a rush on, then workers are often asked to work up to two hours of overtime per weekday or an extra four hour shift on a Saturday. Lately, it is often necessary to have to work a total of at least four hours overtime per week. Indeed, the workers now expect this and are unhappy on the odd occasion that it does not occur. The firm guarantees delivery of orders within ten days of an order being placed. Although the average time for fulfilling an order is nine days, there are a growing number of occasions when the firm is unable to meet its stated delivery time and this is causing problems with customers.

As a batch is being produced, the shells are deposited onto one of the two, small, conveyor belts. It is then the job of one of the workers to stick the relevant brand-name onto the shell, of another to attach the chin straps to the helmet, of a third to put in the cushioning materials and of a fourth to pack the helmets and label the boxes. Workers are moved from one position to another on the same line or to the other line, but there is no doubt that it is tedious work and motivation and morale are not high amongst these workers. On average, one worker is away from work for one day per fortnight. When this happens, production is, obviously, slowed down a great deal. Normally, the workers can keep up with the output of the machines, but, when they are short-handed, they can only assemble and pack an average of 200 units per hour. When the machines are being reprogrammed for a new batch, the assembly workers are expected to prepare the materials necessary to assemble and pack the batch. This is supervised by Howard Pedley.

Because of the nature of the product, quality control is obviously of great importance. The firm has earned the right to use the kitemark logo of the British Standards Institute and there is no doubt that this is an enormous help to sales. It is rare for a consumer to buy a product of this type if it is not carrying the BSI mark. Quality control is considered to be the job of everyone involved in the production process and all of the workers have the right to hold up production if they think that there is

something wrong. They receive a weekly bonus as long as the average reject rate from customers stays below one in one thousand, which it invariably does. The workers take this role very seriously and it acts as a boost to morale.

Lately, the quality of some of the bought-in chinstraps has given some cause for concern. Jamie has just changed to a new supplier, based in Taiwan and the quality of some batches has been rather variable. In order to guard against stock-outs, because of the distance that deliveries have to cover, a large buffer stock is being carried and this is also a concern, since it is tying up capital. However, the prices charged by the Taiwanese firm are considerably lower than European Union (EU) suppliers and this enables Jamie to have lower prices than his competitors with the same profit margins.

Howard Pedley works to a fairly traditional system when he is dealing with the stock control at the firm. He works on a maximum and minimum stock-level basis and, knowing the usual delivery times, he reorders stocks and ensures that these never go below the minimum stock level. Jamie is worried that far too much money is tied up in stocks and he is keen to reduce stock levels. Howard feels that any change might jeopardise output. None of the suppliers is that reliable and there have been occasions where deliveries have taken twice as long as normal to arrive. Current stock-control figures for bought-in components, and some production information, are shown in Table 17.2.

Jamie Pither has noticed an increasing demand from abroad, mostly France and Italy. He feels that this is a very good sign, since he has not attempted to promote his products in these countries. He has now researched the potential markets and has found that all of the activities that he supplies for are popular in France and Italy and that cycling, especially, is much more popular there than it is in the UK. Competition is keen, but Jamie's prices are very competitive. He is keen to expand his market, but he is aware that it would involve a marked increase in weekly production levels. He has estimated that, if things went as planned, he might have to double output over a period of eighteen months.

	Logo transfers	Chin straps	Cushioning materials	Boxes and labels
September 1997	10,000	120,500	12,000	22,000
October 1997	12,000	132,000	15,500	20,500
November 1997	10,000	121,500	14,000	19,000
December 1997	10,500	94,000	18,000	21,000
January 1998	11,000	126,500	22,000	21,500
February 1998	10,500	122,000	25,000	20,500

Table 17.2 Stock figures for bought-in components (figures are for stock held at the start of each month, to the nearest 500)

Average daily production is 1,800 units. Average weekly production is 10,000 units. The usual delivery times, following an order, are as follows:

Logo transfers	3 days
Chin straps	4 weeks
Cushioning materials	1 week
Boxes and labels	2 days

1 (a) Evaluate the production method used at Hard Hats.

(b) Discuss any improvements that you feel might be made to the production method. Explain your reasoning.

2 Identify and explain any economies of scale that Jamie Pither might expect to gain as his firm expands.

3 How would you classify Hard Hats in terms of size? Explain your reasoning.

4 Explain any disadvantages associated with production that might arise from the fact that Hard Hats Ltd is a relatively small firm.

Summary

In this section we have recognised that:

● There are three types of production: primary, secondary and tertiary.

● Firms should try to produce as efficiently as possible, in order to minimise unit costs and to avoid wastage of resources.

● Traditional production methods – job, batch and flow – have been improved in many cases by recent innovations, such as cell and lean production.

● Firms of all sizes exist in the economy.

● Large firms benefit from economies of scale, although diseconomies may also exist.

● It is sensible for firms to utilise as much of their capacity as possible.

● Some firms are capital intensive and others are labour intensive.

● Firms have an obligation to avoid waste, to manage their resources effectively and to protect the environment.

● Firms should strive to protect their workers in the workplace.

Key words

Definitions of Key words can be found in the Glossary on page 236.

batch production
capacity utilisation
capital intensity
cell production
diseconomies of scale
economies of scale
environmental audit

flow production
job production
just-in-time (JIT) production
Kaizen
labour intensity
resource management

18 Controlling operations

On completion of this section you should be able to:

➤ define quality

➤ understand the importance of quality to both suppliers and consumers

➤ identify methods of attempting to ensure quality

➤ understand the difference between inspected and built-in quality control

➤ understand the implications for motivation and training of built-in quality control

➤ describe and understand different approaches to attaining quality, including total quality management, benchmarking, Kaizen and continuous improvement, quality assurance and quality circles

➤ identify the different types of stocks

➤ understand the purpose and costs of holding stocks

➤ appreciate the opportunity costs of holding stocks

➤ construct and interpret stock control charts

➤ define just-in-time (JIT) stock control

➤ understand the implications for the firm and its suppliers of JIT

➤ understand the requirements of successful approaches to JIT

What do we mean by quality?

We live in times when consumers have more choice than ever before and this means that quality, as perceived by consumers, is of enormous importance if firms wish to sell their products. Consumers will make decisions about quality based upon a combination of the following factors:

- physical appearance and image;
- reliability;
- durability;
- special features that set the product apart from its rivals;
- availability of maintenance and repairs, where necessary;
- sales and after-sales service;
- reputation of the supplier and the supplier's 'name';
- perceived value for money;
- experience.

It must be remembered that quality does not mean that a product has to be perceived to be the best in its field, such as Ferrari or Rolls Royce. It actually means that the product is the best to fulfil the particular needs of a consumer, which are determined by the use to which the product is to be put and the price for which it is to be sold. As was stated in Section 9, a 'good' product needs to be functionally sound, aesthetically pleasing and capable of economic production. When making decisions about quality, consumers will consider a combination of these requirements, as well as the factors mentioned in the list above.

So far, we have considered the concept of quality in terms of how consumers will perceive it. However, we should also consider quality from the point of view of the producer. To the producer, a product is quality if it conforms with the specifications to which it was designed and produced. Producers will aim to produce all of their products so that the products lie within the acceptable range of error that will have been decided upon by the designers of the product and the production system. There is an important implication here. Quality is an objective and is not necessarily concerned with excellence. A good example is carpets. The makers of Axminster and Wilton carpets are aiming

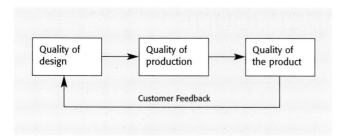

Figure 18.1 Flow chart showing quality improvement resulting from customer feedback

for excellence but the objective of those making 'bedroom' quality is much lower. Each will pursue quality within its own specifications.

It is argued that it is possible to improve quality continuously by taking into account both the consumer's view of quality and the producer's attempts to produce a quality product. The system concerned may be shown in a flow diagram (Figure 18.1).

Quality of design is an essential starting point. The design features of the product must match, as closely as possible, the requirements of the customers. However, they must also allow efficient production to take place. The quality of production is essential. The production process must be capable of manufacturing products that match the design specifications. The quality of the finished product is, obviously, also important. The final product must satisfy the requirements of the consumers as closely as possible. The use of customer feedback closes the chain and enables continuous improvement. Customers will comment on how well the product satisfies their requirements. Design specifications can be altered and the production process can be modified, if necessary, and the final product should be even closer to the requirements of the consumers. This process can continue ad infinitum.

Inspected quality

Traditionally, quality has been checked by inspecting products during the production process. Obviously, it is not possible to check all of the products at all stages of production and so a sampling process takes place. This sampling normally takes place in three stages. First, it is necessary to check the quality of the raw materials and bought-in components the firm purchases in order to produce. Obviously, if inputs are not of a reasonable quality, then the products that are manufactured with

them will also lack quality. The responsibilities and role of the supplier are seen to be of great importance these days.

The second stage of checking takes place during the production process itself. Semi-finished products are checked at regular stages of the production process, so that any faults in the process can be identified. The last stage is the checking of the finished products. This is carried out to ensure that the products conform to the required design specifications, being not too good, which would raise costs, and not too poor, which would lose customers.

Weaknesses of inspecting for quality

The key thing about inspected quality is that it involves a group of quality control inspectors, who check the work of other workers. Although there are still firms where this type of quality control takes place, they are now in the minority and this is because there are a number of problems associated with this type of checking system:

◆ It is negative and may cause resentment. The inspector is considered to be successful if faults are discovered and this may make inspectors too keen to find fault. In addition, the workers in the firm are likely to become wary of the inspectors and to see them as management employees, who are there to find fault. This sort of mistrust cannot be good for working relationships and the overall levels of morale in a firm.

◆ The job of inspection is likely to be boring and so inspectors may become demotivated and not carry out their tasks efficiently.

◆ If checking only takes place at specific points in the production process, then it may well be that faulty products are passing through a number of production stages before they are picked up. Also, it may take a lot of time to discover where the fault is appearing, between different quality checkpoints.

◆ The most important point is that, because inspectors exist, they are taking away the responsibility for checking and upholding quality from the workers. Workers do not see quality as their responsibility and do not feel that it is their duty to ensure that it is being kept up.

As we can see from the above points, inspected quality control has many weaknesses and it is hardly surprising that there has been a move away from it in recent years. The trend has been towards built-in quality control, where the workers are empowered to check quality at all points along the production process and, in many cases, are given the power to stop the production process if the quality is slipping. This empowerment has had beneficial effects upon worker motivation and also upon quality levels. A number of new approaches have been developed to improve quality and quality control, mainly involving the empowerment of the workforce and it is at some of these approaches that we will now look.

Modern approaches to attaining quality

There have been a number of new approaches to attaining higher quality levels over the last few years and we should look at some of the more important ones, if we are to have a good knowledge of recent management thinking in this area.

Total Quality Management (TQM)

The philosophy of TQM is that it attempts to minimise errors in production. It aims to eliminate quality control inspectors and to put the onus for quality control on all members of the firm. In this way, the production process can be monitored at every stage. In a perfect TQM system, the only quality control inspectors would be those who were carrying out specialist scientific tests on the product. An example of this would be in a firm producing bottled mineral water, where there would still be a need for scientifically qualified inspectors to ensure that the water was of the required quality.

TQM uses the concept of the internal customer. The internal customer is the next department in the production process and the relationship between departments is seen as a supplier and customer relationship. When a department passes on semi-finished products, it should be attempting to satisfy the next department (the customer) by passing on the best quality products. Every department is obliged to meet the needs and requirements of its customer(s). These departmental relationships are sometimes known as quality chains. It is fair to say that all businesses can be described as a series of supplier and customer relationships.

In the past, controlling was seen as a cost for the firm and nothing else. Under TQM, achieving high quality levels is seen as a way of cost cutting. If the number of reject products can be reduced, then there will be cost savings. If quality is improved and also guaranteed, demand for the products should rise over time.

However, TQM will only work properly if everyone in the firm is committed to the idea. Too often those at the top of the firm, in senior management, expect the workforce to believe in TQM, but do not adhere to the system themselves. If this is the case, it will not be long before the workforce loses belief in the system.

Benchmarking

The full title for benchmarking is 'best practice benchmarking' and it involves management identifying the best firms in the industry and then using the standards of those firms to set its own desired performance levels.

The first decision that the management needs to make is what areas should be benchmarked. This is discovered by researching customers and finding out what they consider to be important. For example, research amongst customers may reveal that the most important factors to them are quality of the product, speed of delivery and after-sales technical support. These are the areas that the firm would first benchmark. It must then set about identifying the firm or firms in the industry that are considered to be the best. This may be done by asking customers and by seeking expert opinion, both inside and outside the firm.

Once the company that is going to be used as the benchmark has been selected, then it is necessary to gather the necessary information. This is not easy, but there are a number of sources that can be employed, such as customers, suppliers, specialist publications, industrial associations, magazines, newspapers, databases and the Internet. When the information is gathered, it needs to be analysed and the benchmarks need to be established. When these standards have been established and taken as objectives, then the management and workers of the firm need to plan how to match the standards of the benchmarked firm. This will require funding, much consultation, training, control and review.

Firms would love to benchmark the whole production process, but it is very difficult to gain the information from other firms. It does take place, where possible, but firms are understandably reticent to disclose their production details. If a firm becomes the best in an industry, then it has little choice but to benchmark itself and to attempt to increase its own standards. If possible, the firm may look abroad for benchmarking opportunities, but these may not be available. Benchmarking is not limited to the same industry. An engineering firm may find that the best customer-relations skills are found in a mail-order firm.

Kaizen and continuous improvement

Kaizen highlights the difference between western and eastern approaches to problem solving that existed up to a few years ago. Now, the majority of large firms adopt the eastern approach. Traditionally, the western approach involved keeping production up to a certain mark, and then looking for one-off improvements in the form of inventions or alterations to the production process. The eastern approach, the Kaizen approach, has been to strive for 100% perfection by continuously attempting to improve the efficiency of the production process, even if it is only by a barely discernible amount.

This can be shown by means of a diagram; see Figure 18.2. The eastern producers are aware that 100% perfection is not possible to achieve, but they believe that to strive for it must lead to improvement. They also benefit by adjusting their production process in a gradual manner, avoiding much of the unrest and uncertainty that tends to be attached to the managing of more major change. It is for these reasons that many

firms in Europe and the USA have taken up the idea of a Kaizen programme.

In a Kaizen programme, the main target is the elimination of waste of all types. Waste is defined as any activity that adds cost, but not value, to a product. There are three main problem areas identified for production that need to be dealt with and these are:

Muda This is the Japanese word for waste. This is considered to be the most important area and different forms of *muda* are specified. The two most commonly used are 'idling *muda*', which is the time wasted when an employee is idle and waiting for work to arrive, and 'motional *muda*', which is the time wasted through unnecessary movement by an employee during that employee's part of the production process.

Mura This is the inconsistent or non-regular use of a machine or worker.

Muri This is the imposition of excessive demands upon machines or workers.

Kaizen programmes attempt to use the mental abilities of all of the workers and also to improve their manual skills. Workers are expected to assess their roles in the production process and to make suggestions in order to attempt to improve their part of the process. Any idea that cuts half a second or more from the process will be considered and, if possible, implemented.

The process of Kaizen has a knock-on effect and improvements in one part of the production system will require improvements further down the line, if bottlenecks are not to occur. For example, if a worker on a production line that assembles cars finds a way to save 5 seconds from the time it takes to weld the roof panels to the support struts, then the workers who are responsible for the next process must also find a way to save 5 seconds or there will be a build up of work-in-progress stocks. In this case, there would be no increase in production levels. This example highlights the need for all workers to be involved in a Kaizen programme, if a firm is to benefit fully from the process.

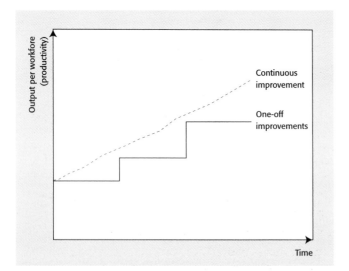

Figure 18.2 Kaizen and 'one-off' responses contrasted

Workers at the Nissan factory in Sunderland finish off Primera cars on the assembly line. Nissan decided that they are to build a new model at the plant from the year 2000 resulting in the creation of 800 jobs and a new investment of £215 million.
Source: Popperfoto/Reuters.

Quality assurance

Many firms now have quality assurance departments that aim to put into place systems that will ensure that agreed quality standards are complied with, throughout the organisation, so that the customers receive products that are up to their desired standards.

The quality assurance department needs to consider all areas of the firm, such as product design, the quality of inputs, quality control, delivery systems, customer service and the commitment and quality of the workforce. They will set quality standards for all members of the firm and all departments and the hope is that, if these quality standards can be reached, then the quality of the final good or service will be guaranteed and will live up to the expectations of the customer.

The quality standards that are set may be devised internally, benchmarked from market leading firms or set by independent bodies, which will then give accreditation if the standards are met. Examples of the latter method of setting standards would be the standards set by the British Standards Institution (BSI), various trade associations, such as the Association of British Travel Agents (ABTA) or the International Standards Organisation (ISO). Obviously, if firms gain accreditation from outside, such as the ISO 9000/9002 quality certification, which is equivalent to the BS 5750 certificate, then customers will know that the company has reached a recognised standard of quality and will have more faith in it.

Quality circles

Quality circles are another Japanese initiative that has gained considerable significance over the last few years. Quality circles are small groups of workers, usually between five and ten, who meet voluntarily in order to discuss methods of improving productivity and quality in their work areas. Usually, an appointed 'facilitator' leads the group. The main aims of the group are to involve workers in problem solving, thus giving them motivation, and to use the expertise of those who are nearest to the production process, the production workers themselves.

Quality circles are not a means of quality control. They are actually a means of quality and productivity

217

improvements and, as such, are often employed as an integral part of a Kaizen programme.

The importance of education and training

It should have been noted that all of the approaches mentioned above, TQM, benchmarking, Kaizen programmes, quality assurance and quality circles, require input and expertise from the workforce. If this is the case, then the approaches will only be successful if the employees are educated and have been trained to understand their role in the firm and the aims of the firm.

Because of this, there has been an emphasis upon the importance of education and training in industry over the last ten years and this will not die down. Management are beginning to realise the real benefits that can accrue from a talented and skilled, even multi-skilled, workforce. Worker participation requires workers who are able to cope with their empowerment and who are able to contribute fully to the chosen quality attainment system.

Activities

1 Define quality.
2 Distinguish between inspected quality and built-in quality control.
3 How important is the shop-floor worker to quality control in modern production units? Use examples to illustrate your answer.
4 Explain the differences between traditional quality control systems and the Kaizen system.
5 In a group, attempt to set up a benchmarking process for your school or educational establishment.
6 Compile a list of firms and products that have managed to gain external quality assurance certification of different types.

Stocks

Firms have a number of different types of stocks that they need to order and control. There are two main types of stocks, product stocks and production process and administrative stocks. The first type, product stocks, are certainly the most important. Product stocks may be split into three distinct categories:

- ◆ stocks of raw materials and bought-in components;
- ◆ work-in-progress stocks;
- ◆ stocks of finished goods.

Stocks of raw materials and bought-in components

These are kept in order to make sure that there are no hold-ups in production caused by late delivery of stocks or by the delivery of faulty stocks. Although the recent trend is to minimise, if not eliminate, these stocks (see the section on Just-in-time [JIT] Stock control), firms do not always do so. JIT involves relatively small, frequent, orders of stocks and it may be that there are large savings to be made by bulk-buying stocks, which will more than outweigh the gains from JIT.

Work-in-progress stocks

These are the stocks of semi-finished products that build up, or are purposely kept, at various stages of the production process. Sometimes, work-in-progress stocks will build up because there is a bottleneck in the production system. At other times, firms will stockpile work-in-progress stocks at certain points on the production system where shortages are known to occur.

Whatever the reason for the existence of these stocks, they signify a production system that is not working efficiently and that should be investigated, analysed and altered. This would be a perfectly appropriate situation for the setting up of a Kaizen programme.

Stocks of finished goods

These are kept to make sure that customers can be supplied, even if there are hold-ups in production or surges in demand. Firms are quite rightly worried that if customers fail to find the product they are seeking, then they will move onto another product that is available and never return to the original choice. There is no doubt that this does happen, but in certain markets this is not the case and firms do try to minimise stocks of finished products. For example, car firms now produce to order and gone are the days when there would be huge numbers of finished cars sitting in parking lots waiting for a customer. In most car firms, it is the order that instigates production and, if orders are not received, then production will not take place.

Production process stocks are maintenance equipment and spare parts that it is necessary to hold in order to keep the production process running. Administration stocks are items that are necessary to run the administration of the firm, such as stationery items and spares for office equipment. These types of stocks are normally much less important than production process stocks, although they can be quite significant in some service industries, such as insurance or banking.

The benefits and costs of holding stocks are summarised in Table 18.1.

Benefits	Costs
They enable the production process to continue when unexpected events occur	Stocks tie up working capital and they have an enormous opportunity cost
Finished goods stocks keep customers happy when they are looking for a product	The actual costs of storing and handling stocks are high
Large-scale buying of input stocks often gains cost advantages through purchasing economies of scale	There is always the danger that stocks may deteriorate, become obsolete, or go out of fashion
Large-scale buying of input stocks reduces the frequency of stock-handling requirements that apply to JIT stock control	Theft of stock is a problem in some businesses

Table 18.1 Benefits and costs of holding stocks

Stock control charts

In situations where firms do hold stocks, then they often use charts to show what their present stock situation is and also to trigger reordering. These charts are frequently computer-generated these days. They are nonetheless useful and should be considered. The traditional chart shows maximum and minimum stock levels, reorder levels, at which point new stock must be ordered, and delivery times. By definition, the charts show a perfect situation and they are based upon three main assumptions:

- all stocks are delivered on time, in the correct quantity;
- there are no faulty stocks;
- stock is used up at a constant rate (see Figure 18.3).

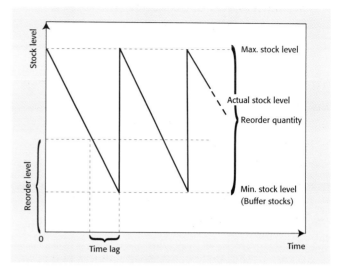

Figure 18.3 A typical stock control chart

After the initial order, stock is used up at a constant rate and when it falls to the reorder level, a new order for stock is placed, equal to the difference between the maximum and minimum stock levels. The delivery should arrive as the stock level reaches the minimum level and should then take the stock level back to maximum.

Usage is very unlikely to be constant, waste will occur and delivery on time cannot be guaranteed. Also, there is no guarantee that the reordering will take place at exactly the right moment, although computer ordering has helped here. However, these types of stock control diagrams can still be very useful, so long as the possible inaccuracies are borne in mind and not ignored.

Activities

1. Distinguish between the different types of stocks a firm may hold. Use examples to illustrate your answer.
2. A firm keeps a stock of brass brackets, which it uses at the rate of 500 a week. No more than four weeks supply of stock is required, but stock must not fall below 1.5 weeks supply. If the initial order is for 1,000 brackets and the delivery time is one week, draw a stockholding chart that shows the minimum and maximum stock levels, the re-order level and the delivery time.
3. If the firm doubles its usage of the brass brackets, redraw the stockholding chart to show the new situation.

Just-in-time (JIT) stock control

JIT started in Japan in the 1960s as an approach to stock management and was first used by the Toyota Car Company. It has since become much more and its birth was very much responsible for the wider philosophy of Total Quality Management.

The basic idea is that nothing should be received, produced or despatched until the precise point at which it is needed. If a firm is able to do this successfully, then it will be able to reduce, or even eliminate, stocks of all types and surpluses of finished goods. This in turn will reduce or eliminate all of the costs that are incurred by stockholding. In order to do this, the whole production process needs to be very closely controlled and this will not be easy. The system works best where the production system is highly automated and computer controlled.

The elimination of buffer stocks should reveal any problems that exist with the flow production system and these problems can then be 'Kaizened', improving the efficiency of the system even further. JIT systems of production are based upon actual demand, i.e. products do not start production until they have been ordered.

The best known approach for doing this is the Kanban system that was developed by Toyota. A Kanban is a card that accompanies a part through every stage of the production process. There are two forms of Kanban card, 'move cards' and 'make cards'. 'Move cards' accompany parts, or groups of parts, as they move between work areas. 'Make cards' are used within a work area in order to initiate production. Parts will not be moved or treated unless a card exists and cards are only generated when orders are received for final products. Thus, there should be no spare movement of materials and parts in the production unit. If orders fall, so will the number of kanban cards in circulation and so will the movement and manufacture of parts.

The advantages in terms of overall efficiency and attitude as well as in terms of costs are considerable, but there are dangers and there are situations in which a JIT approach will not be easy to adopt. Among these are:

- where it is difficult to forecast demand or where it is unpredictable and given to erratic surges;
- where suppliers are unreliable;
- where delivery is unreliable;
- where production processes are erratic.

Over-to-you

Short-answer questions

1. Explain the quality objective which might be established by:
   (a) the makers of cheap ball-point pens;
   (b) the owners of a five-star hotel.
2. Distinguish between quality control and quality assurance.
3. Explain why quality circles may be a good approach to motivation.
4. Why might built-in quality be better than inspected quality?
5. Explain and comment upon two types of built-in quality.
6. What are the problems associated with effective benchmarking?
7. Distinguish between Kaizan and one-off improvements.
8. What is meant by multi-skilling and what part does it play in modern approaches to production?
9. What would you consider to be the advantages of holding an external quality assurance certificate?
10. Explain why JIT may not always be the answer.

Discover and learn

For each of these you may find that contacts made by past students for Assignments will be a good starting point.

1. Work in small groups. Each choose a product. Discuss each product. Comment on its quality.
2. Choose any supermarket. Find out how it controls its stock, what the problems are and how they are dealt with.
3. Choose a small retailer. Consider how it deals with stock control and ways in which stockholding might be reduced.
4. Select a producer in your area. Consider how the firm deals with quality. Comment on its approach.

5 Case study – Hard Hats Ltd

Using the information from the case study, which can be found at the end of Section 17, tackle the following exercises:

(a) ◆ The maximum stock level for cushioning materials is 25,000 sets and the minimum is 10,000 sets. Weekly usage for the four weeks from the 1 February is 10,000 sets. Stating any assumptions that you have made, draw a stock-holding chart for the four weeks to show the maximum and minimum stock levels and the reorder levels. Indicate clearly the points where new orders need to be made.

◆ Evaluate the current stockholding policy for all of the materials held at Hard Hats Ltd.

(b) Hard Hats Ltd is continuing to expand and Jamie Pither has decided that a change in the location of the firm would be of benefit. Evaluate factors that Jamie should take into account when he is deciding upon the new location.

(c) Develop a strategy that Jamie Pither might adopt in order to improve the motivation of the production workers.

(d) Write a report considering the firm's approach to quality and make recommendations for a strategy that might be employed to improve quality control in the firm.

Summary

In this section we have recognised that:

● The concepts of quality, quality control, stocks and stockholding are important.

● Quality as an objective and work must be to specification, neither above it nor below it.

● Firms must supply quality products if they wish to succeed.

● There are many possible ways of attempting to ensure quality, but more recent systems make quality the responsibility of every single member of a firm.

● Inspected quality control is a waste of resources and is also demotivating for the shop-floor workers.

● There are various types of stocks, but holding stocks has high monetary and opportunity costs.

● Stocks can be controlled by means of stock control charts, but the lower the stock levels, the better, in most cases.

● JIT is a method of attempting to do this.

Key words

Definitions of Key words can be found in the Glossary on page 236.

benchmarking
quality
quality assurance

stock control
total quality management
(TQM)

19 Revising effectively

On completion of this section you should be able to:

➤ revise more effectively for your AS modules

➤ understand more completely what examiners look for

➤ have a better understanding of the Levels of Response Approach

➤ obtain some ideas on how to use pre-issued case studies

➤ test yourself on the activities provided

➤ be more successful in the examination

Introduction

In modular courses, examinations come quickly, but if you have made a real effort to prepare for them the results can give you confidence for the rest of the course. In this section we look at the course you are revising, what revision really is and the expectations of the examiners. We also spend some time dealing with pre-issued cases.

What you have to do during the year is to take three compulsory papers.

Paper 1 This is a one and a quarter hour unseen paper with two questions based on a single short story, probably taken from a newspaper or magazine and focusing on a real business situation (see the section *The first module assessment* (page 231)).

Paper 2 This is also a one and a quarter hour paper called Business decisions. It covers your second module of work (see the specification for details). In this paper there are two questions, each based on a different sample of data. It is likely that some calculation will be involved in each of the two questions. You will be required to try and apply your knowledge to make decisions or to comment on decisions that have been provided as part of the question. The section *Business decisions* on page 232 gives you examples of questions to try.

Paper 3 This is a pre-issued case, very similar in nature to the ones you are used to. You will have one and a half hours for this paper in the examination room. The three sections starting with *Using the pre-issued case* on page

225 give you advice on how to respond to pre-issued cases and prepare for using them; The section *Business behaviour* on page 233 gives you an example. The paper draws on the same specification as Paper 2. Note that the examples given here have been prepared by the author and not by the Board. All responsibility for them rests with the author and they are only intended to give you extra relevant practice. You will find a set of Board-prepared specimen papers with the specification.

Revising effectively

You can only revise things you have learnt well. The first key to good revision is therefore good learning. Much of the learning of this subject is concerned with language and techniques.

Language

It will be common practice in the AS papers to ask you questions like:

◆ What do you understand by ... ?

◆ Define ... .

◆ Explain ... .

◆ Give two examples of ... .

◆ Calculate ... .

In all of these cases you will have to know your language. There are good dictionaries of the subject, which you should use from time to time to check that you do understand the idea you have found. However, it is important to express ideas in your own words and then you know you will understand. It has been recommended that you keep a vocabulary book and that in it you define words and phrases as you come across them.

To have knowledge of the language consistently and correctly written in a vocabulary book is simply to write your own dictionary, but if this is all you do it will not be of great use. Once you have acknowledged a word, by writing it in the book, you have to *use it regularly*, because real understanding only comes with use. There are three important reasons for being good at the language of the subject:

1 You will be able to understand the case, which will use such language in the expectation that you can understand it.

2 You will not suffer the indignity of being unable to answer a question because you did not know the language:

   ◆ Working capital is *not* all the capital that is working in the business.

   ◆ Gearing is *not* the extent to which a firm is automated.

   ◆ Market segmentation is *not* the positioning of products in a supermarket.
   All of these misunderstandings, and many more, were offered in exam answers and meant that candidates could earn no marks from their answers.

3 You will be able to write more confidently, more accurately and more concisely about questions that are asked.

You will find that well-understood language will act as a trigger, reminding you of the context in which that language was learnt, thus giving you yet another advantage.

The questions you are asked which ask you to show knowledge of language will frequently require three other things:

Context The question will perhaps read like this:

'What do you understand by ... in the context of the case?'

You must always refer back to the case because it is likely that the normal meaning has been changed in some way by that context. Make sure you find that small difference.

Relevance The relevance of every idea is always within the situation in which it is used. In one context the meaning of a word may be trivial, whilst in another it is right at the heart of the situation. You know how what

people say can sometimes be distorted by taking it out of context. The same is true of what is written. When you are asked to comment upon relevance, make sure you appreciate not just the meaning but also the relevance of the idea you are asked about.

Examples Always give examples where you can. Do not wait to be asked. A definition you have given may be weak or unclear and then the example will show that you do understand.

Activities

1 Find the meaning of each of the following. Give examples where you can:
   ◆ value added;
   ◆ primary production;
   ◆ quality;
   ◆ market penetration;
   ◆ liquidity.

2 Distinguish between:
   ◆ gross and net profit;
   ◆ profit and profitability;
   ◆ production and productivity;
   ◆ Kaizan and Kanban;
   ◆ induction and training.

3 Choose any five words or phrases you think you know. Write down their meaning and then look them up. Correct as necessary. Do this in groups and you will find it is more fun. Repeat as often as you like. It gets tougher if members of the group choose the words for each other.

Techniques

First, look at the following Activities.

Activities

1 Check in the specification the techniques that you should know. Do this yourself, but then check with members of your small group just to make sure that you have found them all.

2 Look in your notes or in a textbook. Work through the technique. Work in groups of four. Change the numbers in the example, so that you are all doing the same new one, and do it again.

3 Check your results with members of the group and, where necessary, seek the help of your teacher. Keep at it until you get it right.

It is not sufficient to be able to use the technique. You must also:

- Show all your working where calculation is involved, because without it you cannot see where you went wrong (if you did) and you cannot get any marks from the examiner if there is a mistake. To miss out the working is effectively saying give me all the marks or none.
- Know all the uses to which this technique may be put.
- Know what the answer means and how it can be used.
- Know what assumptions you make when using the technique.
- Know what the strengths and weaknesses of the technique are.
- Be aware of the limitations of its use.

If you are unsure about any of these things the relevant section of this book should be able to help you.

Activities

List the techniques you agreed in your group. Share them out between members of the group and go through the things you should know and be able to do that are listed above, making appropriate notes on each point. Discuss your ideas with the other members. Correct your notes. Photocopy them so that you all have a full set.

Revising purposefully

There is little benefit in just reading your notes or textbooks. There is some benefit, but not a great deal, in reducing your notes to postcard-sized topic notes. Both of those activities are more concerned with the processes of either reading or making summaries than they are with learning. Your notes and your textbooks should be **resources**, which you use, in purposeful revision. The last three groups of self-assessment tasks are examples of directed revision with a clear purpose. You can use past double-module and business-context papers to revise purposefully, but you will need the help of your teacher in selecting which questions in those papers to use.

You can also use the questions that are posed at the end of this section and others in the book that you have not done. For the first module paper you should select work from Sections 1–7 and for the second two papers

from Sections 8–18. In using case studies, do not try to spot questions but select topics. The example below has selected some from **Hard Hat**, which you can find at the end of Section 17.

1 Hard Hat Ltd

The firm is a private limited company.

- What does this mean?
- What advantages does it confer?
- Who are the stakeholders?
- In the case study are there any finance situations that might arise from being Limited.?
- Are there any suggestions that it should change its structure.

2 Batch production

- What methods of production are there?
- Do you understand them?
- Do you know the kinds of production to which each is best suited?
- Do you know the costs and benefits of each method?
- Do you think that batch production is best suited to the work of Hard Hat?
- If not, how and why should it be changed?

Activities

Work in groups.

1 Each member of the group should choose a different one of the themes in Hard Hat, other than the two examples above, and write down questions about the theme that occur to you.
2 Discuss with the others the list of questions you have made and make any changes you agree upon.
3 Work on these questions. Define where necessary, explain, give examples and write good, useful notes.
4 Discuss your notes together and check with your teacher things you are unsure of or disagree about.
5 Amend your notes in the light of the discussion.
6 Photocopy the notes so that each person in the class has a full set.

Working in groups

Working in groups is simply division of labour. It recognises three things:

- That each of us has strengths and weaknesses and that by working together we therefore support each other.

- That there is less work for everyone to do if tasks are shared, discussed and distributed than if we all try to do everything ourselves.
- That mutual help, in this way, tends to make us responsible towards each other and more motivated to get things done.

It will only work if:

- The work is shared evenly and fairly.
- The strengths and interests of each member of the group are used.
- Everyone pulls their weight.
- The work that is done is carefully discussed to ensure that everyone understands.
- The work done is changed in line with the discussion and the teacher's support.
- Everyone then gets and uses a copy.

Most people in teaching agree that the best way to really learn something is to be in a position where you have to explain it to someone else. This only works if those who do not understand freely admit it and ask for further explanation. This is your examination and you should never pass up an opportunity to ensure that you understand.

Using the pre-issued case

You only have one requirement to do this in the first year and that is with the third paper. The purpose of pre-issue is to give you a sound basis for revision and many of the ideas about revision commented upon above form part of the approach to the pre-issued case.

There is no specific amount of time that is necessary for preparation and the Board *does not guarantee any minimum classroom time* for class study of the cases. It simply determines the dates of the examinations and then a pre-issue date. From that date the case will be available on the Internet, as well as being sent to the centre. Teachers and students may use the case from the time of receipt in whatever ways are considered appropriate.

What follows is one way of using the case. This approach does not have to be used, but it may give you ideas of your own. The method is based upon the assumptions that:

- Two copies of the case will be used, so there will be a need to photocopy.

- The teacher will need some time to study the case before it is issued or worked with.
- Quite a short period of time – two weeks is enough and three weeks is ample – is necessary for preparation. Any lengthening of this period and the work becomes too intensive and counter-productive. There is also an important balance to strike. Short modular studies do not leave large periods of time for revision. Every week used reduces the study time.
- The examination is not competitive. Co-operation between students in the run up to the examination is to everybody's advantage and nobody's loss. By sharing, students can cover much more extensive revision than otherwise and can support each other's efforts. See ideas on working together in the section above on *Working in groups*.

A plan (explained as a set of instructions for students)

Work in small groups of 4–6. If the class is small work in pairs.

You will be given the first copy of the case and have time to read it through. Check on your understanding of it as a piece of English. This is best done immediately and in discussion with your group. Since this is pre-issued, not all of the words or phrases may be within your vocabulary. Don't be shy about this. The examination is yours and it would be silly to lose marks because you had not made certain that your understanding of the English in the case is complete.

The case should be divided into approximately equal units, depending on the number of groups with one unit for each group. Title and the diagrams (tables) should be a part of this division.

The objective is that you should gain a thorough understanding of the case by a combination of reading the whole case and then specialising in part of it. Responsible revision with work shared both within and between groups gets more done and enables you to achieve those marks that are earned by analysis and evaluation. It also helps to ensure that your knowledge and use of the language of the subject is better.

Activities

1 Read the whole case.

2 Read your part and ensure that you understand it. Discuss this with members of your group.

3 Now concentrate on your section alone.

   (a) Highlight all words and phrases in your part that have business-studies meanings.

   (b) Check your list with members of your group and agree.

4 With reference to each of the identified things you should be able to:
   ◆ define it;
   ◆ give examples;
   ◆ explain it;
   ◆ use it in context;
   ◆ understand uses;
   ◆ understand limitations.

5 Bring your completed work back to class. Present it and photocopy it for all students. You should now have a complete portfolio of words and phrases.

6 Read through your portfolio alone and with your group. Highlight anything you do not understand and bring questions back to the next lesson.

7 With reference to your identified words and phrases, trace links backwards or forwards with repetitions of the same idea or with associated ones.

8 Check any association that the ideas may have with the diagrams or tables in the case.

9 Identify the main issues and themes and allocate one/ two as required fairly among members of each group.

10 Revise your area(s) of the syllabus and create notes for the rest of the class. *Do not try to identify any questions. Trying to create model answers is a dangerous waste of time. Do look at past questions of A-level standard that are on your topic and make sure you can answer them* or come back with questions you need to ask and debate in class.

11 Try some questions that require different levels of response.

1 **Explain why (or how) ...**   (4)

This is quite clearly a level-2 answer. You are only expected to show understanding and this may best be done with a definition, a comparison, an example, by stating reasons or by description. For four marks it should not take more than four minutes.

2 **What do you understand by ...? (Line 23)**   (5)

This is still level 2 at best, but there is a clue here. You have been given a line reference to work with. This suggests that it is contextual understanding that the examiner is looking for.

3 **Which of Mr Parker's objectives do you think is most important?**   (8)

The examiner doesn't just want an answer, but for eight marks clearly expects a level-4 answer in which you have argued good reason(s) why one objective is the most important. Here the clue to the level is in the *mark awarded*. You don't get eight marks for just saying growth or for just giving an unsupported reason for growth.

You need practice at these questions before you go into the exam room. There is a time constraint and you need to get straight to the point giving the examiner the kind of answer that was sought. Take some good answers you have written (ones on which you obtained a level-4 mark (16–20 out of 20) and reduce it to 350 words without losing any of the marks.

Good exam results depend more on the following things than on what you know:
   ◆ good technique;
   ◆ good timing, i.e. completing the paper as requested;
   ◆ organising the answer well in the form required;
   ◆ being neat and orderly and showing all working;
   ◆ giving examples as often as you can;
   ◆ always relating your answer to the context of the case;
   ◆ using the subject language well and appropriately;
   ◆ using the English language properly;
   ◆ checking that you have answered the question.

Using the second copy of the case

Analysing the case in the way described above will have left you with a mass of knowledge about the detailed elements of the case. In doing this you will have many detailed notes on the case. You need to clear all of those away, retaining them but trying to forget them for the moment, and concentrate not on the parts of the case but the whole story. You have analysed the trees in the wood and know them well, but now is the time to focus on the wood as a whole. For this you will need to read the specification (syllabus). Ask some general questions that come to mind from your knowledge of the business in the case.

- What legal structure is it?
- How big is it?
- What field of business activity is it in or could it be in?
- What its objectives are or might be?
- What sort of management style and culture is indicated?
- How well it is doing and is it growing or in decline?
- What changes are in progress or likely?
- Is the workforce motivated?
- How is it financed and does it have enough finance?
- What are its strengths and its weaknesses?
- What threats and opportunities are there?
- What problems can you see?

Losing marks in exams

Virtually all candidates manage to lose some marks by the way they complete their papers. Some lose more than a grade. The main reasons for this are set out below. The interesting thing is that they are common mistakes, which all teachers warn about. There are few who can afford to lose marks by carelessness or poor strategy so perhaps these same points, made to you by an experienced chief examiner will not be ignored in the examination papers you take.

These comments are based on significant mark reductions made in actual scripts. To demonstrate them, 50 scripts, chosen at random across a mark range from 15 to 76 out of 100, were read. In 80% of these scripts at least a grade was lost. Four of those where this was not true were either at the very bottom or at the top. What follows concentrates on the mistakes and hence is basically a list of *Don'ts*.

Ignoring the case

The effect of ignoring the case is simple. Since there is no case data in the answer, there is no application and even the very best of answers like this cannot gain a mark above level 2. All the questions arise from, and concern, the case, so you must always use it as the focus of the answer. The market segmentation question and

the non-price one shown below were ones within which several candidates wrote theoretical answers that made no reference to the context. In three cases these were good answers, but were limited to 5 marks out of 15.

Timing

A last question not attempted or with a skeleton for an answer and evidence of haste in one or two of the last questions are all very common. This come from pressure you put upon yourself by spending too much time on earlier questions. Spending more time than it deserves on a question is very foolish. It may increase your marks on that question by one or two, but it is likely to mean that very few marks are earned later in the paper. The net result is a loss of marks.

In your first paper you have 75 minutes and 60 marks. Given that you need some time to read the case and some time to plan the answers, the allocation of time ought to look something like this:

- 10 minutes reading the case;
- 5 minutes total planning time;
- 1 minute actual writing time for each mark awarded to a question.

This is not very much time, but it is enough if you use it well and do not go over time on any question. You may have time left over at the end, which you can profitably use to improve an answer. To make this possible *leave a good long gap between answers* so that any additional points that can be made are made as part of the answer and not elsewhere in the paper.

Read the question

You would, perhaps, be surprised by the frequency with which people do not read the question. In fact there were 168 instances noted in the papers surveyed. It is not possible to refer to them all but here are some examples. See the effect; *this was on average more than three errors in a paper.*

1 **Why is market segmentation an important part of ... strategy?**

There were several misreadings here. Some were because the candidate did not know what market segmentation was. Some just gave a definition of market segmentation and some examples. They gained 2 marks out of the possible 12. Some did not see the word 'strategy' and some did not see the word 'why'.

2 How might non-price competition help the firm to increase sales?

Again there was poor understanding of language here. Several clearly did not know what non-price competition really was. Some answered purely in terms of what it was and did not answer the question. The biggest error was in not seeing the prefix 'non'. These candidates often wrote very good answers about price competition, but they got no marks at all.

3 Discuss the advantages ...

Many answers merely listed and possibly explained the advantages, but did not discuss them. However, the common fault this time was to give something that had not been asked for; 14 of the 50 answers gave the advantages, for which they often got good marks, but then went on to write about the disadvantages which had not been asked for. This did not lose them any marks, but it lost precious time.

4 Discuss the possible methods of production. Select one and say why you think it would be best for the firm.

There are two questions here and not one. Many candidates ignored one or other of them. What you should always do is:

- Take a highlighting pen into the examination room and highlight the trigger words.
- Look at the question and note whether there is a special word or a limitation. This would have avoided the error about non-pricing and the error of writing about disadvantages when only advantages were asked for.
- When you have finished writing the answer, go back to the question and read it again. This should tell you whether you have really answered it.

Show your working

This applies to working with numbers. Most candidates show working when asked to do so, but the paper rarely asks for it. We expect you *always* to show every step of the working and that includes both what you are doing in the line and the performing of it. For example:

Multiply × 2 = 48.

If there is not any working, there cannot be any reward except for the right answer. Anyone who does not show working is totally penalised by one mistake. If a question is out of 6:

- No working but correct answer 6
- Working and one mistake 5
- Working and two mistakes 4
- No working and wrong for some reason 0

In the two calculations on the paper, both of which were simple arithmetic operations that did not really need a calculator, there were 12 candidates who scored 0, having no working on both occasions, and a further 5 who omitted the working and gave the wrong answer on one of the two occasions.

Use the subject language

There were many instances where time was wasted or marks were lost because answers were too long and vague. The students had not taken advantage of the opportunity to make their answers clearer and shorter by using the language of the subject. It is unlikely that a candidate will get a mark better than a grade C unless there is evidence of competent confident use of the language.

Using what you know

Level 2 shows understanding of the subject matter and is the lowest level of use. At this level you are able to define, to compare, to explain and to link together ideas. However, using knowledge is best shown by organising the data. This will show some insight into the question and begins to provide evidence that will support the answer. This is level 3. At the highest level you have to both make a judgement or a decision and support it with facts, theories and opinions that show the judgement to be a good one. The next section is about what examiners really look for in applying levels of response.

Too much knowledge

All the knowledge in the world, the most perfect and most detailed knowledge base, will never get you more than 4 marks out of 16 unless it is used. If it is well used, you will still get an excellent mark but the sheer length of the answer will rob you of valuable time. Remember the golden rule:

- *A few points well argued and supported by relevant evidence is the best approach.*

It is *quality* and not quantity the examiners are looking for.

Lack of planning

What this means is a minute or so reflecting on what the examiner wants and how it can be delivered. It is easy to see when candidates have not planned. Those who just write are not quite sure what the question means or what the answer should be. They often struggle towards the answer and begin to focus after several lines of writing. That focus would be much sharper and more worthy of marks if the first few lines were omitted and the time used to think before writing. You should plan because the answer is always better. You should plan because it is more likely to save time than to waste it. In planning, remember that an answer has three elements:

◆ The question that is asked and the apparent requirements of the examiner. This needs consideration because those expectations are not always clear and are often wider than the writer at first imagines.

◆ The theory. All questions require some use of theory or concept. The chosen theory must be relevant and accurately explained and applied. The chosen technique needs to be the best one for the job. These things also require a little thought.

◆ The case material. What part of that material is relevant and why is it appropriate? Which parts seem to be the most useful to use.

Remember that the examiner is looking for a few points well made and not just for as much as you can think of.

The focus on skills

The philosophy of the approach is that examiners seek to assess and reward the *use of knowledge* much more than its *demonstration*. Four levels are normally defined and examiners assess from the top down, seeking the extent to which an answer gives them what they really want from the question. Only the best candidates will offer that response, so each answer is tested successively against each lower level until the level is found that corresponds to what the candidate has shown. If a level is not found, the candidate has earned no marks. The use of levels of response does not mean that all answers will be assessed in this way. A levels approach is not used where:

◆ The answer required is a straight calculation so that there are stages of working, which can be assessed in the traditional way.

◆ The answer required is visual, e.g. the drawing of a product life cycle or a break even chart.

The fact that a levels approach with four possible levels is used does not mean that there will always be four or that the mark band for each will necessarily be equal. The four levels do, however, represent different kinds of skills, which are identified by reading the whole of an answer. It is sufficient to demonstrate a particular level *once* in an answer and that defines the minimum mark for the whole answer.

If a question is set where the highest level is level 2 and there is one instance of understanding in your answer, you will have achieved level 2. Similarly if the question demands a level-four response and we find a supported judgement in your answer, you will have reached level four and get at least the lowest mark for that level. Out of 12, that is likely to be 10 or 11. To get more than the minimum mark in a band you need to show:

◆ a very good instance of the skill associated with the level; and/or

◆ more than one relevant instance of that skill.

Because the skills at each level are different, you cannot get into a higher level because your skills at the lower level are excellent. Very good understanding cannot be considered as analysis and superb analysis never amounts to evaluation. You have got to show the skill a level demands.

At AS we shall put more emphasis on levels 1 and 2 and less emphasis on levels 3 and 4. This means that good understanding of language and techniques and a good ability to express that understanding can get you a good mark overall. You should, of course, show the higher skills where the mark allocation and the trigger word(s) used show that those higher skills are demanded.

The four skill levels

The FOUR levels are:

◆ Level 4: Reasoning;
◆ Level 3: Analysis;
◆ Level 2: Explanation;
◆ Level 1: Knowledge.

Level 4: Reasoning

The trigger words that might indicate that this skill is asked for might include:

- **discuss** – because a conclusion based upon the discussion is called for;
- devise a **strategy** because a strategy implies a plan that has been produced by analysing and evaluating evidence;
- **evaluate** – because that is a reasoning process;
- **why** – because that too requires reasoning;
- **give reasons for your answer;**
- make and **justify**;
- assess the strategy and comment upon …

The other clue always present with the question is the number of marks that are awarded. Anything over 7, where a multi-part answer is not required, is likely to expect a reasoned answer.

A multi-part answer would be required by something like:

'State and explain three ways in which …' (9)
This is really three times 3 marks, rather than one mark of 9, and will require up to a level 2 response for each of the three parts.

Level 3: Analysis

The trigger words that look only for this skill and which rule out a level 4 response are:

- **analyse**, provided it does not go on to ask for evaluation;
- **critically explain**, which requires the candidate to show an awareness that goes beyond mere explanation, but does not require a reasoned argument;
- **Use of a technique**, e.g. ratio analysis or break even;
- **application of a theory**; human relations theory is most common;
- **application of a concept**, e.g. Boston Matrix or Product Life Cycle.

Questions that seek only a level 3 response will not be common, but, of course, all questions that seek level 4 can be answered in a way that only achieves level 3. Suppose a strategy is asked for but the answer only sifts the evidence upon which a strategy would depend without putting one together. That would be level 3. A discussion that accurately considers both sides of the argument, but does not sum up would also be level 3. A decision where the basis of the decision is well analysed but no decision is made or the decision made is not supported by the analysis is also level 3.

Level 2: Explanation

This is the level at which the candidate shows understanding, rather than using knowledge. Triggger words for this level include:

- **explain**
- **define**
- **what do you understand by**
- **distinguish between**
- **compare**
- **contrast**

Ideas discussed in context or the development of relevant facts in a way that shows understanding without going further are at this level. They will be relatively poor answers to questions demanding evaluation, attracting little more than half the marks available at AS. Every AS exam paper, however, is likely to have some questions that do not look for answers above this level. Such questions usually carry between 3 and 6 marks.

Level 1: Knowledge

Knowing quite a lot and spending time stating it or knowing little and rarely getting beyond a list of the facts is never going to get more than 5 marks out of 20 and on that basis will always fall very far short of a pass.

The effect of the levels approach on learning and revision

You have to be trained to come to terms with the way examiners assess. It requires an entirely different approach from you than you may have used in previous exams. You have to get straight to the question asked and try to home in on the highest level the question demands Answers have to be short. There is no time for an answer much longer than 300 words and that has to be capable of attracting 15 marks out of 15.

The real skills are:

- working out what the question really wants and going directly for that (planning);
- keeping the answers concise – aiming for a level 4 answer inside 300 words (language and timing);
- selecting from the knowledge held and/or available in the case, whichever is more appropriate for the question asked (selectivity and quality);
- using the language of the subject contextually and accurately, both when asked to do so and as a matter of course when appropriate;

- using examples, where appropriate, to illuminate understanding of concepts or situations;
- always showing working step by step in any calculation;
- remembering that the questions are about the case study and finding appropriate ways to use that evidence;
- working co-operatively in preparation for the examination, rather than alone or competitively;
- having a good working knowledge of the local business community and using it as appropriate;
- learning to integrate knowledge in answering questions;

All of these skills have to be built up over time and by the time the first module examination is taken. Once mastered, they become the basis of success in all the other modules.

The first module assessment

- First read the specification for the first teaching module.
- Do some of the short-answer questions in this book.
- Do some of the case studies.

Strong pound forces high street prices down

By Anne Segall, Economics Correspondent

High street prices fell for the first time in 16 years in February as retailers took advantage of the strong pound to buy cheap supplies from abroad, a Confederation of British Industry survey has revealed.

The fall in prices coincided with a surge in high street activity, with 61pc of retailers experiencing rising sales last month and 14pc suffering falling sales. The positive balance of 47pc was the highest recorded by the CBI since November 1996.

The strength of demand took retailers by surprise. They had been expecting a dip in activity after the traditionally strong January sales period.

A positive balance of 17pc of those surveyed said sales were above average for the time of year and 28pc said they expected the business situation to improve in the next six months. Sentiment in the sector rose to its highest level for three years.

The CBI yesterday attributed the fall in prices in the high street to a combination of competitive pressures and the rising share of cheap imports. Import penetration rose faster last month than at any time for the past 10 years, with one in five retailers claiming to have raised the proportion of imports to total goods on offer.

Alastair Eperon, chairman of the CBI distributive trade panel, warned: "The strong pound continues to bite, with retailers buying more of their supplies from abroad." He appealed to the Bank of England to keep interest rates on hold when it meets to review policy next week.

The rising tide of imports is likely to set alarm bells ringing at the Treasury after news earlier in the week of a sharp deterioration in the trade balance last year and evidence yesterday of a marked slowdown in manufacturing activity.

According to the Chartered Institute of Purchasing and Supply, manufacturing companies are struggling to keep their heads above water. An index compiled by the institute to measure the overall health of manufacturing slipped to 51.0 last month from 51.8 in January and a recent peak of 56.4 in December. The index is now just a short distance away from the "break-even" level of 50 which separates periods of expansion from periods of contraction.

The CIPS report points to a deterioration in manufacturing order books, with a decline from 53.1 to 51.8 last month in the new orders index and a fall to 52.1 in the new export orders index – its lowest level since last June.

Source: Daily Telegraph 2 March 2000

Questions The questions are related to the article, but your answers should make use of appropriate aspects of your business studies knowledge.

1 Most retailers are small.
  (a) i. How would you define small in this context? (4)
      ii. What legal structure is most common among retailers? Explain your answer. (10)
  (b) Discuss reasons why a 'strong pound' is said to be forcing High-Street prices down. (15)
2 (a) What does the term 'rate of interest' mean as it is used in the article? (4)
  (b) Discuss objectives that the Bank of England might have in changing the rate of interest? (10)
  (c) What effects would you expect a rise in the rate of interest to have on businesses which sell durable consumer goods? Justify your answer. (15)

Business decisions

The following are some examples of single questions to try.

Bernard's Bikes

Bernard is a cyclist of very high standard who was injured in a race. He has set up a business hiring bikes to people who want to cycle around a large reservoir. It was a good opportunity and his business net profits for the second summer season are shown in Table 19.1. Bernard invested £40,000 in his business two years ago and retained £10,000 profit last year. He has not borrowed any money.

	April	May	June	July	Aug.	Sept.	Oct.
Income	1.2	1.8	4.7	5.9	11.9	5.4	2.4
Expenses	1.9	1.9	1.9	2.2	3.4	2.1	1.9
Net profit	(0.7)	(0.1)	2.8	3.7	8.5	3.3	0.5

Table 19.1 Net income April to October (£'000)

1 Explain what is meant by the term 'net profit'. (4)
2 Calculate Bernard's net profit for the year. (2)
3 Calculate and comment upon Bernard's return on capital employed for the season. (8)
4 Explain possible reasons for the pattern of trade during the season. (5)
5 Discuss ways in which Bernard might increase his net income for the year. (10)

Benson's Hedges

John Benson is a very keen gardener, who was made redundant in 1998. He turned his hobby into a job and set up business as a jobbing gardener, starting in January 1999. By December 1999 it was obvious that he could not take on any more business without employing someone else. He did not really want to be an employer and was afraid that his reputation might suffer so he is considering whether it would be reasonable to raise prices as a way of both restricting the demand for his services and increasing his profits. He found the information in Table 19.2 in an article he read in his newspaper. It referred to a small town very similar in structure and population to his own town.

	1997	1998	1999	2000
Houses in area	2,000	2,100	2,310	2,772
Houses with gardens	1,050	1,120	1,270	1,600
Percentage employing gardeners	1.5%	1.8%	2.4%	3%
Average spending on gardeners (£'s per month)	60	61.8	63.65	65.56

Table 19.2 Increasing demand for gardening services

1 What is meant by the phrase 'made redundant' and what is its possible relevance for John's new business ? (6)
2 Calculate the percentage increase in potential income from gardening in the town in the year 2000 as compared with the year 1997. (4)
3 Define the term 'price elasticity of demand' and give an example. (4)
4 From all the evidence you have available advise John on whether he should employ an assistant or raise his prices. (15)

Business finance

The data given in Table 19.3 was obtained from a survey of 2,000 small businesses. The survey was undertaken to enable a consultant, who specialises in business start-up advice, to advise his clients. The total capital obtained by these businesses in the ways described in the table was £30,000.

Percentage	
Overdrafts	58
Bank loans	22
Hire purchase	10
Leases	3
Other loans	2
Mortgage	3
Factoring	1
Share issue	1

Table 19.3 Sources of finance other than profits and savings

1 Define the term factoring. (4)
2 (a) Calculate the total borrowing from banks. (3)
 (b) Explain the difference between a loan and an overdraft. (4)
3 Explain why this pattern of borrowing is typical of small businesses. (5)
4 Discuss possible reasons why small businesses fail and suggest ways in which they may try to ensure survival. (13)

It is not suggested that these would be actual questions in the Business Decisions paper, but they will give you good practice in:

- reading and interpreting data; you need to learn to do that in 10 minutes;
- answering questions based on that data;
- timing yourself in readiness for the exam.

Business Behaviour

The Business Behaviour paper is based on a pre-issued case study, so the ideas discussed in the earlier sections (pages 000–000) should be read carefully before making use of this case.

The Chequered Flag Hotel Ltd

Introduction to the case The hotel gets its name from its owner's enthusiasm for motor racing. Like most hotels, it has a seasonal pattern of demand. The company has income, cash flow and costing problems arising from this and is looking for marketing plans that might help. Ways of boosting income are considered.

The case The hotel is located in West Sussex about 16 miles from several south-coast resorts, two airports and two channel ports. It became a limited company with

Conrad Jeffs as the majority shareholder when, in 1998, it forged a link with a local tour operator, Angharad Jones, who contributed a capital injection of £80,000 in return for 10% of the shares. Other shareholders are Sarah, John's wife, with 15% and Michael Jeffs, their son, with 12%.

The hotel has accommodation for 100 people, together with a reception area, two large lounges and a large dining room. There are six full-time members of staff in addition to the Jeffs family. Angharad does no work in the hotel, but her firm provides a substantial part of the business through holiday bookings and coach parties. In the high season (June to September) the firm employs students to supplement the full-time staff. For occasional busy times in the rest of the year the company employs a number of part-timers, mostly school students. Conrad takes responsibility for the 'front-of-house' activities, for customer relations, for the bar and for marketing. Sarah oversees all of the financial affairs, the restaurant and the kitchen, whilst Michael is responsible for all housekeeping and personnel functions, as well as general stock control.

At the Board meeting in January 2000 Sarah reviewed the bookings for 1999. The figures showed the usual seasonal variation with the trend being slightly downwards. She also provided a projection for 2000, based on the trend and current advance bookings. The figures are shown in Table 19.4.

Month	Bedspaces 1998	Bedspaces 1999	Projected 2000
Jan.	46	44	44
Feb.	37	33	32
Mar.	46	46	49
Apr.	72	69	69
May	57	54	51
June	63	61	60
July	89	87	85
Aug.	92	90	88
Sept.	77	72	70
Oct.	50	40	36
Nov.	29	24	20
Dec.	52	50	48

Table 19.4 Bookings (Actual figures 1998 and 1999 and projections for 2000)

Sarah argued that the position was even less favourable than the figures suggested because in 1998 only 13% of all visitors were from overseas and last year it was 25%. Given the strong pound, it was to be expected that the number of overseas visitors would fall off more sharply than the trend. Sarah had also found information on the Internet that showed that an increasing proportion of British holidaymakers were going overseas. Angharad pointed out that, whilst this may be true, the tendency to take more than one holiday or to take short breaks was increasing rapidly. She also said that the feedback the firm got from its customers showed more negative comments about the hotel than in the past and that these most commonly referred to facilities available and general standards of service. The meeting agreed that there was a need for market research to pinpoint the segments the hotel could target more aggressively and for action to identify the weaknesses in customer service and improve them.

Whilst Angharad agreed with the need for market research, with which she said her company could help, she also pointed out that the problem was not just about occupying beds. It was about cash flow and profits. 'There are', she said, 'many more ways for this hotel to make real profits than filling the beds, and some of these should be investigated.'

'Do you have any idea of the average amount that clients spend in the hotel over and above their residential costs?', she said. 'What proportion of current income is provided by people who do not stay in the hotel?'

Everyone agreed that these were vital questions to which answers must be sought so that 2000 could be the year in which the trend was reversed. Angharad produced some figures (shown in Table 19.5) to strengthen the case for more careful analysis of the market.

Hotel	Bedspaces	Annual average income (£ million)	Percentage from rooms
Majestic	120		
Palace	100		
Brunswick	94		
Alberta	110		

Table 19.5 Comparative figures for other local hotels

A quick calculation by Sarah suggested that chequered flag business was way behind these figures with about 20% of income generated other than by occupancy and most of that from people who were staying in the hotel.

Further research revealed that the hotel's pricing policy of £60 per person per night was much less flexible that that of other hotels, which varied their prices in terms of some or all of the following:

- single and double/twin rates;
- group bookings;
- differentiating rooms in terms of position/facilities;
- week-ends as compared with weekly rates;
- offers for week-ends and out-of-season bookings.

Questions

1 In the context of the case, explain what is meant by:
   (a) Seasonal? (4)
   (b) Downward trend? (4)
2 Angharad estimates that a reduction in price to £50 per night per person would increase occupancy by 20%.
   (a) Calculate the price elasticity of demand. (4)
   (b) Calculate the change in income for January to March 2000. (4)
   (c) Explain why this lower price strategy should or should not be followed for those months. (8)
3 (a) Explain what contribution cost pricing is. (4)
   (b) Discuss the appropriateness of this strategy for the pricing of the hotel's rooms. (12)
4 Explain why a strong pound might adversely effect the bookings the hotel might receive. (8)
5 Discuss new market segments the firm might enter. (10)
6 Choose one market segment you think might be best for the hotel and explain and justify your choice. (10)
7 What factors would you take into account in planning the market survey? Justify your selection. (12)
8 Clearly, customer service is not as good as it could be. Discuss the issues involved in good customer service and discuss ways of improving performance. (8)

Note   These are some of the many questions that could be asked on this case. A good way of revising would be to think of more potential questions and to research answers to them. You can also use some of the cases at the end of the sections in this book and past cases from OCR exams. In using the latter, remember to stick to issues that are part of the syllabus. The specimen paper will show you what a real paper looks like.

Written communication skills

In the first two modules written communication skills are worth 2 marks per paper. In the third paper 4 marks are at risk. Although not many marks, they are marks you cannot afford to lose. Please be careful in the ways you use the English language and structure your work. Check your work if you can find a little time to do so.

Glossary

above the line Using the media to advertise or promote goods and services for sale.

absenteeism Absence from work which is not acceptably explained.

accountability The fact that workers with responsibilities must be accountable to a supervisor or manager.

accounts The financial records of a business. Accounts should be kept for all activities which have a money value.

acid-test ratio Relates liquid assets (cash and debtors) to current liabilities as a tighter test of the liquidity of a business.

advertising Informing or persuading potential buyers about a product or service. Normally involves one or more of the media. Designed to increase sales.

AIM The Alternative Investment Market through which companies can gain access to further capital. The market is designed to give support to smaller companies.

appraisal Any method of evaluating the performance of an employee, often against set targets with new targets set for the coming period. Appraisal is often two way.

assets employed The assets used in a business. Usually found by adding working capital + fixed assets + intangible assets.

audit A check on the accuracy of the accounting process, the truth and fairness of the accounting statements and the probity with which the cash flows into and out of the business have been undertaken and accounted for.

authority The requirement and the status to get something done. Authority is passed down the line and the delegated is accountable to the delegator for ensuring that it is done.

average rate of return A method of investment appraisal which measures viability in terms of the average return per year (see also pay back period).

balance sheet The view of the value of a business at a point in time. This is usually the end of the trading year. It provides a 'true and fair' view of the position of the business at that time. Can be presented in a variety of forms.

bank overdraft The negotiated right to take more money from a bank account that is in it. An upper limit to the right is always stated.

batch production Simultaneous production or completion of a process, of several units at the same time. Example the cooking of loaves of bread.

below the line Promotion of a product through such methods as 'two for the price of one', demonstrations and displays, special offers.

benchmarking Seeking to identify best practice in any aspect of production and in any organisation and then adopt it in the production process.

book value The value placed on an asset in the accounts of a business. Usually based on original cost less provision made for depreciation.

break-even point The point at which total costs are equal to total revenue. Can be found graphically or by use of a formula. It is a form of forecasting on which production decisions may be made.

Budget (a) A planned allocation of resources (usually money) to a particular purpose, e.g. production costs or a planned target for receipts, e.g. sales revenue.
(b) The (usually) annual plan which the Chancellor of the Exchequer puts before parliament the intended approach for the raising and using of money in the coming year. These plans are embodied in the annual Finance Act and in other appropriate legislation.

business cycle The changing pattern of business activity over a period of time (see diagram of page 77).

capacity The capability of a firm to produce.

capacity utilisation A measure of the efficiency with which capacity is being used. The more fully facilities are being used the less waste and inefficiency there should be.

capital   (a) One of the factors of production, the wealth that makes business possible.
(b) The amount of money used within a business.

capital borrowed   That part of the capital obtained from loans.

capital employed   The capital which a business uses against which the profit can be measured to provide the primary measure of profitability. Consists of capital borrowed plus capital owned or the net assets of the business.

capital expenditure   Money which is spent out to increase the assets of a business. This is in contrast to revenue expenditure, see below.

capital intensity   The extent to which capital is used in preference to other factors of production. For example the Docklands Light Railway is fully automated and has no drivers. It is highly capital intensive.

capital owned   That part of the capital which belongs to the owner(s) or to shareholders.

cash flow   The movement of cash into and out of the business. The business needs a positive cashflow to survive, i.e. inflows greater than outflows.

cash flow forecast   A cash budget which plans or forecasts the likely flow of cash into and out of a business in a given period of time.

cell production   The workforce is divided into a number of self-contained units (cells). Each cell produces the whole of the product or at least several stages of it.

centralisation   The tendency to keep control within a central office or among the management team. It is common to centralise financial matters and often buying decisions.

chain of command   The levels of hierarchy within an organisation. Command passes down the levels from the top to the bottom. The chain is the linked levels in a line from top to bottom.

civil law   The law which regulates relationships between two or more people and provides a means of settling non-criminal disputes.

cluster sample   Relatively intense sampling of the same small area, e.g. sampling a single constituency in a general election.

communication   Any process, by any method, which is designed to influence the behaviour of someone, or the actual processes by which this is done.

competition   The situation where there is more than one firm in the market for the same goods or for close substitutes.

competition-based pricing   Setting a price for a product or service by taking into account prices charged by competitors.

conservation   The act of saving resources or areas and of using them wisely. An example is the careful maintenance of stocks of fish by limiting catches.

consumer marketing   Attempting to sell to consumers rather than to businesses.

consumers   Those who use a product or service. They are not always the buyers, e.g. baby clothes.

contract   A legally binding agreement between two parties. Contracts need not be in writing but it is normal to have some evidence of their existence, e.g. a receipt for a purchase. Some contracts have to be written, e.g. one to buy a house or business.

Contract of Employment   A legally binding agreement to provide work (employer) and to undertake that work (employee). An employee must be given particulars of the contract but does not always have to be given an actual, formally written contract.

contribution costing   Costing which ignores fixed costs and bases decisions only on the difference between the sale price of a unit and its variable cost. This difference is called the contribution.

corporation sole   A company consisting of one person. Often a personality like a pop singer. Bishop's are another example.

corporation tax   The tax levied on the profits of companies.

cost-based pricing   Determining price by adding a mark-up to the unit cost. There is a traditional mark-up associated with many industries.

creditors   Those who are still to be paid for goods or services. It is usual to distinguish between trade creditors, e.g. for raw materials, and expense creditors, e.g. for advertising. Creditors help to finance business by providing time to pay.

criminal law   The law which establishes which acts are punishable and the means, through the criminal courts, of bringing wrong doers to justice.

current assets   Those assets of a business which constantly change their nature in the flow of daily business activity. The main elements of current assets are stock, debtors and cash.

current ratio   The most familiar of the ratios which measure liquidity. It relates total current assets to current liabilities. A tighter ratio best suited to firms with high stock values, is the acid test ratio (see above).

debentures   Loan certificates. Usually long-term loans at a fixed rate of interest, sometimes secured against a specified asset in which case they are mortgage debentures.

debtor days ratio   Calculates the number of days taken to collect debts. Helps to measure the extent to which debts are really a liquid asset. A business would normally look for a ratio below 30 days. However it is frequently much longer.

debtors   Those who owe a firm money. Some businesses try to avoid debtors (cash and carry) and most will wish to see some evidence of credit worthiness before granting credit.

decentralise   The tendency to spread control and to delegate authority, e.g. from head office to the branches of a business.

decision accounting   That part of the accounting process, sometimes called management accounting, which prepares accounting data and analyses it, in order to enable decisions to be made. It also monitors processes to ensure progress towards objectives is maintained.

delegation   The passing down the line of authority to do something. The responsibility remains with the delegator.

demand   (a) The desire for a good or service backed by the ability and willingness to pay for it.

(b) The amount of a commodity actually purchased per unit of time at a given price.

demand-based pricing   Often called 'what the traffic will bear' it is based upon the amount the consumer will pay.

depreciation   The way accountants assess the fall in value of an asset as a result of use and passage of time. Shown as an accumulated amount in the balance sheet and as an annual provision in the profit and loss account.

development   Often used in conjunction with research. Taking something which has been invented or discovered a stage further with a view to production.

direct costs   Costs which are attributable to a particular product, process or service.

directives   Decisions made by the EU which national parliaments must bring into their own law. An example is the Directive on working hours.

direct taxes   Taxes levied directly on income, e.g. income tax and corporation tax.

diseconomies of scale   Factors in a production situation resulting from the increasing scale of operations which increase unit costs of production, e.g. having to work overtime or holidays.

dismissal   The act of terminating a contract of employment. It is a formal procedure in most cases and, if not carried out in accordance with procedure, may be unfair.

disposable income   What is left of net income after all necessary payments have been made. The income earner has a choice as to how disposable income will be spent. For many people disposable income is very small.

distribution channels   The route taken from producer to consumer. The shortest is direct selling and the commonest through an agent, dealer or wholesaler to the retailer and then the customer.

dividend   Part of the disposable profit of a company is paid out to shareholders. This is worked out on a per share basis and is a dividend on each share. Preference shares receive a fixed dividend. Ordinary shares carry no entitlement to receive a dividend but actual dividend is unlimited.

double entry   Reflects the fact that every transaction has two sides and that both should be recorded, e.g. if I buy a kilo of sugar, the cash of the retailer is increased by its price and the stock of sugar reduced by one kilo.

economies of scale   Factors which lead to a falling unit cost as output rises. The major factor here is usually the spread of fixed costs over an increasing number of units as output rises. But there are also economies which arise from specialisation, from greater capacity utilisation or from bulk buying.

efficiency ratios   Those ratios which focus on the measurement of efficiency, e.g. how well fixed assets are utilised can be shown by relating gross profit or net profit to fixed assets.

employment law   All legislation which regulates contracts of employment, conditions of work and ways in which employees can be dismissed.

empowerment   Transferring authority to act to workers. A form of delegation but it is less specific, offering choice to the worker in many situations.

environment   All aspects of the surroundings, conditions and circumstances within which business operates.

environmental audit   Methods intended to assess a company's corporate responsibility by costing the contributions it might make to environmental damage against the benefits which accrue from exercise of corporate responsibility towards the environment.

equilibrium point   The point when the market is in balance, i.e. the amount demanded is equal to the amount supplied.

equity   Share capital but often used to refer to the whole of the shareholders' funds in a company.

ethics   A set of moral principles by reference to which we would expect our own lives and the practices of business to be conducted. There is no universal agreement about what these principles should be.

European Union   The union of countries in Europe who have agreed to act collectively rather than nationally. The number of countries in the Union has grown considerably since the Treaty of Rome in 1957. The Union is set to grow even bigger.

exchange rate   The rate at which one currency is traded for another.

excise duties   Taxes on commodities, e.g. cars, beers, cigarettes.

export duties   Taxes which would be levied on selling goods to other countries by the home countries.

factors of production   The inputs upon which production of goods and services is dependent. These are land (natural resources), capital, all forms of work (labour) and managerial skill (enterprise). There is an increasing tendency for capital to be more and labour less significant in the combinations which producers create.

factoring   The process of selling an outstanding debt to a debt collecting business. Often undertaken when a business needs to avoid cash flow problems. Most businesses factor high purchase debts at the time the HP agreement is made.

favourable variance   A difference between budgeted and actual results which is to the benefit of the business, e.g. sales greater than budgeted would be regarded as a favourable variance as would costs less than forecasted.

final accounts   Those documents and reports which collectively sum up the activities and position of a business at the end of a trading period. Minimum requirements in this respect are laid down for public limited companies by the Companies Acts.

finance   Support for business which enables activity, usually money but it is sometimes time.

financial accounting   That aspect of accounting which records all the day-to-day transactions of the business, audits, records and completes the periodic financial statements.

fixed assets   Those assets whose purpose and nature do not change over time. They are recorded at historical cost (what was paid for them) and revalued as required, in various ways. Premises, vehicles and machinery are examples.

fixed costs   Those costs which, in the short run, do not vary with output.

flow production   In its major form it is mass production. Producing by completing the stages on an assembly line. Flow production may not produce the whole article.

formal groups   Groups which have been deliberately created, e.g. the classes in a school or the Health and Safety Committee at work. They exist only to complete their function and their objectives are determined from outside the group. Membership is often by appointment.

full costing   An approach to costing which allocates all the costs of production to cost centres to ensure that everything is taken into account.

goodwill   As an accounting concept it is the difference in value between the price for which a business is sold and the value of the assets. It is a reflection of the trading value or reputation of the business.

grants   The provision of finance in a way which does not expect repayments. Grants and charitable institutions often give support in this way.

gross income   Personal income before any deductions. The full amount earned.

gross profit   The profit made on actual trading activities before considering the expenses of running the business. Found by subtracting cost of goods sold from net sales revenue.

growth   The extent to which an economy or a business adds value to itself. In money terms growth means increases in money values which are above the rate of inflation.

health and safety   It is a legal requirement that employers or providers of facilities and services ensure that their premises are a safe and healthy place to work in accordance with the established code of practice. It applies to most activities and institutions as well as places of work, e.g. schools, churches and entertainment places. The main legislation is the Health and Safety at Work Act and the Food Safety Act.

Herzberg, F.   Developed the two factor theory of motivation at work. The development of his work was through job enrichment (see below).

hire purchase   A form of medium-term credit purchase involving a deposit followed by regular monthly payments. The goods are not owned by the purchaser until the last payment is made.

human resource management   Modern term for the personnel function which includes a wide range of activities designed to recruit, train and efficiently use human resources.

import duties   Taxes levied in this country on goods bought from abroad.

income tax   The tax on personal incomes which is determined each year by the amount of income earned and the budgetary decisions of the Chancellor.

incremental budgeting   Budgeting on the basis of a change (usually an increase) on the budget for the previous period.

indirect costs   Costs which must be covered but which cannot be directly attributed to producing a particular product, process or service.

indirect taxes   Taxes levied through the spending of money, e.g. VAT.

induction   The process of introducing new employees to their place of work, the culture and operational methods of the business, the roles they are meant to adopt and those within which they will work. Poor induction or no induction are often reasons why people leave firms.

industrial marketing   Attempting to find customers among other businesses as opposed to consumer marketing.

inflation   A fall in the value of money. It is a government objective to keep inflation low.

informal groups   Usually arise rather than created. Have no roles defined from outside and membership is determined by the norms of the group. Examples are a friendship group or a group of those who play cards in the lunch hour.

inputs   The resources which are brought together to produce goods and services.

insolvency   The firm is unable to meet its immediate financial commitments.

intangible assets   Those assets which have no physical form but which are of monetary value to the business, e.g. goodwill, copyright and patents.

investment goods   Those goods and services which are bought to enable production. Machines and raw materials are examples.

job description   Details the nature of a job. Often the basis of an advert and usually sent out to potential employees. Should be part of the contract of employment and should be changed whenever an employee's job is changed or redesigned.

job enlargement   Making a job bigger so that it is more complete or more challenging.

job enrichment   Developing the characteristics and requirements of a job so that the job gives greater satisfaction to the worker and hence provides greater motivation.

job production   Producing one unit at a time. This is often customising the product at the same time.

job rotation   Increasing the flexibility of the work force and the variety of the work they do by moving them from one job to another on a regular basis.

joint venture   A co-operative activity between two or more organisations or countries. Concorde and the Channel Tunnel were both produced by joint ventures.

just-in-time   Part of a lean production attitude. It tries to avoid holding stock of any kind. Just-in-time seeks delivery of stock, or work in progress or finished goods just when they are needed and not before.

Kaizen   Continuous improvement rather than improvement in lumps (see diagram on page 216).

labour intensity   The extent to which production depends upon labour as a factor of production. Craft industries, the arts and many of the professions are labour intensive.

labour turnover   The number of people who leave an employment as a proportion of total employed. High labour turnover has substantial costs for a business.

leadership   The fact of leading, the role adopted when workers have to be guided towards the achievement of objectives. There are many styles of leadership and the appropriate one must be found for any given situation.

lean production   Not really a method, this is more an attitude of mind or a culture within which the objective is to eliminate waste of all kinds from original stock order through to customer service.

leasing   Renting a service, an asset or a property. It reduces the capital required to use an asset but carries the risks of non-ownership.

legal personality   Conveyed on companies by incorporation it gives them rights and responsibilities, treating them as people in the eyes of the law.

legislation   The means by which new law is brought into being. We are subject to laws made by our regional and national assemblies as well as those made by the EU (see directives above).

lenders   Those who provide funds to a business without rights of ownership. Money borrowed must be repaid and attracts a rate of interest in most cases.

limited liability   Reduces the risks of ownership for shareholders in companies, to the investment they have made in the company and prevents any claim on their personal assets.

line and staff   Line workers are those who work in a given position in the chain of command of a given department. Staff workers do not work in the line but may be called into it to give support, advice or to maintain a common policy or approach. There is often conflict between the two.

liquidity   The speed with which the current assets of a firm can be converted to cash without a reduction on their book value. The ratios which measure this are the current ratio and the acid test ratio (see above). The ability of a firm to pay its short-term creditors.

liquidity ratios   Those ratios which measure the ability of a firm to pay its short-term creditors. The main two are the acid test and the current ratio.

management accounting   An alternative phrase for decision accounting (see above).

management by objectives   Determining the required outcome and managing the efforts of a worker or workers towards its achievement. The method often sets up individual short-term targets to guide workers more easily towards success.

McGregor Author of Theory X and Theory Y (see below).

management style The approach to management adopted by a single manager or by all within the culture of an organisation.

marginal costing Costing in terms of the cost of the last unit produced. If 100 units are produced and output is raised to 101 units, the marginal cost is the cost of producing that 101st unit.

marketing All the processes and practices which link producers and potential buyers.

marketing objectives The particular objectives which a marketing team will pursue in order to meet the objectives of the business as a whole, e.g. market penetration or market leadership.

marketing mix The combination of marketing variables which is put together to form a plan or strategy.

market orientation Focusing on the markets and the needs and wants of the consumer.

market positioning Placing a product within the market in terms of an image, e.g. young and fashionable.

market segment A part of the market for a good or service which has its own characteristics and which can be identified and targeted. Segmentation can be by any variable, e.g. sex, age, occupation, region.

market standing The reputation of a firm among its suppliers and customers.

mark up The amount added to the unit cost of products to determine the price at which they will be sold.

Maslow Best known for his hierarchy of needs as a basis for pinpointing and satisfying human needs and hence motivating people at work (see diagram page 177).

Mayo, E. Concluded from experiments at the Hawthorne works that co-operation with, and supportive observation of, people at work can increase their productivity. Also undertook research into the effects of fatigue and boredom.

motivation The desire which people have to work well. Not easy to measure except through careful observation of behaviour.

movement A concept developed by Herzberg. Movement is those processes which take people to work, putting them in a position to do it. People who are at work are not necessarily motivated.

net current assets Another name for working capital. Measured by subtracting current liabilities from current assets. It indicates the sufficiency of the funds with which the firm is carrying on its day to day transactions.

net income Personal income after tax and national insurance payments have been made.

net profit That profit which remains after all the expenses and provisions of running the business have been deducted and any additional incomes have been added in.

niche market A small segment of the market which a firm can target and hold successfully against competition. Sock shop is an example of a niche approach.

noise Any form of disturbance which makes communication difficult.

objectives The outcomes which a firm or organisation attempts to achieve. Overall objectives normally include survival, profit and growth. There may be others. Departments will develop objectives designed to ensure achievement of corporate ones.

observation A direct method of research. Has the advantage that what is seen has actually happened.

off-the-job training Training which takes place away from the job. This often takes place in a firms own training school or in colleges following appropriate courses.

on-the-job training For many jobs the only way to train is by doing the job, usually under controlled or observed conditions. Examples are teaching, medicine and bus driving. A great many training programmes are a combination of both on- and off-the-job training.

operating profit The actual profit earned from what the business does.

opportunity cost The cost of something in terms of the next-best alternative. Example: if I can buy either a pop disc or a dance ticket but not both, the cost of one can be expressed in terms of the other. The cost of the disc is the ticket I could not have.

organisation (a) A work unit not necessarily a business one, e.g. a church or a golf club. (b) The process of structuring work and workers so that activities are efficiently undertaken.

organisational objectives The pattern of objectives which an organisation decides upon and attempts to fulfil (see Objectives above).

organisation charts Diagrams which represent the way a firm is organised and define the inter-relationships between workers. The most common form divides and organises work by function, but it is also possible to organise by product, by team, by system or by a matrix approach.

overheads The costs of running a business over and above those of producing specific products. Overhead costs can be either fixed, e.g. office premises, or variable, e.g. telephone calls.

pay back period The length of time it takes for an original investment to be paid back by the net inward cash flows involved.

planning The process of organising how things should be done to achieve a given objective.

price elasticity of demand The responsiveness of demand to a small change in price. Measured by the percentage change in demand/percentage change in price.

price stability Keeping prices stable. In part this is a matter of controlling inflation. In part it may be a deliberate policy by businesses or by the State, to avoid price wars.

price wars Competition by businesses which uses price as a major weapon. Particularly common when there is over-supply of a good or service.

pricing strategy The plan of action through which a price or prices are determined or changed, normally part of an overall marketing strategy.

primary activity Business activity in the primary sector using national resources. Fishing, agriculture and mining are examples.

primary information Often called field research and is collected with specific reference to the matter being investigated.

product development Making the product or the product range more suited to the needs of the market place. Sometimes used to mean the development stages before the production and launch of a new product.

productivity Not to be confused with production. This is a measure of efficiency. Measurement can be in terms of the use of any of the factors of production and is still commonly expressed in terms of productivity per employee hour. Productivity per £ of capital invested is often more significant.

product life cycle The stages through which all products which survive the launch, go through to the end of their natural life (see diagram on page 112).

product positioning Places a product in the market in terms of its rivals (see diagram on page 115).

production The process of adding value when inputs are used to create outputs of goods and services.

product orientated When the focus of a firm's activities is on what is being produced rather than on the consumer.

profit The difference between the total costs and total revenue of a business. The word has no precise meaning on its own.

profitability ratios Ratios which focus on the profits made in relation to assets used. The leading ratio of this kind is the Return on Capital employed (ROCE) which is net profit/capital employed.

profit and loss account The account in which the net profit or net loss made by the business in a specific trading period is calculated, part of the final accounts of a business. Has three elements: (i) the calculation of the gross profit often called the Trading A/c, (ii) the calculation of the net profit after tax and interest deductions, (iii) the decision as to how the disposable profit is used or distributed often called the appropriation account.

promotion strategy Promotion is any activity designed to persuade a successful sale. The strategy is the total approach in line with a given objective.

published accounts Accounts of companies which are available to shareholders and the general public. They consist primarily of the final accounts of a business. Most businesses now make them available on the Internet.

qualitative information Information of a non-numerate kind, often based on judgments, opinions, attitudes or experiences.

quality Some goods like Thornton's chocolates are meant to be of a high standard of excellence. Others like cheap ballpoint pens are meant to be as cheaply produced as possible as long as they do their job. From this it is clear that quality is a variable standard which once established at a given level, the production line will work to achieve.

quality assurance Giving assurances to the buyer, which may be an internal one, that required specifications have been met.

quality circles Groups of workers involved in different stages of work who meet together at regular intervals with the objective of ensuring or improving the quality of work done.

quality control Sometimes built in and often statistical it seeks to control quality by testing and then rejecting sub-standard goods. Often demotivating where it involves an inspector rejecting and criticising.

quantitative information Information which is collected in numerate form and can be meaningfully aggregated and interpreted.

questionnaires A means, through direct questionning of respondents, of collecting information. Questions may be open or closed.

quota sample When a demographic pattern of the population is known and samples are drawn from it in proportion to the characteristics of the pattern. Example: If 70% of shoppers are women then 70 out of every 100 interviews in a shopping survey should be women.

random sample When every person in the population being surveyed has the same chance of being selected.

rate of interest The cost at which money can be borrowed.

ratio analysis The technique which relates two bits of accounting information so as to enable interpretation of a reported situation.

recruitment The process of finding the employees needed. Good recruitment is based upon effective workforce planning and carefully designed selection procedures.

recycling Processing waste products so that they may be used again in some form, now a major industry applying to a wide range of used materials.

redundancy A worker is redundant when dismissed because there is no longer any work for the worker to do. Dismissal followed by the employment of someone else to do the same job is not redundancy. Under certain circumstances workers receive redundancy payments related to their average weekly wage and their length of service.

research Discovery activities. Market research looks for market information; technological research looks for new ways of doing things.

resource management The quality of the management of resources of all kinds, and the extent to which waste can be reduced or eliminated.

retained profit That part of the disposable profit of a business which is retained by the business. It is sometimes called 'ploughed back' profit and is one of the major sources of finance for companies.

return on capital employed The relationship between net profit and capital employed (ROCE). Considered the most important profitability ratio.

revenue expenditure Expenditure incurred to meet the day-to-day expenses of the business. It does not add to asset values, it simply pays for costs which are incurred. Examples are payment of wages and advertising expenditure.

role An employee's expected function within the total workforce.

role reversal When roles in one situation are the opposite of roles in another. Jennifer may be a Secretary to John at work but she may be his leader as Mayor of a council of which he is a member.

role conflict When two or more roles are such that the proper completion of one makes it difficult or impossible to complete the other.

sale of assets The conversion of assets to cash often followed, in the case of fixed assets by lease back. Organisations will sell assets which have come to the end of their useful life. They will also sell as an internal source of finance.

sales turnover May be expressed in money in which case it is net sales for a period or it may be expressed in volume and is the number of units of product(s) sold.

sampling The process of collecting information from a population which is either unknown or too large to ask everyone (see definitions of the different kinds of sample).

sales promotion A promotion strategy which is focussed on a sales target. Commonly it sets out to attract the consumer with sales-based promotions, such as 'buy one get one free' or demonstrations.

secondary activity Business activity which uses natural resources and other inputs to construct or manufacture.

secondary information Often called desk research, this is information which already exists and is not specific to the matter being investigated.

semi-variable costs Costs which have both a fixed and a variable element, e.g. salaries which have an element of commission payment in them, or costs which vary with output but not proportionately, e.g. use of power.

services Activities which satisfy consumers needs. Services may be personal, e.g. hairdressing, or financial advice or public, e.g. transport and telephones.

shareholders People who own shares and hence are part owners of a company.

social costs Measures the cost to society as a whole of a decision or activity. Examples might be pollution of the atmosphere, the closing of a school or the dumping of waste materials.

social responsibility Accepting accountability for the social and environmental consequences of a process or a decision, taking into account the objectives and interests of all stakeholders.

span of control The number of subordinates for whom a supervisor or manager is responsible. There is no perfect span it varies widely within the circumstances.

specialisation Concentration on part of a process or activity. Usually increases standards because specialists are good, or become good, at what they do. Businesses may also specialise, e.g. in certain segments of a market.

stakeholders Those who have an interest in something. Used to indicate all those different groups who have an interest in the activities of a firm. Examples are employees, customers and the State.

stock Goods held for manufacture or for sale. There are three kinds of stock: (i) the stock of components and raw materials held for manufacture or processing, (ii) the stock of products which go through several stages and which take time to complete or mature (this is work-in-progress), (iii) the stock of finished goods ready for sale.

stock control Finding a method of controlling stock where it is held. This varies from the completely manually and physically controlled to that which is totally computerised as in supermarkets. Good stock control is crucial where it may deteriorate, or be stolen or simply become rapidly obsolete.

Stock Exchange The major market for shares in most countries. The shares of all the major companies are quoted and traded on the Stock Exchanges of the world.

stock turnover ratio Measures the rate at which stock is sold or the number of days it takes to sell average stock. The lower the number of days the more efficiently the firm is using its working capital.

stratified random sample A population is divided in accordance with the proportions in which its known and relevant characteristics exist. Each of the identified groups is then randomly sampled.

supply The amount offered for sale at a given price over a given period of time.

suppliers Those from whom goods and services are obtained.

SWOT analysis A technique which critically assesses strengths, weaknesses, threats and opportunities in a given situation. It clarifies problems and issues and enables decisions but it does not make them.

tangible assets Those assets which have a physical form, e.g. all fixed and current assets.

Taylor Father of the Scientific Approach to management. He used work study to establish what might be expected from workers and how it should be rewarded. Saw production as a combined effort and hence did not see a role for unions.

taxation   The amount drawn from personal and business incomes by the state. This may be through direct taxes or indirect taxes (see above).

team working   A modern approach to business activity which puts the emphasis on workers working together and their responsibility to and for each other within that team, the approach is said to give greater empowerment and satisfaction to workers and hence to be more motivating and productive.

tertiary activity   Business activity which provides services for consumers, retailing and refuse collection are examples.

Theory X and Y   McGregor argued that management attitudes to workers varying from the extremely positive position of Theory Y, in which workers are seen as wanting to work and seeking responsibility, to the extremely negative position, in which they are viewed as disinclined to work without close control and under instruction.

training   Necessary when a firm wishes an employee to undertake something new which cannot be done without increased information, skill or experience. Some training is specific and other training is developmental.

unemployment   Applies to all resources but most commonly applies to the workforce and to being economically active but unable to find a job.

unfavourable variance   A difference between budgeted and actual costs or revenues which are to the disadvantage of the firm, e.g. lower sales or higher costs than planned for.

unfair dismissal   Dismissal which has not followed procedures or which has not treated the worker fairly as compared with other employees. Employees may take the matter to a tribunal if they consider dismissal has been unfair. It is a matter of fact, to be decided by the Tribunal, whether dismissal has been unfair.

unique selling point   A feature of a product or service which can be promoted to attract customers for it. Most businesses try to find or develop a USP for their product.

unlimited liability   Applies to sole traders and partners. They risk everything they own if a business venture fails.

value added   The difference made by production. The difference between the value of inputs and the value of output from them.

value added tax   A tax which is paid on the value that is added at each stage of a production process. It is reclaimed at all stages except the final one of sale when the tax is levied on the consumer. Some goods like food are exempt.

variable costs   Those costs which vary relatively proportionately with output. Examples are raw material costs and wages paid on piece rates.

variance analysis   The technique which enables management accountants to identify cause of differences between budgeted and actual figures for a given period.

watchdog bodies   There are three kinds:
(a) Self-created: These are created by organisations themselves. Good examples are the Law Society and the Association of British Travel Agents (ABTA)
(b) Government bodies such as OFTEL and OFSTED
(c) Pressure groups such as the Consumer Association and Greenpeace.

waste   The extent to which resources and goods of all kinds are lost. One of the biggest wastages in our society is unemployment.

work in progress   Part-finished goods whose value has been assessed. A necessary part of construction industries in particular where completion may extend over two or more financial years.

workforce planning   Working out the overall human resource requirement and the way the jobs of the personnel will interact. This is the basis for effective recruitment.

working capital   The net current assets of a business. It uses these to transact its day-to-day business in the conversion of stock into products, products into debtors and debtors into cash. It is measured by deducting current liabilities from current assets.

zero budgeting   Assumes there is no budget and requires a justification for each expenditure as it is planned or occurs. Prevents the assumption that budgets will rise each year.

zero defects   Part of the lean production approach. The assumption is that quality will be tested continuously so that there are no defects and hence no waste of finished or part finished products.

Index